The future of the British conurbations

The future of the British conurbations

policies and prescription for change

edited by
Gordon C. Cameron

Longman
London and New York

Longman Group Limited London

*Associated companies, branches and representatives
throughout the world*

*Published in the United States of America
by Longman Inc., New York*

© Longman Group Limited 1980

First published 1980

British Library Cataloguing in Publication Data

The future of the British conurbations.
 1. Metropolitan areas – Great Britain
 I. Cameron, Gordon Campbell
 309.1′41   HT334.G7   79-40544

ISBN 0-582-44389-X
ISBN 0-582-44390-3 Pbk

Printed in Great Britain by
Richard Clay (The Chaucer Press) Ltd.,
Bungay, Suffolk.

To the memory of my father,
Archibald Arthur Cameron

Contents

List of contributors

Gordon C. Cameron Professor, Department of Land Economy, University of Cambridge; formerly Professor, Department of Town and Regional Planning, University of Glasgow. Urban Policy Consultant and Economic Consultant to Secretary of State for Scotland.

Alan W. Evans Reader, Department of Economics, University of Reading.

John R. Firn Member of Strategy Division, Scottish Development Agency and formerly Lecturer in Applied Economics, University of Glasgow.

Christopher D. Foster Director, Coopers and Lybrand; visiting Professor of Urban Economics, London School of Economics and formerly Director, Centre for Environmental Studies.

Eric Gillett Secretary, Scottish Development Department.

Peter Hall Head and Professor, Department of Geography, University of Reading.

Peter M. Jackson Director, Public Sector Economics Research Centre and Head of the Economics Department, University of Leicester.

Richard M. Kirwan Assistant Director of Research, Department of Land Economy, University of Cambridge.

J. Douglas McCallum Senior Lecturer, Department of Town and Regional Planning, University of Glasgow.

Malcolm L. McKenzie Senior Lecturer, Department of Education, University of Glasgow.

John N. Randall Economic Adviser, Scottish Economic Planning Department.

Ray Richardson Reader in Industrial Relations, London School of Economics.

John D. Stewart Professor and Director, Institute of Local Government Studies, University of Birmingham.

Foreword

The theme for this book was suggested by Alastair Hetherington then Controller of BBC Scotland and formerly Editor of the *Guardian*. Like all good ideas it took shape over an excellent lunch. (Only later does one realise the folly of wine-affected commitments!) The BBC generously provided funds so that all the authors could meet to discuss initial drafts and also encouraged the *Glasgow Herald* to be associated with the project. I am especially grateful to the BBC and to the *Herald* for their continual encouragement and especially to David Martin of the BBC, who, despite his scores of other commitments always had a lively interest in the book and its possible contribution to public understanding.

Unlike many other collected essays on a theme, every one of the following chapters has been written as an 'original' for this book. Our objective has been to provide succinct, readable essays which bring out the underlying causes at work. In so doing we have sought to look at the future of the British conurbations with as dispassionate an eye as possible. In this we have tried to steer a course between spurious optimism and unfounded pessimism. The outcome, we believe, is a series of balanced and perceptive essays which treat policies for these important parts of national space in a truly comparative way.

Gordon C. Cameron
January 1979

Acknowledgements

The Editor wishes to acknowledge the debt he owes to many colleagues in the Centre for Urban and Regional Research, University of Glasgow. He also received valuable research assistance from Derrick Johnstone. The index was compiled by Anne Carey. Secretarial assistance by Miss Audrey Graham and Mrs. Hilda Walker as always, was provided efficiently. The Editor wishes to record his thanks to all those mentioned above and to Longman staff for their sensitive and timely handling of the complex of decisions associated with the book.

Maps

Conurbations

① Greater London
② West Midlands (Birmingham)
③ S. E. Lancashire (Manchester)
④ Central Clydeside (Glasgow)
⑤ W. Yorkshire (Leeds)
⑥ Merseyside (Liverpool)
⑦ Tyneside (Newcastle)
● Cities over 200 000

Map 1 Conurbations in the United Kingdom

Map 2 Greater London conurbations

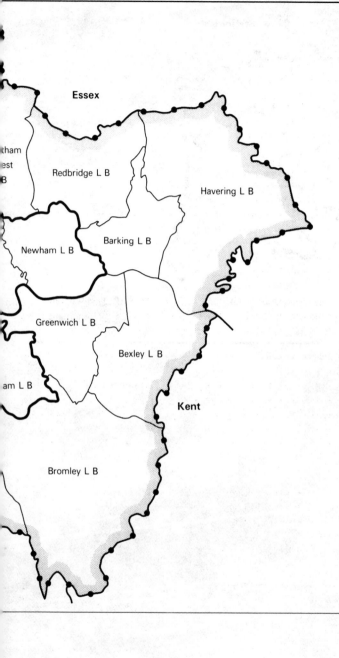

Essex

tham
est
B

Redbridge L B

Havering L B

Newham L B

Barking L B

Greenwich L B

Bexley L B

am L B

Kent

Bromley L B

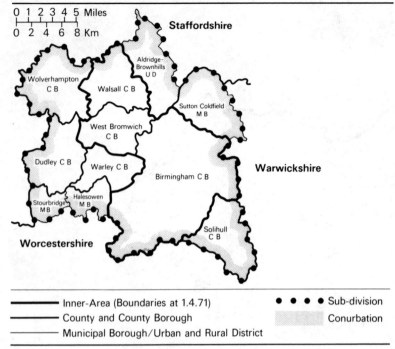

Map 3 West Midlands conurbation

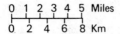

| | | | | | Miles |
|0|1|2|3|4|5|

| | | | | |
|0|2|4|6|8| Km|

Lancashire

Turton U D

Ramsbottom U D

Whitworth U D

Wardle U D

Littleborough U D

Blackrod U D

Horwich U D

Tottington U D

Bury C B

Rochdale C B

Milnrow U D

Bolton C B

Heywood M B

Crompton U D

Little Lever U D

Radcliffe M B

Royton U D

Yorkshire

Westhoughton U D

Farnworth M B

Middleton M B

Chadderton U D

Oldham C B

Kearsley U D

Whitefield U D

Lees U D

Worsley U D

Swinton and Pendlebury M B

Prestwich M B

Failsworth U D

Ashton Under Lyne M B

Mossley M B

Eccles M B

Salford C B

Droylesden U D

Audenshaw U D

Stalybridge M B

Dukinfield M B

Irlam U D

Urmston U D

Stretford M B

Manchester C B

Denton U D

Hyde M B

Sale M B

Bredbury and Romiley U D

Altrincham M B

Stockport C B

Marple U D

Bowdon U D

Hale U D

Cheadle and Gatley U D

Hazel Grove and Bramhall U D

Disley R D

Derbyshire

Bucklow R D

Wilmslow U D

Cheshire

Knutsford U D

Alderley U D

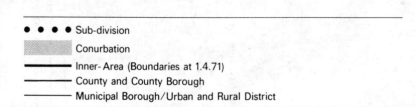

● ● ● ● Sub-division

         Conurbation

━━━━ Inner- Area (Boundaries at 1.4.71)

──── County and County Borough

──── Municipal Borough/Urban and Rural District

Map 4 South East Lancashire conurbation

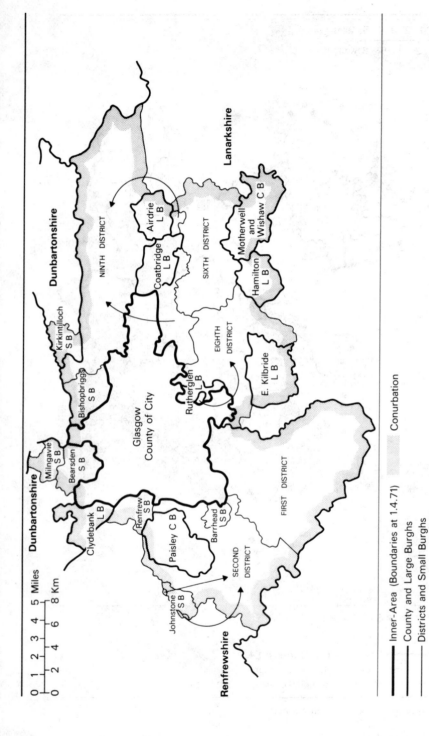

Map 5 Central Clydeside conurbation

— Inner-Area (Boundaries at 1.4.71) ▨ Conurbation

— County and Large Burghs

— Districts and Small Burghs

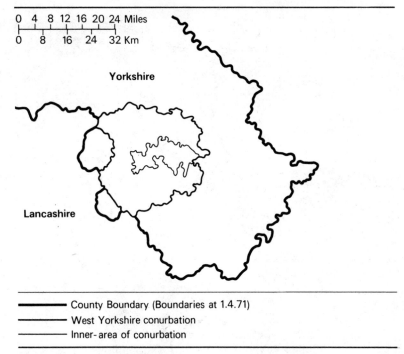

0   4   8   12   16   20   24   Miles
0   8   16   24   32 Km

Yorkshire

Lancashire

━━━━━━ County Boundary (Boundaries at 1.4.71)
─────── West Yorkshire conurbation
─────── Inner-area of conurbation

Map 6 West Yorkshire conurbation

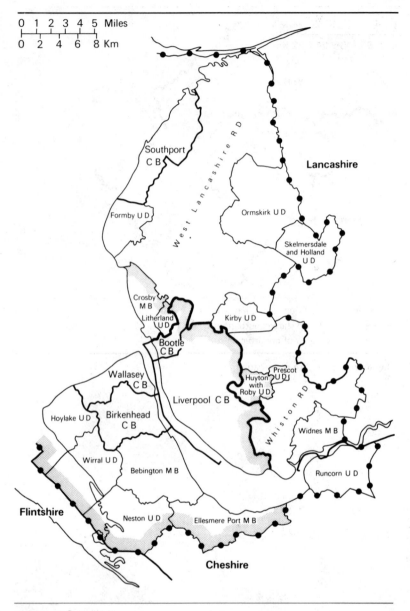

Map 7 Merseyside conurbation

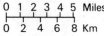

0 1 2 3 4 5 Miles

0 2 4 6 8 Km

Northumberland

Ashington
U D

Newbiggin-by-the-sea U D

Bedlingtonshire
U D

Blyth M B

Seaton Valley U D

C a s t l e W a r d R D

Whitley Bay
M B

Longbenton
U D

Gosforth
U D

Tynemouth
C B

Newburn U D

Wallsend
M B

Newcastle upon tyne
C B

Hebburn
U D

South
Shields
C B

Ryton U D

Jarrow
M B

Gateshead
C B

Felling
U D

Blaydon U D

Whickham
U D

C h e s t e r - l e - s t r e e t R D

Boldon U D

Washington U D

Sunderland
C B

Stanley U D

Consett U D

Chester-le-
street
U D

Houghton-
le-spring
U D

Seaham
U D

Hetton U D

L a n c h e s t e r R D

D u r h a m R D

Brandon and Byshottles
U D

Durham
and
Framwelgate
M B

Durham

• • • • Sub-division

Conurbation

Inner Area (Boundaries at 1.4.71)

County and County Borough

Municipal Borough/Urban and Rural District

Map 8 Tyneside conurbation

Introduction

The term 'conurbation' is a statistical artefact, not a precise legal or political entity. First used by Patrick Geddes in 1915, it is defined simply and rather vaguely by the Oxford Dictionary as an 'aggregation of urban districts'. Officially it embraces seven urbanised areas ranging from Britain's largest urban concentration and a true 'world city' – Greater London – with a 1971 population of almost $7\frac{1}{2}$ million, down to Tyneside which with 800,000 inhabitants was nine times smaller and only marginally larger than several other urbanised areas.[1] And yet although the term has a rather imprecise cut-off point, it creates an unmistakeable image of scale, of large stretches of contiguous built-up areas, of dense and highly varied concentrations of economic activity, of population of every social and ethnic hue, of political power and of pulsating cultural influence. Here we are clearly dealing with the 'heavy-weights' of the British urban system all of which grew to dominate national manufacturing, national trade and national servicing, during the explosive population growth of the nineteenth century. Thus, although we cannot measure the population of these areas at the beginning of that century, since only Greater London's population has been recorded in this way, we can show that by 1891 four out of every ten persons in England and Wales lived in one of the six English conurbations (Hall *et al.*, 1973, p. 64).

Though the precise factors varied city by city, as Asa Briggs has shown so clearly in his *Victorian Cities* (1968), the underlying causes behind the emergence of these dominant centres were very similar. Nineteenth-century economic growth was based upon factory production. There were marked economic advantages in concentrating this production close to areas of raw material extraction, a varied labour supply, locally available finance and diverse transport opportunities, particularly rail linkages. The outcome was the concentrated creation in specific locations of key manufacturing industries, their ensuing growth through technical change and innovation and the exploitation of internal and external economies of scale and ultimately an urbanised domination of whole regions as primary manufacturing and servicing linkages were initiated and extended. By the end of the Victorian period the nation had become a set of specialist regions linked in ever-expanding trade and led by a few key urban centres. Internally these same centres had grown in haphazard leaps and bounds, creating huge peaks of dense economic activity in the areas of highest productivity and lowest linkage cost around their central core railway terminals with a dense, largely unplanned admixture of dwellings, public buildings and work-places, elsewhere.

Then, as now, the growth of these urban gargantua was condemned by some, praised exuberantly by others. For the 1858 *Chambers's Edinburgh Journal*, the large urban areas represented 'the very symbol of civilization, foremost in the march of improvement, a grand incarnation of progress'. Here was a wonderful mechanism for creating riches, where man could exploit his energy and his intelligence and where personal pride in achievement went hand in hand with the growth of civic pride and civic achievement.

Others disagreed violently, pointing to the ugliness, the insanitary overcrowding, the anonymity and the alienation of man from man as functional work relationships replaced the cohesive social, historical and cultural bonds so typical of smaller communities. The city became, in the words of the Hammonds, not the 'refuge of civilization but the barracks of an industry'. Or, as George Gissing the nineteenth-century novelist expressed it in an even more compelling phrase, the place where 'men ... toil without hope and yet with the hunger of unsatisfied desire'.

Anti-urbanism

This anti-urbanism has always been present in British thought, both official and unofficial. Ruth Glass in her brilliant article on this theme (1972, p. 65) has argued that the town 'was not, as in other societies the home of reason, intellect and a symbol of civic pride, but merely a place of new resources for the impoverished landed upper class and one where manufacturers and merchants could make money to buy their tickets of admission into the polite circles of the shires'. But if the town was a scene of exploitation and personal gain for the few, it was not a stable entity. The explosive growth of the major cities was '... a change charged with a menace to the future. They dread the fermenting, in the populous cities, of some new, all-powerful explosive, destined one day to shatter into ruin all their desirable social order' (Masterman, 1904, p. 61).

But could the catastrophe be avoided? For Salt, Howard, Geddes and Mumford the answer was 'yes', but only by rejecting the big city and creating an urban form which emphasised entirely different social values. Thus the giant cities could not be tamed unless their populations were prepared to turn their backs on them and rediscover the joys of small community living, in decent houses, with close-at-hand work, clean environments and benign paternalistic employers. Small scale and the beneficial effects of a good environment were the ingredients – a recipe allegedly proven by Owen in New Lanark even before these urban excrescences had emerged.

The prophets did not go unheeded. Anti-urbanism or, more precisely, the desire to dismantle the big city by diverting population and economic activity away from its growing grasp, was given a tangible shape in a set of post-Second World War legislation. The conceptual foundation of much of this legislation lay in the findings of the Royal Commission on the Distribution of the Industrial Population (Cmnd. 6153, 1940). The Royal Commission was set up in 1937 under the chairmanship of Sir Anderson Montague-Barlow, and the Commissioners were given explicit terms of reference. They were to enquire into the causes of the geographical distribution of industry and population, to consider the disadvantages – social, economic and strategic – of the concentration of population and economic activity within the large centres and, finally, to report remedies, in the national interest, for changing the patterns of spatial distribution which had emerged or were likely to emerge. The dice was loaded. The clear intention was for the Commission to provide evidence of the disadvantages of spatially concentrated growth and to suggest how the urban gargantua should be controlled. Nevertheless, despite its unbalanced origins the Report deserves its reputation as the most authoritative policy statement ever written on the British space economy. Three of its findings were crucial. First, the Commissioners contended that the redistribution of national population over national space which had occurred in the twentieth century and, in particular, the overwhelming growth in the number of insured workers in London and the Home Counties and the very slow growth in the old industrial areas of the North, Wales and Scotland, was caused by economic forces which shaped the locational preferences of industrialists. Thus whilst nineteenth-century preferences had been moulded by the location of raw material deposits, both as inputs in the process and for fuel, the growth of electricity power and the drawing of raw material supplies from all over the world freed many of the newer industries to locate closer to the most prosperous markets in the south. In direct contrast, the areas which were not growing rapidly were locked in with specialist economic activities for which demand had collapsed. Given the preferences of the industrialist in the newer industries, there was no likelihood that sufficient new capital would flow into these older specialist regions to employ their unemployed labour. Barlow's second conclusion related to the large urban centres themselves. All the Commissioners were unanimous in finding that these centres were unsafe on strategic grounds, more unhealthy than alternative small urban or rural areas, and involved their workers in tedious journeys to work. Furthermore, due to high land values, public authorities could not afford to offset these inherent disadvantages by acquisition of land and compensatory public spending.

Though the Commissioners disagreed upon the precise remedies required they all agreed that regional employment growth had become imbalanced and that a more 'balanced' distribution of employment opportunities over national space was essential. They agreed, in addition, that the biggest urban centres must be thinned out, preferably through a policy of new town development and schemes which would allow public authorities to capture some of the increments in urban land values.

The disagreement of the Commissioners over remedial strategies did not inhibit Government. Powerful measures were introduced to control industrial (and later office) development in the South East and East and West Midlands of England and to induce investment to flow into the development areas of Wales and the North. The growth of the major urban centres was to be controlled and planned by a series of interrelated measures – land use controls within a development plan framework, decanting and dispersion of population to new and expanded towns within contiguous metropolitan regions, the creation of green belts to prevent urban coalescence and massive clearance of central city slums accompanied by major schemes of urban renewal, peripheral housing development and, latterly, investment in the rationalisation and development of the metropolitan road system.

Few would deny that these policies generated social benefits. Slums were cleared, inner city population densities lowered, new towns built, the average age of the public housing stock dramatically reduced, green belts established and integrated planning of local public facilities set in train. At an inter-regional level, regional policy caused sizeable decreases in regional unemployment disparities, in regional *per capita* earnings and in the inter-regional migration from north to south.

From spatial goals to equity

And yet by the end of the 1960s there was a growing consensus that many of these measures were, at best, inadequate, or at worst, perverse in their effect. To continue with them, so the argument ran, would not cut at the root of the continuing urban malaise.

Some have seen the origins of this dissatisfaction in the importation of American ideas. During the 1960s, US cities had experienced racial tension, the growth of ethnic ghettoes, the persistence of mass unemployment for minorities and a growing division of the metropolis into suburban 'haves' and central city 'have-nots'. It is true that these urban problems in the United States did generate a very marked growth in sophisticated urban analysis and later in urban policies, both at the federal and state levels. It is also true that most British researchers interested in urban problems at the time would have acknowledged the intellectual leadership of their American counterparts and especially their stress upon processes which cause urban problems, and their analytical rigour in specifying alternative policy solutions. But when it comes to the origins of British dissatisfaction with British urban and regional policies we must note some significant differences in the nature of the two urban systems. Unlike Britain, the US has experienced the growth of very large urban centres this century, especially in the South and West of the country. This has been caused by major shifts in the distribution of economic activity over national space, in the case of the South lured by low wages, but also associated with population movements to gentler climates, especially in the South and West, and the urbanisation of rural populations freed from the land by the growth in productivity of capital intensive agriculture. Thus, if we take a city like Houston, we find that its 1900 population was 44,633. Seventy years later it had topped 1,320,018, and was continuing to grow at a rapid pace. Houston is not alone, for several metropolitan areas reached 'millionaire status' in 1970, though in 1901 none had over 100,000 inhabitants. A second major difference relates to migration flows and the nature of the housing market. The shift of capital to the South was accompanied by an opposite shift of black rural population to the older northern cities. This movement was caused by the continuing lure of an allegedly more free society, the expectation of wider employment opportunities and the comforting feeling that welfare supports were much more generous than in rural, low tax base, states.

Given the nature of the northern housing markets, the vast majority of this black population was housed in the older residential parts of the central cities, especially in private rental property. Discrimination in the private owner-occupier sector and a poorly developed public housing sector meant that very few of the black migrants or longer-resident blacks were able to find a house in suburban areas. In contrast, the wealthier whites flowed out of the central city as road systems improved, suburban areas were developed and an increasing proportion of employment opportunities were suburbanised. This movement in the location of employment opportunities was partly an accompaniment to the residential shifts but also was encouraged by lower tax rates, the reduction in the need for face-to-face contacts and the lowered costs associated with more land-extensive production technologies. The outcome was a fiscal and political crisis. The central city increasingly became an enclave of blacks and other ethnic minorities, many of them without work and many suffering from disabilities such as low levels of schooling, or fatherless homes. Beleaguered central city governments had to face this radical alteration of client groups at the same time as their economic base was under threat from decentralisation of economic activity, and all they could rely upon was a narrow and unpopular tax base based on property values, and precious little compensatory support from the State or federal level.

Seen in this light the scale of British urban problems are infinitely less dramatic. We have not created new metropolitan areas in the twentieth century. We have not permitted major shifts in the distribution of national population and of economic activity between the nation's regions. We have not witnessed the numerical domination of central cities by ethnic minorities. We have not lured people to the cities by major differences in the operation of the rule of law, political freedom and the level of welfare benefits. We have planned the intra-regional decentralisation of population and of economic activity directly through public provision of facilities and indirectly through land-use planning ultimately backed by central Government approval. And, perhaps of most significance, central Governments have tried to compensate local authorities for differences in their taxable resources and in their spending needs.

The new policy dimension

But if the magnitude and context of Britain's urban problem was different, why did our urban policies come to be seen as deficient? There is no answer to this question, no single point in time when Governments accepted that a change in direction was necessary. None the less several diverse though related strands are discernible. Perhaps the most significant was the realisation that Government, and especially local government, had grown to such an extent that the life chances of individual citizens could be altered by the precise way in which public spending decisions impacted on urban space. Not surprisingly this general awareness was interpreted in a number of ways. Conservative thinkers drew from it the conclusion that the individual's liberty was in peril, that the social wage had grown too large relative to the private wage and that Government should be reduced or at least its continued growth held in check. In terms of urban development goals they tended to emphasise traditional objectives such as improvements to infrastructure to buttress local economic growth, the enforcement of green belts to preserve separation between town and country and the cost savings associated with conserving rather than destroying the built environment. Those on the left, in contrast, increasingly attacked the prevailing planning ideologies which saw physical planning as a value-free and technocratic implementation of goals which everyone subscribed to. Such critics argued that planning was not value-free, that it was part and parcel of the political process in which scarce public resources are allocated and that the result of urban planning certainly had not favoured the weakest groups in urban society. Thus new schools and other public facilities were awarded to the areas of population growth and especially the suburbs; the new towns, through a variety of mechanisms, kept out the sick, the aged and the unemployed; urban renewal both excluded the poorest through bureaucratic rules and resulted in new housing environments which few residents had any control over in advance or could tolerate living in afterwards.

Three official actions at this time signified the acceptance that the rewards of urban development perhaps were biased in an unacceptable way. Following the publication of the Plowden report into the operation of primary schools, the Government accepted that certain schools within defined areas in which educational attainment was stifled by poor school facilities and a deprived local environment, should be given special financial and other assistance. These Education Priority Areas (EPAs) represented the first serious attempt to discriminate positively in favour of deprived groups.

A second commitment by Government, that of the Urban Programme, suggested another level of concern. Spurred into action by Enoch Powell's inflammatory speech on the 'rivers of blood' which would flow if Government did not reduce non-white immigration from overseas into some of the nation's largest centres, the Home Office, in 1968, introduced a limited programme of financial aid to several urban areas under an Urban Aid Programme. The objective was to supplement local resources in aiding citizens in the most deprived areas of cities and towns, and, by a discriminatory use of funds, arrest the cycle of decline which affected these areas. Allocations were to be made flexibly and anything from children's play areas to consumer advice centres were to be eligible for support. One year later the Home Office established an applied research experiment over a five-year period – the National Community Development Project. This was started in twelve areas, with teams of researchers and community workers whose job it was to explore appropriate and practical methods of better meeting the needs of people living in areas of high social deprivation.

The Urban Programme and the Community Development Projects were based on an implicit view that Britain's most deprived urban citizens lived in those areas of British cities which could also be described as deprived, environmentally, socially and economically, and that policies to ameliorate the socio-economic conditions of these deprived people must be conceived on an area or community basis. Leaving aside the question of whether Government has ever provided sufficient resources to really prove or disprove the validity of this small area approach – a question we return to later – this theme of tackling personal deprivation as an area phenomenon is one which was at the root of the Callaghan Government's approach to urban problems as exemplified in the Inner Areas White Paper and Inner Urban Areas Act.

The cost of population decline

However, we are moving too far ahead chronologically. At the time of their inception the Urban Aid Programme and the National Community Development Project were thought of by most commentators as interesting experiments in the potential amelioration of some of the conditions of the worst casualties of the urban process but hardly likely to have a fundamental impact on the basic objectives for, and the planning of, the nation's great cities. It was David Eversley who, as Chief Planner (Strategy) in the Greater London Council, raised the whole tenor of the debate and placed the future of the British conurbations in the centre of the policy stage (1972). Seen in a context in which Greater London's population had fallen from 8.6 million in 1939 to 7.4 million in 1971 and was expected to fall to 6.5 million in 1981, Eversley argued that the *per capita* costs of operating London as a public entity were bound to rise whereas incomes, both public and private, were bound not to rise commensurately. On the cost side Eversley's argument was straightforward. Part of the extra cost burden was associated, he asserted, with fulfilling London's role as a national capital which would have to continue regardless of its population size. Part arose from the need to replace outdated public infrastructure and to pay exceptionally high land values in any public development. But the most significant argument was that public services could not be scaled down rapidly to match a declining population, since many services were provided in indivisible units. In any event even when population did decentralise for residential reasons this did not reduce the demand for access to London-located jobs, so that transport services would require to be provided for the same decentralised population. Finally he argued that since net migration losses were selectively biased towards the young, skilled and productive, then London's population would become increasingly dependent upon the provision of social services of all kinds. In necessarily responding to these more dependent clients, London would face increased *per capita* service costs.

On the tendencies in incomes, Eversley's argument was even more straightforward. As the highest income groups leave, the average capacity of the remaining residents to support a given level of services through local taxation diminishes. If we add a further tendency, namely for the most productive economic activity to decentralise out of London (or not start up there) under the twin influence of Government regional policy and of the inherent advantages of an off-centre site with low rental cost and adequate access to London itself, then this too, over time, reduces the fiscal capacity of London.

Taken together, these two basic tendencies of rising costs of public operation plus an inadequately rising fiscal capacity to support the requisite services could only lead, so Eversley argued, to a growth in the number of areas of poverty within London and a generally reduced capacity to improve its environment. Three alternative solutions were offered. London could expand its territory by integrating surrounding political jurisdiction and tax-payers within one larger administrative framework; central Government could shoulder any increased share of London's expenditure by augmenting its allocation under the Rate Support Grant and/or London could be given an augmented capacity to raise local revenue as, for example, through a local income tax.

In presenting these arguments to the Greater London Development Plan Enquiry, Eversley and his colleagues at first suggested that London's population should not be allowed to fall below a certain population size. Later, when no optimal population size could be defended statistically or logically, the GLC changed its plea and asked for a reduced rate of population decline. The Panel, in reviewing these propositions, found that they had no merit,

> ... We emphatically recommend rejection of the GLC view that there is any particular danger in either a lower level of population to which the present rate of decline of population is likely to lead, or the particular rate of change itself. The arguments put forward in support of the view that the decline should be retarded are either ... illogical or are unsupported by the evidence. In any case we see very little likelihood that policies could be successful in restraining any particular rate of change (DOE, 1972).

In scrutinising the GLC's evidence (and that of Eversley) many commentators have come to similar conclusions as the Layfield panel. Foster and Richardson (1973) could find no evidence that there had been any major imbalance in either the number or the type of jobs which had decentralised relative to the working force which had decentralised. As a general conclusion they were able to argue that '... it is not easy to discern extensive hardship in London arising from declining city size (or) a strong empirical case which would justify a dramatic change in policy designed to alter the existing emigration forces'. Holtermann (1973) in an even more wide-ranging review also remained sceptical. She found no evidence that land costs had risen faster in London as compared to the South East or to Great Britain as a whole. Very few local authority services seemed subject to diseconomies of scale and although the structure of London's population had been affected by net migration losses, the overall effect had been very modest.

These reviews notwithstanding, Eversley's analysis continues to raise fundamental questions about the consequences of central city decline in London and all other declining conurbations for the welfare of residents, the fiscal base, the economic vitality and the political health of these declining core cities. Is emigration imbalanced? Are there unwanted labour market effects, if not at a level of the central city as a whole, then in terms of pockets of unemployed who are unable to join in the outward migration and face reduced service employment opportunities as residents shift out? And what of the effects of economic activity decentralisation? Has this resulted in the withdrawal of high productivity, high paying activities from the central city? Does this in turn cause local linkages to be severed, thus destroying external economies and thereby making it more likely that other plants will decentralise? Should this occur, then what are the effects upon the taxable base? Does decentralisation of the most productive parts of the base result in a reduced capacity to draw upon local finance and thereby create a growing dependence upon central Government funding? Alternatively is the decentralisation of some activity more than compensated for by the growth of other activity with a capacity to pay high central city rents, as, for example, some parts of service (office) activities? And if net migration forces are imbalanced and the central city does increasingly contain a more public-service dependent population, what are the effects on the costs of running existing services and what new service requirements have to be supplied to the new client groups? And if there are additional *per capita* operating costs and new services to be provided, does the central Government have sufficiently subtle mechanisms for identifying these marginal costs and appropriate grant régimes to compensate for the needed expenditure?

If equity arguments were at the root of the concern in the Educational Priority approach and the Urban Programme, then arguments about the costs of adjustment, both short term and long term, as population and economic activity decentralise from the conurbations, are at the core of Eversley's concern. Accordingly, the management of urban decline forms the second of the principal concerns of this volume.

The conurbation economies

Our third focus point relates to the structure and performance of the conurbation economies. Unlike the other two broad areas of interest, concern for the likely future of conurbation economies has not been the subject of any official enquiry or official report or, for that matter, of significant academic research. But now the situation has changed. Gone are the days when it was felt that the conurbation economies could look after themselves. Didn't they possess marked agglomeration economies, which would guarantee low-cost production? Didn't they have the most sophisticated communication networks which would guarantee the attraction of office activities as the sectoral balance of the economy shifted in this direction? Were not the recent internal road and rail improvements sufficient to diminish the threat to the costs of operation from congestion or diminished worker mobility? And above all, couldn't they cope better with their problems of adjusting land uses for economic activity if some of the growth pressures were taken off by a diversion of growth to new towns and other planned growth centres?

Such arguments now read very strangely. In part the new concern reflects the persistence of the deepest economic recession the UK has experienced since the 1930s. This has affected the level of employment throughout the country; and the conurbations, as major labour markets, have experienced absolutely large numbers of unemployed seeking work. In part it reflects the fact that unemployment is heavily concentrated amongst the young and ethnic minorities and the latter, in particular, have tended to concentrate in the major urban centres. But there are other deeper causes for disquiet. Manufacturing and service investment flows, which regional policy has sought to divert to the northern conurbations and especially Merseyside, Newcastle and Glasgow, have been constrained by the recession. Furthermore, the equalisation of unemployment over the nation's regions has pressured the Government into a relaxation of industrial and office controls in the south of the UK and into making an increasing range of investment incentives available throughout the country. The net effect is that the northern conurbations are liable to be at a comparative disadvantage in attracting new investment – especially investment opportunities generated by activities outside of their immediate areas of influence.

Of more general concern is whether the conurbations as such increasingly are likely to lose investment opportunities to alternative smaller centres within the urban system. We have already touched upon the factors causing decentralisation from the central cities of the conurbations to their surrounding regions. But the process of movement down the urban hierarchy is a separate, though related, phenomenon. If the conurbations have always been the locations for innovation and unstandardised decision-making, can they cling on to this status if communications improvements allow not only access to the agglomeration economies of the big city but also a capacity to obtain pleasanter living environments and lower operating costs? Is the continued economic vitality of the conurbations, so dependent in recent years upon the growth of Government activities, at risk in an era of restraint in public expenditure growth? And can the conurbations really compete for investment opportunities if local governments have highly limited powers and even less experience in the promotion of local economic development?

The Inner City

These three levels of concern – the distributional consequences of planning, the welfare, political and fiscal implications of intra-regional decentralisation, and the apparent weakness in conurbation economies – were welded together in the last Labour Government's thinking about the Inner City. Though the Inner City was never defined geographically, the Callaghan Government accepted the general findings of consultants who had looked at a number of parts of several conurbations in a series of Inner Area studies. The theme running through all of the resulting reports was that much of the central cities at the core of the conurbations were in urgent need of publicly-initiated revitalisation. They had become the areas of lowest public investment, most inadequately provided public services and most squalid environments. Increasingly they were areas which modern private economic activity had shunned and had become the living places for all of those who were excluded by reason of income from the tolerable parts of the private rental and owner-occupied sector. Increasingly too, as public urban renewal and new-town policy had filtered off the young, the skilled and the vigorous, the public sector housing stock within such areas had come to contain an ageing population and, in some instances, a population heavily weighted by ethnic minorities.

Both the Callaghan and now the Thatcher Governments have sought to shift more public resources into some of these areas. But here is the rub. Most of the public resources which have to be applied are under the control of local authorities. Thus the central Government must initiate 'partnerships' and with the lubrication of some earmarked central Government funds under the Urban Aid Programme, convince local authorities of the need to place a higher priority upon the allocation of local funds to the Inner City. This central Government involvement, albeit on a financial basis which is explicit and limited, creates obvious difficulties. It cuts across the avowed intention of central Government to free local authorities increasingly to make their own investment decisions. It can be interpreted as unnecessary pressure upon local authorities at precisely the time when local corporate planning processes, which have been encouraged by the central Government, are reaching into fundamental questions of service efficiency, area management, and the delineation of needs. And it can be viewed as a yet more elaborate blurring of responsibilities at a time when locally elected authorities are trying to cope with the crop of semi-autonomous non-elected agencies which central Government has created and inserted into the operational domain of local government. Above all else it may give too sharp a geographical definition to deprivation and decay which is not isolated but instead is spread throughout local authority areas. The result could be a diversion of too much administrative and political attention, as well as financial resources, to areas which have genuine needs but are not uniquely in this position.

The objectives of this volume

We have come along a path strewn with complex ideas. And yet the objectives of the volume are very simple. The British conurbations have not been studied in depth on a comparative basis before. What we have is a series of regional and sub-regional studies and the occasional in-depth portrayal of the crucial policy issues facing individual conurbations. However, the twin assumptions which underlie this volume are, firstly, that the economic, social and political forces which are shaping the direction of these urban 'heavy-weights', are worthy of detailed consideration from a national viewpoint. And, secondly, because there is sufficient similarity in the nature of the forces shaping the pattern of conurbation development, it is a valid exercise to study these forces comparatively.

In this study we have eschewed the pattern of so many other comparative books – namely that of describing and analysing the forces at work and the policy choices facing each conurbation on a one-by-one basis. Apart from a case study of one conurbation and a comparative statistical chapter, we have ordered all the contributions around a number of key themes. Thus we will look at the emerging shape of the conurbation economies, and the financial resources which will underpin their development. We will scrutinise the provision of key public services, in a context where efficiency and equity considerations have to be weighed and given priority. We will examine a selection of critical urban problems and especially the incidence of poverty, local area decay, urban unemployment and urban economic adaptation. Finally, we shall look at the governance of the conurbations, highlighting the ways in which local corporate responsibilities are being perceived, and we shall investigate the complex financial and political interactions between central and local government made necessary by the changing perceptions of the role of the conurbations.

Notes

1. The English conurbations are Greater London, Merseyside, South East Lancashire, West Yorkshire, West Midlands and Tyneside. The seventh conurbation is Central Clydeside in Scotland.

References

Briggs, A. (1968) *Victorian Cities*. Penguin Books, Harmondsworth.
Cmnd. 6153 (1940) *Report of the Royal Commission on the Distribution of the Industrial Population*. HMSO.
Department of the Environment (1972) *Report of the Panel of Inquiry into the Greater London Development Plan*. Chairman: F.B. Layfield. (SBN 11 75061.5 X)
Eversley, D.E.C. (1972) 'Rising costs and static incomes: some economic consequences of regional planning in London', *Urban Studies* **9** (3), pp. 347–68.
Foster, C.D. and **Richardson, R.** (1973) 'Employment trends in London' in Donnison, D., and Eversley, D.E.C. (eds) *London: Urban Patterns Problems and Policies* Ch. 3. Heinemann, London.
Geddes, P. (1915) *Cities in Evolution*. Williams and Norgate, London.
Glass, R. (1972) 'Anti-Urbanism' in Stewart, J.M.W. (ed) *The City*. Penguin Books, Harmondsworth.
Hall, P., Thomas, R., Gracey, H. and **Drewett, R.** (1973) *The Containment of Urban England*, vol. 1. Allen and Unwin, London.
Holtermann, S. (1973) 'The Decline of London: Some Evidence', South East Economics Working Note No. 19 (Mimeo). Department of the Environment.
Masterman, C.F. (1904) *The English City*. Johnson, London.

Chapter 2

Statistical trends of the British conurbations

In terms of official statistics, the British conurbations were born in the 1951 Census and died in the 1974/75 reorganisation of local government. Most of our data, therefore, cover only a twenty-year period encompassing the 1951, 1961, and 1971 Censuses.[1] However, the two decades between 1951 and 1971 saw enormous structural change in the country's space-economy, and it is in these changes that lie the origins of so many of today's urban policy problems. This makes it crucial to explore as fully as possible the available statistical information about the conurbations. In doing so, this chapter will provide a broad view of the characteristics of the conurbations, and their changes over time, both to contrast the conurbations with the rest of the country and to highlight different features of individual conurbations.

Population trends

Table 2.1 shows the population of the conurbations for the period 1901 to 1974; Table 2.2 converts these to rates of change, and Fig. 2.1 illustrates graphically the overall time profiles of population change. The seven conurbations as a whole grew nearly as fast as Great Britain's total population 1901 to 1921, and in the decade 1921–31 grew about one-and-a-half times as fast: by 1931 the seven conurbations held just over 40 per cent of the nation's population.[2] It was in the period 1931–51 that things began to change. The conurbations as a whole grew only very slowly, whereas the population of the rest of Great Britain grew substantially. In the 1951–61 decade the conurbation population scarcely grew at all, while the population elsewhere grew even more rapidly than before. In the 1961–71 period the conurbations began to lose population (−958,000) at the same time as population elsewhere in the country was increasing more rapidly than in any ten-year period in the century (+3,653,000). Finally, according to the 1974 estimates, the 1961–71 trends continued into the early 1970s, with a somewhat more rapid decline of conurbation population and a somewhat slower increase of non-conurbation population.

Four of the conurbations – Central Clydeside, Greater London, Merseyside, and Tyneside – exhibited broadly similar time patterns of

Table 2.1 Population of the conurbations, 1901–1974 (in millions)

Conurbation	1901	1911	1921	1931	1951	1961	1971	1974
Central Clydeside	1,374	1,498	1,618	1,688	1,759	1,802	1,728	1,658
Greater London	6,586	7,256	7,488	8,216	8,348	8,183	7,452	7,174
Merseyside	1,030	1,157	1,263	1,347	1,382	1,384	1,267	1,207
South East Lancashire	2,117	2,328	2,361	2,427	2,423	2,428	2,393	2,376
Tyneside	678	762	816	827	836	855	805	781
West Midlands	1,483	1,635	1,773	1,933	2,237	2,347	2,372	2,353
West Yorkshire	1,524	1,590	1,614	1,655	1,693	1,704	1,728	1,737
Total: 7 conurbations	14,792	16,226	16,933	18,093	18,678	18,703	17,745	17,286
Rest of Great Britain	22,208	24,605	25,836	26,702	30,176	32,581	36,234	37,132
Total: Great Britain	37,000	40,831	42,769	44,795	48,854	51,284	53,979	54,418

Source: English conurbations 1901–51 from *1951 Census England and Wales, General Tables*, Table 3.
Scottish conurbation 1931–51 from *1951 Census of Scotland, General Tables.*
English conurbations 1961 from *1961 Census England and Wales.*
Scottish conurbation 1961 from *1961 Census Scotland.*
All conurbations 1971 from *1971 Census Great Britain, Age Marital Condition & General Tables.*
Scottish conurbation 1901–21 estimated from constituent area data in the relevant Census volumes 1901, 1911, and 1921.
All conurbations 1974 data are from Registrar General Estimates, Office of Population Census and Surveys.

Note: In many cases there were small changes in conurbation boundaries between censuses; this is not generally significant, except that for Greater London the fall in population 1961–71 is somewhat exaggerated because of the change in definition consequent upon the creation of the GLC.

Table 2.2 Rates of population change in the conurbations, 1901–74
(Percentage change over period shown)

Conurbation	1901–11 (%)	1911–21 (%)	1921–31 (%)	1931–51 (%)	1951–61 (%)	1961–71 (%)	1971–74 (%)	1951–74 (%)
Central Clydeside	+ 9.0	+ 8.0	+ 4.3	+ 4.2	+ 2.4	− 4.1	− 4.1	− 5.7
Greater London	+ 10.2	+ 3.2	+ 9.7	+ 1.6	− 2.0	− 8.9	− 3.7	− 14.1
Merseyside	+ 12.3	+ 9.2	+ 6.7	+ 2.6	+ 0.1	− 8.5	− 4.7	− 12.7
South East Lancashire	+ 10.0	+ 1.4	+ 2.8	− 0.2	+ 0.2	− 1.4	− 0.7	− 1.9
Tyneside	+ 12.4	+ 7.1	+ 1.3	+ 1.1	+ 2.3	− 5.8	− 3.0	− 6.6
West Midlands	+ 10.2	+ 8.4	+ 9.0	+ 15.7	+ 4.9	+ 1.1	− 0.8	+ 5.2
West Yorkshire	+ 4.3	+ 1.5	+ 2.5	+ 2.3	+ 0.6	+ 1.4	+ 0.5	+ 2.6
Total: 7 conurbations	+ 9.7	+ 4.4	+ 6.9	+ 3.2	+ 0.1	− 5.1	− 2.6	− 7.5
Rest of Great Britain	+ 10.8	+ 5.0	+ 3.4	+ 13.0	+ 8.0	+ 11.2	+ 2.5	+ 23.1
Total Great Britain	+ 10.4	+ 4.7	+ 4.7	+ 9.1	+ 5.0	+ 5.3	+ 0.8	+ 11.4

Source: As for Table 2.1.
Note: All periods are ten years, except 1931–51 (twenty) and 1971–74 (three); hence, rates of change are not exactly comparable between the ten-year inter-censal periods and the other periods.

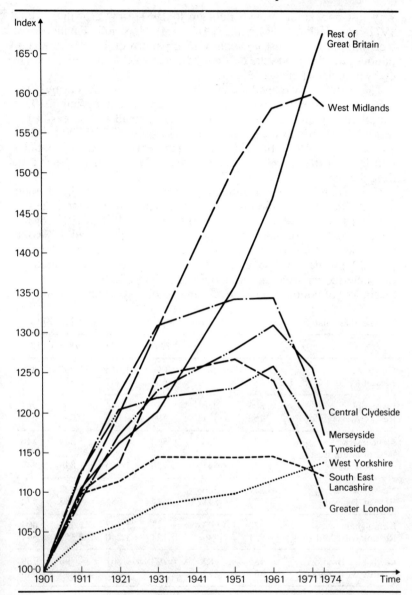

Fig 2.1 Index of population growth: Conurbations

change: fast growth 1901 to 1931; slow growth 1931 to 1951 or 1961; and heavy decline 1961 through 1974. South East Lancashire exhibited a different pattern, with rapid growth only in the 1901 to 1911 period; slow growth 1911 to 1931; no growth 1931 to 1961; and slow decline 1961 to 1974. The West Midlands, on the other hand, showed very fast population growth right up to 1961, slow growth 1961 to 1971, and decline only in the 1971 to 1974 period. Finally, West Yorkshire has the most non-conforming pattern of all: slow but continuous growth – it was the only conurbation which recorded growth in every period, including 1971–74.

The pattern of expansion and contraction has meant that by 1974 the seven conurbations contained *fewer* people than they had in 1931: conurbation population was 807,000 (4.5%) smaller, whereas in the rest of Great Britain the population in 1974 was 10,430,000 (39.1%) greater than in 1931. In 1931 over 40 per cent of the British population lived in the seven conurbations; by 1974 less than 32 per cent lived there.

If the conurbations are disaggregated into, on the one hand, their central cities, and on the other hand, the outer areas, quite different patterns emerge. Table 2.3 presents the data for 1921 to 1974 for the six conurbations outside of London.[3] Between 1931 and 1974 the population of the conurbation central cities dropped by 886,000 (−18.5%) while at the same time the population of the outer areas of the same six conurbations grew by 1,121,000 (+22.0%). Clearly, the recent loss of population (relatively and absolutely) from the conurba-

Table 2.3 Populations of conurbation central cities and remainders, 1921–1974

	1921	1931	1951	1961	1971	1974
Glasgow	1,034	1,088	1,090	1,055	897	816
Rest of Central Clydeside	584	600	669	747	831	842
Liverpool	805	856	789	746	610	561
Rest of Merseyside	458	491	593	638	657	646
Manchester	736	766	703	662	544	516
Rest of South East Lancashire	1,625	1,661	1,720	1,766	1,849	1,860
Newcastle	277	286	292	270	222	209
Rest of Tyneside	539	541	544	585	583	572
Birmingham	922	1,003	1,113	1,107	1,015	1,004
Rest of West Midlands	851	930	1,124	1,240	1,357	1,349
Leeds plus Bradford	755	782	797	807	790	789
Rest of West Yorkshire	859	873	896	897	938	948
Total: 6 conurbation 'Cities'	4,529	4,781	4,784	4,647	4,078	3,895
Total: Remainder of conurbations	4,916	5,096	5,546	5,873	6,215	6,217
Total: 6 conurbations	9,445	9,877	10,330	10,520	10,293	10,112

Source: Censuses for 1951, 1961, and 1971; Registrar-General Estimates for 1974 (OPCS).

tions has been the result of concentrated and massive loss from their central cities, only partially offset by gains in the outer areas.

The population changes of the conurbation cities can also be contrasted with the experience of large non-conurbation cities; this is shown in Table 2.4. Although the 12 cities only began to suffer absolute population loss in the 1971–74 period, they experienced practically no growth in the 20 years 1951 to 1971. Thus, the 12 non-conurbation cities occupied a middle position between the decline of the conurbation central cities and the growth of the conurbation outer areas. The relative rates of change of population are summarised in Table 2.5.

It is also true that population densities in the conurbation central cities have been significantly higher than those in other large cities, which might suggest a greater need to lose population in order to rebuild at lower, more acceptable modern densities. In 1961, when the conurbation central cities began to lose population rapidly, the average density was some 50.7 persons per hectare (ranging from Bradford's

Table 2.4 Population of Major Great Britain cities, 1921–1974 (in thousands)

	1921	1931	1951	1961	1971	1974
Non-conurbation cities:						
Bristol	382	404	443	437	427	419
Cardiff	221	227	245	257	279	276
Coventry	153	178	258	306	335	334
Edinburgh	420	439	467	468	454	450
Kingston/Hull	291	314	299	303	286	279
Leicester	238	257	285	273	284	287
Nottingham	264	276	306	312	301	288
Portsmouth	248	252	234	215	197	200
Plymouth	214	213	227	230	239	251
Sheffield	516	518	513	494	520	507
Southampton	161	176	190	205	215	213
Stoke-on-Trent	268	277	280	277	265	258
Sub-total: 12 non-conurbation cities	3,376	3,531	3,747	3,777	3,802	3,762
Conurbation cities:						
Birmingham	922	1,003	1,113	1,107	1,015	1,004
Bradford	292	299	292	296	294	290
Glasgow	1,034	1,088	1,090	1,055	897	816
Leeds	463	483	505	511	496	499
Liverpool	805	856	789	746	610	561
Manchester	736	766	703	662	544	516
Newcastle	277	286	292	270	222	209
Sub-total: 7 conurbation cities	4,529	4,781	4,784	4,647	4,078	3,895

Source: Censuses for 1951, 1961, 1971 Registrar General Estimates for 1974 (OPCS)

Table 2.5 Rates of population change, conurbation cities, outer areas, and other large cities, 1921–1974

	1921–31 (%)	1931–51 (%)	1951–61 (%)	1961–71 (%)	1971–74 (%)
Greater London Conurbation	+ 9.7	+ 1.6	− 2.0	− 8.9	− 3.7
Cities of other 6 Conurbations	+ 5.6	+ 0.1	− 2.9	− 12.2	− 4.5
Outer areas of other 6 conurbations	+ 3.5	+ 8.8	+ 5.9	+ 5.8	0.0
12 large non-conurbation cities (>200,000)	+ 4.6	+ 6.1	+ 0.8	+ 0.7	− 1.1
Total: 7 conurbations plus 12 large non-conurbation cities	+ 6.5	+ 3.7	+ 0.2	− 4.2	− 2.3
Rest of Great Britain	+ 3.2	+ 14.1	+ 9.0	+ 12.6	+ 2.9

Source: As for Table 2.4.

28.7 to Glasgow's 67.2) as compared to 35.4 in the 12 large non-conurbation centres (ranging from Sheffield's 26.9 to Portsmouth's 57.3). But by 1974 the gap had been greatly reduced, and population density in the conurbation cities was down to 42.5 persons per hectare compared to 35.3 for the non-conurbation cities. However, the relationship between density and population change is sometimes ambiguous, as shown by Table 2.6. For example, Coventry, Leicester and Southampton had higher than average densities in 1961 but still increased their populations 1961–74. Equally, Edinburgh and Stoke-on-Trent had lower than average densities yet lost population. Further, Birmingham with a very high 1961 density of 53.0 persons per hectare only declined by 9.3 per cent to 1974, while Newcastle with a lower 1961 density of 49.1 persons per hectare lost a massive 22.6 per cent of its population in the same period.

Migration

The very heavy recent population losses of the conurbations cannot be explained in terms of variations in natural increase; they can only be understood in the context of large and sustained migration flows. In the five years 1966–71, for example, there was a net out-migration of 891,180 people from the seven conurbations (excluding international migration). In gross flows, that five year period saw 809,620 people move into the conurbations, but at the same time 1,700,800 moved out (again excluding international movements). Interesting differences in migration show up on Table 2.7, which shows that 55 per cent of people moving into the conurbations came from outside the conurbations

Table 2.6 Population and density, conurbations, conurbation central cities, and non-conurbation cities, 1961–1974

	1971 area (ha)	Population density (Persons per hectare)		Population Change
		1961	1974	1961–74 (%)
Bristol	11,000	39.73	38.09	− 4.1
Cardiff	8,000	32.13	34.50	+ 7.4
Coventry	8,100	37.78	41.23	+ 9.2
Edinburgh	13,500	34.67	33.33	− 3.8
Kingston/Hull	7,100	42.68	39.30	− 7.9
Leicester	7,300	37.40	39.32	+ 5.1
Nottingham	7,400	42.16	38.92	− 7.7
Portsmouth	3,750	57.33	53.33	− 7.0
Plymouth	7,900	29.11	31.77	+ 9.1
Sheffield	18,400	26.85	27.55	+ 2.6
Southampton	4,900	41.84	43.47	+ 3.9
Stoke-on-Trent	9,300	29.78	27.74	− 6.9
12 large non-conurbation cities	106,650	35.41	35.27	− 0.4
Birmingham	20,900	52.97	48.04	− 9.3
Bradford	10,300	28.74	28.16	− 2.0
Glasgow	15,700	67.20	51.97	− 22.7
Leeds	16,400	31.16	30.43	− 2.3
Liverpool	11,300	66.02	49.65	− 24.8
Manchester	11,600	57.07	44.48	− 22.1
Newcastle	5,500	49.09	38.00	− 22.6
6 conurbation central cities	91,700	50.68	42.48	− 16.2
Conurbations outside of central cities:				
Central Clydeside	62,150	12.02	13.55	+ 12.7
Merseyside	28,150	22.66	22.95	+ 1.3
South East Lancs.	87,300	20.23	21.31	+ 5.3
Tyneside	17,950	29.81	31.87	+ 6.9
West Midlands	46,900	26.44	28.76	+ 8.8
West Yorkshire	98,800	9.08	9.60	+ 5.7
Sub-total	341,250	17.21	18.22	+ 5.9
Central Clydeside	77,850	23.15	21.30	− 8.0
Greater London	157,950	51.81	45.42	− 12.3
Merseyside	39,450	35.08	30.60	− 12.8
South East Lancs.	98,300	24.70	24.17	− 2.1
Tyneside	23,450	36.46	33.30	− 8.7
West Midlands	67,800	34.62	34.71	+ 0.3
West Yorkshire	125,500	13.58	13.84	+ 1.9
Total 7 conurbations	590,300	31.68	29.28	− 7.6

Source: 1971 Census; Table 2.4.

Table 2.7 Internal (Great Britain) migration, 1966–1971, conurbations

Conurbation	From conurbation to same region	From same region to conurbation	Net between conurbation and same region	Ratio: out-migration to in-migration	From conurbation to other GB	From other GB to conurbation	Net between conurbation and other GB	Ratio: out-migration to in-migration
Central Clydeside	77,850	33,600	− 44,250	2.32	50,120	21,550	− 28,570	2.33
Greater London	589,500	187,890	− 401,610	3.14	261,950	189,080	− 72,870	1.39
Merseyside	96,080	25,410	− 70,670	3.78	47,770	28,950	− 18,820	1.65
South East Lancs.	78,150	36,630	− 41,520	2.13	97,380	72,220	− 25,160	1.35
Tyneside	39,380	17,670	− 21,710	2.23	36,980	20,880	− 16,100	1.77
West Midlands	124,020	36,120	− 87,900	3.43	88,860	58,620	− 30,240	1.52
West Yorkshire	40,870	27,630	− 13,240	1.48	71,890	53,370	− 18,520	1.35
Total 7 conurbations	1,045,850	364,950	− 680,900	2.87	654,950	444,670	− 210,280	1.47

Source: 1971 Census, 5-year migration tables.

Note: 'Same Region' is as follows: Central Clydeside = Scotland; Greater London = South East; Merseyside and South East Lancs. = North West; Tyneside = Northern; West Midlands = West Midlands; West Yorkshire = Yorkshire and Humberside.

region, whereas only 38.5 per cent of people leaving conurbations went outside the region. The net *intra*-regional migration was over three times as great as net inter-regional migration. In other words, most of the domestic migration has been from the conurbations to other locations in the same region. Table 2.8 converts the absolute

Table 2.8 Rates of migration, 1966–1971, conurbations

Conurbation	1966 population	Migration, 1966–71, Per 1,000 base 1966 population			
		Net to/from same region	Net to/from all other GB	Net to/from total GB	Into conurbation from outside GB
Central Clydeside	1,766,000	− 25.06	− 16.18	− 41.24	+ 8.70
Greater London	7,671,000	− 52.35	− 9.50	− 61.85	+ 38.56
Merseyside	1,338,000	− 52.82	− 14.07	− 66.89	+ 9.64
South East Lancs.	2,404,000	− 17.27	− 10.47	− 27.74	+ 16.20
Tyneside	832,000	− 26.09	− 19.35	− 45.44	+ 6.66
West Midlands	2,374,000	− 37.03	− 12.74	− 49.77	+ 19.60
West Yorkshire	1,708,000	− 7.75	− 10.84	− 18.59	+ 17.62
Total 7 conurbations	18,093,000	− 37.63	− 11.62	− 49.25	+ 24.60

Source: 1971 Census, 5-year migration tables.

Note: No data are available on migration from conurbations to areas outside Great Britain, and therefore no net total migration figures are available.

migration figures into rates, based on 1966 population. The highest rate of domestic migration loss was from Merseyside (−66.9 per 1,000), closely followed by Greater London (−61.85 per 1,000); at the low end of the scale were West Yorkshire (−18.6) and South East Lancashire (−27.74). Significantly, the three top conurbations in terms of net losses to other regions (that is, excluding intra-regional migration) are those located in the most economically depressed regions: Tyneside, Central Clydeside, and Merseyside.

Systematic data on migration from the conurbations to overseas destinations is unfortunately not available, but the final column of Table 2.8 shows the extreme variations in overseas migration into the conurbations. Greater London is the principal recipient, and its overseas immigrants were coming in between 1966 and 1971 in volumes which radically reduced its overall net outmigration rate. Predictably, the least attractive destinations for overseas immigrants were Tyneside, Central Clydeside, and Merseyside.

Population characteristics

The population of the conurbations has been characterised at all three Censuses 1951–1961–1971 by lower than national average proportions

Table 2.9 Age distribution of the population, conurbations, 1951–1961–1971 (per cent distribution)

Conurbation	1951 Census			1961 Census			1971 Census		
	0–14	15–59F 15–64M	60+F 65+M	0–14	15–59F 15–64M	60+F 65+M	0–14	15–59F 15–64M	60+F 65+M
Central Clydeside	25.3	63.7	11.0	26.9	61.3	11.8	27.3	58.9	13.8
Greater London	20.6	66.0	13.4	20.2	65.2	14.7	21.1	62.5	16.4
Merseyside	25.4	62.7	11.9	26.1	60.8	13.1	25.6	58.8	15.6
South East Lancashire	21.8	64.6	13.5	23.3	62.2	14.5	24.5	59.4	16.0
Tyneside	23.6	64.1	12.3	24.9	61.5	13.6	23.8	60.0	16.2
West Midlands	23.9	64.6	11.5	23.3	64.3	12.4	24.7	61.0	14.3
West Yorkshire	21.2	64.5	14.3	22.9	61.7	15.4	24.2	59.0	16.8
Total: 7 conurbations	22.1	65.0	12.9	22.5	63.5	14.0	23.4	60.8	15.8
Rest of Great Britain	22.6	63.3	14.1	23.7	61.2	15.1	24.2	59.2	16.6
Total: Great Britain	22.4	64.0	13.6	23.3	62.0	14.7	24.0	59.7	16.3

Source: Censuses of 1951, 1961, 1971,
Note: Totals do not always add to exactly 100 per cent because of rounding.

Table 2.10 Size distributions of private households, conurbations, 1951–1961–1971 (per cent distribution)

Conurbation	1951 Census household size:			1961 Census household size:			1971 Census household size:		
	1 or 2	3 or 4	5 +	1 or 2	3 or 4	5 +	1 or 2	3 or 4	5 +
Central Clydeside	33.6	43.1	23.4	39.0	40.6	20.4	45.3	35.3	19.3
Greater London	42.0	43.3	14.6	47.0	39.6	13.5	54.5	33.0	12.5
Merseyside	33.4	43.1	23.6	37.7	41.0	21.3	46.5	34.8	18.6
South East Lancashire	40.1	44.5	15.4	45.4	40.5	14.0	51.2	34.6	14.1
Tyneside	35.8	45.1	19.0	42.1	41.5	16.4	50.4	35.5	14.0
West Midlands	33.4	46.4	20.3	39.0	43.2	17.8	47.5	36.8	15.8
West Yorkshire	43.3	42.7	14.0	48.2	39.2	12.7	52.9	33.8	13.2
Total: 7 conurbations	39.4	43.7	17.0	44.4	40.3	15.3	51.4	34.2	14.3
Rest of Great Britain	37.2	44.2	18.5	42.3	41.6	16.1	49.0	36.8	14.2
Total: Great Britain	38.0	44.1	17.8	43.1	41.1	15.8	49.8	36.0	14.2

Source: Censuses of 1951, 1961, 1971.
Note: Totals do not always add to exactly 100 per cent because of rounding.

of children and older people and by consistently higher than average proportions in the working ages (see Table 2.9). Amongst the seven conurbations, however, there is more variation. Merseyside and (especially) Central Clydeside have had well above average proportions of children, whereas Greater London has had proportions well below average. Central Clydeside and West Midlands have consistently had below average shares of people over retirement age, while West Yorkshire has had above average shares.

More differentiation shows up when the size distribution of households is examined (Table 2.10). Taken as a whole, the conurbations have had higher than average proportions of small households (1 or 2 persons), and by 1971 over one-half of conurbation households were in this size category. In contrast, although the conurbations had lower than average proportions of large households (5+ persons) in 1951 and 1961, by 1971 the proportion was slightly above average. Even so, by 1971 in the conurbations, only about one household in seven had more than four persons and this proportion had declined steadily over the period.

Amongst the individual conurbations, household size variations follow in many ways those of age distribution. Central Clydeside and Merseyside have much higher than average shares of large households, as would be expected from the high proportions of children in their populations. Central Clydeside, Merseyside and West Midlands all have lower than average shares of small households, consistent with their relatively smaller shares of older people. West Yorkshire had the highest proportion of one- and two-person households in 1951 and 1961 but was overtaken by Greater London in 1971.

Labour force characteristics

Social characteristics of the population are difficult to determine statistically, both because of limited data availability and because of fundamental problems of definition. Since social class is normally assigned in the Census on the basis of occupation of the (presumedly male) head of household, our principal data here are related to the male labour force, not to the population at large.[4] In Table 2.11 the categorisations by socio-economic group (s.e.g.) are presented, with a selected further analysis in Table 2.12. The six conurbations outside London are totalled separately from Greater London in Table 2.11 because of the enormous differences in socio-economic structure. For example, in 1971 fully 62.3 per cent of working men in the six conurbations were in manual occupations, whereas in Greater London the figure was only 46.1 per cent. Comparing the six conurbations to non-conurbation Great Britain, we can see that they have a lower proportion of men in

Table 2.11 Male labour force, by socio-economic group, by conurbation (per cent distribution)

	1961 Census							1971 Census						
	S.e.g. 1,2, 3,4	S.e.g. 5,6, 7,12	All non-man-ual	S.e.g. 8,9	S.e.g. 10,11	All man-ual	Other	S.e.g. 1,2 3,4	S.e.g. 5,6 7,12	All non-man-ual	S.e.g. 8,9	S.e.g. 10,11	All man-ual	Other
Central Clydeside	9.6	20.5	30.1	41.9	26.4	68.3	1.7	13.4	20.7	34.1	38.5	25.0	63.4	2.5
Merseyside	11.8	21.6	33.4	33.9	29.9	63.8	2.8	13.3	21.9	35.2	33.0	28.6	61.6	3.1
South East Lancashire	12.9	21.8	34.8	37.6	25.6	63.2	2.0	15.9	22.9	38.9	35.5	23.2	58.7	2.4
Tyneside	11.2	19.3	30.4	41.4	25.9	67.3	2.3	12.7	20.4	33.1	40.4	23.9	64.3	2.7
West Midlands	11.5	17.2	28.7	44.3	24.4	68.7	2.6	14.1	18.7	32.8	40.1	24.0	64.9	2.3
West Yorkshire	12.7	19.2	31.9	40.0	25.1	65.0	3.0	14.8	21.1	35.9	38.1	23.6	61.7	2.4
Total: 6 conurbations	11.7	19.9	31.6	40.1	26.0	66.0	2.4	14.3	20.9	35.2	37.8	24.4	62.3	2.5
Greater London	16.7	28.2	44.9	31.0	21.1	52.1	3.0	19.9	30.7	50.6	27.4	18.7	46.1	3.3
Rest of Great Britain	12.5	18.7	31.2	34.7	22.9	57.5	11.3	16.5	21.9	38.4	33.7	19.8	53.5	8.1
Total: Great Britain	13.0	20.6	33.6	35.2	23.2	58.4	8.1	16.5	22.9	39.5	33.6	20.5	54.1	6.4

Source: Censuses of 1961 and 1971.

Note: S.e.g. 1,2,3,4 = Professional and managerial.   S.e.g. 5,6,7,12 = Other non-manual.
S.e.g. 8,9 = Foremen and skilled manual.   S.e.g. 10,11 = Semi-skilled and unskilled manual.
Other = S.e.g. 13,14,15,16,17 = Agricultural, Armed Forces, and not adequately specified.
Rows may not add exactly to 100 per cent due to rounding.

Table 2.12 Selected aspects of socio-economic structure, conurbations, 1961–1971 (Male economically active population resident in area, per cent distribution)

	Foremen (8) and skilled manual (9) as % of all manual		Professional and managerial (1–4) as % of all non-manual		Foremen (8), skilled manual (9) and professional and managerial (1–4) as % of all economically active	
	1961 (%)	1971 (%)	1961 (%)	1971 (%)	1961 (%)	1971 (%)
Central Clydeside	61.3	60.7	31.8	39.4	51.5	51.9
Merseyside	53.1	53.6	35.4	37.8	45.7	46.4
South East Lancashire	59.5	60.5	37.2	41.0	50.5	51.5
Tyneside	61.4	62.9	36.9	38.4	52.6	53.1
West Midlands	64.5	63.0	40.1	43.0	55.8	55.0
West Yorkshire	61.5	61.7	39.9	41.2	52.7	52.9
Total: 6 conurbations	60.7	60.8	37.1	40.7	51.8	52.2
Greater London	59.6	59.5	37.2	39.3	47.8	47.3
Total: 7 conurbations	60.3	60.3	37.2	40.0	50.0	50.1
Rest of Great Britain	60.3	63.1	39.9	42.9	47.1	50.2
Total: Great Britain	60.3	62.1	38.8	41.8	48.2	50.2

Source: as for Table 2.11.

the top socio-economic groups (1, 2, 3, 4) and a higher proportion in the lower socio-economic groups (10, 11). Moreover, the professional and managerial men as a proportion of the total male labour force in the conurbations (excluding Greater London) increased more slowly 1961–71 than in the rest of Great Britain: the skill gap widened over the 10 years. In 1961 two conurbations (South East Lancashire and West Yorkshire) had proportions of socio-economic groups 1–4 above the average for non-conurbation Britain; by 1971 all six had lower proportions. In Greater London, the greatest difference was not in the proportion of top socio-economic group males (s.e.g. 1–4) but in the proportion of other non-manual occupations (s.e.g. 5, 6, 7, 12 – clerks, junior non-manual, etc.).

Table 2.12 highlights the changes 1961–71 in the structure of manual and non-manual occupations. For the seven conurbations, in both years, over 60 per cent of male manual workers were foremen or skilled, with less than 40 per cent being semi-skilled or unskilled. The only exception was Merseyside, with a strikingly high proportion of semi-skilled and unskilled labour. In the seven conurbations again, the proportion of male non-manual labour who were professional or managerial increased from 1961 to 1971, but remained lower than in the rest of Great Britain. Merseyside was once more the conurbation characterised by the lowest proportions of higher-skill occupations. When both manual and non-manual occupations are combined, the conurbation average of higher-skill occupations, while greater than in the rest of the country in 1961, was virtually the same in 1971. The proportion remained at 50 per cent for the conurbations, but rose from 47 to 50 per cent elsewhere. Merseyside and Greater London were the areas with the lowest proportions, the latter because of its disproportionate numbers of clerical and junior non-manual workers, the former because of its lower skill mix in both manual and non-manual categories.

Table 2.13 shows the structure of the labour force by national origin of economically active persons.[5] Immediately obvious is the concentration of immigrants – from all origins – in London and, to a lesser degree, the West Midlands. Equally striking is the fact that in 1971 there were relatively fewer immigrant workers in Central Clydeside, Tyneside, or Merseyside than in non-conurbation Britain. (Both of these features are consistent with the patterns of in-migration shown in the last column of Table 2.8.) Of the relatively few immigrants in the three conurbations, moreover, the greatest number were Irish; only about one-half of 1 per cent of the population were immigrants from the Commonwealth. Taking the seven conurbations together, a substantially greater proportion of workers had both parents born outside the UK than was the case in non-conurbation Britain: 11.3 per cent as opposed to 3.5 per cent. But this average hides variations ranging from Greater London's 15.7 per cent down to Tyneside's 1.4 per cent.

Table 2.13 National origin of labour force, by parents' birth place, 1971 (per cent of economically active persons.)

	One or both parents born in the UK (%)	Both parents born in:				
		Common-wealth (%)	Irish republic (%)	Other EEC (%)	Other Europe (%)	All other Countries
Central Clydeside	97.8	0.5	1.1	0.3	0.2	0.1
Greater London	84.3	7.1	4.1	1.2	1.8	1.6
Merseyside	97.1	0.6	1.6	0.2	0.2	0.3
South East Lancashire	93.6	2.1	2.6	0.5	0.7	0.5
Tyneside	98.6	0.5	0.3	0.2	0.2	0.2
West Midlands	89.7	6.0	3.2	0.3	0.4	0.3
West Yorkshire	92.7	3.7	1.5	0.5	1.0	0.6
Greater London plus West Midlands	85.5	6.8	3.9	1.0	1.5	1.3
Other 5 conurbations	95.3	1.7	1.6	0.4	0.5	0.4
Rest of Great Britain	96.5	0.9	1.0	0.5	0.6	0.5
Total: Great Britain	94.1	2.2	1.7	0.6	0.7	0.6
Total: 7 Conurbations	89.7	4.6	2.9	0.7	1.1	0.9

Source: 1971 Census of Population, special tabulation DT 1746 and Economic Activity Table 2, as published in *The Role of Immigrants in the Labour Market*, Department of Employment Unit for Manpower Studies, 1976, p. 112.

Note: Totals do not always add to exactly 100 per cent because of rounding.

Employment structure

Much about the economy of the conurbations can be seen from the structure of employment; Table 2.14 presents the data for 1961 and 1971 in terms of percentage shares by broad grouping of Standard Industrial Classification Orders. The six non-London conurbations had nearly one-half of their employment in manufacturing in 1961, as compared to about one-third in Greater London and in non-conurbation Britain. At the same time, only 21.2 per cent of the six conurbations' employment was in Services, as contrasted to 34.7 per cent in Greater London and 27.8 per cent in non-conurbation areas. In three of the conurbations, over 50 per cent of the 1961 workers were in manufacturing, with a peak of 59.6 per cent in the West Midlands and figures of 51.1 and 50.3 per cent for West Yorkshire and South East Lancashire. Merseyside had an unusually low manufacturing share in 1961 (34.9%), but this was partly because of its very high concentration in the utilities/transport/communications sector (reflecting its port and related activities). None of the six conurbations had more than Merseyside's 25.9 per cent of its workers in services and in the West Midlands the figure was only 17.7 per cent. Over all, the 1961 employment structure still reflected the historic role of the conurbations as the industrial workshops of the nation.

By 1971, however, the situation had changed in a number of important ways. The share of manufacturing dropped in all the conurbations, most sharply in Greater London, West Yorkshire, and South East Lancashire. The manufacturing element of the six conurbations combined dropped from 48.9 per cent in 1961 to 43.8 in 1971; but at the same time, the manufacturing share in the non-conurbation areas actually rose, from 32.3 to 33.6 per cent. By 1971 the manufacturing share in Greater London dropped to 27.1 per cent. The services share rose in all conurbations, in Greater London from 34.7 to 40.8 per cent, and in the other six from 21.2 to 27.7 per cent. But it also rose in the non-conurbation areas, from 27.8 to 32.6 per cent.

The changes in the actual numbers working in the various employment categories 1961–71 are given in Table 2.15 and illustrate the dynamics behind the structural shifts of Table 2.14. For example, all of the conurbations lost employment in manufacturing: Greater London suffered a traumatic loss of 23.8 per cent, with heavy losses also in South East Lancashire (−19.0 per cent) and Central Clydeside (−16.9 per cent). At the same time, however, manufacturing workers in the non-conurbations increased by 9.2 per cent. All the conurbations also experienced a heavy loss in primary jobs, but the absolute numbers were small in all cases. The losses in distribution jobs were fairly uniform across the conurbations. In terms of services, the conurbations tended to converge, those with higher shares in 1961 (such as Greater London and Merseyside) growing most slowly (+10.7 and +16.9 per cent respectively), and those with lower shares (West Midlands) growing

Table 2.14 Industry structure of the working population, conurbations, 1961 and 1971 (per cent distribution)

	1961						1971					
	Primary (%)	Manufac-turing (%)	Construc-tion (%)	Utilit. Transp. Commun. (%)	Distri-bution (%)	Services (%)	Primary (%)	Manufac-turing (%)	Construc-tion (%)	Utilit. Transp. Commun. (%)	Distri-bution (%)	Services (%)
Central Clydeside	1.4	43.3	6.9	10.4	15.6	22.4	0.6	38.4	7.7	9.4	13.9	29.9
Greater London	0.3	33.5	4.7	11.6	15.1	34.7	0.2	27.1	6.2	12.0	13.6	40.8
Merseyside	0.4	34.9	5.7	16.2	16.9	25.9	0.2	33.7	7.3	12.9	14.2	31.7
South East Lancashire	1.1	50.3	4.6	7.4	15.9	20.7	0.6	43.4	6.3	7.5	14.8	27.5
Tyneside	4.6	39.7	5.5	9.4	15.8	25.0	2.4	36.8	7.0	8.1	13.7	32.1
West Midlands	0.4	59.6	4.5	6.0	11.8	17.7	0.2	53.7	5.7	5.9	11.1	23.4
West Yorkshire	2.2	51.1	4.3	6.9	14.4	21.1	1.3	44.9	5.8	6.8	13.5	27.7
Total: 6 conurbations excluding Greater London	1.3	48.9	5.1	8.6	14.7	21.2	0.7	43.8	6.5	8.0	13.4	27.7
Greater London	0.3	33.5	4.7	11.6	15.1	34.7	0.2	27.1	6.2	12.0	13.6	40.8
Rest of Great Britain	10.7	32.3	8.2	8.1	12.9	27.8	6.7	33.6	7.5	7.2	12.4	32.6
Total: Great Britain	6.7	36.1	6.9	8.8	13.7	27.7	4.4	34.5	7.1	8.2	12.8	33.0

Source: Censuses of 1961 and 1971.

Note: Statistics are for persons working at time of Census, excluding those with inadequately described industry and those working outside the UK.

Industry categories are by industry order: Primary = I + II (1961 and 1971); Manufacturing = III–XVI (1961) and III–XIX (1971); Construction = XVII (1961) and XX (1971); Utilities, transport and communications = XVIII + XIX (1961) and XXI + XXII (1971); Distributive Trades = XX (1961) and XXIII (1971); Services = XXI–XXIV (1961) and XXIV–XXVII (1971).

Totals do not always add to exactly 100 per cent because of rounding.

Table 2.15 Changes in numbers working in conurbations, by industry group, 1961–1971

	Primary (%)	Manufacturing (%)	Construction (%)	Utilit. Transp. Commun. (%)	Distribution (%)	Services (%)	Total all Workers (%)
Central Clydeside	− 57.2	− 16.9	+ 4.3	− 15.9	− 16.2	+ 24.9	− 6.4
Greater London	− 31.8	− 23.8	+ 23.1	− 2.2	− 15.3	+ 10.7	− 5.8
Merseyside	− 45.0	− 7.8	+ 22.7	− 23.5	− 19.6	+ 16.9	− 4.4
South East Lancashire	− 50.2	− 19.0	+ 27.0	− 4.3	− 12.7	+ 25.2	− 6.0
Tyneside	− 47.5	− 6.4	+ 27.7	− 13.2	− 12.6	+ 29.3	+ 0.9
West Midlands	− 59.3	− 9.4	+ 27.3	− 0.3	− 6.0	+ 33.0	+ 0.5
West Yorkshire	− 41.5	− 14.7	+ 32.9	− 4.7	− 9.1	+ 27.6	− 2.8
Total: 6 conurbations Excluding Greater London	− 48.7	− 13.4	+ 22.5	− 10.9	− 12.3	+ 26.3	− 3.3
Greater London	− 31.8	− 23.8	+ 23.1	− 2.2	− 15.3	+ 10.7	− 5.8
Rest of Great Britain	− 34.4	+ 9.2	− 3.0	− 6.0	+ 0.9	+ 23.4	+ 5.2
Total: Great Britain	− 34.9	− 2.9	+ 4.3	− 6.1	− 5.4	+ 20.9	+ 1.4

Source: Censuses of 1961 and 1971.

most rapidly (+33.0 per cent). This was in the context of a decline in the total of workers in the conurbations: down 3.3 per cent in the six conurbations and down 5.8 per cent in Greater London.

By 1971, the differences amongst the conurbations themselves were in many cases extreme. Merseyside, for example, had more or less the same proportion of its workers in manufacturing, services and construction as did non-conurbation Britain. The West Midlands, in contrast, had a manufacturing share 20 percentage points greater, with below average shares in every other sector. Greater London had 52.8 per cent of its workers in services, utilities, transport and communications, as compared to 39.8 in non-conurbation Britain and only 35.7 in the other six conurbations. Perhaps most interesting in terms of its contrast to conventional images is the fact that of the seven conurbations, Merseyside, Central Clydeside and Tyneside most resembled the national average in shares of workers in the various sectors.

Housing

The basic information about housing tenure is given in Tables 2.16 and 2.17. In both 1961 and 1971 the shares of public sector rental are most nearly alike in the conurbations and in non-conurbation areas; there is much greater difference in the shares of owner-occupied and private rental housing. However, the seven conurbation average in this case hides a great deal of individual variation. In 1961, for example, the share of owner occupation ranged from Central Clydeside's 19.8 per cent to West Yorkshire's 44.8, while the range of public sector rental ranged from Greater London's 18.3 per cent to Central Clydeside's 45.1. Unfurnished private rental was substantial in all conurbations (from West Midlands' 22.8 per cent to Merseyside's 37.6), but furnished private rental varied greatly from Central Clydeside's 2.1 per cent to Greater London's 8.8.

In 1971 the range was nearly as great in owner occupation (between Central Clydeside's 25.0 per cent and West Yorkshire's 52.3) and in public sector rental (from Greater London's 24.9 per cent to Central Clydeside's 59.1). Unfurnished private rental shares were down everywhere to a range between West Midlands' 11.5 per cent to Greater London's 23.6, while the range in furnished private rental had lengthened, with Central Clydeside's share remaining at 2.1 per cent while Greater London's share rose to 10.5.

The rates of change in Table 2.17 show interesting underlying patterns. Most notable is the consistency of the increase in public sector rental: the number of households in that tenure increased between 1961 and 1971 from a low rate of 22.3 per cent (West Midlands) to a high rate of 39.1 (South East Lancashire) for a conurbation average of 31.5 per cent, which can be compared to the non-conurbation average

Table 2.16 Housing tenure, 1961 and 1971, Conurbations (per cent distribution)

Conurbation	Per cent of households 1961 Living in				Per cent of households 1971 living in			
	Owner-occupied	Public sector rental	Unfurnished private rental	Furnished private rental	Owner-occupied	Public sector rental	Unfurnished private rental	Furnished private rental
Central Clydeside	19.8	45.1	33.1	2.1	25.0	59.1	13.7	2.1
Greater London	36.6	18.3	36.3	8.8	40.4	24.9	23.6	10.5
Merseyside	32.1	26.8	37.6	3.5	39.9	33.4	23.5	3.2
South East Lancashire	44.2	21.9	30.7	3.2	51.0	29.7	15.7	3.5
Tyneside	28.2	32.8	36.4	2.6	31.5	43.5	22.5	2.4
West Midlands	38.1	35.4	22.8	3.8	45.3	39.6	11.5	3.6
West Yorkshire	44.8	23.9	29.0	2.3	52.3	30.8	14.2	2.7
Total: 7 conurbations	36.4	25.0	33.0	5.6	41.8	32.5	19.1	6.3
Rest of Great Britain	43.2	25.8	28.3	2.8	51.5	29.3	15.5	3.5
Total: Great Britain	40.6	25.5	30.1	3.8	48.3	30.4	16.7	4.5

Source: Censuses of 1961 and 1971.

Note: For 1961, unfurnished private rental also includes tied houses and houses rented with farms, and businesses and houses supplied with employment.

Rows may not add exactly to 100 per cent due to rounding, and because in 1971 'other tenures' and 'tenures not stated' are not included.

Table 2.17 Changes 1961–1971 in private households by tenure, conurbations

Conurbation	Per cent change in number of private households in					Total number of Private households
	Owner-occupier	Public sector rental	Unfurnished private rental	Furnished private rental		
Central Clydeside	+ 28.0	+ 32.5	− 60.0	+ 0.5		+ 1.1
Greater London	+ 7.8	+ 32.9	− 36.5	+ 16.9		− 2.3
Merseyside	+ 23.9	+ 24.2	− 37.7	− 8.2		− 0.2
South East Lancashire	+ 18.5	+ 39.1	− 47.5	+ 12.8		+ 2.6
Tyneside	+ 14.1	+ 35.1	− 36.9	− 5.7		+ 1.9
West Midlands	+ 30.2	+ 22.3	− 44.7	+ 2.0		+ 9.3
West Yorkshire	+ 21.9	+ 34.5	− 48.9	+ 24.2		+ 4.5
Total 7 conurbations	+ 16.1	+ 31.5	− 41.6	+ 13.6		+ 1.0
Rest of Great Britain	+ 42.0	+ 35.1	− 34.9	+ 51.9		+ 18.9
Total: Great Britain	+ 33.3	+ 33.8	− 37.7	+ 31.0		+ 12.2

Source: Censuses of 1961 and 1971.

of 35.1. Owner-occupier households also increased everywhere, but not nearly so consistently. In the West Midlands their numbers went up faster than public sector rental, and in Central Clydeside and Merseyside nearly as fast; this can be contrasted with relatively small increases of 7.8 per cent in Greater London, 14.1 in Tyneside and 18.5 in South East Lancashire.

Also consistent was the substantial fall in households living in unfurnished private rental. In the conurbations in just 10 years their numbers dropped 41.6 per cent – fully 60 per cent in Central Clydeside. Only in furnished private rental do we see a mixed pattern. There were

Table 2.18 1971 Private households, by tenure, conurbation cities and remainders

Area	Per cent of Private households living in:			
	Owner-occupier	Public sector rental	Unfurnished private rental	Furnished private rental
Glasgow	22.1	53.9	20.6	3.3
Remainder of Central Clydeside conurbation	28.4	65.0	5.9	0.7
Liverpool	31.7	36.2	27.8	4.2
Remainder of Merseyside conurbation	47.4	30.8	21.1	2.2
Manchester	33.4	35.5	22.9	8.1
Remainder of South East Lancashire conurbation	51.4	28.1	13.6	2.2
Newcastle	28.3	41.0	25.4	5.3
Remainder of Tyneside conurbation	32.8	44.5	21.4	1.3
Birmingham	42.3	38.2	13.6	5.9
Remainder of West Midlands conurbation	47.6	40.6	10.0	1.8
Leeds and Bradford	46.9	34.5	14.3	4.3
Remainder of West Yorkshire conurbation	56.8	27.7	14.1	1.4
Total: 6 conurbation cities	35.3	40.3	19.2	5.0
Remainders of 6 conurbations	47.9	37.1	13.3	1.7
Total: Great Britain	48.3	30.4	16.7	4.5

Source: 1971 Census.
Note: Rows do not necessarily add to exactly 100 per cent due to rounding.

absolute decreases in the numbers of households in this tenure in Merseyside and Tyneside, but substantial increases in Greater London and – especially – West Yorkshire.

As Table 2.18 indicates, there are significant differences between the housing tenure patterns of the central cities of the conurbations and those of the outer conurbation areas. The differences are *not*, however, in the shares of public sector rental, which in 1971 were very similar at 37.1 and 40.3 per cent. Indeed, in three of the six conurbations the outer areas had *greater* proportions of households in public sector rental than did the inner cities (Central Clydeside, Tyneside, and West Midlands). The significant differences are in the other tenures. There is a substantially higher percentage of households in owner occupation in the outer areas of the conurbations, both on average and in every conurbation individually. Similarly, private rental (furnished and unfurnished) is consistently more concentrated in the central cities than in the outer areas. In unfurnished rental the differences are not great (except in the case of Central Clydeside), but in furnished rental the concentration in central cities is strong.

The basic measure of housing quality available in the statistics relates to the proportion of households lacking exclusive use of hot water and/or fixed bath and/or inside w.c.; the data are presented in Table 2.19. The proportion lacking basic amenities is subdivided by tenure, as there are systematic differences amongst them. For example, for owner-occupier and public sector tenures, the Great Britain averages of households lacking amenities are 11.7 and 7.3 per cent, respectively; for unfurnished private rental, however, the average is 43.2. Looking first at the averages for the seven conurbations, we find that for owner occupation the percentage lacking amenities is exactly the same in the conurbations and in the non-conurbation areas: 11.7 per cent. With the exception of Central Clydeside (where 20.3 per cent lack amenities) and South East Lancashire (16.2 per cent), the conurbations have a stock of owner occupied housing which is better (by this measure) than that in the rest of the country. The variation in the public sector stock is similarly small, on average: the seven conurbations have a proportion lacking amenities of 8.2 per cent, only slightly above the 6.8 per cent average for non-conurbation areas. The only significantly variant conurbation is West Midlands, where 17.0 per cent of the public sector stock lack amenities; this is an extraordinarily high proportion, and it also makes West Midlands the only conurbation in which the public sector stock is worse than the owner-occupier stock. For unfurnished private rental, the conurbation average stock is worse (at 49.3 per cent) than the stock in the rest of Great Britain (at 39.4). But the picture is grim everywhere, from the West Midlands (with its low of 39.1 per cent) to Central Clydeside (with its high of 61.0).

When the three main tenures are combined in a weighted average for the conurbations, a picture of striking consistency emerges. The seven conurbations all lie within a tight range from 14.4 per cent (West

Table 2.19 Households lacking basic amenities, 1971, by tenure, conurbations

| Conurbation | Per cent of households without exclusive use of hot water and/or fixed bath and/or inside w.c.: | | | | |
	Owner-occupier	Public sector rental	Unfurnished private rental	Furnished private rental	Overall average, first three tenures only
Central Clydeside	20.3	3.2	61.0	67.1	15.7
Greater London	10.3	8.0	46.7	65.3	19.3
Merseyside	10.4	9.3	50.5	66.9	19.8
South East Lancashire	16.2	7.2	57.8	66.1	20.2
Tyneside	9.9	4.5	58.1	57.2	18.6
West Midlands	8.9	17.0	39.1	64.4	15.8
West Yorkshire	10.7	5.3	48.0	65.5	14.4
Total: 7 conurbations	11.7	8.2	49.3	65.3	18.1
Rest of Great Britain	11.7	6.8	39.4	42.2	14.7
Total: Great Britain	11.7	7.3	43.2	53.1	15.8

Source: 1971 Census.
Note: Since furnished rentals tend to be bedsitters and similar multi-occupancies, the criteria of exclusive use of facilities are not relevant; hence, this tenure is excluded from the overall average.
Rows do not necessarily add to exactly 100 per cent due to rounding.

Table 2.20 1971 Private households, by density of occupation, conurbations

Conurbation	Per cent of private households living at					
	More than 1½ persons per room	1 to 1½ persons per room	¾ to 1 persons per room	½ to ¾ persons per room	Less than ½ persons per room
Central Clydeside	10.7	14.7	26.9	33.9	13.8
Greater London	2.9	5.5	23.5	39.2	28.9
Merseyside	1.9	6.4	20.6	35.9	35.2
South East Lancashire	1.5	5.1	19.4	40.2	33.8
Tyneside	2.3	7.3	21.6	41.1	27.7
West Midlands	2.2	5.7	21.3	37.5	33.2
West Yorkshire	1.7	5.2	20.9	41.1	31.1
Total: 7 conurbations	3.1	6.4	22.4	38.7	29.3
Rest of Great Britain	1.2	4.7	20.4	39.0	34.6
Total: Great Britain	1.8	5.3	21.1	38.9	32.8

Source: 1971 Census.

Note: Rows do not necessarily add to exactly 100 per cent due to rounding.

Yorkshire) to 20.2 (South East Lancashire), giving an average of 18.1, which can be compared to the 14.7 per cent average in the non-conurbation areas. In other words, in 1971 the housing in the conurbations (by this particular measure) was good absolutely (81.9 per cent of households had exclusive use of basic amenities) and was good relative to non-conurbation areas (where the figure was only slightly higher at 85.3 per cent).

Since 1971 the picture will almost certainly have changed in favour of the conurbations, because it is the private unfurnished rental sector which is the main source of inadequate housing and which is heavily concentrated in conurbations (and their central cities) but which is rapidly being eliminated by urban redevelopment programmes.

A rather different measure of housing adequacy is shown in Table 2.20, which presents the 1971 data on density of occupation of private households. In general, households living at more than 1 person per room are considered 'overcrowded', and those living at more than $1\frac{1}{2}$ persons per room, acutely so. Central Clydeside stands out as the one conurbation suffering from widespread overcrowding: 25.4 per cent of its households were living at densities over 1 person per room, as compared to a Great Britain average of 7.1 per cent. The other six conurbations had overcrowding percentages ranging from 6.6 per cent in South East Lancashire to 9.6 in Tyneside. Even including Central Clydeside, the seven conurbations averaged only 9.5 per cent as compared to the 5.9 average for the non-conurbation areas. It would appear, therefore, that overcrowding is not a problem (at the conurbation level) except in Central Clydeside.

Car ownership and commuting

Levels of car ownership provide a direct indication of the availability of personal transport; they also provide an imperfect, but useful, indirect indicator of income.[6] Table 2.21 shows the situation as it existed in 1966 and 1971. Taking the conurbations as a whole, a much higher proportion of households had no car as compared to non-conurbation Britain, in both years; moreover, the proportion decreased more slowly in the conurbations than elsewhere, widening the gap. Not even the West Midlands – which had the highest proportion of households with cars – came very close to the proportion which obtained outside the conurbations. Equally, none of the conurbations had proportions of households with 2 or more cars as high as the average for non-conurbation areas, and this gap also widened between 1966 and 1971.

As would be expected, the central cities of the conurbations have even lower car ownership: two-thirds of households in the six central cities had no car in 1971, as contrasted to only 54 per cent in the outer conurbation areas (see Table 2.22). However, even the outer areas of

Table 2.21 Households with cars, 1966 and 1971

	1966 Per cent of private households with			1971 Per cent of private households with		
	No car	1 car	2+ cars	No car	1 car	2+ cars
Central Clydeside	72.7	24.9	2.4	67.0	28.9	4.1
Greater London	58.1	36.1	5.8	53.7	38.5	7.8
Merseyside	66.2	29.9	3.8	59.3	34.8	6.0
South East Lancashire	63.6	32.3	4.1	58.0	35.7	6.3
Tyneside	69.4	27.8	2.8	65.8	30.4	3.8
West Midlands	54.9	38.8	6.3	51.3	40.5	8.2
West Yorkshire	64.8	31.6	3.6	59.9	34.5	5.6
Total: 7 conurbations	61.5	33.7	4.8	56.7	36.6	6.8
Greater London plus West Midlands	57.4	36.7	5.9	53.2	39.0	7.8
Other 5 conurbations	66.8	29.8	3.4	61.1	33.5	5.4
Rest of Great Britain	51.8	41.3	6.9	45.2	45.1	9.7
Total: Great Britain	55.3	38.6	6.2	49.1	42.2	8.7

Source: Censuses of 1966 and 1971.
Note: Central Clydeside in 1966 excludes two small areas under 15,000 population for which data was not published; the estimate for Central Clydeside for 1971 is for the new local authority areas (Glasgow plus 10 districts).
Rows may not add to 100 per cent because of rounding.

Table 2.22 Ownership of cars, 1971

	Per cent of households having		
	No car	1 car	2 + cars
Central Clydeside	67.0	28.9	4.1
Conurbation centre	n.a.	n.a.	n.a.
Central city	76.5	21.2	2.3
Remainder	56.1	37.7	6.2
Greater London	53.7	38.5	7.8
Conurbation centre	72.5	23.4	4.1
Central cities	66.8	30.0	3.2
Remainder	44.1	45.5	10.4
Merseyside	59.3	34.8	6.0
Conurbation centre	82.7	16.0	1.3
Central city	67.4	28.5	4.1
Remainder	51.8	40.6	7.6
South East Lancashire	58.0	35.7	6.3
Conurbation centre	64.6	31.2	4.2
Central city	68.4	27.7	3.9
Remainder	55.0	38.0	7.0
Tyneside	65.9	30.4	3.8
Conurbation centre	72.4	24.4	3.2
Central city	70.0	26.5	4.5
Remainder	64.2	31.9	3.9
West Midlands	51.3	40.5	8.2
Conurbation centre	63.2	29.2	7.6
Central city	57.7	36.2	4.2
Remainder	46.5	43.8	9.7
West Yorkshire	59.9	34.5	5.6
Conurbation centre	–	–	–
Central cities	64.8	30.9	4.3
Remainder	55.9	37.6	6.5
All 7 conurbations	56.7	36.6	6.8
Conurbation centre (5)*	72.4	23.4	4.2
Central cities	66.8	29.0	4.2
Remainder	49.8	41.7	8.5
Great Britain	49.1	42.2	8.7

* Excluding West Yorkshire (which has no conurbation centre) and Central Clydeside (for which figures were not published).

Source: 1971 Census, England and Wales, Availability of Cars;
1971 Census, Scotland, Housing.

Table 2.23 Commuting in the conurbations, 1961 and 1971

	1961			1971		
	Non-residents as % of total working in conurbation	Per cent of conurbation residents who work outside of conurbation	Net in-commuting as % of total working in conurbation	Non-residents as % of total working in conurbation	Per cent of conurbation residents who work outside of conurbation	Net in-commuting as % of total working in conurbation
Central Clydeside	5.9	2.6	3.4	8.7	5.0	4.0
Greater London	9.4	2.2	7.3	13.2	3.0	10.6
Merseyside	8.3	7.5	0.9	15.0	9.5	6.1
South East Lancashire	5.4	2.9	2.6	7.4	4.0	3.5
Tyneside	11.3	6.5	5.1	16.9	7.0	10.7
West Midlands	6.7	2.3	4.5	10.1	3.0	7.3
West Yorkshire	5.3	2.2	3.1	7.1	3.2	4.0
Total: 7 conurbations	7.9	2.9	5.1	11.4	3.9	7.8

Source: Censuses of 1961 and 1971.

Table 2.24 Commuting into the conurbations, by socio-economic group, 1971

	Non-residents as per cent of total persons working in conurbation					
	Managers employers professionals (1–4)	Other non-manual (5–7)	Foremen, skilled manual (8–9)	Unskilled and semi-skilled manual (10–11)	All other (12–17)	All s.e. groups (1–17)
Central Clydeside	15.9	8.1	9.3	5.7	4.7	8.7
Greater London	27.5	12.6	10.8	4.6	3.7	13.2
Merseyside	23.3	14.1	17.8	11.0	7.0	15.0
South East Lancashire	14.1	7.3	7.5	4.3	3.9	7.4
Tyneside	26.8	18.3	16.4	10.9	8.0	16.9
West Midlands	19.7	10.8	9.5	6.1	5.1	10.1
West Yorkshire	13.3	8.0	6.1	4.6	3.3	7.1
Total: 7 conurbations	23.1	11.5	10.2	5.7	4.1	11.4
6 conurbations excluding Greater London	17.6	10.2	9.8	6.3	4.7	9.9

Source: Census 1971.

Table 2.25 Composite matrix of indices, conurbations (see p. 48)

	A. 1951–74 pop'n change index, (GB = 100)	B. 1971 % of Pop'n aged 15 to 59/64 (GB= 100)	C. 1971 % of house-holds with 5+ persons (GB= 100)	D. 1971 % of male labour force in seg. 1–4 (GB= 100)	E. 1971 % of male labour force in s.e.g. 10–11 (GB= 100)	F. 1971 % of labour force both parents foreign born (GB= 100)	G. 1971 % of total workers in manuf. (GB= 100)	H. 1971 % of total workers in services (GB= 100)	I. 19 % o hoï hoï in puï sec rerï (Gï 10(ï
Central Clydeside	84.6	98.7	135.9	81.2	122.0	37.3	111.3	90.6	194
Greater London	77.1	104.7	88.0	120.6	91.2	266.1	78.6	123.6	8ï
Mersey-side	78.4	98.5	131.0	80.6	139.5	49.2	97.7	96.1	10ï
South East Lancs.	88.1	99.5	99.3	96.4	113.2	108.5	125.8	83.3	9ï
Tyneside	83.8	100.5	98.6	77.0	116.6	23.7	106.7	97.3	14ï
West Midlands	94.4	102.2	111.3	85.5	117.1	174.6	155.6	70.9	13ï
West Yorkshire	92.1	98.8	93.0	89.7	115.1	123.7	130.1	83.9	101
Average index (unweighted)	85.5	100.4	108.2	90.1	116.4	111.9	115.1	92.2	122
'Expected' direction of index	<100	<100	>100	<100	>100	>100	>100	<100	>1ï
Source of data – see Table:	2.1	2.9	2.10	2.11	2.11	2.13	2.14	2.14	2

the conurbations were worse off in this respect than non-conurbation areas, in which only 45 per cent of households had no car.

Commuting into and out of the conurbations can be interpreted as a measure of decentralisation of jobs and people. Table 2.23 illustrates the gross and net flows in 1961 and 1971. The first column in each year relates to the inflow of workers: the percentage of jobs in the conurbation filled by people living outside the conurbation. The second column relates to the outflow: the percentage of conurbation residents who work outside the conurbation. The first column – which results from decentralisation of homes – and the second column – which results from decentralisation of jobs – are combined to produce the net figure of the third column. This represents the *net* inflow of workers as a percent of jobs in the conurbation. The degree of self-containment of

1971 % of households in owner-occupied housing (GB=100)	K. 1971 % of households lacking basic amenities (GB=100)	L. 1971 % of households over-crowded (GB=100)	M. 1971 % of households with no car (GB=100)	Number of indices						
				In the 'Expected' direction:			GB average:	In the 'Contrary' direction:		
				more than 25% +/-	15% to 25% +/-	5% to 15% +/-	less than 5% +/-	5% to 15% +/-	15% to 25% +/-	more than 25% +/-
				100	100	100	100	100	100	100
51.8	99.4	357.7	136.4	5	3	2	2	0	0	1
83.6	122.2	118.3	109.4	1	4	1	1	2	4	0
82.6	125.3	116.9	120.8	3	5	1	3	0	0	1
105.6	127.8	93.0	118.1	2	2	3	4	2	0	0
65.2	117.7	135.2	134.2	5	3	1	3	0	0	1
93.8	100.0	111.3	104.5	4	1	5	3	0	0	0
08.3	91.1	97.2	122.0	1	4	2	3	3	0	0
84.4	111.9	147.1	120.3	1	5	6	1	0	0	0
<100	>100	>100	>100							
2.16	2.19	2.20	2.21							

the conurbations was substantial in both years, although gross and net in-commuting increased everywhere between 1961 and 1971. Even by 1971, however, net in-commuting accounted for only 7.8 per cent of conurbation jobs on average. The two conurbations with greatest net in-commuting in 1971 were Greater London (10.6%) and Tyneside 10.7%); at the other end of the scale were South East Lancashire (3.5%) and West Yorkshire and Central Clydeside (both 4.0%). The most significant changes between 1961 and 1971 were in Merseyside (0.9% up to 6.1%) and in Tyneside (5.1% up to 10.7%). It is significant that in every conurbation both inward and outward commuting increased 1961–71, although inward commuting generally increased more rapidly.

Finally, Table 2.24 shows that while gross in-commuting was biased toward higher-status socio-economic groups, there was still substantial in-commuting in other groups. The proportion of non-residents in the conurbation labour forces was 23.1 per cent amongst managers, employers and professionals, 11.5 for other non-manual workers, and 10.2 for foremen and skilled manual workers; for the unskilled and semi-skilled the figures dropped to 5.7 per cent.

Conclusions

The various statistical measures analysed here show that the conurbations, taken as a group, are different from the rest of the country in many important ways, although on some measures (for example, age structure) they are similar to the country as a whole. Equally clear however, is the evidence which shows how wide are the variations among the seven conurbations, how much they sometimes differ from one another. Both of these points have crucial implications for urban policy.

Table 2.25 (p. 46–7) brings together some of the statistics from the earlier tables, with individual conurbation measures converted to indices based on the Great Britain average. This form of composite analysis is not, of course, theoretically rigorous or systematic; it is, instead, a convenient classificatory device which helps to highlight patterns of variation amongst the conurbations. The table is also structured to illustrate the ways in which the conurbations do or do not conform (on the statistical measures available) to what might be termed the popular image or stereotype. For example, the stereotype of the conurbations would see them characterised by: high proportions of children and the elderly; high proportions of large households; a rapidly declining population; a labour force of relatively low skills; an employment structure weighted toward manufacturing; a relatively high proportion of immigrants; bad housing, with low quality and high overcrowding; a predominance of public sector housing; and low car ownership. The direction of the index numbers (GB=100) for the conurbations which would be predicted by this stereotyped view is shown, for each measure, in the next-to-last row of Table 2.25. The right-hand part of the table then summarises the information by showing, for each conurbation, the number of indices which are in the direction 'expected' by the stereotype, the number which are in the 'contrary' direction, and the number which are at or very close to the national average.

The picture which emerges is consistent, however the results are scored or averaged. There is a group of four conurbations – Central Clydeside, Merseyside, Tyneside, and West Midlands – which have the most conurbation-like (or 'expected' or stereotyped) characteristics. There is a second group – comprising South East Lancashire and West Yorkshire – which exhibit many 'expected' characteristics, but more weakly and inconsistently than the first group. Finally, there is Greater

London, which simply doesn't fit the stereotype; it seems to have as many characteristics opposite to those of the other conurbations as it does characteristics which parallel them. Naturally, a different choice of indices might have given a different picture in some respects. But the consistency of results suggests that whatever the exact mix of statistical measures used, so long as it encompasses a broad range of indicators (covering housing, employment, population, etc.) then the basic group-ings and rankings of the conurbations will be the same.

The four conurbations with the most 'expected' or stereotyped characteristics, however, do not form a homogeneous group; rather, they fall naturally into a sub-group of three (Central Clydeside, Merseyside, and Tyneside) on the one hand, and West Midlands by itself on the other. The key point is that these two sub-groups acquire their conurbation-like characteristics in different ways. West Midlands fits the stereotype in terms of, for example, workers with foreign-born parents, percentage of labour force in manufacturing, and percentage of labour force in services; the other three conurbations fit the stereotype in terms of percentage of households with no car and per-centage of households in owner-occupied housing. The natural group-ings become clearer when the rankings of the seven conurbations on each of the 13 indices are arrayed, as in Table 2.26.

Table 2.26 Rankings of the conurbations, by grouping

Index: (from table 2.25)	Central Clydeside, Merseyside, Tyneside	West Midlands	South East Lancashire, West Yorkshire	Greater London
A	2, 3, 4	7	5, 6	1
B	1, 2, 5	6	3, 4	7
C	1, 2, 5	3	4, 6	7
D	1, 2, 3	4	5, 6	7
E	1, 2, 4	3	5, 6	7
F	5, 6, 7	2	3, 4	1
G	4, 5, 6	1	2, 3	7
H	4, 5, 6	1	2, 3	7
I	1, 2, 4	3	5, 6	7
J	1, 2, 3	5	6, 7	4
K	2, 4, 6	5	1, 7	3
L	1, 2, 4	5	6, 7	3
M	1, 2, 4	7	3, 5	6

Ranking is done so that the conurbation with the most 'expected' characteristic is ranked 1st; in some cases this means the conurbation with the lowest index score on Table 2.25.

The clear four-way grouping indicated by Table 2.26 is also consis-tent with other known features of the conurbations. Central Clydeside, Merseyside, and Tyneside are historic 'problem areas' of long standing; they are all designated Special Development Areas, the highest level for regional policy assistance. South East Lancashire and West York-shire have never posed economic problems in the same way, having been consistently more prosperous than Central Clydeside, Mersey-side, and Tyneside, albeit equally consistently less prosperous than most of the South or Midlands. South East Lancashire and West Yorkshire are designated Intermediate Areas, the lowest level for regional policy assistance. The West Midlands and Greater London both have histories of economic good health, with unemployment well below national averages (except for the short time in the mid 1970s in the West Midlands).

The point, however, is not simply to classify, for the sake of classification. Instead, the concern is to emphasise once again the diversity amongst the conurbations. Averaged together, they are unquestionably different from the rest of the country, in many of the ways in which the popular stereotype would suggest. But these averages conceal large and significant variations – variations which must be comprehended before any sensible analysis can be made of the so-called 'urban problem' and therefore before any effective policy responses can be framed.

Notes

1. Basic population data have been extended back to 1901 (see sources for Table 2.1) by aggregating constituent units, and the Office of Population Censuses and Surveys has carried its series of annual estimates forward to 1974. The bulk of the statistical information, however, is still restricted to the 1951–71 period. Moreover, some data is available in compatible form only for the more recent two Censuses, 1961 and 1971, further restricting the time series available. Another complication is that some data are available only for the conurbations in England and Wales, as the Censuses of Scotland publish somewhat different tabulations. The 1966 Sample Census has only been sparingly utilised, reliance being placed wherever possible on the full Censuses of 1961 and 1971. Finally, because of severe problems of non-comparability and incompleteness, data from outside official Census sources have not been used. For those interested in carrying statistics forward, Appendix Table A2.1 compares the old conurbations and cities with the new reorganised local authority areas.
2. It was this continued growth of the conurbations – especially in the 1921–31 period when their combined population grew twice as fast as population in the rest of Great Britain – that was in the minds of the Barlow Commission during their deliberations in the late 1930s and which explains the great emphasis they put on restraining further concentration into the conurbations.
3. Greater London conurbation has no analogous central city core and so cannot be analysed in the same way. (For instance, the population density of the Greater London conurbation as a whole was slightly *above* that of the other six conurbation central cities in 1974: 45.4 persons per hectare as opposed to 42.5.) Indeed, it may be that the GLC area (the defined conurbation) should have been considered as a 'central city' with the conurbation boundary being extended to encompass the outer metropolitan ring of commuter areas. Such a modification, however desirable, is none the less clearly outside the scope of this analysis of existing statistics.
4. This classification is unsatisfactory as an indicator of social class, for a number of reasons, including: the difficulty of attaching social class significance to rapidly changing occupations; the inaccuracy of ignoring other, non-occupational, indicators; and the confusion of assigning on the basis of a male head of household when more and

Appendix Table A2.1 Comparisons of old (pre-1973/74) and new (post-1973/74) statistical areas

Statistical area	Land area (ha)	Population (000's)				Population change (%)		
		1961 Census	1971 Census	1974 Est.	1976 Est.	1961–71	1971–74	1974–76
Central Clydeside conurb.	77,850	1,802	1,728	1,658	n.a.	− 4.1	− 4.1	n.a.
10 Districts (Strathclyde)	160,950	n.a.	1,857	1,795	1,751	n.a.	− 3.3	− 2.5
Merseyside conurbation	39,450	1,384	1,267	1,207	n.a.	− 8.5	− 4.7	n.a.
Merseyside Metro. County	64,800	1,718	1,657	1,606	1,578	− 3.6	− 3.1	− 1.7
South East Lancs. conurb.	98,300	2,428	2,393	2,376	n.a.	− 1.4	− 0.7	n.a.
Greater Manchester Met. Co.	128,650	2,720	2,729	2,711	2,684	+ 0.3	− 0.7	− 1.0
Tyneside Conurbation	23,450	855	805	781	n.a.	− 5.8	− 3.0	n.a.
Tyne and Wear Metro. Co.	54,000	1,244	1,212	1,189	1,183	− 2.6	− 1.9	− 0.5
West Midlands Conurbation	67,800	2,347	2,372	2,353	n.a.	− 1.1	− 0.8	n.a.
West Midlands Metro. Co.	89,950	2,732	2,793	2,780	2,743	+ 2.2	− 0.5	− 1.3
West Yorkshire Conurbation	125,500	1,704	1,728	1,737	n.a.	+ 1.4	+ 0.5	n.a.
West Yorkshire Metro. Co.	203,900	2,005	2,068	2,083	2,073	+ 3.1	+ 0.7	− 0.5
6 Conurbations	432,350	10,520	10,293	10,112	n.a.	− 2.2	− 1.8	n.a.
6 new statistical areas	702,250	n.a.	12,316	12,164	12,012	n.a.	− 1.2	− 1.2

Sources: 1971 Census England & Wales, New County Reports; 1971 Census Scotland, New Local Authority Areas Report; Office of Population Censuses and Surveys; Registrar-General for Scotland.

n.a. = not available.

Appendix Table A2.1 (Continued)

Statistical area	Land area (ha)	Population (000's)				Population change (%)		
		1961 Census	1971 Census	1971 Est.	1976 Est.	1961–71	1971–74	1974–76
Glasgow City of County	15,700	1,055	879	816	n.a.	– 15.0	– 9.0	n.a.
Glasgow District (new)	19,750	n.a.	982	905	856	n.a.	– 7.8	– 5.4
Liverpool C.B.	11,300	746	610	561	n.a.	– 18.2	– 8.0	n.a.
Liverpool District	11,300	746	610	561	540	– 18.2	– 8.0	– 3.7
Manchester C.B.	11,600	662	544	516	n.a.	– 17.8	– 5.1	n.a.
Manchester District	11,600	662	544	516	490	– 17.8	– 5.1	– 5.0
Newcastle C.B.	5,500	270	222	209	n.a.	– 17.8	– 5.9	n.a.
Newcastle District (new)	11,200	336	308	297	296	– 8.3	– 3.6	– 0.3
Birmingham C.B.	20,900	1,107	1,015	1,004	n.a.	– 8.3	– 1.1	n.a.
Birmingham District (new)	26,450	1,183	1,098	1,086	1,059	– 7.2	– 1.1	– 2.5
Leeds C.B.	16,400	511	496	499	n.a.	– 2.9	+ 0.6	n.a.
Leeds District (new)	56,200	713	739	749	745	+ 3.6	+ 1.4	– 0.5
Bradford C.B.	10,300	296	294	290	n.a.	– 0.7	– 1.4	n.a.
Bradford District (new)	37,000	453	462	461	459	+ 2.0	– 0.2	– 0.4
7 conurbation centres	91,700	4,647	4,078	3,895	n.a.	– 12.2	– 4.5	n.a.
7 new statistical areas	173,500	n.a.	4,743	4,575	4,445	n.a.	– 3.5	– 2.8

more women are working in their own occupations and in an increasing number of cases are heading their own households. To obtain a time series disaggregated to conurbations on a consistent basis, however, we have no choice but to use the Census and its categorisation of the male labour force by socio-economic group.

5. This indicator is not the same, of course, as other classifications of immigrants as a proportion of the total population. In particular, a labour-force-based measure does not accurately reflect the possibly greater impact which immigrant populations have through relatively greater numbers of children. On the other hand, it does focus more directly on the impact on local labour markets. And in any event, shares of total population will closely follow the shares in the labour force.

6. There are factors other than income which affect car ownership, most notably the availability and price of public transport. As public transport is more extensive and well developed in the conurbations than elsewhere, there is less 'need' of a car. Nevertheless, there can be little doubt that low car ownership in Clydeside, Merseyside and Tyneside, for example, is strongly income related.

Chapter 3

The economies of the conurbations

Introduction

Historically the economies of the British conurbations have been shaped by five distinct, though related, locational processes. Manufacturing activities grew up there initially because of the location of raw materials and of natural features such as navigable waterways, but at a later stage so that they could gain access to the inputs of other producers and to obtain plentiful supplies of labour. Business and professional services tended to cluster in conurbations not only because their major markets in manufacturing and in government were there but also because of their need for each other as suppliers of inputs. Consumer services of a specialist nature which required to draw their support from a large population, found that the conurbations were the best locations for consumer access. Similarly many governmental activities were focused there not only because decision-makers for metropolitan-wide or regional services found it easiest to congregate at a point central to their various residential locations but also easiest for contacts between the governed and those making decisions. And finally this diversity and density of activity gave rise to a huge demand for transport, communications and distribution facilities, many of which were provided in 'lumpy' units and drew their users from beyond the economic activities and the population of the conurbation itself.

The cumulative effect of these processes was, and is, a structure of economic activity significantly different from that of the rest of the country. Changes in census methods of recording economic structure prevent us from showing the full nature of this conurbation specialisation, but Table 2.14 has already highlighted some of the differences. It showed that in 1961 in every conurbation except Greater London and Merseyside, manufacturing dominated employment to a far greater extent than elsewhere in the country. Indeed in no less than three conurbations – West Midlands, West Yorkshire and South East Lancashire – the majority of the employed labour force was in manufacturing. The only other noticeable form of conurbation specialisation was in distribution, with every conurbation except the West Midlands having a heavier concentration of employment than that of the rest of Great Britain. By contrast the conurbations had a weak representation in two land-extensive activities – primary and construction – and, perhaps surprisingly, in other services. However, if we split services into those which primarily serve local consumers and those which serve business, then there is a marked tendency for the latter group to locate within the conurbations.

In this chapter we will seek to explain why the structure of activity in the conurbations has emerged with these particular specialisms. We will look especially at manufacturing and business and professional services since transport activities are covered separately in Chapter 7 and Government activities in Chapter 14. Thereafter we will consider those major changes in the structure of activity which have occurred in the last decade or so, and explore the factors which have caused a major re-sorting of the location of economic activities within the conurbations. In later sections we will speculate on the future structure of conurbation economic activity and their future locational pattern, especially the role of their central cities.

Manufacturing in the conurbations

Why should manufacturers be willing to pay the high rentals or high land prices which are an inevitable feature of every conurbation economy? One possibility is that the prices of other factors of production might be lower than elsewhere. In fact, we know that for a given skill and level of proficiency, workers are paid marginally *more* in the conurbations than elsewhere, primarily as compensation for longer average work journeys (Evans, 1973). Similarly, there is no evidence that for given projects the price of capital is lower in the conurbations than elsewhere. The real answer lies in history and in current economic realities.

The historical reality is that manufacturing has dominated the conurbation economies since the nineteenth century; it follows that in those industries where technical linkages are crucial to low-cost operation – chemicals is sometimes an example – new plants may replicate the patterns of history. In addition there are three factors – all embraced under the broad and rather vague notion of agglomeration economies – which are now much more central.

The first relates to those activities where demand is volatile, production methods are constantly changing, and the product itself is often modified in a time scale which extends over hours rather than weeks or months. The fashion trades, where a buyer's preferences may result in a complete re-design of a line of dresses, or newspaper publication where a news story may break and cause a complete re-setting of the front page, are both good examples. It is here that the conurbations, with their dense array of communication facilities, have a clear advantage in bringing producers into instantaneous contact with these key economic, political and social agents who mould the nature of product demand by their opinions, their buying patterns and their influence over others.

That the conurbation is the best locale for producer–market contacts in these volatile product industries is not, in itself, always a sufficient reason for a production facility to be located there. The crucial additional ingredient is a spatial cluster of varied suppliers who free the company facing volatile demand to concentrate upon product assembly. They supply the necessary inputs as the product changes, and are always near enough to guarantee the arrival of inputs. This relationship is symbiotic. The company facing volatile demand has limited control over the inputs necessary to produce the ever-changing product. It can either attempt to predict its input pattern, store materials to supply its needs and undertake all production itself, or else it can rely on an array of closely accessible specialists, thus freeing itself from storage and from specialist production. But in their turn the specialist suppliers require a sufficient array of demanders in order to reap the advantages of specialisation. The physical consequence is a spatial cluster of demanders and of suppliers locked together by the mutually advantageous principle of specialisation. The economic consequence is lowered unit costs for all producers.

A second set of advantages – more often referred to as urbanisation economies since they apply throughout the urban area – may also affect locational choice. The large urban area, by definition, contains an absolutely large number of workers. This in itself may be a sufficient enticement to those industries in which internal economies of scale result in very large plant size and a consequent demand for thousands of workers. Even more important is the fact that large urban size is associated with economic diversity, especially diversity of employee skills. Thus, even though wages paid for a given skill are likely to be higher in the conurbation than elsewhere, the costs of hiring that labour, whether by advertising, job centre notification, word of mouth or whatever, could well be lower. This is because for any given level of unemployment, there may be a greater range of skills on offer in the large diversified as compared to the smaller less diversified labour market. Thus the employer is more likely to be able to hire locally without having to incur the additional expense of hiring from other labour markets.

This example of the advantages which urban scale and diversity can bring, could be multiplied many times over. The larger urban area, served by rail, road, air and telecommunications connections to the outside world, is much less prone to linkage failure should any one of these modes be out of action, or any part of each mode be inoperative. Essentially this is a point about close substitutes in conditions of supply withdrawal or supply failure – substitutes which are as effective and cost much the same as the service withdrawn.

Urbanisation economies may take a different form. Large size may generate the conditions in which suppliers of all kinds themselves gain internal economies of scale which can be passed on to all other producers in the urban area. Thus an inter-regional transport operator, for example, facing large and continuous demands from conurbation producers, may generate economies in terminal handling facilities, in size of vehicle and in utilisation of capacity, economies which are then passed on as lowered freight rates.

Thirdly, the conurbation may be an appropriate locale in which to initiate the development of new products or new technologies, especially in the context of the small new business (Thompson, 1965). Here the argument is that newness implies riskiness – the product may not be popular, the technology inoperative – and therefore the location which minimises risk is one with an array of close-at-hand labour skills, a range of specialist services, such as in marketing, finance, accounting, legal, promotional, technical, all of which can be called upon to cope with unforeseen difficulties. The conurbation may also present a dense and varied market in which to estimate demand potential.

Thus the conurbation economy is most likely to be appropriate for those activities where technical linkages are relevant and where there is already a concentration of the 'linked' industry, where product demand is highly volatile, where large quantities of varied labour are required, where reliance upon one mode of supply or delivery is to be avoided, and where product or technology innovation, especially in small firms, requires an unpredictable set of inputs and, or, of market conditions. All of these types of activity are most likely to be prepared to compete for high-cost conurbation space in order to gain the desired advantages and agglomeration economies which such areas possess.

Business services

Business and professional services, one of the other marked conurbation specialisms we identified, embrace all those activities which serve manufacturing, governmental and other industries, often with products which vary markedly day by day. As such they represent a particular form of external economy activity typically characterised by small firms, labour-intensive production, much of it of a skilled nature and serving markets which change frequently in their geographical spread, their product range and their size of order. Banking, finance, broking, insurance, accountancy, legal services, business consultancy, trade associations, advertising, property advice, publicity, computing services, printing, employment agencies, these and many more have a strong tendency to congregate in the major urban areas. Typically they choose a location within or close to the inner urban core, where they provide their highly varied services to the headquarters of the major British and international companies, to government, sometimes to their own membership and to the population at large. Once again these activities typically have a symbiotic relationship to the industries which use their products – a relationship which frequently demands close physical access, face-to-face communication and frequent changes in the form of the finished outputs. In addition, these are the kind of activities which have a technology which can use a high labour-to-space ratio, so that the high rental costs of the urban core can be absorbed.

Some major changes

Up to this point we have looked at the principles which seek to explain why the structure of conurbation economic activity developed as it did. In this section we focus on the factors which have been changing these patterns of conurbation activity.

The most obvious point is that the conurbations have ceased to be centres of employment growth. Table 3.1 shows clearly that between

Table 3.1 Employment in the conurbations and the rest of Great Britain 1951–1971 (thousands)

	1951	1961	1966	1971
Central Clydeside	n.a.	808	797	740
Greater London	4,288	4,490	4,326	4,086
Merseyside	596	608	609	562
South East Lancashire	1,236	1,224	1,205	1,123
Tyneside	367	386	400	378
West Midlands	1,122	1,223	1,261	1,198
West Yorkshire	842	857	859	811
Total 7 conurbations	n.a.	9,596	9,457	8,898
Rest of Great Britain	n.a.	13,744	14,712	14,834

Source: Censuses of 1951, 1961, 1966, 1971.

1951 and 1961 employment did continue to grow absolutely though probably at a rate markedly slower than the rest of Great Britain. Between 1961 and 1966, when one million people were added to the total number in employment in the rest of Great Britain, conurbation employment actually fell back by 140,000. Indeed only Tyneside and the West Midlands managed to run counter to this downward trend. When we look at the period from 1966 to 1971, this downward movement had become absolutely clear-cut, since every single conurbation lost employment, even though the rest of Great Britain continued to experience employment growth. The net effect was that whereas more than four out of every 10 workers had their work-place in a conurbation in 1961, only three out of 10 were working there 10 years later.

When we look at the absolute decline in conurbation jobs, which between 1961 and 1971 numbered 700,000, the striking fact is that over 80 per cent of the loss was caused by a fall in manufacturing employment. This occurred at the same time as a growth of half a million manufacturing jobs elsewhere in the country. In contrast, many of the conurbations experienced a rate of growth in other services similar to that in the rest of Great Britain. Indeed whereas all conurbation employment between 1961 and 1971 fell by 8 per cent, manufacturing actually dropped by no less than 18 per cent, whilst other services increased by 19 per cent.

The consequence of all of these tendencies was that by 1971 the structure of conurbation employment which, in 1961, had been 'over-represented' in manufacturing and 'under-represented' in other services, had moved closer to that of the rest of Britain (Table 2.14).

The decline of manufacturing

The structural explanation

Several factors might explain this relative and absolute shift of manufacturing away from the conurbations. One possibility is that they were dominated by the kind of manufacturing industries which shed labour everywhere in the country and not just in the conurbations. One way of testing this explanation is the 'shift-share' method. Briefly this assumes that every local employment change may be ascribed to national growth pressures, a structural or individual industry growth effect and a differential local residual unaccounted for by the other two factors. Thus, a local industry which experienced a 10 per cent employment growth between two dates could be said to have achieved this because of national (overall) growth of 4 per cent, a particularly rapid growth nationally in the industry in question of 2 per cent above the overall growth rate, and therefore a differential local growth performance of 4 per cent. Applied to the performance of every sector in a local area, this shift-share approach can be used to detect local 'growth performance'.

We must treat this approach with due caution. Indeed this method is really a standardisation procedure which allows us to ask questions in a more refined way and is in no sense a causal or explanatory model.

A shift-share study by Lever (forthcoming) is the most relevant to our purposes. He analysed the relative shifts in conurbation employment using data drawn from employment exchange areas. Though these areas do not exactly match census conurbation boundaries, they can be made to fit fairly closely. Lever was also concerned with a wider range of employment than just manufacturing, and included mining, quarrying, construction, public utilities, retail and distribution activity. Thus in 1973 his total of conurbation employment, excluding West

Yorkshire, was 4 million, whereas the corresponding conurbation total in manufacturing was only about 2.6 million.

Lever's analysis shows that between 1952 and 1973 conurbation employment declined by over a million, from 5.1 million to 4.1 million. Some of this might have been expected because national employment declined over this period. However, taken as a whole, the conurbations contained industries which had a favourable structure for growth and so we would have expected an employment trend more favourable than that of the nation. In fact, and as we have noted, instead of positive growth the conurbations declined quite rapidly. The reasons seem to lie in a local employment performance which was markedly worse than could have been expected. Thus the figures show a decline of one million jobs; we would have expected a loss of 100,000 jobs because national employment declined, but since the structure of conurbation activity was favourable to growth we should have expected 400,000 jobs to be added to the conurbation employment total, making a net growth of 300,000 jobs. Instead we have a local negative differential performance of 1.3 million jobs.

There are three crucial points to note about Lever's findings. First, London's performance massively affects the overall conurbation local differential and actually accounts for three-quarters of the negative result. Second, every conurbation except Newcastle had a negative local differential performance, though none approached London's relative loss. Third, not all of the conurbations started with an unfavourable structure of activity. Indeed not only London but Merseyside and also the West Midlands could have expected employment growth because of their structure. Finally, except in the case of London and of Newcastle, the poor local performance was entirely associated with what was happening to economic activities in the inner city, here defined by Lever as the employment exchanges covering the major cities at the core of the conurbation area (e.g. Glasgow, Liverpool). The outer part of every single conurbation except London performed marginally better than could have been anticipated given their structure.

Two other pieces of research confirm Lever's findings. Dennis (1978), in analysing manufacturing change in London between 1966 and 1974, suggests that only 30,000 of the estimated absolute employment decline of 390,00 could be accounted for by structural factors. Instead he argued that the main causes of London's decline were associated with a high closure rate of plants, a shrinkage of employment at plants which remained open and, to a lesser extent, a movement of plants to Assisted Areas, to overspill and new towns and elsewhere. He also confirmed Lever's conclusion that London is unusual in having a negative local employment performance in both its inner and outer areas.

A second confirmation of Lever's findings comes in Fothergill's and

Gudgin's work (1978). They used British sub-regional data to delineate their conurbations, so that they include the census areas and typically much more besides; none the less they showed that over the period 1959 to 1971 the six conurbations and London had a negative local employment performance. But they also found that this negative performance was worst between 1959 and 1966. Thereafter, whilst it was negative, it was not markedly so, except, once again, in London. They also paint an interesting picture of the opposite side of the coin – the strong absolute and relative growth in all other areas: on their specification the major free-standing cities, the small free-standing cities, the industrial non-cities, the urbanised but non-industrial areas, the rural and semi-rural areas.

Summarising all of these findings we can see that London has experienced an especially rapid relative manufacturing decline which occurred throughout the 1960s and early 1970s and affected both inner and outer areas. Here the major explanation seems to lie in factors other than industrial structure, since this particular conurbation appeared to have a structure favourable to growth in the initial years. With the other conurbations the almost uniformly poor local growth performance was overlaid on an already weak industrial structure in some cases, or in others occurred despite a favourable structure. But in all cases, except Tyneside, the local performance weakness was associated with the inner areas and probably became less important in the latter part of the 1960s.

Other explanations

There are many possible reasons other than structure why manufacturing employment has declined in the conurbations but grown elsewhere. The most obvious is that regional policy inducements have changed factor prices to the detriment of areas such as London and Birmingham, and to the benefit of the 40 per cent or so of the country which is assisted, both by financial inducements and by infrastructural provision, under the government's regional policy.

Evidence gathered by Dennis suggests that London has indeed lost employment due to the effects of regional policy, but that this loss has been relatively small. Only 9 per cent of all London's total decline in manufacturing, 1966–74, was associated with moves to the Assisted Areas. Even if we allow a generous amount for the subsequent expansions of these plants, expansions which might conceivably have occurred in London had there been no moves induced by regional policy, we are not likely to be able to explain away much of London's manufacturing decline. A different possibility is that some new developments might have located in London had there been no regional inducements and industrial development certificate controls. There is no direct way of measuring this, though it is relevant that few industrial development proposals actually were refused in London even at the peak of the period of 'tough' control.

Another possibility is that factor prices in London and the other conurbations and especially their land, labour, and communication costs have risen more rapidly than in alternative locations. If this were the case, then we would expect a shift of manufacturing investment to other locations where costs were rising less steeply. There is no reliable evidence on changes in communication costs across national space but the evidence on rentals and on wage costs, which we will look at later, does not appear to support this contention.

Dennis, in reviewing the evidence for London, found that the principal form of employment decline was not in terms of movement of plants. Instead there was a massive imbalance between new company job formation and the losses from plant closure, as well as heavy *in situ* employment shrinkage. We cannot assume that this finding holds good for all conurbations. Thus Firn's and Hughes's (1975) evidence for Glasgow, for a slightly earlier period, suggests that *in situ* shrinkage was exactly offset by *in situ* growth, so that the real difference came with a lower growth in new company jobs as compared to losses from closures. None the less Dennis's delineation of these components of decline helps us to refine our questions. We can ask why did London experience large losses from closure and *in situ* shrinkage? Why was there a marked imbalance in both Glasgow and London, in the jobs created by new firms setting up as compared to the jobs lost in closures? And why, in London, was there a marked shrinkage of jobs *in situ*?

The only detailed study of job shrinkage and of closure has been made by Massey and Meegan (1978). In examining the effects of the Industrial Reorganisation Corporation's restructuring activities in the engineering industries they noted that the major cities of London, Birmingham, Liverpool and Manchester suffered particularly large redundancies and closures. Employment losses were far higher than could have been anticipated from the initial incidence of plants. Unfortunately their evidence is not sufficient to show why this was so, though one inference is that the conurbation plants were larger, employed a lot of labour and were particularly suitable for rationalisations which could generate major cost savings. What this might imply is that the conurbations contained a heavy concentration of old plants which could only be made competitive by major substitutions of capital for labour: or alternatively that they were so outmoded that the companies were forced to close them in order to maintain their overall corporate viability. Whilst this vintage of capital argument is reasonably convincing it tells us nothing about whether the conurbations have become *generally* less attractive locations for new investment.

On this question we have to develop a different set of arguments. We concluded, in an earlier section, that the principal justification for manufacturers to locate in the conurbations was the need for agglomeration economies, for large labour complements and for technical linkages. But two factors are loosening the necessity for close physical proximity to achieve these advantages. Transport and communications costs have tended to fall relative to net output and a growing number of industries are organised around three or four major corporate groupings which provide the necessary externalities for the individual production unit from within the corporate organisation. The first tendency frees the company to opt for lower rentals in those areas where there is less competition for land but close enough to the needed externalities of the conurbation; the second reduces the need for urban agglomeration benefits. And both result in a freeing of the industry to consider a range of locations different from the conurbation. Some, like Keeble (1976), have also argued that non-economic variables such as a physically and socially attractive environment are increasingly liable to play a critical role in many location choices, and certainly Fothergill's and Gudgin's data does tend to suggest an increase in the range of feasible production locales.

The whole thrust of this argument then is that there has been a fall in the demand for urban agglomeration economies. This fall is likely to be expressed through some plants with expansion plans, but presently operating on congested conurbation sites, seeking an appropriate labour force in areas where rental costs are lower than in a conurbation site. It is also likely to be expressed through a reduction in the proportion of new companies which seek the special externalities of the large urban area. As the advantages conferred by agglomeration economies diminish, it is likely to be expressed in a continuous substitution of capital for relatively high-cost conurbation labour and an increased opening of conurbation economies to imports of goods and services from elsewhere.

This process of employment de-concentration is unlikely to be random. The industries which continue to require close contact with buyers and physical proximity to a varying range of suppliers may still require a conurbation core location. Those industries in which plant size is large and employment needs large and very varied are liable to seek a decentralised conurbation site. But for other types of activity the conurbation, and particularly the conurbation 'fringe' areas, are liable to become only one of several types of location suitable for production.

The growth of business and other services

Whilst manufacturing has shown unmistakeable signs of decentralising from the conurbation to other parts of the urban hierarchy, the other services category has shown no similar tendency. Unlike manufacturing, service employment was growing rapidly between 1961 and 1971.

In absolute terms this growth was heavily concentrated within the rest of Great Britain (one million jobs between 1961 and 1971), whereas the conurbations, as a whole, only picked up one-third of a million extra jobs. However, leaving aside London, which, in fact, had a modest rate of growth, the overall conurbation employment growth rate in services (23%) was close to that of the rest of Great Britain (26%) (Table 2.15). Moreover, when we allow for the fact that overall conurbation employment and population was declining between these years whereas there was growth in the rest of Great Britain, this suggests *relatively* fast service growth in the conurbations. Indeed Table 3.2 confirms that other services employment per thousand resident population grew more rapidly in all the conurbations, excluding London, than in the rest of Great Britain. As a result by 1971 only the West Midlands had an other services employment/population ratio lower than the rest of the country, and two conurbations, London and Tyneside, had ratios markedly higher than that of the rest of Great Britain.

Table 3.2 Other services employment per thousand resident population

Conurbation	1961	1971
Central Clydeside	100	128
Greater London	197	220
Merseyside	112	139
South East Lancashire	103	128
Tyneside	112	150
West Midlands	92	117
West Yorkshire	105	129
Total 7 conurbations	141	167
Rest of Great Britain	117	133

Source: Censuses of 1961 and 1971.
Other services = Industry Orders XXI–XXIV (1961) and XXIV–XXVII (1971).

This services growth varied markedly sector by sector. In two sectors, professional and scientific services and public administration, growth in the conurbations was especially strong. The professional and scientific sector, which is dominated by publicly-provided educational and medical activities, had a national employment growth of over three-quarters of a million jobs. This was distributed as a relatively low growth in London (17%) but an almost exactly equivalent growth in the other conurbations and elsewhere (40% and 42% respectively). But this equivalence of growth rate should be set against the fact that population in the conurbations declined whereas it grew elsewhere. As a result the ratio of jobs per thousand resident population moved up sharply in London and in the other conurbations and not quite so markedly elsewhere (Table 3.3). In public administration neither London nor the rest of Great Britain showed any marked change in the service/population ratio, but the other conurbations experienced a sharp growth in the ratio.

The changes in both of these sectors clearly reflect factors other than simple population growth or decline. Generalising, they appear to show that the major urban areas were spending heavily, *per capita*, upon publicly-provided services such as education and were also receiving large financial allocations for health expenditure from the central government. These expenditures fed through to employment in the professional and scientific employment grouping and also to local

Table 3.3 Service sectors per thousand resident population

Sector	Greater London		Rest of conurbations		Rest of Great Britain	
	1961	1971	1961	1971	1961	1971
Insurance, banking, finance	30	51	10	16	7	11
Professional and scientific services	54	68	37	53	40	51
Miscellaneous services	73	60	38	38	42	42
Public administration	40	42	17	22	29	29

Source: Censuses of 1961 and 1971.

public employment, in particular to employment by local governments.

In the other major sectors a different pattern emerged. London's domination of the insurance, banking and finance employment remained unchallenged even though there was sizeable employment growth in the other conurbations and elsewhere. In miscellaneous services London experienced a very large absolute reduction both in employment and in the employment/population ratio, whereas this ratio remained unchanged elsewhere.

The net outcome of all of these tendencies was that London continued to be attractive to a wide range of service activities, though population reduction there clearly affected the demand for miscellaneous services. The other conurbations increasingly came to resemble the rest of Great Britain with regard to service employment. All of the conurbations experienced a relative growth in professional and administrative skills rather than clerical skills, the net effect being to upgrade the range of work undertaken (Daniels, 1977).

The consequences of employment decline

Up to this point we have looked at the causes of employment decline and structural change within the conurbations without commenting upon whether they are likely to weaken the economic role of the conurbations over the long run or adversely affect the welfare of conurbation residents and employees. We will look at a number of indicators which will help us to answer these questions. The first point to note is that conurbation job decline has been mostly accompanied by a roughly commensurate drop in the labour force. This was partly achieved by a fall in activity rates for males; but since this occurred in the rest of Great Britain as well, the fall in the labour force was primarily associated with migration losses. One consequence of this roughly proportionate drop in both the labour force and the level of employment is that the conurbations, as a whole, have not contained a growing proportion of the nation's unemployed. Thus in 1961, 43.2 per cent of the male unemployed were recorded as conurbation unemployed. Ten years later, when unemployment was absolutely larger, the proportion of the nation's male unemployed within the conurbations had risen only marginally to 44.9 per cent (see Ch. 10). Over this ten-year period the proportion of female conurbation unemployed remained virtually constant (Department of Employment, 1977).

Another way of indicating the relative strength of the conurbation is in terms of their dependency ratios. This measures the number of economically inactive persons living in an area as a percentage of the number economically active there, the latter including the unemployed. In London there was a drop in the percentage from 1951 to 1977 and the same is true of Merseyside, Tyneside and the West Midlands. On Clydeside the percentage remained unchanged, but it increased in South East Lancashire and West Yorkshire. The rest of Great Britain has shown no clear trend though there was a small fall in 1977 as compared to 1951. What this seems to suggest is that the conurbations as a whole have not moved to a position where fewer and fewer economically active persons have to 'support' those who are inactive.

An additional reasonably comforting finding emerges if we scrutinise changes in the socio-economic composition of the male labour force of the conurbations. Generally speaking the conurbations have tended to contain a relatively large proportion of skilled manual workers but a low proportion of managers and professionals; the one exception to this rule is London where the reverse position holds good. Over the years between 1961 and 1971 there is no evidence that the conurbations experienced a process of de-skilling (Table 2.12). Indeed there is contrary evidence of an upgrading of the British labour force including that of the conurbations, over these years (Department of Employment, 1977).

Our final measure – incomes – is perhaps the best single indicator of personal welfare. Inland Revenue data for the conurbation in the 1960s suggests that conurbation (tax-case) income rose at a rate equivalent to that of the nation as a whole (Cameron, 1973). New Earning Survey data for a later period 1970–75 (and for areas typically bigger than Census conurbations), shows that only the West Midlands and Merseyside have failed to keep up in terms of average earnings with Great Britain, and even here the disparity was only noticeable for full-time males rather than females. Thus we can see that for given broad earning groups there are no substantial differences between conurbation earnings, the earnings of those in contiguous regions, and the earnings of the same group in the country.

Taken as a set, these indicators allow us to be reasonably content at the way in which the conurbation economies have adjusted to changes in the absolute level of employment and in the structure of economic activity. The labour force has adjusted downwards, there has been no marked growth of a dependent population, there is no evidence of a growing proportionate concentration of unemployment, de-skilling has not occurred, and incomes, in most conurbations, have grown at a rate commensurate to that of the nation. But before we become too sanguine we must recognise that our data are very deficient. For example we have no data on conurbation productivity, or conurbation rates of return on capital invested, or upon the net contribution to (or receipts from) the Exchequer. Furthermore, although we have argued that the conurbations as a whole have done relatively well vis-à-vis the nation, particular parts of the conurbations, and particularly their inner cities, may not have shared in this relative progress. And finally we should judge whether these relatively favourable trends for the conurbations as a whole are likely to continue.

Inner city economic decline

For a considerable period of time economic activity has been shifting away from the dense centres of the conurbations and from their core cities such as Glasgow, Liverpool or Birmingham (see Ch. 7). Thus between 1961 and 1971 the ratio of conurbation employment in the centres, rest of core cities and remainder of the conurbations changed from 24:32:44 to 23:29:48.

The most substantial shifts have occurred in manufacturing, and here we know that the principal 'cause' is that new plants have tended to avoid setting up in the inner parts of the central city, preferring instead surburban or peripheral sites. The actual closure of plants in the inner city and their physical removal to suburban sites has not been a major mechanism of decentralisation. This is not to argue that no new plants have chosen the inner city, but probably that a declining proportion have done so, and that those which have so chosen, have been relatively small employers of labour (Cameron, 1979).

There are a great number of reasons why new plants and some existing activities have decentralised. Developments in telecommunications have replaced the need for many face-to-face contacts. A shift in manufacturing technology to favour single-storey extensive layouts has increased the land-to-output ratio. The growing substitution of road for rail transport for materials and product delivery has reduced the dependence on city rail terminals. The decentralisation of urban population has reduced the access to labour advantages of the urban core and the desire to avoid continuous tussles with planning authorities over development permission has encouraged the acquisition or renting of land in excess of immediate production requirements.

Each one of these factors has tended to reduce the desirability of operating in a central location and has encouraged industries to seek non-central (and lower rental) sites. Many have argued that two consequences have ensued. First, resident employees in the inner city who do not possess the skills necessary for the growing central city service economy are alleged to have become spatially separated from the kinds of manufacturing jobs which they are able to do. The consequence, in the absence of explicit policies to bring labour closer to jobs, either through transport policies, rehousing of the unemployed in public housing closer to available jobs, or by shifting manufacturing jobs to inner city locations, is alleged to be a localised inner city unemployment problem. The evidence on this is reviewed by Richardson in Chapter 10 but at this point it is worth emphasising that the case does not seem proven. Essentially this is because it rests upon rather mechanistic assumptions about spatial disequilibrium in a labour market which is in practice fluid, well served by changing public transport facilities, and in which market information about job opportunities can be assumed to be fairly readily transmitted throughout the system. Moreover there is a danger that spatial disequilibrium may be falsely detected in a context which more truly reflects a *general* rise in unemployment *throughout* the urban area.

A second consequence is more generally accepted. As economic activity has shifted away, large areas of central city land, much of it in a derelict state, have been left abandoned. Whilst it is difficult to generalise about the possibilities for redeveloping this space in every conurbation, there are two broad possibilities. First it could be argued that decentralisation has been caused by the blighted conditions and the current inappropriateness of land use in the areas around the central areas. If such conditions were removed, economic activity would flow back to the redesigned central sites on a large scale. This would argue for relatively large allocations of land use for economic activity in any redesigned central sites. The opposite argument is that the real causes of decentralisation are not inner city blight and shortages of appropriate land, but a fall in the demand for close physical access to the central area and to central producers. Thus even if the blighted sites are redeveloped, they will not attract much new activity. This would suggest that redevelopment should concentrate, in the main, upon residential, environmental and social facility improvements.

Pushed to the extreme, neither of these arguments is likely to be correct. There are real and permanent reasons for decentralisation of economic activities. Equally there are industries which continue to want close physical access to the central area, and the centre itself may, in particular instances, require physical expansion to cope with service growth. This suggests that an increasing proportion of economic activity will seek decentralised urban sites, but that there will also be a continuing requirement for inner city sites especially by small-scale manufacturing and other activities.

The future of the conurbations

All the evidence points to a continued dispersal of manufacturing employment away from the conurbations and to employment trends less favourable than those of the rest of the nation. In part this reflects the continued operation of regional policy, the rapid growth of new plants already dispersed and the declining need for urban externalities by manufacturing activity. But it also reflects the depressing effects on employment growth of cut-backs in local authority expenditure, and the increasing propensity by many service industries to raise output through productivity increases rather than through employment increases (Harris and Taylor, 1978). However, the critical question is whether the *per capita welfare* of conurbation employees and residents is liable to be affected adversely by continued absolute declines in the level of conurbation employment. We can see no particular reason why this unfavourable outcome is likely. This suggests that the management of urban decline in a context of a declining local economic base is the crucial dimension. What is needed is new land-use policies to counteract dereliction and environmental decay; employment and economic policies to raise the level of demand for labour particularly in the conurbations experiencing heavy unemployment and sensitive public capital expenditure policies especially for housing in conditions of population decline. These are the major areas of economic management which will require relevant solutions.

Conclusions

The economies of the conurbations have undergone major change over the last fifteen to twenty years. They now employ fewer of the nation's workers, their dominance over manufacturing has been challenged and, London apart, they have increasingly developed economic structures which conform to that of urban Britain as a whole. In particular, the growth in employment in services, which has been such a marked feature of the national picture in the 1960s and 1970s, has shaped the growth pattern of the conurbations as well, so that services now employ almost as many workers as does manufacturing.

The factors causing the absolute decline of conurbation manufacturing employment can be separated into those which policy-makers themselves have encouraged and those which arise from changing locational preferences by private decision-makers. Public policies have deliberately and successfully sought to spread population and economic activity away from dense and congested urban centres. But policy has been working with the natural trend because a decline in the demand for urban agglomeration economies has been hastened by a combination of transport and communication improvements, by changes in manufacturing technology, by a growing concentration within key industrial sectors and by an increased preference for working environments which are attractive living environments as well.

All of these forces have tended to increase the range of areas thought suitable for efficient production (industrial dispersal) and, even for those activities which wish to remain in the conurbations, have tended to highlight the operating advantages of suburban locations (urban decentralisation).

Although we have insufficient data to make a full evaluation, it does appear that this absolute decline in the level of conurbation employment has not been accompanied by undesirable effects upon the welfare of conurbation employees nor upon the relative strength of conurbation economic activity. Income growth has mirrored that of the nation, the proportion of the nation's unemployed residing within the conurbation has not increased, dependency ratios have not worsened and, in common with the nation as a whole, there has been an upgrading of the skills of the labour force. Where there is greater doubt is whether this economic dispersion and decentralisation has created pockets of localised unemployment within the inner cities of the conurbations. This decentralisation of economic activity has also called into question the longer-term economic role of those parts of the conurbation immediately outside of the city centres. These could either be redeveloped primarily for commercial and manufacturing activity or reused principally for housing, social facilities and environmental improvements.

For the immediate future the continued absolute decline of conurbation employment seems probable. Thus employment dispersal will be a natural accompaniment of continued population dispersal. Employment dispersal will also reflect the relatively rapid growth of new facilities recently installed in non-conurbation locations. But the most critical factors are likely to be the employment-depressing effects of reductions in the real rate of growth of local authority expenditure and the less easily reversible reduction in the demand by manufacturers for agglomeration economies. Both point to employment growth trends considerably less buoyant than for the nation as a whole; trends which will be offset only to a marginal extent by the continued demand of high level service activity for the communications advantages of the city centres. Within this overall picture the evidence points to continuing employment difficulties in some of the 'northern' conurbations, Merseyside, Tyneside and Clydeside in particular, none of which have managed to throw off their unenviable record of persistently high unemployment and heavy out-migration.

In general, however, it is probable that absolute declines in activity will not be accompanied by conurbation *per capita* welfare deterioration vis-à-vis the rest of Great Britain. The real uncertainties lie in whether this continued and predictable absolute decline will be managed by public authorities with skill or with ineptitude. Falls in local tax revenue, public capital spending in conditions of change in the number and structure of city population, the appropriate local policies needed to support the adaptation of city land uses, the transport system, the labour force and the local economic structure, these are the economic issues which will crowd in on the decision-makers. For if the old urban 'heavy-weights' are going to compete they will have to be slimmed down to a new weight and learn some new tricks in the process.

References

Cameron, G.C. (1973) 'Economic analysis for a declining urban economy' in Cameron G.C. and Wingo L. (eds) *Cities, Regions and Public Policy*, Oliver and Boyd, Edinburgh, pp. 209–22.

Cameron, G.C. (1980) 'The inner city – new plant incubator?' in Evans, A.W. and Eversley, D.E.C. (eds) *The Inner City: Employment and Industry*. Heinemann, London.

Daniels, P.W. (1977) 'Office location in the British conurbations', *Urban Studies* **14** (3), Oct., pp. 261–74.

Dennis, R. (1978) 'The decline of manufacturing employment in Greater London : 1966–74', *Urban Studies* **15** (1), Feb., pp. 63–74.

Department of Employment (1977) 'Employment in Metropolitan Areas'. Project report by the Unit for Manpower Studies.

Evans, A.W. (1973) 'The pure theory of city size in an industrial economy' in Cameron and Wingo (eds) op. cit., pp. 49–78.

Firn, J.R. and **Hughes, J.T.** (1975) *Employment Growth and Decentralisation of Manufacturing Industry.* Centre for Environmental Studies 1973 Urban Economics Conference, London.

Fothergill, S. and **Gudgin, G.** (1978) *Regional Employment Change : A Sub-Regional Explanation?* Centre for Environmental Studies Working Note 488. London.

Harris, D.F. and **Taylor, F.J.** (1978) *The Service Sector : Its Changing Role as a Source of Employment.* Centre for Environmental Studies Research Series, 25. London.

Keeble, D. (1976) *Industrial Location and Planning in the United Kingdom.* Methuen, London.

Lever, W.F. (Forthcoming) *Employment Change in British Conurbations 1952–1973.* Department of Social and Economic Research, University of Glasgow.

Massey, D.B. and **Meegan, R.A.** (1978) 'Industrial restructuring versus the cities', *Urban Studies* **15** (3), Oct., pp. 273–87.

Thompson, W.R. (1965) *A Preface to Urban Economics.* Johns Hopkins University Press, Baltimore.

Chapter 4

The fiscal context

The changing structure of the urban public economy

From growth to crisis

The mid 1970s in Britain were a watershed in the development of urban fiscal policy. For 20 years or more local government expenditure had grown at an exceptionally rapid rate. From little more than 8 per cent of the Gross Domestic Product in 1955, the call on real resources had grown to 14.5 per cent by 1975, while the volume of locally-administered transfers (subsidies, grants, debt interest, etc.) had more than doubled its share of the national income. At the same time the number of employees in the local authority sector had nearly doubled, as had the proportion of the total labour force employed in the sector. It could not continue. Politically and economically the progression had reached crisis point. Reform seemed inevitable.

The political crisis came to a head during 1974, when in a closely-fought campaign between two general elections local taxation and the system of local finance emerged, together with housing policy, as one of the most strongly felt issues. The political parties rivalled one another with more or less specific promises to reform the system. The Conservative manifesto for the October election that year, for example, went so far as to state that 'within the normal lifetime of a Parliament we shall abolish the domestic rating system and replace it by taxes more broadly based and related to people's ability to pay'. The Liberals promised site value taxation.

Economically the crisis was quickly reflected in attempts to cut back local programmes and staff recruitment. But its symptoms were not confined to the local level. The structure of local public finance, with its high ratio of centrally-distributed funds and predetermined apportionment of the liability for outturns, ensured that the impact of local fiscal stress was at once transmitted to national public expenditure and borrowing requirements. Local freedom to meet the escalating cost of urban services by increasing local rates or through borrowing threatened the national counter-inflationary strategy as seriously as the need for additional direct assistance strained Exchequer revenues and net borrowing. Evidently there was a fundamental flaw in the system.

The problems were not wholly new. As the Layfield Committee was to point out (Department of the Environment, 1976), 'the character of the problems reviewed in 1902, 1911, 1918, 1922, 1925 and 1929, to cite only a few occasions, bears a strong family likeness to that of the present' (Ch. 2, para. 72). But there were new elements that reflected the peculiar circumstances of the period. The secular growth of expenditure and the steady rise in the proportion absorbed by central government – itself the product of an attempt during the mid 1960s to tackle the underlying problems – left the system much more exposed than hitherto, particularly from the standpoint of central government. Without direct powers to control local spending (on current account), yet expected to meet, at the peak, over two-thirds of its costs, central government could foresee its power to manage the macroeconomy being undermined by the unrestricted spending of the local authorities. This was not simply a question of the Government of the day failing to impose its political will: the administrative power of central government (in the guise of Treasury) was as fundamentally threatened as the authority of the executive. There was no balking the call for action.

The immediate crisis centred on counter-inflation policy. For, on top of the long-term growth in local spending, four factors had coincided to generate an unprecedented rate of increase in expenditure and tax demands. There was firstly the rate of inflation which grew to over 25 per cent during 1974–75 and which was especially strongly and rapidly reflected in the labour-intensive costs of the government sector. (In the period 1970–76, for example, the real cost of output in the government sector is estimated to have grown at a cumulative annual rate 1.5 per cent above that of total domestic expenditure.) This was matched by a steep rise in interest rates, which for local authorities rose to over 13 per cent in 1975. (They were to rise even more steeply again two years later.) Though the impact of these increases on current spending was dulled by the practice of consolidating local borrowing within an internal loans fund, the high proportion of short- and medium-term debt in local authority portfolios meant that through refinancing the effects were bound to be felt before long. There was too the reorganisation of local authorities which took effect in 1974 and entailed not merely a redistribution of costs within the newly-amalgamated areas but also a sizeable once-for-all increase due to the staffing and setting-up costs of the new authorities. And finally, there was the transfer of responsibility for sewerage infrastructure to the statutory water authorities, with new pricing policies and powers to levy separate charges.

The combined effect on local tax demands was dramatic. And for many areas it was made worse, early in 1974, by the newly-elected Labour Government's honouring of a pledge to redistribute central funds (through the Rate Support Grant) in favour of the large metropolitan areas. As a result, in many of the less-urbanised areas rate demands that year were more than twice as large as the previous year's, while the average increase was in excess of 30 per cent (before the hastily-assembled programme of special reliefs).

Meanwhile, the economic recession triggered by the rise in commodity prices and the realignment of international exchange rates had brought about a rapid fall in national income and output and in the volume of real resources available to central government. With the progressive assimilation of monetarism into government policy, local spending was no longer viewed as the ideal Keynesian solution to recession: deficit financing only threatened to fuel the already raging fires of inflation. So attention was directly focused on the issues of the power to control local spending and the appropriate role and form of local taxation.

The immediate political response was characteristic: tough action to regain control of the public economy; faltering steps towards more fundamental reform. Public expenditure was severely cut; local capital expenditure previously free from central control (e.g. local authority house improvement and new house-building – the latter initially through indirect controls but eventually through the institution of formal programmes) was brought within the system of centrally-administered allocations; the central government share of local current expenditure was reduced and strict cash limits were imposed. Meanwhile, resisting the temptation to promise unrealistic reforms, the Labour Government established the Layfield Committee 'to review the whole system ... and to make recommendations' and a new consultative forum to discuss the day-to-day issues of expenditure control with the local authorities. Yet despite this rash of initiatives, as the intervening years have demonstrated, there was little real commitment to reform.

The view from the cities

Britain was not alone at this time in experiencing a fundamental shock to the structure of its urban public economies. Few public finance systems were proof against the combination of hyper-inflation and recession which struck the developed economies of the West during this period. In the United States, for example, the fiscal crisis brought many cities, and not only New York, close to bankruptcy. By contrast, the major British metropolitan areas survived the crisis better than might have been feared. For exactly those features of the system which made the management of the urban economies into an issue of *national* concern and *national* political debate served to protect the cities themselves from the consequences of their spending policies. But the signs of strain were sufficient to justify anxiety about the future.

The United States provides a convenient bench-mark, as it shows what can happen in a system that retains a high degree of autonomy in local fiscal affairs. There the cities' borrowing is not automatically underwritten by the Federal Government; and each city is expected to finance a much higher proportion of locally-required services out of local tax revenues (including welfare payments). The combined effect of recession and inflation, therefore, was to undermine seriously the fiscal viability of all except a few of the major metropolitan areas. By comparison, the structure of urban public finance in Britain incorporates a number of features which helped to soften the impact of the overall crisis on individual urban areas. There is, first and foremost, the much higher proportion of local current expenditure that is absorbed by central government. Though this has been changed from year to year for most of the last decade, since 1970 the percentage has never fallen below 55 per cent; and in 1975/76 it reached a peak of 67.3 per cent. There is too the fact that, with the exception of highways and a few minor services, the central government contribution to capital expenditure takes the form of a grant to debt service payments on current account rather than capital grants. As a result, central government absorbs a high proportion of the costs due to increases in interest rates. This has proved especially important in the light of the high proportion of short- and medium-term obligations in the local authorities' debt: in 1977, for example, 39 per cent of the outstanding external debt (in England and Wales) had a residual maturity of less than one year and a further 35 per cent a maturity of 1–5 years. In a period of rapid inflation and rising interest rates the advantages to the cities are manifest.

Moreover, the larger role played by central government, than for example in the United States, has two significant corollaries. The first is that central government exercises greater supervision and control over local fiscal policy. Formally this is restricted to capital expenditure; but central government also wields considerable informal power over local spending generally, albeit, as the mid 1970s revealed, not sufficient to meet its objectives in a time of profound economic crisis. The second corollary is that there is more scope for a centrally-administered policy of redistributing the fiscal burden between areas. And this in turn has been the main source of the relatively favourable situation of London and the major metropolitan areas throughout this period.

Equally significant has been the comparative ease with which boundaries have been periodically adjusted in Britain to reflect changes in the spatial structure of urban economic activity. This too has played an important part in limiting the strain on the public economies of the larger metropolitan areas. (Here the most obvious examples are the creation of the Greater London Council in 1964 and of the English metropolitan and Scottish regional authorities a decade later.) None the less, changes in the spatial structure of the urbanised communities of Britain remain a major source of concern. Indeed the main problem to emerge in recent years throughout the major metropolitan areas has been that of *absolute* population decline, first dramatically brought to the forefront by publication of the 1971 Census results and following hard on the heels of the concern with *relative* decentralisation identified during the mid 1960s. For the foreseeable future, as Eversley

(1972) was among the first to point out, the fiscal health of British cities will be intimately bound up with their success at adjusting to the loss of population.

The fiscal impact of urban decline

The adjustment of costs

Loss of population and economic decline are not new phenomena. The last hundred years and more have witnessed many shifts in the relative prosperity of different areas of Britain and in the spatial distribution of the population. Ever since the Second World War there have been many examples of the painful process of adjustment to reduced population size; one has only to think of rural communities in Scotland and Wales or the mining villages of Durham or the tight-knit industrial towns of north-east Lancashire. What is new is the scale of the change in the metropolitan areas and more importantly its potential political impact.

The essence of the fiscal problem, so the argument goes, is simple: loss of population and loss of business tend to reduce taxable income (and capital) faster than the cost of urban services. The operating costs of a wide range of activities, from education through police and fire services to street maintenance and refuse collection, cannot be reduced in line with population loss without an abrupt reduction in the quality of service,[1] while the costs of maintaining the physical fabric of the city remain largely unchanged and may even be raised by the relative increase in the volume of commuting. Decline also tends to entail an increase in the proportion of the population dependent on public assistance (the unemployed, old people, low-income families, students, the victims of racial or sexual discrimination) as well as changes in the composition of the active labour force. And this in turn has a significant effect on the demand for the publicly-financed social and other services. Moreover, as Peterson (1976) has observed, the maintenance of the fabric of an ageing city may actually require a higher *per capita* capital expenditure than is needed in an area of growth.

So the declining city, left to its own resources, faces a cruel dilemma: higher tax rates, which would permit a higher quality of service, are likely to encourage the exodus of businesses and upper income households; lower tax rates are likely to be insufficient to prevent a deterioration in services and physical conditions, itself an alternative cause of the 'flight to the suburbs'. In Britain, it is true, the dilemma is not as severe as in the United States, for the total volume of central government funds (however distributed) leaves a much smaller amount to be raised through local taxation. (The rate levied even on industrial and commercial property is typically less than 1 per cent of the true market value in Britain, compared with something closer to 2–4 per cent in the

United States – and cities there are likely to have local sales and business taxes in addition.) The local tax burden is therefore less likely to be a major determinant of business or household location.

In essence, however, this whole account rests on the presumption that local public sector costs cannot in fact be reduced in line with the loss of population and business. The assertion is admittedly tendentious. What does the evidence suggest? As yet, the indications in Britain must be judged scrappy. The phenomenon of metropolitan decline is after all relatively recent and there is a lack of thorough analysis. Certainly one could point to the example of London where political resistance to reductions in education and hospitals and public transport suggests that reductions in cost are unlikely to be achieved without a struggle. But there are also some signs that the central premise may have been given too much weight: with the major part of health and welfare costs borne nationally, it may prove easier to adjust the level of urban services to the shifting pattern of population. As yet it is too early to tell.

Some indices of fiscal health

It would be convenient if Britain's urban areas could be simply divided between declining and expanding communities. Unfortunately, as Webber and Craig (1978) have shown us, the pattern is more complex. Decline is not uniquely the lot of the major metropolitan areas; nor is it necessarily linked to a weak economic base, as the examples of London and the West Midlands show. Urban expansion similarly must at least be divided between the areas of suburban residential growth and the areas of growth in productive activity.

None the less, in an attempt to illustrate how the declining metropolitan areas have fared in relation to other types of city and suburb, I have looked at the experience of a sample of 29 urbanised areas[2] since the first half of the 1960s. The results of this analysis are presented in Tables 4.1, 4.2 and 4.3 and are discussed below. The detailed evidence of this small sample should be compared with the results of a cross-sectional analysis of all authorities recently undertaken by Jackman and Sellars (1978).

(a) *Total expenditure*: There can be little doubt that total expenditure per head has increased in recent years much more rapidly in the major metropolitan areas, and especially in London, than in most other types of urban area. The figures quoted in Table 4.1, for example, reveal that outlays more than doubled between 1965 and 1977 *in real terms* in parts of Inner London (such as Camden and Wandsworth) and in Manchester, with increases well in excess of 50 per cent throughout the declining metropolitan areas. This contrasts with limited increases, and in many cases real reductions, in total expenditure (not merely resource expenditure) in most other urban communities.

Table 4.1 Comparative fiscal performance : selected urban and metropolitan areas

	Estimated population Mid 1976 ('000)	Population change 1964–76 (%)	Estimated actual rateable value (£m)		Change in tax base per head at const- ant prices 1965–77 (%)
			as at 31 March 1965	1977	
1. Declining metropolitan areas					
London:					
Camden	185.8	− 23.7	33.6	104.0	+ 30.3
Wandsworth	284.6	− 14.7	15.6	41.5	+ 0.4
Newham	228.9	− 12.7	14.6	35.2	− 11.2
Barnet	305.2	− 4.0	22.1	57.5	− 12.9
Croydon	330.6	+ 0.5	18.4	66.3	+ 15.0
West Midlands:					
Birmingham (92%)	1,058.8	− 4.3	49.9	157.9	+ 6.2
Coventry (99%)	336.8	+ 2.7	13.1	42.3	+ 1.2
Wolverhampton	266.4	+ 77.4	7.5	40.1	− 3.6
Greater Manchester					
Manchester (99%)	490.0	− 24.0	27.7	71.2	+ 8.8
Merseyside					
Liverpool	539.7	− 26.0	26.6	71.3	+ 16.5
South Yorkshire					
Sheffield (91%)	558.0	+ 13.7	21.0	62.9	− 15.4
2. Areas of expansion					
Blaby (Leics.)	77.3	+ 22.7	2.1	8.2	+ 1.5
Fareham (Hants.)	86.3	+ 25.6	2.5	10.2	+ 3.0
Gillingham (Kent)	93.9	+ 21.8	2.5	9.7	+ 2.9
3. Established high— status residen- tial areas					
Epsom and Ewell (Surrey)	70.7	− 1.4	3.7	10.8	− 4.8
Oxford	117.4	+ 7.8	6.6	19.7	− 10.5
4. Areas of old heavy industry					
Stoke-on-Trent	256.2	− 7.7	9.2	29.2	+ 10.5
Rhondda	85.4	− 13.8	1.6	3.7	− 12.5

Total rate and grant-borne expenditure per head (£)			Change in expenditure per head at constant prices 1965–77 (%)	Government grants (excluding Housing Revenue Account) as percentage of total expenditure	
1965	1974	1977–8		1965–6	1977–8
90.50	315.09	586.11	+ 108.0	33.9	24.5
38.06	115.33	258.79	+ 118.4	60.7	66.7
50.45	133.12	302.79	+ 92.7	24.1	62.6
48.03	115.49	235.97	+ 57.8	33.2	53.1
46.34	128.77	243.60	+ 68.8	39.8	54.0
46.64	130.31	252.89	+ 74.1	44.2	61.3
45.94	127.63	244.65	+ 71.0	48.3	63.6
45.18	116.55	232.18	+ 70.0	46.1	61.1
51.73	156.77	345.23	+ 114.3	49.0	58.2
50.44	154.13	283.15	+ 80.3	59.3	68.5
44.41	129.51	260.40	+ 88.3	44.1	63.3
42.63	n.a.	111.77	− 15.8	57.9	53.9
42.78	105.58	136.96	+ 2.8	53.1	45.0
37.69	98.69	123.47	+ 5.2	56.6	58.2
46.79	n.a.	134.29	− 7.8	42.0	26.1
49.76	126.88	141.74	− 8.5	32.0	14.7
48.43	126.70	150.05	− 0.5	58.4	42.9
33.41	135.04	180.53	+ 73.5	69.6	81.7

	Estimated population Mid 1976 ('000)	Population change 1964–76 (%)	Estimated actual rateable value (£m) as at 31 March		Change in tax base per head at const-ant prices 1965–77 (%)
			1965	1977	
5. *Modern indus-trial areas*					
Gloucester	91.6	+ 27.8	2.7	12.0	− 20.6
Luton (Beds.)	164.5	+ 11.3	9.3	27.9	− 13.6
Scunthorpe (Humberside)	68.1	− 2.2	5.2	12.4	− 22.4
Thurrock (Essex) (101%)	127.7	+ 7.9	7.1	30.5	+ 27.8
6. *Medium-sized manufacturing cities*					
Derby	213.7	+ 64.4	6.7	27.9	− 18.3
Ipswich	121.5	+ 1.2	5.1	18.0	+ 13.0
7. *Regional service centres*					
Bristol	416.3	− 3.7	20.2	56.9	− 6.1
Kingston-upon Hull	276.6	− 7.9	8.9	27.1	+ 5.9
Nottingham	280.3	− 10.1	14.7	39.4	− 4.0
Southampton	213.7	+ 2.4	10.7	29.5	− 13.6
York	101.9	− 3.1	3.7	10.6	− 4.9

Source: CIPFA statistical series, based on annually prepared budget estimates.

Notes: (a) Percentages in brackets relate to population of former area as per cent of post-1974 reorganisation total: if not cited, the total was unchanged.

(b) *Tax base*: By contrast, the majority of the major metropolitan areas in the sample experienced a real fall in the value of their tax base (per head of population) over the same period. Given the British practice of infrequent revaluations, the evidence of a real fall is not surprising (though the period embraced one major revaluation). It is the relative experience of the different types of area that is more significant. Here it is noteworthy that the real fall in the major metro-politan areas was not generally worse than that experienced by other areas analysed. Apparently the loss of tax base has not occurred at a rate much faster than the loss of population. Set against the real increase in expenditure, however, the picture still suggests a steadily worsening fiscal balance in the declining metropolitan areas.

Total rate and grant-borne expenditure per head (£)			Change in expenditure per head at constant prices 1965–77 (%)	Government grants (excluding Housing Revenue Account) as percentage of total expenditure	
1965	1974	1977–8		1965–6	1977–8
50.08	111.56	125.57	− 16.9	51.1	33.9
44.50	124.20	166.15	+ 39.9	44.1	13.7
n.a.	138.56	154.18	n.a.	54.2	11.1
65.99	149.10	178.72	− 13.0	48.8	13.2
44.60	113.10	143.56	+ 3.4	43.3	35.5
41.29	109.00	130.28	+ 1.3	49.1	26.3
45.00	128.52	156.42	+ 11.6	45.0	32.1
52.29	119.63	144.80	− 11.1	61.6	56.4
43.99	127.05	165.57	+ 20.9	46.7	40.8
49.05	127.36	157.09	+ 2.8	43.7	28.8
44.62	n.a.	133.26	− 4.1	54.8	52.5

(b) Tax base estimates and expenditures reduced to constant prices by Consumers' Expenditure Deflator.

(c) Expenditure includes expenditure of other authorities financed by precept.

(d) Area categorisation adapted from Webber and Craig (1978).

(c) *Reliance on central government finance*: The gap implied by real increases in expenditure and real reductions in rateable value has of course been filled in part by increased taxes and in part by transfers from central government. Here the period since the mid 1960s has witnessed a very dramatic shift in the direction (as well as the volume) of central government assistance. While the major metropolitan areas have enjoyed a significant increase in the proportion of their expenditure absorbed by central government, most of the medium-sized cities have been required to meet a significantly higher proportion of their expenditure from local resources. The only exception, the sample evidence suggests (apart from the special case of the urban communities of Wales), seems to have been the areas of relatively new growth.

Table 4.2 Comparative credit rating: selected urban and metropolitan areas

	Estimated actual rateable value (£m) as at 31 March		Outstanding debt (£m)	
	1965	1977	1965	1977
1. *Declining metropolitan areas*				
London				
Camden	33.6	104.0	n.a.	295.0
Wandsworth	15.6	41.5	n.a.	188.7
Newham	14.6	35.2	n.a.	204.9
Barnet	22.1	57.5	n.a.	118.3
Croydon	18.4	66.3	n.a.	126.0
West Midlands				
Birmingham (92%)	49.9	157.9	237.9	718.7
Coventry (99%)	13.1	42.3	61.0	185.0
Wolverhampton	7.5	40.1	28.9	146.4
Greater Manchester				
Manchester (99%)	27.7	71.2	159.1	476.4
Merseyside				
Liverpool	26.6	71.3	152.8	350.0
South Yorkshire				
Sheffield (91%)	21.0	62.9	111.5	312.0
2. *Areas of expansion*				
Blaby (Leics.)	2.1	8.2	3.7	13.5
Fareham (Hants.)	2.5	10.2	8.2	15.5
Gillingham (Kent)	2.5	9.7	7.2	17.9
3. *Established high-status residential areas*				
Epsom and Ewell (Surrey)	3.7	10.8	4.6	13.0
Oxford	6.6	19.7	29.6	8.6
4. *Areas of old heavy industry*				
Stoke-on-Trent	9.2	29.2	47.6	106.5
Rhondda	1.6	3.7	7.4	27.6
5. *Modern industrial areas*				
Gloucester	2.7	12.0	14.5	19.6
Luton (Beds.)	9.3	27.9	30.4	82.1
Scunthorpe (Humberside)	5.2	12.4	16.0	33.4
Thurrock (Essex) (101%)	7.1	30.5	13.0	57.0

Outstanding debt per £ actual rateable value		Resource deficiency (R.S.G. definition) as % of actual tax base (R.V.)
1965	1977	1977/8
n.a.	2.84	0
n.a.	4.55	19
n.a.	5.81	12
n.a.	2.06	0
n.a.	1.90	0
4.77	4.66	16
4.66	4.42	39
3.84	3.66	15
5.75	6.69	19
5.74	4.93	32
5.31	4.97	54
1.75	1.66	64
3.23	1.53	47
2.89	1.86	69
1.24	1.19	12
4.51	0.44	3
5.18	3.64	52
4.66	7.48	300
5.41	1.65	33
3.26	2.95	2
3.05	2.69	0
1.83	1.87	0

	Estimated actual rateable value (£m) as at 31 March		Outstanding debt (£m)	
	1965	1977	1965	1977
6. *Medium-sized manufacturing cities*				
Derby	6.7	27.9	28.5	70.0
Ipswich	5.1	18.0	17.5	30.9
7. *Regional service centres*				
Bristol	20.2	56.9	103.6	204.0
Kingston-upon-Hull	8.9	27.1	59.3	144.8
Nottingham	14.7	39.9	49.9	208.9
Southampton	10.7	29.5	52.6	96.5
York	3.7	10.6	15.0	39.0

Source: CIPFA statistical series, based on annually prepared budget estimates.

Notes: (a) Percentages in brackets relate to population of former area as per cent of post-1974 reorganisation total: if not cited, the total was unchanged.

Central government assistance has tended to be directed to the areas of growth and decline, at the expense of the more stable communities.

(d) *Debt ratios*: A common symptom of fiscal stress is an increase in the ratio of outstanding debt to available resources. Indeed under conditions of inflation it is extremely difficult to avoid. Nonetheless, the figures in Table 4.2 suggest that most of the metropolitan areas have managed to avoid massive increases in debt ratios, albeit that they remain at a higher level than in the smaller cities.[3] In this respect the fiscal system has undoubtedly successfully protected the major cities from the sudden collapse of credit-worthiness that has become associated with New York's slide towards bankruptcy. Not of course that the British cities are so dependent on credit-ratings as American cities: with their debts fully underwritten by the State, the risks of default are negligible. Lenders are more likely to be influenced by an area's potential share of the Rate Support Grant than by its unassisted wealth or indebtedness. None the less, the capital market cannot be assumed in the long run to be blind to all such indicators of fiscal viability.

(e) *Local tax rates and payments*: During the period 1965/66 to 1974/75 the combination of the increase in central government funding and the revaluation of rateable property was broadly sufficient to enable local authorities to meet their needs without increasing rate

Outstanding debt per £ actual rate-able value		Resource deficiency (R.S.G. definition) as % of actual tax base (R.V.)
1965	1977	1977/8
4.28	2.52	33
3.46	1.73	18
5.13	3.58	27
6.65	5.41	79
3.40	5.32	23
4.91	3.26	25
4.08	3.68	66

(b) Tax base estimates and expenditures reduced to constant prices by Consumers' Expenditure Deflator.
(c) Expenditure includes expenditure of other authorities financed by precept.
(d) Area categorisation adapted from Webber and Craig (1978).

poundages. During 1974, however, and subsequently, the impact of inflation led to significant increases in rate poundages in all types of community (a phenomenon largely explained by the timing of the property revaluation). But these increases were not so large as to raise the burden on domestic ratepayers *in real terms* (after allowance for the Government's special relief for the domestic ratepayer) over the longer period: indeed, as the example of the 29 selected urban areas in Table 4.3. illustrates, the real burden on householders has in fact fallen since the mid 1960s across a wide spectrum of urban communities. Within the major metropolitan areas the experience seems to have varied. Generally speaking, however, it is clear that it has predominantly been Londoners who have benefited from the largest reductions in local taxes, while in most other metropolitan areas there have been moderate increases.

It must be stressed that the detailed figures quoted here relate only to a small sample of urbanised areas and that not necessarily a strictly representative one. A more authoritative account must await the results of studies currently under way. But the indications outlined above are in line with others' assessments and it is unlikely that more exhaustive analysis will greatly alter the picture.

What therefore may we conclude? Despite the well-founded fears of many observers, it appears that metropolitan decline in Britain has not so far been accompanied by a significant deterioration in the fiscal

Table 4.3 Comparative burden of local taxation: selected urban and metropolitan areas

	Local tax rate (Rate poundage) (pence)			Average domestic rates paid (£)			Change in average domestic rates paid at constant prices 1965-6–77-8 (%)
	1965-6	1974-5	1977-8	1965-6	1974-5	1977-8	
1. Declining metropolitan areas							
London							
Camden	45.33	49.00	90.78	77.66	138.85	259.23	+ 7.2
Wandsworth	50.08	43.96	73.81	52.88	83.35	137.70	− 16.4
Newham	50.67	54.10	84.50	38.30	87.71	134.20	+ 12.5
Barnet	45.42	44.17	71.83	70.65	121.32	193.11	− 12.2
Croydon	50.00	47.00	69.08	53.50	109.16	151.81	− 8.9
West Midlands							
Birmingham (92%)	60.17	56.32	77.55	35.22	94.44	116.29	+ 6.0
Coventry (99%)	60.00	53.76	82.84	37.77	90.28	124.55	+ 5.9
Wolverhampton	45.83	49.60	77.90	29.56	85.88	120.43	+ 30.8
Greater Manchester							
Manchester (99%)	65.00	66.60	108.90	35.11	93.94	147.94	+ 35.3
Merseyside							
Liverpool	60.33	64.60	82.50	35.06	85.18	100.28	− 8.1
South Yorkshire							
Sheffield (91%)	55.67	62.23	91.42	26.69	66.83	91.99	+10.7

2. Areas of expansion						
Blaby (Leics.)	50.08	48.70	64.05	38.08	84.76	92.82	−21.2
Fareham (Hants.)	50.83	51.00	78.90	44.22	104.70	135.63	− 1.5
Gillingham (Kent)	50.17	40.06	67.98	30.50	59.26	91.45	− 3.7
3. Established high status residential areas						
Epsom and Ewell (Surrey)	50.50	n.a.	85.75	64.89	n.a.	209.18	+ 3.5
Oxford	25.17	51.60	83.30	50.31	98.47	150.63	− 3.9
4. Areas of old heavy industry						
Stoke-on-Trent	60.33	61.30	85.50	26.15	79.35	96.95	+19.1
Rhondda	65.50	69.50	99.00	19.87	25.00	39.15	−36.7
5. Modern industrial areas						
Gloucester	65.00	51.10	75.50	35.64	69.96	93.22	−16.0
Luton (Beds.)	40.00	52.75	96.00	35.90	100.52	182.09	+62.9
Scunthorpe (Humberside)	50.42	65.50	75.76	35.01	87.18	75.06	−31.2
Thurrock (Essex) (101%)	55.50	45.30	72.26	33.76	85.19	102.47	− 2.5
6. Medium-sized manufacturing cities						
Derby	50.25	53.80	79.00	26.65	79.22	100.83	+21.5
Ipswich	50.33	51.30	78.70	32.62	79.37	109.99	+ 8.3

Table 4.3 Comparative burden of local taxation: selected urban and metropolitan areas

	Local tax rate (Rate poundage) (pence)			Average domestic rates paid (£)			Change in average domestic rates paid at constant prices 1965-6-77-8 (%)
	1965-6	1974-5	1977-8	1965-6	1974-5	1977-8	
7. Regional service centres							
Bristol	50.58	62.59	85.24	37.00	92.84	113.19	−28.1
Kingston-upon-Hull	70.00	60.00	72.39	27.97	64.14	79.49	− 8.7
Nottingham	50.33	62.39	79.90	29.23	75.50	90.41	− 0.7
Southampton	50.75	58.00	86.19	40.80	87.01	158.80	+25.0
York	64.00	n.a.	73.30	28.80	n.a.	70.22	−21.7

Source: CIPFA statistical series, based on annually prepared budget estimates.

Notes: (a) Percentages in brackets relate to population of former area as per cent of post-1974 reorganisation total: if not cited, the total was unchanged.
(b) Tax base estimates and expenditures reduced to constant prices by Consumers' Expenditure Deflator.
(c) Expenditure includes expenditure of other authorities financed by precept.
(d) Area categorisation adapted from Webber and Craig (1978).

situation of the major cities. Debts have been kept within bounds (with only a few possible exceptions) and the burden of taxation has been limited, despite a rapid increase in expenditure. This has been achieved primarily by the transfer to central government of an increasing share of the cost of urban services. Amongst the major metropolitan areas, London has been favoured more than most, while the domestic ratepayer has been effectively insulated against the real and inflationary increase in the cost of servicing urban communities.

The structure of fiscal relations

Fiscal exploitation

A central thesis of urban fiscal analysis is that the spatial sub-division of jurisdictions within a metropolitan area creates the conditions for the fiscal exploitation of the inner areas by the residents of the outer areas. Suburban residents tend to include a high proportion of commuters who work in the central and inner areas, typically with higher average incomes than the majority of inner area residents; and these commuters, it is alleged, are able to enjoy the employment and other benefits of the inner area while contributing less to the tax revenues than equivalent inner area residents. If this thesis is true, the prospect of continuing metropolitan decentralisation would leave the inner areas (in the absence of specific corrective measures) at an increasing fiscal disadvantage.

The theory can in fact be specified in two ways. In one, the concern is simply with the costs imposed on the public sector, and the taxes contributed, in the inner areas by workers resident elsewhere. The question is: are commuters a net cost or a net benefit to the public economy of the inner area? Alternatively, the theory can be formulated in terms of fiscal equity, by comparing the total taxes paid by residents in the inner and outer areas (including the taxes paid by commuters in the suburbs) with the overall value of the services enjoyed. The underlying hypothesis in the second case is that suburban residents are able to pay less absolutely, or in relation to their incomes, than inner area residents for an equivalent standard of local public service.

How one should measure equity is not immediately obvious. Where, as in the United States, a major part of local taxes takes the form of a property tax, which is explicitly viewed as a form of wealth tax, there is a case for judging equity in terms of equivalent *tax rates*. In Britain, however, where rates, though specifically a tax on the beneficial occupation of real property, are more typically seen as a contribution to local costs, equivalence of *taxes paid* seems a more acceptable basis of comparison.

Unfortunately, there are as yet no published studies in Britain to match those undertaken in the United States of the net fiscal impact of commuters and residents on the inner areas of the major cities. The situation is in any case more complex. For in the absence of local income and sales taxes, the contribution of non-residents to local revenues has to be imputed from the value of their employment and their purchases as a source of the taxable real wealth of the area – difficult concepts in theory as well as practice. Some American studies have adopted an alternative strategy of estimating the effective incidence of local public sector costs and benefits through a measure of willingness-to-pay (Greene *et al.*, 1974) but, as I have argued elsewhere, it is not clear that such a quasi-market model is appropriate to the analysis of local fiscal relations (Kirwan, 1973)

We are left therefore in the unsatisfactory position of being unable to state clearly whether or not at the metropolitan level there is a spatial bias in the incidence of the current British system of local finance. We have to make do with partial indications. Analysis of London data in another context revealed no systematic relationship between rate poundages and the pattern of commuting (Kirwan, 1973). In practice, moreover, the systems of inter-area redistribution (through the Rate Support Grant) and inter-personal redistribution (through rate rebates) appear to have lifted the relative tax burdens of inner and outer area residents out of the arena of current political dispute. There is no immediate *sense* of inequity about the current arrangements. The issue of 'fiscal exploitation' remains important, however, both because it has implications for local tax reform (i.e. for the choice between wealth- and income-based taxes) and because it is not politically inconceivable that there will in future be an attempt to shift back on to local taxation a major part of the expenditure currently shouldered by central government.

Fiscal zoning

Another outcome of the recognition of the significance of urban decline has been to focus attention on the control of urban development as a means of strengthening the local tax base. In practice the scope is limited. Given the complexity of the system of fiscal redistribution between central and local government it is in any event not an easy matter to estimate the likely fiscal impact of new development in Britain. Whereas in the United States zoning is used to reserve districts for categories of land use which are likely to minimise locally-incurred net costs, in Britain the case-by-case approach to planning control calls for a specific fiscal calculus. Moreover, once again the high proportion of local costs absorbed by central government reduces the incentive to give great weight to fiscal impact. Nonetheless, there are signs that rateable value is increasingly being regarded as the most significant factor in most of the major metropolitan areas whenever inner area commercial and residential schemes come to planning appeal or inquiry.

There are many well-established examples too: the redevelopment of central business districts which was undertaken in most medium-sized cities during the 1960s and early 1970s; or outer metropolitan areas' reluctance to accept public housing because of the potential need (social considerations apart) for a rate fund contribution to the Housing Revenue Account and associated social service costs.

What is clear is that growth and decline generate different conflicts. In a period of expansion, communities may attempt to select between value categories of land use, such as upper- and lower-income housing. But most forms of development contribute in some measure to the fiscal health of the area. Within the inner areas of the declining cities, by contrast, real conflicts exist: the interaction between fiscal and planning policies cannot be side-stepped. For, as local community groups protest, stemming the outward flow and revitalising the productive economy requires new investment in housing and jobs for local residents; but strengthening the local tax base in order to undertake essential expenditure, as the conservative business interests are quick to point out, may necessitate accepting commercial development mainly oriented to non-residents (offices for commuters, hotels for tourists, etc.). It is a conflict which stems directly from the structure of the land market, on the one hand, with its essential tension between the use-value and market-value of redeveloped sites, and of the fiscal system, on the other, with its reliance on property values and value-increments. Its seeds are deeply embedded.

The expansion of the urban public sector

The outward migration of firms and households apart, perhaps the most remarkable feature of the development of the metropolitan areas since the Second World War has been the growth of the local public sector. Directly and indirectly the prosperity of the metropolitan areas now depends heavily on the state of the urban public economy. Nationally imposed reductions in public expenditure, such as those experienced after 1976, are severely felt in the metropolitan economies. How then should one interpret this expansion? Is it likely to be renewed and what if it is not?

As Baumol (1967) pointed out over a decade ago, we would expect the relative size of the local public sector to increase in a world where local public services are relatively labour-intensive and where productivity increases are mainly achieved in private and manufacturing industries and trades unions demand wage-comparability between public and private sector employees. And undoubtedly the rapid increase in the cost of such services as education and the police can partly be explained by their labour-intensity. But, as Howick (1977) has recently demonstrated, labour costs do not account for the whole expansion. Baumol's analysis does not go far enough: the growth of the sector is more than a mere mathematical identity.

Another underlying factor has been the changing social and physical fabric of the cities. For, while selective migration has created a concentration of the more disadvantaged households in the inner city (Department of the Environment, 1977) who look to the public sector for financial and material assistance, the ageing of the housing stock has increasingly necessitated an injection of public funds to encourage maintenance, improvement and redevelopment. But need, like cost, is not an adequate explanation. The need existed long before it began to be satisfied.

In fact, to understand the growth of the local public sector we need to set it in its macroeconomic context. For the forces that have shaped urban public services in Britain in the last two decades have to a very significant extent originated at the national rather than the local level. Indeed, as local authorities are prompt to remind us, the scope for purely local initiatives in expenditure has been very limited. In the field of capital expenditure this came to be recognised explicitly with the separate identification of a 'locally-determined sector'. But more generally urban public expenditure has been affected by an increasing volume of national legislation covering such widely-differing matters as the establishment of social service departments and the raising of the school-leaving age.

Many interpretations have been put on this interaction.[4] Some have pointed to the growth of national income as the most significant factor in enabling the community to broaden the range of public services – a necessary condition perhaps, but scarcely a sufficient one. Some have stressed the complementarity between public and private expenditure, especially in the establishment of new communities. Others have seen the growth of the local public sector more in terms of the political struggle for improved facilities for lower-income groups and the disadvantaged. And certainly it is significant that in the last decade the 'compensatory' or redistributive services tend to have expanded faster than many of those, like highway construction, which might once have been thought to have a high social income-elasticity of demand. Others again have focused on the legitimation function of public expenditure, seeing the growth of urban services as a means of reducing the potential for conflict that the failure of the system to tackle deep-seated inequities would otherwise engender; or as an aspect of the general assistance afforded by the State to protect capital in the private sectors against a secular fall in the rate of profit.

The structure of urban finance in Britain, however, immediately lifts this discussion above the purely urban or metropolitan dimension. For there is little in the effective fiscal policy pursued *at the local level* to which any of these perspectives is uniquely relevant. This is not of course to say that they are invalid: merely that the point of response to the structural requirements of the evolving economic situation during the post-war period in fiscal affairs in Britain has consistently been the national level. Indeed it would probably be necessary to look back to the last quarter of the nineteenth century to find a period of sufficient autonomy in local fiscal affairs to give substance to this form of analysis.

Moreover, at the urban scale, and more particularly within the Labour-dominated inner metropolitan areas, the contrast implicit in many accounts between successful political struggle by the working class, on the one hand, and State-sponsored support for the needs of capital, on the other, cannot so easily be established. For many of the improvements in services which urban authorities have been required or empowered to provide since, say, 1960 – comprehensive education, improved social services provision, subsidised public transport and so on – have been legitimate parts of a progressive local and national political platform, even though from an alternative viewpoint they can be seen to have assisted in the maintenance of profitable opportunities for investment in the urban context. It would require a detailed histori- cal analysis of the evolution of urban fiscal policy in the different metropolitan areas truly to throw more light on these interpretations. And more importantly the theoretical framework – essential to the coherence of any interpretation – would have to be national rather than purely local.

The structural weakness of the fiscal system

In the same terms I think we are bound to conclude that there is no necessary tendency to crisis in the fiscal system *at the urban level* in Britain, even though the Layfield Committee has pointed to the fre- quency of its recurrence. The Marxist theory of recurrent crises has recently been revived and applied to the urban fiscal system by O'Connor (1973) and others, who argue that the need to create profit- able opportunities for investment in the major urban communities and to maintain the legitimacy of the system place an increasing burden on local taxation which in turn threatens the dynamic of the local economy and the scope for the accumulation of productive capital. In the United States the thesis is more credible. On the one hand, there is a very wide range of local taxes which impinge on economic activities in a number of different ways – taxes on property, income, sales, business turnover, etc.; while on the other hand local communities have been expected to play a much larger role than in Britain in stimulating local employment and the growth of the local economy. The recent tax revolt in California provides ample evidence of how precarious the balance is between maintaining the economic attrac- tiveness of an area and meeting its real needs in a highly mobile and individualistic society. In Britain, crises that are the product of the structural *role* of the urban public economy, rather than of the *form* of the local fiscal system, must be seen primarily as a reflection of the character of fiscal relations at the national scale. Nonetheless there are some signs of an emerging conflict at the local level, for example where local councils (as in Wandsworth and Newcastle), faced with pockets of high local unemployment, have attempted to pursue policies of more extensive intervention in the local labour market than are usual. Typically, however, once the need is recognised and the signs of stress detected, central government has moved in (through the Inner Areas Act, 1978) to absorb a major part of the additional expenditure.

Local fiscal crisis in Britain has been avoided at the cost of national fiscal stress. A rapid expansion of local services has been achieved only by dint of an equally rapid and massive transfer of resources from the central to the local level. But the years of uncontrolled expansion are over. Without a more rapid growth in the level of macroeconomic activity it is difficult to see how it will be possible to achieve further real increases in the amount or quality of urban services. The effect of this end to a period of continuous expansion will be to remove the potential for specifically fiscal crisis – that is, a conflict between the level of local public expenditure and the amount of revenue that can be raised through taxation – and to put in its place intensified conflict over the allocation of resources.

Policy issues

Local tax reform

In the mid 1970s the apparent crisis in urban fiscal relations seemed to point to an urgent need for reform of the system. But little genuine reform has followed. Despite the lengthy analysis of the Layfield Committee, the Labour Government gave every appearance of wanting to avoid the real underlying issues. But the shortcomings of the system have been demonstrated; with a change of circumstances many of the same issues are likely to return to prominence.

Take the issue of local tax reform. Despite the guarded recommendations of the Layfield Committee, the Government rejected innovation. But a change of government may bring new thinking. From the standpoint of the declining metropolitan areas the case for tax reform remains the inappropriateness of relying solely on property values as a source of revenue. A declining economy is bound to suffer from a declining tax base, as the experience of American cities with their much larger range of taxes demonstrates: the metropolitan economy can only fully be protected against the diseconomies of reducing size – if such they really are – by transfers from outside its own fiscal net. But there are disadvantages in relying on a single tax and these are likely to be increased by the shift to capital values as the basis for rating valuation. For where urban decline is anticipated there is always the likelihood that capital values will reflect only weakly the short-run buoyancy of sales and income generation associated with particular inner area sites, while the capitalised value of future expected increases in the income potential of properties escapes across the boundaries along with the higher-income residences and expanding industry. Conversely, where sites in inner areas are regarded as having future development potential, the existing occupiers face a level of taxation quite out of proportion to the value of their current activity. At the extreme, as in many United States cities, this could lead to the abandonment of properties, even though they are not yet regarded as ripe for conversion to their new use. The potential for disruption and hardship is worrying. True, a wide difference between present and future use-values is generally more characteristic of expanding areas; but even in declining cities the land market tends to identify some sites as having greater long-run development potential. Moreover, the growing importance of the local public sector, especially in inner areas, itself tends to reduce the volume of taxable real property. So reliance on property-related taxes risks being both inadequate in total and inequitable in incidence.

Rate Support Grant and the distribution of central government funds

Rate Support Grant and the system of distributing central government funds, on the other hand, must be judged in the broadest terms a considerable success. It has enabled the major metropolitan areas to absorb a rapid increase in real outlays without imposing an intolerable burden on businesses or households. And it has prevented the emergence of a wide disparity between the quality of urban public services in different areas (though differences clearly exist). Rate Support Grant has proved a flexible instrument able to accommodate both changes in political intention and changes in the real circumstances of different areas. But in doing so it has become increasingly complex. And this complexity and flexibility, together with the strong bias in favour of the declining metropolitan areas in recent years, may ironically be the cause of its abandonment or modification.

The system has been manipulated (through the inclusion of carefully selected variables and the special treatment of London) to favour the big cities: indeed this has been the explicit intention of recent Labour governments. But as Jackman and Sellars (1977) have pointed out, of itself this cannot make clear whether or not the massive shift (of some £350 million a year, by their estimates, in the three years 1974/5 to 1977/8) was justified by differential need.

The combination of flexibility and complexity in the system has generated two types of response. One is the Government's own proposal for simplification, namely a Unitary Grant to replace the Rate Support Grant's separate 'needs' and 'resources' elements. This is designed to compensate for differences in needs and tax bases by a single formula and would have the outstanding merit of equalising the resource potential of different areas instead of, as at present, merely bringing the below-average up to the mean. As a consequence some of the wealthier inner-city areas would lose.

The other type of response, arising mainly from the less urbanised areas, is for a radical simplification of the distribution formulae. Introduction of a Unitary Grant would make the issue of needs assessment even more important than at present, since the proposal is to base the distribution of grant on an absolute assessment of the overall requirement for assistance in cash terms. Though the semblance of local autonomy is to be preserved, the effect of this will be to increase central government's control over the composition of local expenditure as well as over its total.

The issue of needs is raised in an acute form by the situation of the declining metropolitan areas. On the one hand, there is the strongly argued case that needs do not decline, and in some instances may even increase, as the size of the population is reduced. On the other hand, there is the risk, pointed to by Jackman and Sellars, of misinterpreting a high level expenditure (made possible by generous central government assistance) as evidence of a high level of need. That the needs of different areas vary is undeniable. Historical endowments, the structure of the population, the nature of the industrial and commercial base, the age of the building stock and the condition of the physical infrastructure all affect the requirement for urban services. The problem is one of identification and measurement.

Or is it? Perhaps the main failure of the Rate Support Grant has been to attempt to link too closely the technical problem of measuring need and the political problem of determining appropriate allocations. The result has been, on the one hand, the inclusion of an increasing number of relevant factors in the formulae, and on the other, the accusations of manipulation. Though the metropolitan areas happen to have done well out of this in the recent past, the demand from other areas for reform of the system is likely to grow. So one is bound to ask whether alternatives are possible.

Consider one such. This might be based on the differentiation of types of areas. Statistical analysis might be used to guide the process of grouping authorities into a small number of clusters and to help to determine appropriate differentials in expenditure levels. But it would be left to political decision both how many categories of differentiation (or deviations from the mean) to accept and how large the differences in funding should be. This would of course be to adopt a radically different approach from the Unitary Grant, which by enhancing the status of the measures of need will require more rather than less substantial backing for their identification and costing than under the present system. It would differ also from the notion favoured by some members of the Layfield Committee of the specific identification and costing of minimum standards for individual services.

I quote this merely as an example. I cannot pretend that such a system would not also generate serious disagreements. But this is because conflict is intrinsic to the task of allocating resources between areas, the more so if the total is not growing in real terms and the amount to be distributed is a high proportion of the recipients' disposable income. There is an unavoidable tension between the desire for a simple and clearly-understood system that is above charges of manipulation and one that reflects the minutiae of differential circumstances. The development of revenue-sharing in the United States has illustrated how simple *per capita* formulae are not adequate to reflect genuine differences in needs (Reischauer, 1975; Nathan and Adams, 1977). There, ironically, the movement has been towards the introduction of more complex variables. But there has been little attempt to make them 'representative': they have been selected unashamedly to achieve a politically-determined distribution. By contrast, the British Rate Support Grant system, with undoubted success to its credit, nonetheless illustrates the risk inherent in attempting to meet political objectives through an over-complex technical assessment of needs.

Central/local relations

More money and less interference is the cry from the metropolitan areas. But the reality is likely to be very different. If the British system of urban public finance has achieved a very significant measure of redistribution between the cities, the price has been the severe curtailment of local autonomy. In the opinion of the Layfield Committee, local responsibility and participation depended on a well-defined area of local financial autonomy. But the Committee seems to have failed to appreciate the impossibility of central government, within the North European tradition, confining its attention to *minimum* standards of service *per se*. The central concern of governments is bound to be with deviations from the mean and with equality. This is partly for sound reasons of economic management – to take account, for example, of the effects that spill over between areas and of the needs of the macroeconomy. But it also, and more significantly, reflects a balance of political forces which has been achieved through long struggle and is not likely lightly to be altered.

What does this imply for the future of the relations between central and local government in fiscal affairs? We should not underestimate the mood of disenchantment with bureaucratic control and regulation that has grown up at all levels in recent years. The forces that point in the direction of the simplification of financial controls and greater local autonomy are not going lightly to be disregarded. However, it is hard not to feel that the more significant developments in urban fiscal relations are all likely in the foreseeable future to reinforce the dominant role of central government. Poor macroeconomic performance combined with a severe restraint on the expansion of the share of urban public services in the economy as a whole will exacerbate the problems of allocation. And this is likely to call for more rather than less central government supervision of the allocation process, both between activities and between areas. Even under a Conservative administration, nominally more committed to the decentralisation of authority than Labour government, central government is unlikely to stand idly by if it sees what it regards as a serious misallocation of resources between services. Ironically, the Conservative proposal to replace domestic rates by other forms of taxation, and in particular to transfer the cost of educational manpower to central government, would seem to imply a return to the categorical allocation of funds that would.be bound to entail greater central control. Moreover, metropolitan decline itself, with its implications for a continuing need for urban growth management, makes conscious political control over the distribution of resources to the cities almost inevitable. In the short run it is conceivable that there will be a serious attempt to redress the balance of central government assistance in favour of the smaller and less urbanised communities. But if this is taken to an extreme, the prospect of serious political conflict and unrest in the major cities clearly underlines the inevitability in the longer run of the maintenance of strong central control over urban resource allocation.

Conclusions

Thus far the major metropolitan areas in Britain have reason to be content with the way in which they have been supported by the fiscal system. Of course they would have liked greater assistance, but, set against the potential for financial disaster in a period of major economic recession, the system has served them well. By transferring the greater part of the financial responsibility for local services to central government, Britain largely avoided the urban fiscal crisis that hit the United States. As a redistributive mechanism, the Rate Support Grant system has proved very effective. There is little evidence of fiscal exploitation of the inner city by the suburbs. And successive modifications of the system have revealed a genuine concern to improve the identification of the needs of the cities and to meet the particular circumstances of metropolitan decline.

But the effect of relieving the major cities of such a large part of the cost of providing their own services has undoubtedly been to take the political initiative away from the local context. It would be hard, for example, in present circumstances to imagine a tax revolt as serious as that of California in 1978 striking one of the major British cities. The corollary of the feeling that local bureaucrats and politicians are in league with Whitehall and Westminster to impose policies over which local residents have next to no control is that there is little purpose to be served by financial revolt. While the demands on the domestic ratepayer (in the large cities) remain relatively moderate, it is better to keep quiet.

But the future may not be so easy. The end to the growth of urban public expenditure, on the one hand, and the demands for a simpler system of distributing central government assistance, less biased in favour of the big cities, on the other, will create a more hostile climate for the metropolitan authorities. Limited budgets will mean more controversy over their allocation. The pressure may grow as a result for faster increases in local rates which in turn will generate greater internal resistance. The prospect must be faced of a heightened conflict between the declining metropolitan areas and central government and within their own communities.

And this could well be worsened if there is a national swing in favour of tax reductions. For an ironic side-effect of attempts to reduce national taxation may yet prove to be an increase in the level of local taxation and in the share of local expenditure borne locally. If this entails the creation of new sources of local revenue – sales taxes or income taxes, for example – it may in some ways be beneficial to the major metropolitan areas. But at the same time it could open up the possibility of exactly those problems of fiscal exploitation, incentive to decentralisation and inherent fiscal crisis which the present system has successfully avoided.

Notes

1. This is not necessarily inconsistent with the growing belief that economies of scale in metropolitan administration are illusory. For there is an important difference between the comparative economies and diseconomies of scale of communities of different sizes and those related to changing the size of given areas. It seems likely also that the effects of changes in population on costs are not the same in upwards and downwards directions.
2. The main criterion for the selection of areas, apart from representation of different types of urbanisation, was that the area was substantially unaffected by the 1974 local government reorganisation. The exact relationship between the 'before' and 'after' populations is shown in the relevant table.
3. The figures quoted are affected by the transfer of assets from non-metropolitan districts to shire counties after the 1974 reorganisation.
4. For a selection of recent interpretations of American experience, see Cloward and Piven (1974), Mollenkopf (1977), Peterson (1976), and O'Connor (1973).

References

Alcaly, R. and **Mermelstein, D.** (eds) (1977) *The Fiscal Crisis of American Cities*. Vintage Books, New York.
Baumol, W. (1967) 'Macroeconomics of unbalanced growth: the anatomy of the urban crisis', *American Economic Review* **57**, pp. 415–26.

Cloward, R. and **Piven, F.F.** (1974) *The Politics and Turmoil: Poverty, Race and the Urban Crisis*. Pantheon, New York.

Department of the Environment (1976) *Local Government Finance*. Report of the Layfield Committee. HMSO, London.

Department of the Environment (1977) *Inner Area Studies: Summary of Final Reports*. HMSO, London.

Eversley, D.E.C. (1972) 'Rising costs and static incomes: some economic consequences of regional planning in London', **Urban Studies 9**(3), pp. 347–68.

Greene, K., Neenan, W. and **Scott, C.** (1974) *Fiscal Interactions in a Metropolitan Area*. Lexington Books, Lexington, Mass.

Howick, C. (1977) *Local Authority Manpower Growth: an Historical Perspective*. Centre for Environmental Studies Review No. 2. London.

Jackman, R. and **Sellars, M.** (1977) *The Distribution of Rate Support Grant*. Centre for Environmental Studies Review No. 2. London.

Jackman R. and **Sellars, M.** (1978) *Local Expenditure and Local Discretion*. Centre for Environmental Studies Review No. 3. London.

Kirwan, R.M. (1973) 'The contribution of public expenditure and finance to the problems of Inner London' in Donnison, D. and Eversley, D. (eds) *London: Urban Patterns, Problems and Policies*. Heinemann, London.

Mollenkopf, J. (1977) 'The crises of the public sector in America's cities' in Alcaly, R., and Mermelstein, D. (eds), op. cit.

Nathan, R. and Adams, C. (1977) *Revenue-Sharing: the Second Round*. The Brookings Institution, Washington D.C.

O'Connor, J. (1973) *The Fiscal Crisis of the State*. St Martins Press, New York.

Peterson, G. (1976) 'Finance' in Gorman, W., and Glazer, N. (eds) *The Urban Predicament*. Urban Institute, Washington D.C.

Reischauer, R. (1975) 'General revenue-sharing – the program's incentives' in Inman, R., et al (eds) *Financing the New Federalism*. Johns Hopkins Centre for Resources for the Future. Baltimore.

Webber, R. and **Craig, D.** (1978) *The socio-economic classification of local authority areas*. Office of Population Censuses and Surveys Studies on Medical and Population Subjects, 35, HMSO.

Chapter 5

Central Clydeside –
a case study of one conurbation

Introduction

This chapter considers the development and prospects of the Clydeside conurbation and in particular its central city Glasgow over a period of some two hundred years of dramatic shifts in population. Most attention is given to the efforts of planners during the post-war years to improve the social and economic conditions of the conurbation's population, and to the nature of the problems which face the area now or which can be foreseen over the rest of this century. Clearly the perspective is a very broad one, and it is only possible to give a general account of some of the main features of social and economic change. The focus is on the interrelationship of population and employment trends and on the implications for public service provision: in this way the chapter may serve as a context for the more detailed treatment of individual themes which follow. Of course Clydeside has a number of distinctive features which mark it out from other British conurbations, each of which have their own particular characteristics (Ch. 2). Nonetheless, in the broad outline of its history Glasgow's experience is relevant to other major British cities, and indeed the extreme form which many of the trends have taken in Glasgow may serve as a useful means of highlighting issues of more general concern.

Development up to the Second World War

In addition to Glasgow, the Clydeside conurbation extends over a much wider area of the central Clyde valley, encompassing previously separate burghs such as Paisley, Motherwell and Wishaw, Clydebank, Coatbridge, Hamilton, Airdrie and Rutherglen. In the 1951 Census the population of the conurbation was about 1.75 million, of which nearly 1.1 million (just under two-thirds) was accounted for by the former City of Glasgow area. The Clydeside conurbation in turn accounted at this time for nearly three-quarters of the population of 2.4 million in the larger West Central Scotland region (which includes

(The views expressed are personal to the author and do not necessarily reflect those of the Scottish Economic Planning Department or the Scottish Development Department).

the whole of the counties of Lanarkshire, Renfrewshire, Dunbarton-shire and Ayrshire).

Estimates by Webster in the mid eighteenth century suggest that fewer than 200,000 people (only 14% of the estimated Scottish popu-lation) lived in West Central Scotland (Kyd, 1952). During the eight-eenth century and throughout the nineteenth century a whole series of major industrial developments occurred – textiles, coal, iron, shipbuild-ing, steel, heavy engineering – which were to transform the Clyde valley into the most heavily populated region of Scotland. This growth partly reflected the availability of natural resources appropriate to the new technologies based on metal manufacture and the steam engine, but also the ability of a number of exceptional individuals to seize opportunities and frequently to overcome severe problems. While individual towns can trace their period of most rapid development to particular industries (for example textiles in Paisley, iron-making in Coatbridge), the growth of interlinked manufacturing processes in the latter half of the nineteenth century and their associated transport networks produced an integrated industrial region (Slaven, 1975). In all these developments a unifying force was the role played by the city of Glasgow which was not only the commercial and organisational centre of the region but also a major location of manufacturing activity in its own right.

The phenomenal scale of Glasgow's growth, reflecting the city's economic success, is illustrated in Table 5.1. Because of boundary changes a consistent series of estimates is not possible but the general

Table 5.1 Population change in Gasgow 1801–1951

Year	Definition		Area in acres (000's)	Population (000's)
1801	Area approx. equal to Parliamentary Burgh created in 1832		*c.* 5.1	77
1811	,, ,, ,, ,,		*c.* 5.1	103
1821	,, ,, ,, ,,		*c.* 5.1	140
1831	,, ,, ,, ,,		*c.* 5.1	193
1841	Parliamentary Burgh		5.1	256
1851	,, ,,		5.1	329
1861	,, ,,		5.1	396
1871	,, ,,		5.1	478
1881	Parliamentary Burgh		5.1	489
	Municipal Burgh of 1872		6.1	511
1891	Municipal Burgh		6.1	566
1901	Municipal Burgh (enlarged)		12.7	762
1911	,, ,, ,,		13.0	784
1921	,, ,, ,,		19.2	1,034
1931	,, ,, ,,		29.5	1,088
1951	,, ,, ,,		39.7	1,090

Source: Cunnison and Gilfillan (1958).

pattern of sustained growth throughout the nineteenth century from about 77,000 in 1801 to well over half a million (over seven times as much) by 1891 is clear. During the latter part of the period illustrated in Table 5.1 more significant changes in boundary occurred and a more reliable picture of changes between 1871 and 1951 is likely to be provided by the estimates in Table 5.2 (after Robertson) for the 1951

Table 5.2 Estimated population change in Glasgow 1871–1951

Year	Definition	Area in acres (000's)	Population (000's)
1871	Municipal Burgh (1951)	39.7	600
1901	Municipal Burgh (1951)	39.7	950
1921	Municipal Burgh (1951)	39.7	1,056
1931	Municipal Burgh (1951)	39.7	1,093
1951	Municipal Burgh (1951)	39.7	1,090

	Average population change p.a. (000's)
1871–1901	+ 12
1901–21	+ 5
1921–31	+ 4
1931–51	0

Source: Robertson (1958).

area of Glasgow Municipal Burgh. A marked slowing up in the rate of population growth after 1901 is indicated, as in most of the burghs of Clydeside (Abercrombie and Matthew, 1949). This appears to coincide with the crucial shift from net in-migration to net emigration noted by Robertson. Up to 1901 Glasgow appears to have gained population both from in-migration (with the movement of people to seek job opportunities) and from a high rate of natural increase (reflecting the relatively young age structure of the in-migrants); after this date migration flows have acted to reduce the population resulting from the city's natural change.

During the middle decades of the nineteenth century the largest flow of in-migrants to the West of Scotland was from Ireland, while other major movements took place from the Highlands and from other parts of central Scotland (Slaven, 1975). About 16 per cent of Glasgow's total population was Irish-born in 1841, and when account is taken of the natural increase of migrants it is possible that about one-third of the city's population was of Irish descent in the middle years of the century (although it has been estimated that at least half of the Irish in-migrants were Protestants) (Handley, 1964). Many of the migrants from Ireland and the Highlands were to all practical purposes destitute on arrival in West Central Scotland, particularly after the 1840s, seeking accommodation in the already overcrowded tenements of central Glasgow and other urban areas and predominantly unskilled work in industries such as textiles, coalmining, iron and steel, and construction. A massive programme of private house-building for rent was carried out, mainly taking the form of four-storey stone tenements. But appalling conditions of overcrowded and insanitary housing, periodic outbreaks of typhus, cholera and other epidemics and widespread poverty are well documented in the worst parts of Clydeside throughout the nineteenth century (Slaven, 1975; Handley, 1964 and Checkland, 1976).

The counterpart to these dramatic changes was paradoxically a growing sense of industrial and civic progress and prosperity in the latter half of the century. The West of Scotland was in the forefront of new developments in iron-making, shipbuilding, and locomotive engineering, and leading industrialist families such as the Bairds, Elders and Tennants amassed large fortunes. The Corporation of Glasgow showed enterprise and determination in promoting facilities such as a public supply of water, gas and electricity, electric tramways and subway, art galleries, parks and exhibitions, and a resplendent City Chambers. Following the City of Glasgow Improvements Act of 1866 a trust was established to clear some of the worst slums, although the efforts made on this front proved inadequate to the scale of the problem. There was thus a sharp contrast between the conditions of the working classes (and particularly those living in the poorest areas) and the prosperous middle class, and this pattern was reinforced by geographical segregation. But Checkland (1976) has argued that there was also a strong sense of common identity among Glaswegians which stemmed from a shared pride in the city's industrial achievements and public services. Reflecting prevailing religious attitudes, there was a belief in and desire for material progress, and a confidence that Glasgow would prosper.

The change from net in-migration to net emigration from Glasgow around the turn of the century seems accurately to reflect a faltering in the city's economy which occurred at this time, although with a continuing growth in population and relatively low unemployment this was only apparent in retrospect. Despite some pioneering efforts in motor-car and aircraft manufacture Clydeside was not able to establish a sufficiently large involvement in the new technologies of the twentieth century, and the world depression of the inter-war period hit the traditional industries with exceptional severity. It is difficult to underestimate the impact of this drastic change in economic fortunes. Clydeside, which had staked its pride on industrial enterprise and success, now faced the realisation of failure. The shock was deeply psychological, and was reflected in a far-reaching shift in political attitudes. During the 1920s heavy emigration of about 20,000 per annum from the West of Scotland took place (Abercrombie and Matthew, 1949), but in the 1930s this moderated and unemployment reached staggering proportions. Between 1931 and 1933 the unemployment rates in each of Lanarkshire (including Glasgow), Renfrewshire and Dunbartonshire were continuously in excess of 30 per cent compared with about 20 per cent in Great Britain as a whole. Unemployment in Clydeside remained above 20 per cent until 1936 (Fogarty, 1945).

The reaction to this crisis was mainly by Clydeside businessmen and consisted of attempts firstly to rationalise the heavy industries to improve efficiency in readiness for an upturn in demand, and secondly to diversify the economy by attracting the newer light engineering industries from outside the region. Both faced serious difficulties. Rationalisation, as Checkland (1976) has noted, called for co-operation rather than competition, a fundamentally different challenge from the demands of the nineteenth century. The attraction of new firms, aided by the Government's Special Areas legislation of 1934 and 1937 which enabled financial inducements and factory provision to be offered in the whole of Clydeside except the City of Glasgow, was hampered by the relatively small amount of mobile industry and to some extent by the need to overcome Clydeside's recently acquired image of industrial unrest and depression.

If the inter-war period marked the first steps toward a Government regional policy, public intervention was more marked in the field of housing policy. Under a series of Housing Acts from 1919 onwards, Glasgow Corporation showed their determination to improve housing conditions by building local authority housing estates on a considerable scale both at the periphery of the built up area (as at Knightswood and Mosspark) and on inner city redevelopment sites (as at Blackhill). This emphasis on local authority housing at low rents was reinforced by the Labour party gaining control of Glasgow Corporation in 1933. Between 1919 and 1939, 76,360 houses were authorised to be built in the city, but of these only 9,106 (about 12%) were privately built, a much lower proportion than in most English cities at this time (Checkland, 1976). A similar pattern developed in the other industrial burghs in Clydeside, with most of the relatively low level of private house-building which did take place being concentrated in the county areas on the periphery of Glasgow. But Glasgow's natural increase was sufficient to lead to a slow growth of population in the city during the 1930s, and it is estimated that the peak population of 1,128,000 was reached in 1939 (Cunnison and Gilfillan, 1958).

From the Clyde Valley Plan to the West Central Scotland Plan

The urban and economic development of Clydeside in the post-war period has been shaped to an increasing extent by the planning and policies of public sector agencies, and many of the general lines of approach were set out in the Clyde Valley Regional Plan 1946 (Abercrombie and Matthew, 1949). This advisory plan, prepared by a team

of consultants under Sir Patrick Abercrombie for an Advisory Committe of representatives of the local planning authorities in West Central Scotland, inevitably reflected many of the prevailing assumptions
of professional planning at the time, but its basic tenets and recommendations were to prove remarkably influential even when the underlying circumstances of Clydeside changed. The plan was prepared
largely by physical planners and, although it stressed the links between
land use and economic change and contained a substantial discussion
of the background and prospects of the main industries, the Plan did
not attempt to make aggregate regional employment projections.
Economic planning, it was stressed, was the responsibility of the Government and it was felt inappropriate for the town planner to enter the
field of industrial planning. While a shift in employment and population from Lanarkshire to the western part of the Clyde Valley was
thought probable as a result of the decline of coalmining and the
possible relocation of the steel industry, at regional level it was
assumed that Government economic policy would be able to sustain a
stable population. After a discussion of the uncertainty of population
projections, the Plan concluded in the light of contemporary demographic trends and prospects that it was 'prudent to assume for the
Region for the purposes of the preparation of the Regional Plan a total
population substantially the same as existing for the next 40 or 50
years'.

The chief concern of the Clyde Valley Plan was the poor housing
conditions and extremely high residential densities in the urban centres
and particularly Glasgow. Some 700,000 people lived on 1,800 acres
in the central part of Glasgow, an average gross residential density of
nearly 400 persons per acre. In some areas, densities were as high as
700 persons per acre and industrial congestion added to the problem.
In order to reduce densities to more acceptable standards (gross residential densities below 60 persons per acre in all parts of the region) it
was estimated that over 700,000 people in the region (of whom
550,000 were in Glasgow – half the city's population) would need to be
displaced from redevelopment areas. For the burghs outside Glasgow
it was suggested that most of the people displaced could be accommodated by local peripheral development, while approximately 250,000
of those displaced from inner Glasgow might be rehoused in planned
communities on the outskirts of the city, partly inside and partly outside the city boundary but within the inner line of a proposed Green
Belt. This left an 'overspill' of some 250,000–300,000 people displaced
from Glasgow alone who would need to be accommodated away from
the city, and the Plan recommended that a first step should be the
planning of four New Towns at Cumbernauld, East Kilbride, Bishop-
ton and Houston (the latter two possibly to form one new town with a
double focus). Population moving to the New Towns was expected in
the main to be drawn from the lower income groups.

The New Towns were planned to be industrial centres in their own right rather than dormitory areas. Industry was to come primarily by the steering of some of the incoming industry expected to be attracted to Scotland by Government inducements, and secondly by a limited amount of decentralisation from the congested urban areas. Given the high densities in Glasgow and population decentralisation policy recommended, the Plan felt it would be wrong to encourage industrial expansion in the city on any appreciable scale. Apart from the New Towns, a series of industrial estates to provide the region with modern factory accommodation was planned at strategic locations such as Newhouse and Wishaw within reasonable travel-to-work distance of the older industrial centres.

The advisory recommendations of the Clyde Valley Plan did not initially find universal acceptance. During the preparation of the Plan, a contrary analysis was produced by the City Engineer of Glasgow Corporation (the 'Bruce Plan') which argued that with a carefully phased redevelopment programme involving the rebuilding of some existing estates at higher densities and some incursion into the proposed Green Belt it was possible to rehouse the whole of Glasgow's population at acceptable densities within the city boundary (Glasgow Corporation, 1945). This report impressed the City Council who, mindful of Glasgow's historic status as the Second City of the Empire, were not convinced that the Green Belt and overspill were in the city's interest. When the Advisory Committee of local authorities considered their response to the Clyde Valley Plan in 1947 they were clearly divided and expressed no opinion on the principal recommendations concerning the level of overspill from Glasgow and the building of New Towns (West Central Scotland Plan Team, 1972). Contrasting with this neutral response by the local authorities, the Government were sympathetic to the Plan's recommendations, the Secretary of State for Scotland designating East Kilbride New Town in 1947 and also developing other industrial estates outside the congested centres.

Glasgow Corporation's attitude towards overspill changed in 1952 following a report by their newly appointed City Architect and Planning Officer (Glasgow Corporation, 1952) which calculated that to rehouse Glasgow's population adequately it would be necessary to find sites for 135,000 houses outside the city boundary, equivalent to an overspill population of 400,000–500,000, even higher than the estimate made by the Clyde Valley Plan six years previously. The Advisory Committee of local authorities was reconstituted and suggested a further new town be built at Cumbernauld; this was designated by the Secretary of State for Scotland in 1956. Following the Housing and Town Development (Scotland) Act of 1957, Glasgow Corporation also reached agreements with a number of local authorities throughout Scotland to provide housing for Glasgow overspill families. During the 1960s the Government's support for the New Towns was confirmed in a 1963 White Paper (Cmnd 2188). This identified a number of 'growth areas' in Central Scotland (including East Kilbride and Cumbernauld) which it was thought had particular advantages for economic growth and where it was planned to concentrate public infrastructure provision.

Meantime within Glasgow the Corporation had embarked on a major programme of new local authority house-building to meet the still desperate need for housing. The housing waiting list in Glasgow has been estimated at about 80,000–90,000 families in the early 1950s (Checkland, 1976), and the numbers stayed stubbornly high. The main response was a series of very large estates on greenfield sites on the periphery of the urban area particularly at Drumchapel, Easterhouse and Castlemilk. These took the form predominantly of three- and four-storey tenement flats, built at higher densities than proposed by the Clyde Valley Plan or the 'Bruce Plan', and often with few community facilities and amenities. There was of course substantial public investment in schools for the relatively young age structure of the population of the new estates, but information contained in a Corporation report of 1972 suggests that in some cases the provision of associated playing fields and open space fell below standard. Some of the estates were well located in relation to the electrified suburban railway system in which investment had taken place at the start of the 1960s; but others had to rely on lengthy bus trips for public transport to Central Glasgow.

The start of a major effort to improve housing conditions in the older parts of Glasgow was made in 1957 with a comprehensive development scheme for the Gorbals-Hutchesontown area, and the Corporation's 1960 Development Plan outlined proposals for no fewer than 29 Comprehensive Development Areas within the city. Densities on average rather higher than proposed by the Clyde Valley Plan were planned, although even so approximately 60 per cent of the previous residents of the redevelopment areas would need to be rehoused on other sites. The emphasis throughout the 1960s was overwhelmingly on the clearance rather than improvement of older housing. This inevitably brought social disruption of previous communities on a large scale. A considerable part of the house-building programme during the decade took the form of multi-storey flats, as in other British cities. By 1969 163 blocks had been brought into occupancy, accounting for some 15,000 housing units or over 10 per cent of the local authority housing stock (Checkland, 1976).

The redevelopment of inner Glasgow had the effect of transforming the physical appearance of the city. Familiar landmarks were swept away, street patterns were changed. Inadequate financial resources to support the massive scale of the plans and problems in co-ordinating the clearance and re-building of the older areas frequently meant vacant and derelict sites for lengthy periods which detracted from the city's environment. In 1977, 17 years after the introduction of the 1960 Development Plan, only 9 of the 29 Comprehensive Development Areas were completed or nearing completion, although clearance had also occurred on a considerable scale outside the CDAs. The second major instrument of physical change was a motorway programme, much of which was originally proposed in the Clyde Valley Plan, but whose implementation stemmed from the recommendations of the Greater Glasgow Transportation Study in 1965 (Scott *et al.*, 1964–74). This report suggested a system of three concentric roads and several radial routes, only a relatively small part of which has been built. But even the construction of half the proposed Inner Ring Road, involving a new motorway link across the heart of the city through former residential areas and a new bridge across the Clyde, has produced a townscape often unrecognisable to those who last saw Glasgow 10 years ago.

The main themes of post-war development in Clydeside – redevelopment, overspill, New Towns, new housing, transport and social infrastructure – can all be traced more or less directly to the Clyde Valley Plan, but over the 25 years up to 1970 the underlying conditions were changing markedly from those envisaged by this plan. Firstly, the economy of West Central Scotland experienced severe difficulties in adapting to changing conditions and it became clear that the Clyde Valley Plan had been too sanguine in its assumption that the Government's regional policy would be able to maintain employment levels and avoid high unemployment. During the 1950s when the traditional heavy industries experienced a relatively high demand for their products, unemployment was kept low but market shares tended to fall, sometimes drastically. For example, the output of Clydeside shipbuilders remained almost stationary at about 400,000 tons per annum between the end of the war and the late 1950s but during this time their share of the rapidly expanding world tonnage fell from 18 per cent to under 5 per cent (Slaven, 1975). During the 1960s the region's position deteriorated, even relative to the slow-growing Great Britain economy. Between 1959 and 1968, West Central Scotland's employment declined by about 10,000 or 1 per cent at a time when employment increased by 5 per cent in Great Britain as a whole. This unfavourable performance can be attributed partly to the region's disadvantageous industrial structure but partly also to a tendency for individual industries on Clydeside to grow more slowly or decline more rapidly than their counterparts elsewhere in Britain (West Central Scotland, Plan 1974b). The shortfall of jobs was most marked in Glasgow, particularly reflecting more job losses through closures and fewer new job gains from incoming industry than the rest of the region (Firn and Hughes, 1975). The amount of direct decentralisation of firms from Glasgow to the New Towns was much more limited (Henderson, 1974). The service industries and office jobs in particular followed a more favourable employment trend, and central Glasgow experienced an office boom after 1963 (Checkland, 1976), but even in these sectors employment growth was more modest than in most British cities (West Central Scotland Plan, 1974b).

Lagging employment was associated with an increase in regional unemployment rates and high and increasing net emigration from West Central Scotland. Between 1951 and 1961 the region lost nearly 15,000 people per annum as a result of net emigration, and between 1961 and 1970 this increased to over 21,000 per annum, just under half of which was in respect of overseas movement (West Central Scotland Plan Team, 1972). Net emigration from the City of Glasgow increased even more rapidly from about 13,000 per annum over the period 1951–61 to about 24,000 per annum between 1961 and 1971 (Registrar General, 1951, 1961, 1971), although in this case an important part of the movement would seem to consist of families moving to a house within the region and commuting back to Glasgow to work. Census of Population figures show that the daily net travel-to-work inflow to Glasgow increased from about 38,000 to 62,000 over the period 1961–71.

Government responded to these economic problems with strengthened measures of regional policy in the 1960s and the whole of Clydeside has been designated a Development Area since 1966 and a Special Development Area since 1970. It has been estimated that regional policy may have generated an additional 60–80,000 jobs in the whole of Scotland in the period 1963–70, mainly from incoming industry (Moore and Rhodes, 1974); perhaps one-third to one-half of these may have been in Clydeside. The need to attract new job opportunities to West Central Scotland was an important factor behind the emphasis placed on 'growth areas' in the 1963 White Paper (Cmnd. 2188). Over time the role which New Towns could play in generating new job opportunities has played an increasingly important part in Government thinking compared with the traditional objective of providing accommodation for population overspill (Scottish Economic Planning Department, 1975), and further New Towns at Livingston and Irvine were designated during the 1960s. The concept of 'growth areas' of the kind identified in the 1963 White Paper has been criticised on the grounds that the whole of Central Scotland can be considered a closely integrated industrial area in which New Towns and the older centres play a complementary role (Cameron and Reid, 1966). Recent research has demonstrated that over the period 1951–70 the Scottish New Towns experienced a much higher rate of annual manufacturing job increases than in the rest of Scotland even when measured in terms of gross job changes at individual establishment level, and this favourable performance was particularly marked for incoming industry (Scottish Economic Planning Department, 1978). While the New Towns do not seem to have developed closely interlinked industries and it cannot be shown that the jobs would not have been created without the New Towns, there can be little doubt that they have proved themselves attractive locations to incoming industrialists. How far they have diverted industry which might otherwise have located in Glasgow is extremely difficult to determine. During the 1950s and

1960s there were few attractive industrial sites available in Glasgow and, reflecting the thinking behind the Clyde Valley Plan and overspill policy, little attention was given to promoting the city as a location for new industry.

A second important respect in which circumstances during the post-war period differed from the assumptions made in the Clyde Valley Plan was in the trend of population and household formation. Up to the mid 1960s the rate of natural increase was more rapid than expected and went a considerable way to offset the loss of population from Glasgow through migration during the 1950s (Table 5.3). Until about 1961, therefore, the city's population level declined at only a modest rate and estimates of overspill requirements and the gross housing shortage remained high. The demand for public sector housing was reinforced by a falling average household size and a low rents policy. A smaller proportion of households in all income bands became owner-occupiers in Scotland than in England. The supply of privately rented property in Glasgow continued its long-run decline as in other parts of the country, reflecting Government taxation and rent control policy and a heavy loss of substandard property through clearance when redevelopment got under way in earnest. All these factors help to explain the continuing acute shortage of local authority housing throughout the 1950s which led to pressure for the maximum number of new housing units and construction of the peripheral estates.

A relatively high rate of natural increase and continuing acceptance of a Green Belt around the city strengthened the need for population decentralisation from Glasgow. But after 1964 the birth rate turned down and continued to follow a downward trend into the 1970s, while the level of annual migration loss from Glasgow almost doubled after 1961. As a result, the rate of population decline in Glasgow was much more marked in the 1960s than in the preceding decade, and even greater in the 1970s (Table 5.3). The implications of this large and accelerating population decline for regional planning strategy were not immediately evident. Public sector house-building and investment in transport and other social investment in Glasgow continued at a high level throughout the 1960s. Even as late as 1970 it was estimated that there was a need for further planned overspill capacity for Glasgow families who could not be adequately accommodated within the rebuilt city, and additional housing at Erskine in Renfrewshire and another New Town at Stonehouse in Lanarkshire were planned (Glasgow Corporation and Scottish Development Department, 1970).

The composition as well as the sheer scale of population loss from Glasgow during the 1960s was at variance with the assumptions of the underlying planning strategy. The 1960 Quinquennial Review of the Development Plan was geared to a projected population of 997,000 in the former City of Glasgow Municipal Burgh area in 1970. It was estimated that 10,000 people per annum would leave the city as part of the planned overspill programme with an additional 6,000 per annum

Table 5.3 Estimated components of past and projected population change in Glasgow 1951–1986*

Definition	Period	Population start of period* (000's)	Net migration per annum (000's)	Natural increase and other (minor) changes† per annum (000's)	Total change per annum (000's)	Population at end of period* (000's)
City of Glasgow Municipal Burgh	1951–61	1,093	– 13	+ 9	– 4	1,056
City of Glasgow Municipal Burgh	1961–66	1,056	– 25	+ 10	– 15	980
City of Glasgow Municipal Burgh	1966–71	980	– 23	+ 6	– 17	894
City of Glasgow District‡	1961–71	1,142	– 25	+ 9	– 16	979
City of Glasgow District‡	1971–77	979	– 24	– 1	– 25	832
City of Glasgow District‡	1977–86	832	– 16	– 2	– 18	672

Source: Registrar-General for Scotland. Mid-Year Estimates of Home Population: 1977-based projection and census of Population, 1951 and 1961.

* Estimates of home population differ slightly from those of total population used in Tables 5.1 and 5.2.
† Apart from natural increase changes, minor changes may result from factors such as changes in the number of merchant seamen and armed forces. The new City of Glasgow District has been in operation since 1975. It is estimated that the area of the new District contained about 85,000 more
‡ The new City of Glasgow District has been in operation since 1975. It is estimated that the area of the new District contained about 85,000 more population than the area of the previous Municipal Burgh in both 1961 and 1971.

through 'unplanned' or 'voluntary' movement. In practice net migration averaged nearly 25,000 people per annum and the actual 1970 population was only 908,000 (nearly 10% fewer than projected). However, the planned overspill programme accounted for the loss of only about 6,300 people per annum, many fewer than originally estimated, while 'unplanned' movement occurred at the rate of about 18,500 people per annum, three times more than expected. The reasons for the very high level of 'voluntary' migration from Glasgow can only be guessed. It is probable that between one-half and two-thirds of this flow was to destinations outside West Central Scotland altogether, much of it to England and overseas, and for this element it seems likely that the unfavourable economic performance of Clydeside was a prime factor. But a substantial number – as many as in the planned overspill flow – appear to have moved to other parts of the region, often commuting back to work in Glasgow. That this flow has remained high even when Glasgow's crude shortage of houses above the tolerable standard has been much reduced suggests that there are more complex issues involved, perhaps connected with the type and tenure of housing which the city can offer or with wider environmental and social preferences.

Finally, the pattern of migration from Glasgow has been more selective in relation to age and socio-economic group than envisaged. Between the Census years of 1966 and 1971 a disproportionately large part of the net migration loss was concentrated in the younger age groups (under 45 years) and in the professional, clerical and skilled socio-economic groups. The proportion of Glasgow's population above the retirement age is estimated to have increased from about 12 per cent in 1961 to 15 per cent in 1971 and 18 per cent in 1976, a more rapid change than in Scotland or Great Britain as a whole, and the city's dependency ratio (the proportion of residents in the non-working to working age groups) has increased from well below the Scottish average in 1951 and 1961 to above average in 1976. While the proportion of employers, managers and professional workers in the population increased slightly in Glasgow between 1966 and 1971, the city's share of these groups in Clydeside and the rest of Scotland fell. The contrast with the age structure and social composition of the New Town areas is particularly marked. For example, the estimated proportion of the population aged 60 or more in 1976 in Glasgow (21%) was more than double that in East Kilbride District (10%) and Cumbernauld and Kilsyth District (9%) (Registrar General). Only 10 per cent of Glasgow's economically active resident males were employers, managers and professional workers in 1971, compared with nearly 18 per cent in East Kilbride and Cumbernauld New Towns. Marked and growing social polarisation is also evident when Glasgow is compared with suburban areas such as Bearsden and Milngavie, reflecting the city's low proportion of owner-occupied housing and the location of almost all new private house-building outside the city in the post-war period. There are clearly implications for the pattern of public service provision required in Glasgow, for example in the balance between public and private transport and in the needs of the elderly. How far the trends also pose problems for the quality of life in Glasgow, for example through the possible effects on the education system, cultural life, and community leadership, must perhaps remain more a matter for political judgment.

An inadequate economic performance, a rapidly declining population, social polarisation – all these factors contributed to the need for a re-examination of planning strategy for Glasgow and its conurbation. While the Springburn Study (MacBain and Forbes, 1967) queried some of the basic premises of the Clyde Valley Plan and its subsequent development, arguing for greater attention to the employment needs and potential of Glasgow as a complement to the growth areas, the most fundamental reappraisal came in 1974 with the publication of the West Central Scotland Plan (1974a). This was an advisory regional economic and physical plan, prepared for a Steering Committe of representatives of the local authorities, Government and others appointed from industry, trade unions and the universities. Compared with the Clyde Valley Plan, it placed much more emphasis on the economic issues. Although it suffered from weaknesses in presentation and has received much less attention in the general or professional press than contemporary regional plans in England or the Clyde Valley Plan, the West Central Scotland Plan on its record to date can fairly claim to have had at least as much impact on decisions that have subsequently been taken and on prevailing views as any of the better known regional plans.

The West Central Scotland Plan placed particular emphasis on the factors other than industrial structure which appeared to be affecting economic performance and on the need to improve the competitiveness of existing industry in the region at individual plant level through product and market diversification and better labour relations. It seems significant that all of this formed the core of Labour Government strategy for industry at the national level. Secondly, the Plan highlighted the scale of recent population and employment declines in the region and particularly in Glasgow and pointed to the need to give particular attention to the regeneration of the urban centre of Clydeside. In view of the changing population trends and projections, further overspill capacity at Stonehouse New Town seemed unnecessary; the existing New Towns already had substantial scope for further employment and population growth, and the marginal cost of expansion in these cases was likely to be lower. Thirdly, emphasis was placed on the need to improve the urban environment of much of Clydeside, and to widen the type and quality of housing opportunities through more rehabilitation of older housing and increased owner-occupation in the conurbation. Much of this general thinking has been accepted and can be seen reflected in the policies of the new local authorities (notably Strathclyde Regional Council and Glasgow District Council which came into being after local government reorganisation in 1975) and of Government: for example, the establishment of the Scottish Development Agency in December 1975 to encourage an improvement in industrial performance through more direct means than the mainly financial inducements, available from Government Departments, and with a responsibility for environmental improvement; the decision taken in 1976 not to proceed with Stonehouse New Town; the Glasgow Eastern Area Renewal project; and a more general interest in rehabilitating older housing and diversifying the pattern of housing tenure in Glasgow. What was chiefly lacking from the West Central Scotland Plan was a detailed analysis of the feasibility of influencing trends in the direction it had charted, and of the effect which new policies could be expected to have on aggregate employment and population trends within particular time periods. It is perhaps not unexpected to find that the same uncertainties dominate any assessment of recent trends and future prospects – to which we now turn.

Recent trends and future prospects

Since 1971 there are signs that the rapid rate of employment decline experienced in Glasgow during the 1960s has moderated (Table 5.4). Between 1971 and 1976 a net decline of approximately 4,000 jobs per annum occurred; even after taking account of cyclical factors it is clear that this rate of decline was considerably less than the fall of about

Table 5.4 Employment change* in Glasgow 1961–1976 (000's)

Industrial sector	1961–71† per annum	1971	1971–76 per annum	1976
Primary	− 0.1	2.3	− 0.0	2.1
Manufacturing	− 7.2	172.0	− 5.6	144.2
Construction	+ 0.4	33.1	+ 0.2	33.9
Services	− 0.9	286.1	+ 1.8	295.0
Total for Glasgow‡	− 7.8	493.5	− 3.7	475.1
Total for Strathclyde§	− 3.3	1,009.6	− 0.6	1,006.6

* Employees in employment.
† 1961–71 estimates are based on a count of national insurance cards and are not directly comparable with estimates for 1971 and 1976 from the Annual Census of Employment.
‡ Department of Employment local office areas covering Glasgow, Clydebank, Rutherglen and Cambuslang; this area approximates to but is slightly larger than Glasgow District.
§ Department of Employment local office areas approximating to Strathclyde Region.

Source: Department of Employment (unpublished data).

8,000 jobs per annum over the period 1961–71. As in the past the main part of the decrease was in manufacturing employment (and predominantly in respect of jobs held by men), but since 1971 there has been a stronger growth in services, reflecting both an increase in private services (insurance, banking, finance and miscellaneous services) and in the public sector (professional and scientific services such as education and health, and public administration in central and local government). Some further decline in manufacturing employment may occur as a result of rationalisation in the steel and other industries into the 1980s, but the more modest rate of fall recorded in recent years may be maintained. The greater attention now being given to the provision of industrial sites and advance factories in Glasgow (as in the Cambuslang Recovery Area) should enable the city to compete more effectively with other areas for the limited supply of incoming industry. While some costs (e.g. land costs, rates, insurance) are likely to be higher in Glasgow than other parts of the region, these may not be overriding considerations for industrial location if the urban environment is improved, suitable sites and premises provided for existing firms experiencing redevelopment or expansion as well as incomers, and account is taken of offsetting inducements such as rent concessions. Aggregate employment levels seem likely to depend mainly on the future of the service sector and particularly the extent to which Glasgow can maintain its position as a leading office centre. The improvements which have taken place in the city's road, rail and air transport links should have a favourable effect in this respect, although further population decline is likely to have implications for more local services in Glasgow.

Official estimates suggest that population continued to fall rapidly between 1971 and 1977 (Table 5.3) at a rate of some 25,000 people per annum. For the first time in many years there was no natural increase over this period but almost all the fall can be attributed to net emigration. Although the economic activity rate of the remaining population is likely to have increased since 1971, particularly for married women, in line with trends in other parts of Great Britain, it seems clear that the decline in the economically active population of Glasgow has been greater than the fall in employment. The net travel-to-work inflow to the city is therefore likely to have increased substantially since 1971. Despite a more favourable balance between jobs and labour force resident in the city, the male unemployment rate of Glasgow residents appears to have remained well above that of the region as a whole –an estimated 13.7 per cent in March 1978 compared with 11.0 per cent in Strathclyde (Strathclyde Regional Council, 1978), reflecting the adverse age, occupational and skill characteristics of Glasgow residents in relation to the new job opportunities. In particular small areas of the city, unemployment can reach much higher rates, mainly as a result of the residential concentration of the unskilled (Wood, 1977). High unemployment in Glasgow therefore reflects both an overall deficiency in the demand for labour (which it shares with most of Strathclyde) and a residential concentration of those who are least able to compete for those job opportunities which are available.

All the indications are that population is likely to continue to leave the city in considerable numbers for the foreseeable future if at rather less rapid rates than have occurred since 1971. For example, the Registrar General's 1977–based projections envisage a net population reduction of 18,000 per annum over the period 1977–86 (Table 5.3). The prospect of a slower rate of decline in jobs in the city is consistent with further large increases in travel-to-work inflow. If these trends continue, there could be some improvement in the unemployment rate in Glasgow compared with other parts of Scotland, and a reduction in that part of net migration from the city which takes place for job-related reasons, although the timing and extent of such a change is very uncertain. Even more problematic is the question of how far emigration from the city will continue at a high level even in the new situation facing Glasgow in the latter half of the 1970s and 1980s when the long-standing quantitative housing problem has been overcome. Strathclyde Regional Council (1976) has argued that the prospect of eliminating almost all the sub-tolerable housing stock before 1981 and of introducing new policies to improve the urban environment gives grounds for suggesting a much reduced rate of population decline. The key issue really concerns the time scale within which new policies can be expected to have a big impact on aggregate migration trends. A number of factors, for example the availability of substantial areas of land with planning permission for private housing outside the city, the realistic scale of possible new building and housing improvement within Glasgow, and the large areas of unsightly derelict land within the city, suggest caution on this point. The Registrar General's projections assume a significantly reduced level of emigration compared with recent trends but are consistent with a rather less optimistic view on the scope for the impact of policies in the short term, and with the importance of wider factors such as housing tenure, housing type and social attitudes towards city life. Certainly a large proportion of the existing population of the city still live in areas of poor environment and it must be expected that those residents who wish to will continue to move to other areas when the opportunity arises.

The above discussion suggests that the critical element in future planning strategy for Glasgow is the likely rate of population decline. A number of factors will influence this, of which the most important seems to be the attractiveness of the housing environment in the widest sense which Glasgow will be able to offer. It must be acknowledged that large uncertainties attach to the speed with which new policies can influence the overall migration trends, and particular attention should therefore be given to measures which are as far as possible able to operate with different population levels. But the probability seems to be for further population decline. For example, the Registrar General's projection set out in Table 5.3 suggests a population for Glasgow of around 672,000 in 1986. Although this implies a lower population for the city than the projections of Strathclyde Regional Council, the Registrar General's projection represents a significant reduction in the rate of net emigration from the early 1970s, and it is worthwhile examining some of the implications of this possibility. If population were to fall less (or more) steeply than suggested by the Registrar General's projection the detailed implications for service provision would change, but it seems generally unlikely that the overall prospect discussed below would be much altered.

Clearly there would be important repercussions on the demand for public services. This is most obvious in the case of housing in Glasgow for which, as a result of the house-building programme since the war and the recent decline in population, there is already no longer a crude shortage in relation to estimated household numbers. Further population decline (and any further increase in the number of housing units), even though partially offset by an increase in the number of households, can be expected to lead to an increase in vacancy rates well above those required for a normal turnover of houses. This is already a feature of some local authority estates, reinforcing difficulties of multiple deprivation and vandalism for the remaining residents, and the problem could grow to much larger proportions. With an increased demand for owner-occupation, available information on preferences (Glasgow District Council, 1978) suggests that vacancies will be concentrated in parts of the public sector stock such as the post-war peripheral housing estates, unpopular inter-war schemes and some multi-storey flats. The phenomenon of concentrated urban deprivation in certain areas of Clydeside, and the need to exercise positive discrimination in public expenditure so that existing inequalities are not reinforced by public service provision, has received growing attention in recent years. Measures of income support and improvements to services and the physical environment may in the last resort be ineffective unless they can be accompanied by an improved morale and sense of confidence on the part of local residents.

Unless radical new rent policies were to be introduced, a surplus of housing units is paradoxically likely to coexist with an excess demand for the more popular housing types, for example houses with gardens, houses of larger size or specially designed for the elderly, and in more attractive areas with good accessibility to employment centres. In this situation one course of action would be to hold back on new construction and concentrate on improving existing housing to make it more attractive to households increasingly able to exercise their preferences; this could entail reduced densities in some of the peripheral schemes, better social and community facilities, and the sale of council houses, with the use of much of the vacant land in inner city areas for non-housing purposes. Alternatively, the approach might be to encourage selective new house-building of the right type in the inner areas where this can meet rising aspirations, special needs and other preferences, particularly through the supply of private housing, houses with gardens, and sheltered housing for the elderly; the corollary of this approach would be very high vacancy rates in the more unpopular estates and the need for demolition, possibly on a substantial scale. The rate of future income growth and policy towards the setting of relative rent levels for different types of house can be expected to have an effect on the level and pattern of demand.

There has also been substantial new investment in recent years in improving transport facilities in Glasgow (e.g. Clyderail, the modernised subway, new roads). Unless offset by the effects of income growth and other factors, falling population is likely to dampen the demand for transport, and lead to a situation of overcapacity. There would be a particular risk of increased operating losses in public transport and the need for additional subsidies to maintain services. As in the case of housing, however, there would not necessarily be a decline in demand in all sectors. We have already noted that there is a probability of big increases in the daily travel-to-work inflow to Glasgow from areas outside the city, although unfortunately the peaked nature of this demand might actually intensify the problem of achieving financial viability for the public services. Decentralisation of population, along with increased car ownership if incomes rise, could similarly maintain demand on the road system and lead to pressure for further improvements in some areas.

Change in the age structure of the population is an important determinant of the demand for other public services. Even if educational standards were to be increased, pressure on school buildings, for example, can be expected to fall very markedly indeed unless there is an unexpectedly large upturn in the birth rate, as the trend towards a greater proportion of elderly households reinforces the falling overall population level. On the other hand the need for hospital and other services used disproportionately by the elderly might fall only slightly if at all. On the Registrar General's 1977-based projection, for example, it is estimated that the number of children between the ages of 5 and 19 could fall from 216,000 in 1977 (26% of Glasgow's population) to about 133,000 (20% of the population) in 1986. In contrast the same projection suggests the population aged 60 and over might decline much more slowly from about 177,000 in 1976 (21% of the population) to about 159,000 (24%) in 1986. An actual increase from 80,000 to 82,000 is projected for those aged 70 and over.

Trends in the distribution of population between different parts of the city are a crucial consideration, particularly for facilities such as primary schools or local shopping where relevant population in the immediately adjacent local catchment area is the key determinant of demand. For those activities, the balance of future population between the peripheral housing areas and inner city sites is of critical importance. In a situation of great uncertainty it seems sensible to place emphasis on flexibility and wherever possible to avoid committing resources which are in danger of being under-used if the situation changes. While it may be possible in some services to invest in facilities which can be adapted to changing requirements at local level – for example bus transport where routes can be adjusted as population patterns change – this may not always be the case. As throughout the post-war period, there is no alternative but to formulate a planning strategy for the new situation which is emerging. The lessons of the past point strongly to the need for realism in taking a view on future trends.

The prospect of substantial further population decline also brings with it the possibility of a deteriorating financial position as local revenues fall more rapidly than costs, although the effect of the resource element of the Rate Support Grant may be to place a major part of the increased burden on the Government. It is already the case that Glasgow's costs and particularly its housing costs (which accounted for over 80% of the city's capital debt in 1977 (CIPFA, 1977)) are higher than in most other parts of Scotland and increasing more rapidly. While loan charges per local authority house in Glasgow are close to the Scottish average, the city's total housing revenue account costs per house are significantly above the Scottish average as a result of very high repair and maintenance costs – in 1977/78 Glasgow was spending £104 per house per annum on repairs and maintenance compared with the average in Scotland of £77, reflecting special problems such as the high cost of lift maintenance in multi-storey flats, vandalism, and other factors. The system of Exchequer housing subsidies in operation in 1977/78 gave Glasgow a rather lower level of assistance per house than in Scotland as a whole (£159 per house compared with £169), although with the introduction of the new Housing Support Grant this difference should be narrowed or eliminated. The result of above-average housing costs and below-average Exchequer subsidy in 1977/78 was both a relatively high level of local authority rents in Glasgow (£232 per house compared with £207 on average in Scotland) and a higher local rate contribution to the housing revenue account than in other parts of Scotland (£66 per house compared with £62).

Despite favourable treatment in the allocation of Rate Support Grant, the effect of higher costs is that Glasgow District's rate poundage is amongst the highest in Scotland, placing both Glasgow residents and industrialists at a disadvantage compared with the surrounding parts of Clydeside. While this problem has been partly reduced by the 1978 revaluation (which resulted in a smaller increase in rateable value in Glasgow than other areas) and the differential impact on manufacturing is, in any case, lessened when the Regional rate and industrial de-rating are taken into account, nonetheless the incentive to locate outside the city remains. The differential in rates could well widen again if population and industrial decentralisation continue, exacerbated by the selective nature of these processes, unless costs can be reduced or the Government becomes responsible for a larger share of the burden. Some further increase in the Government's contribution seems inevitable, although equity and efficiency criteria could be in conflict. The danger is that attempts to remedy Glasgow's problems through high investment could perpetuate the process of population and employment decline through a further increase in debt charges and local rates. In these circumstances the case is strengthened for careful review of expenditure needs with emphasis on spending which allows flexibility in the face of uncertain trends and wherever possible avoids over-commitment (and the associated risk of mounting operating losses).

Conclusions

This chapter has reviewed Clydeside's and particularly Glasgow's recent experience and future prospects in the context of the region's history over a much longer time span. Glasgow's history has been marked by periods of dramatic change, and rapid change is bound to create stresses and problems. This was certainly the case during the nineteenth century when rapid industrial growth, prosperity and in-migration of population was associated with severe housing conditions, overcrowding and lack of amenities. In the post-war period, and particularly since 1960, the city has also experienced changes in population and physical redevelopment on a scale which seems at least as great as has occurred at any time in the past; and further rapid change must be expected in the foreseeable future. But there are crucial differences. Recent changes have taken place, not against the background of nineteenth-century growth and confidence, but in a situation of economic weakness and relative decline; and psychologically the fact of decline has made the inevitable problems created by rapid change much more difficult to tackle. Post-war change has also taken place in the context of a public-sector physical planning system. A more centralised vision of the future has influenced but not controlled the pattern of development, and there have been problems in identifying and adapting to underlying economic and demographic trends in a flexible manner.

In its post-war planning, as throughout its history, Glasgow has always demonstrated a determination to tackle formidable problems in a forthright manner. Planning policy for the West of Scotland has recently emerged from a fundamental re-examination of the assumptions and thinking behind the Clyde Valley Plan, and the broad aims of policy are now more in keeping with current economic and demographic realities. On the employment side, there is a new awareness and sensitivity towards the needs of industry, for example through the provision of more sites and the planning of urban renewal. The establishment of the Scottish Development Agency with the particular emphasis given to indigenous industry is a recognition of the important part which existing establishments could play in achieving increased employment opportunities. In housing policies, there have been moves to consider the possibility of council-house sales and greater private house-building. Housing improvements now form a much larger proportion of the housing programme than formerly. There is greater awareness of the detrimental effect which a poor environment can have on all aspects of urban life.

While the goal of making the city more attractive to industry and people seems clearly right, the chief danger lies in underestimating the strength of the forces leading to further employment and particularly population decline in Glasgow, and thus in overestimating the scale of the impact which policies may make in the short run. If population continues to leave the city for its surrounding areas there is a danger that overcapacity in parts of the social infrastructure will lead to financial losses, a growing gap between revenue and costs, and an increased burden on Government or Glasgow's remaining residents and employers. But, as we have seen, the prospect is not one of declining demand for services across the board. The changing age structure, rising incomes and the increasing aspirations of the population are leading to an increased demand for some facilities, for example services for the elderly, private housing and houses with gardens.

A reduction of pressure on some services and in some parts of the city may open up new opportunities to meet the demands that exist at reasonable cost. To adapt to changing circumstances rather than to attempt to reverse aggregate trends may not require a massive reconstruction on the scale witnessed over the last thirty years, although the cost is bound to be substantial and Government will need to ensure that the burden is shared equitably. It may be possible to get better value for money in constructing an improved general environment, both for residents and to attract industry, by greater emphasis on the adaptation of existing buildings to new uses, and through pricing and financial policies (e.g. the sale of council houses in some circumstances) which more closely reflect the underlying pattern of demand. Environmental improvement and other policies which can operate in a range of circumstances have a particular attraction in conditions of considerable uncertainty about the future level and distribution of population. Investment in new facilities such as in the Glasgow Eastern Area Renewal project and other areas of urban deprivation must be seen as part of a city-wide strategy, with particular attention to the types of housing and other facilities for which there is excess demand at current prices. A realistic aim might be to improve at a reasonable cost the urban environment and help meet the aspirations of those residents who remain. This may mean more attention to the planning of services in the most flexible and efficient manner. It will also mean a greater involvement by residents in the planning and implementation of policies. The lessons of history suggest that above all what is needed in the uncertain period ahead is a greater sensitivity, flexibility, and realism.

References

Abercrombie, P. and **Matthew, R.** (1949) *The Clyde Valley Regional Plan*. HMSO, Edinburgh.

Cameron, G.C. and **Reid, G.L.** (1966) *Scottish Economic Planning and the Attraction of Industry*. University of Glasgow Social and Economic Studies Occasional Paper No. 6. Oliver and Boyd, Edinburgh.

Checkland, S.G. (1976) *The Upas Tree, Glasgow 1875—1975*. Glasgow University Press.

CIPFA (Chartered Institute of Public Finance and Accountancy – Scottish Branch) (1977) *Rating Review*. Glasgow.

CMND. 2188 (1963) *Central Scotland: A Programme for Development and Growth*. HMSO, Edinburgh.

Cunnison, J. and **Gilfillan, J.** (1958) (eds) *The Third Statistical Account of Scotland: Glasgow*. Collins, Glasgow.

Firn, J.R. and **Hughes, J.T.** (1975) *Employment Growth and Decentralisation of Manufacturing Industry*. Centre for Environmental Studies, 1973. Urban Economics Conference, London.

Fogarty, M (1945) *Prospects of the Industrial Areas of Great Britain*. Methuen, London.

Glasgow Corporation (1945) *The First Glasgow Development Plan*. Report by the City Engineer. Glasgow.

Glasgow Corporation (1952) *Report on Housing Needs*. Report by the City Architect and Planning Officer. Glasgow.

Glasgow Corporation (1960) *Development Plan Quinquennial Review*. Report by the City Planning Officer. Glasgow.

Glasgow Corporation (1972) *Area of Needs Report*. Report by the City Planning Officer. Glasgow.

Glasgow Corporation and Scottish Development Department (1970). *Report by the Glasgow Housing Programme Working Party*. Glasgow.

Glasgow District Council *(1978) Housing Management Department Report*. Glasgow.

Handley, J. (1964) *The Irish in Scotland*. John Burns and Sons, Glasgow.

Henderson, R. (1974) 'Industrial overspill from Glasgow 1958–68', *Urban Studies*, **11** No. 1., pp. 61–79.

Kyd, J.G. (ed.) (1952) *Scottish Population Statistics including Webster's Analysis of Population 1755*. Scottish History Society, Edinburgh.

MacBain, I. and Forbes, J. (eds) (1967) *The Springburn Study: Urban Renewal in a Regional Context*. Glasgow Corporation, Glasgow.

Moore, B. and **Rhodes, J.** (1974) 'Regional policy and the Scottish economy', *Scottish Journal of Political Economy*, vol. XXI, pp. 215–35.

Registrar General for Scotland (1951) *Census of Population: Scotland*. HMSO, Edinburgh.

Registrar General for Scotland (1961) *Census of Population: Scotland*. HMSO, Edinburgh.

Registrar General for Scotland (1971) *Census of Population: Scotland*. HMSO, Edinburgh.

Registrar General for Scotland (1977) *1977-based Projection of Home Population*. HMSO, Edinburgh.

Robertson, D.J. (1958) 'Population, past and present', in Cunnison, J. and Gilfillan, J. (eds) *The Third Statistical Account of Scotland: Glasgow*. Collins, Glasgow.

Scottish Economic Planning Department (1975) *New Towns in Scotland: A Consultation Document*. Edinburgh.

Scott, Wilson, Kirkpatrick and partners (1964–74) *Greater Glasgow Transportation Study, Volumes 1—5*. Glasgow Corporation, Glasgow.

Scottish Economic Planning Department (1978) 'Annual gross changes in manufacturing employment in the Scottish new towns and the rest of Scotland 1950–70', *Scottish Economic Bulletin*, No. 14. HMSO, Edinburgh.

Slaven, A. (1975) *The Development of the West of Scotland 1750—1960*. Routledge and Kegan Paul, London.

Strathclyde Regional Council (1976) *Regional Report*. Glasgow.

Strathclyde Regional Council (1978) *Monthly Estimates of Residential Unemployment Rates*. Department of Physical Planning, Glasgow.

West Central Scotland Plan Team (1972) *Components of Regional Change*. Technical Memorandum 4. Glasgow.

West Central Scotland Plan Team (1974a) *West Central Scotland Plan——A Programme of Action*. Glasgow.

West Central Scotland Plan Team (1974b) *The Regional Economy*. Supplementary Volume 1. Glasgow.

Wood, C. (1977) *Urban Unemployment Differentials in Scottish Cities*. Unpublished Central Research Unit (Scottish Development Department) Paper.

Chapter 6

Housing in the conurbations

Since the Second World War, the principal objective of British housing policy has been to reduce the housing shortage by adding to the housing stock, and in this the conurbations have been no exception. Much of the residential building in the conurbations has been to replace housing demolished because it was in too poor a condition for rehabilitation or because the land was needed for another use. Even so, the main indication of achievement has been the net increase in housing stock – after allowing for replacement.

Does it still make sense to go on increasing the housing stock in the conurbations? The answer given in the first section of this chapter is that, as far as we can judge from incomplete and uncertain information, in most conurbations it probably does not. But even if future demand is underestimated, the time has surely come for a change in emphasis and a major shift of interest to policy on the use and improvement of the existing stock. These issues are particularly important in the conurbations because housing there is generally older and more likely to be in need of improvement; because there is generally a high proportion of local authority stock where improvement and changes in utilisation pose specially difficult questions; and because a more varied mix of dwellings and households means greater problems in securing good utilisation than is generally the case in more homogeneous areas.

The stock of dwellings increased in every conurbation throughout the period, but in all cases by much less (12% in 1951–61; 5% in 1967–71) than in the rest of Great Britain (21% and 22% respectively). Such a net increase in dwellings is the sum of increases in stock because of constructions and conversions, and of decreases due to demolition and conversion (Table 6.1).

It is interesting to compare stock changes with increases in demand. Table 6.2 shows the changes in both population and households. Population was stationary in the conurbations between 1951 and 1961 while it rose by 8 per cent elsewhere in Britain. It fell in the conurbations by 4 per cent in the 1960s; while the rate of increase elsewhere rose to 11 per cent. Between 1961 and 1971 all the conurbations lost population except West Midlands which had a static population, and West Yorkshire where it increased by only 1 per cent (See Ch. 2).

More pertinent in estimating housing need is the change in the

Table 6.1 Dwellings

	1951/61 increase as a % of 1951 dwelling stock	1961/71 increase as a % of 1961 dwelling stock
Central Clydeside	n.a.	7.2
Greater London	13.2	3.5
Merseyside	11.8	4.8
South East Lancashire	8.9	4.4
Tyneside	13.6	5.1
West Midlands	14.8	13.2
West Yorkshire	9.0	3.4
Conurbations	12.1*	5.1
Rest of Great Britain	21.4	21.6

* Six in first column because 1951 Clydeside data unavailable; seven in second.

Source: Censuses of 1951, 1961, 1971.

number of households. Conurbation households increased throughout the period except in London where they hardly changed in number, and in Merseyside where they levelled out in the 1960s after a 5 per cent increase in the 1950s. With affluence, more young and old couples, as well as single people, were setting up separate households either in their own dwellings or by sharing. More households were also created by divorce and separation. The proliferation of households is usually held to be commonest in city centres, because that is where the old, the young, childless couples, the separated and divorced tend to be disproportionately large segments of the population. While this may be true of central cities, it is not of conurbations as a whole. Households grew much faster outside the conurbations (16% in 1951–61; 18% in 1961–71) than within them (3%; 2%). In the 1950s the rate of conurbation household formation was far below the average for the rest of Britain, except only in the West Midlands and Tyneside where it was

Table 6.2 Population and household change 1951–1971

	% population increase		% household increase	
	1951–61	1961–71	1951–61	1961–71
Tyneside	2	−6	9.4	1.8
West Yorkshire	1	1	5.6	4.5
Merseyside	0	−8	5.2	0
South East Lancashire	0	−1	5.1	2.6
West Midlands	5	0	10.2	9.4
Greater London	−3	−7	2.1	−0.2
Central Clydeside	3	−4	9.8	1.1
Conurbations	0	−4.4	3.4	2.0
Rest of Great Britain	8.0	10.7	16.1	18.2

Source: Censuses, of 1951, 1961, 1971.

10 per cent and 9 per cent respectively. As the rate of household formation increased slightly in the 1960s elsewhere, it fell in all the conurbations – very dramatically in Tyneside to less than 2 per cent. Only in the West Midlands did its growth stay reasonably high – at 9 per cent. West Yorkshire had the steadiest growth of around 5 per cent in both periods.

As it happens, population and household formation moved more or less in parallel in the conurbations, that is, the conurbations with population growth (or least decline) tended to be those with the highest rate of household formation and vice versa. Conurbations did not differ much from each other in the rate of change in their average household size. In any case, it is more meaningful to compare the net increase in households with the net increase in dwellings to get a measure of changes in housing deficits – that is, in the shortfall in the number of dwellings below the number of households – over the period (see Table 6.3).

Table 6.3 Increases in households and dwellings 1951–1971

	1951–61		1961–71	
	% household increase	% net dwelling increase	% household increase	% net dwelling increase
West Midlands	10.2	14.8	9.3	13.2
Tyneside	9.4	13.6	1.9	5.1
West Yorkshire	5.6	9.0	4.5	3.4
Merseyside	5.2	11.8	−0.2	4.8
South East Lancs.	5.1	8.9	2.6	4.4
Greater London	2.1	13.2	−0.2	3.5
Central Clydeside	9.8	n.a.	1.1	7.2

Source: Censuses of 1951, 1961, 1971.

In the first period there is a fairly good correspondence between net dwelling increase and the increase in the number of households. All were building between about 3.5 per cent and 4.5 per cent more than their rate of household formation except Merseyside which built 6.5 per cent more, and London which was at a very high rate in spite of no change in its number of households. In the second period the relation between the two rates of increase becomes much weaker. The West Midlands, Merseyside and Tyneside, joined now by London, are still building roughly from about 3.5 per cent to 4.5 per cent more than the rate of household formation. South East Lancashire was building less than 2 per cent more; and West Yorkshire was actually building less than the household formation rate. Only Clydeside was building very much more.

However, some of these changes should not surprise us. An economist is likely to argue that some version of a stock adjustment principle determines housing investment. The larger the shortfall of dwellings relative to households, the more dwellings will increase; but as the gap closes and passes into surplus so one would expect the rate of net increase to die away. This reflects a relationship between the supply and demand for housing. In the private sector one would expect the closing of the gap between the number of households and dwellings to reduce the incentive to provide more housing. The shortening of effective waiting lists should have a similar effect in the local authority sector.

If the principle is valid, one would expect Greater London and Merseyside to have had the largest percentage housing deficits in 1951. Table 6.4 shows that this was so. Indeed, if one compares the excess of the net dwelling increase rate over the household formation rate with the percentage housing deficit in 1951, there was an almost perfect correspondence. Only Tyneside was building more houses than one would expect. The same crude version of the stock adjustment principle seems to have worked in the second period as well. Merseyside followed by West Midlands had the highest excess of net dwelling increase over household formation rate and had the greatest 1961 housing deficit outside London. South East Lancashire and West Yorkshire had the lowest 'excesses' and had the largest housing surpluses. In that period Greater London was an exception because it was building fewer dwellings than one would expect, given the size of its deficit; while at the other extreme, Central Clydeside was adding to its stock at the highest rate of all, relative to its rate of household formation, though it already had a 2 per cent surplus.

By 1971 all the conurbations were in surplus except London. Thus the stock adjustment principle would indicate a further decline in the rate of housing investment in the conurbations during the 1970s. But before probing the fragmentary figures we have since 1971, one must consider what meaning to attach to housing deficits and surpluses. A position where there is neither surplus nor deficit does not mean every household has a home. There are second homes though they are unlikely to be important outside London. Even with a conurbation there can be local shortages in contrast to surpluses elsewhere. Moreover, to be efficient the housing stock needs a proportion of vacant homes to allow mobility and permit the major repair and rehabilitation of the stock. The difficult question is what percentage of vacant dwellings is desirable. In 1971 it was 3.75 per cent (excluding second homes) in England and Wales. In 1976 it was estimated to have risen to 4.5 per cent (DOE, 1977). It is difficult to guess what the vacancy rate would be if there were no shortage of housing. 1881 may well have been the last Census year when the vacancy rate was highest at 5 per cent, but it was less than 4 per cent in 1901, also a year when the vacancy rate was determined by market forces in the almost complete absence of a local authority sector (DOE, 1977). One might hazard that in any case the local authority sector ought to be able to work with a lower vacancy rate than either the private rented or owned sectors because of the relative long-distance immobility of its tenants,

Table 6.4 Housing in the conurbations: various comparative statistics 1951/1961/1971 (000's)

	1951			1961			1971		
	Number of dwellings	Number of households	Surplus (+)/ shortfall (−) of dwellings over households and as a % of dwellings	Number of dwellings	Number of households	Surplus (+)/ shortfall (−) of dwellings over households and as a % of dwellings	Number of dwellings	Number of households	Surplus (+)/ shortfall (−) of dwellings over households and as a % of dwellings
Conurbations									
Tyneside	243	249	− 6(2%)	276	272	+ 4(1/)	288	277	+ 11(4%)
West Yorkshire	547	548	− 1(0%)	596	579	+ 17(3%)	628	605	+ 23(4%)
Merseyside	356	386	− 30(8%)	398	406	− 8(2/)	417	405	+ 12(3%)
South East Lancashire	752	767	− 15(2%)	819	806	+ 13(2%)	853	827	+ 26(3%)
West Midlands	615	648	− 33(5%)	706	714	− 8(1%)	799	781	+ 18(2%)
Greater London	2,180	2,659	− 479(22%)	2,468	2,658	− 190(8%)	2,555	2,652	− 97(4%)
Clydeside	n.a.	493	n.a.	553	541	+ 12(2%)	573	547	+ 26(5%)
Total Conurbations	4,693*	5,257*	− 564(12%)	5,816	5,976	− 160(3%)	6,113	6,094	+ 19(0%)
England and Wales	12,389	13,118	− 729(6%)	14,646	14,641	+ 5(0%)	17,024	16,510	+ 514(3%)
Scotland	1,375	1,436	− 61(4%)	1,627	1,570	+ 57(4%)	1,809	1,686	+ 123(7%)
Great Britain	13,764	14,554	− 790(6%)	16,273	16,211	+ 62(0%)	18,833	18,196	+ 637(3%)
Rest of Great Britain†	9,071	9,297	− 226(2%)	9,904	9,694	+ 210(2%)	–	–	–
Rest of Great Britain*	10,457			10,457	10,235	+ 222(2%)	12,720	12,102	+ 618(5%)

* Excluding Clydeside
† Includes Clydeside
Source: Censuses of 1951, 1961, 1971.

the greater administrative ease with which it should be able to place the next tenant, and its ability to plan and undertake major repairs and renewal before or when an occupier leaves, not having to wait until after a sale, as is usual in the owner-occupied sector.

The Department of Environment (1977) forecasts a 6 per cent vacancy rate nationally by 1986; but one can doubt whether it will, even more whether it should, be so high. A range of 4 to 5 per cent would seem less excessive for planning purposes.

If we were to accept 4 to 5 per cent as a reasonable margin, we can compare it with the balances shown in Table 6.4. In Great Britain as a whole there was a 3 per cent surplus in 1971. In Great Britain in the conurbations there was a balance between dwellings and households. But at such aggregate levels the net percentages are meaningless since they hide great geographical differences. Clydeside, Tyneside and West Yorkshire already had surpluses of 4 per cent or more.

There are many problems in continuing the calculation of dwellings–households balance past 1971. The first complication is the result of the change-over in 1974 from conurbations to metropolitan county as a basis for presenting statistics. The approach we have adopted is basically to assume that from 1974 to 1976 the conurbations' statistics moved as the metropolitan counties have done, and that they would have retained the same share of population, households and dwellings as they had in 1971. If anything, it is probable that this share of households has declined with the decentralisation of population, though what has happened to its share of dwellings is more doubtful.

The second problem is that we have no figures on households since 1971 except for England and Wales as a whole. We have had to assume for 1976 – the year for which we have made the comparison – that household formation has increased at the same rate in the conurbations as in England and Wales as a whole. But again this is likely to be an overestimate since we know that between 1951 and 1961, and 1961 and 1971, the ratio of household to population growth increased faster outside the conurbations than within them.

While recognising its drawbacks, the calculations give some idea of the relationship between the net increase in household formation and in dwellings between 1971 and 1976 (see Table 6.5).

The relationships are less clear than they used to be since the greatest additions to the stock are now associated with the smallest increases or even falls in the number of households – except on Clydeside. But this is not unexpected given the surplus situation in which almost all conurbations were in 1971. Interestingly, West Yorkshire and South East Lancashire built fewer houses than they had increases in households.

If one compares the excess of net dwelling increase over the household formation rate with the 1971 surplus, both were then in substantial surplus (4% and 3% respectively). Clydeside almost seemed to have put the brakes on building in response to its 1971 5 per cent

Table 6.5: Changes in household formation and in dwelling stock 1971–1976.

	% assumed increase in household formation	% net increase in dwellings
West Yorkshire	4.0	2.1
West Midlands	2.3	2.8
South East Lancs.	2.3	2.2
Tyneside	1.8	3.8
Greater London	1.6	4.4
Merseyside	−0.7	3.1
Central Clydeside	−0.7	0

Source: Regional Statistics, 1977, HMSO.

surplus. Again, as the stock adjustment principle would suggest, Greater London built at the highest rate relative to its household formation rate, having had the only deficit left in 1971. More difficult to interpret – so far as our figures allow – are Merseyside and Tyneside, and to a lesser extent the West Midlands, whose additions to the stock seem to have been high when judged by the same principle.

All this experience is reflected in Table 6.6 which shows the estimated housing surplus for 1976. One must be careful to show they are illustrative. Households may have risen more than estimated in the conurbations, especially in those anticipated to show the highest 1976 deficits, if only because a local authority with vacant stock will make every effort to fill it and so encourage the formation of more households.

Nevertheless, the prima facie conclusion is that, as one would expect given their building policies, Tyneside (6%) and Merseyside (7%) may have large surpluses relative to their needs, as may have Clydeside (5%). West Yorkshire may have the smallest surplus (2%) and South East Lancashire a small one (3%) because of the cautious building policies pursued. West Midlands has a moderate surplus of 3 per cent. Greater London was the last to move into surplus (2%). The only surprise suggested by the stock adjustment principle could be that neither Tyneside nor Merseyside have been quick enough to attack their housing programme. Much depends elsewhere on the planned vacancy rate assumed; but short of an unexpected increase in household formation one would be surprised in the light of past policies to find much net increase in the stock in any of the conurbations outside Greater London, except possibly to remedy geographical deficiencies or deficiencies of particular types of stock. That is a bold prediction and it may well be possible for a particular metropolitan county to challenge the relevance of the estimates used in its particular case.

Nevertheless it seems a sufficiently robust basis for the argument that in future improvement and utilisation of the stock in the conurbations will matter more than its net increase.

Table 6.6 Number of households and dwellings in 1976 (000's)

Old-style conurbation	Number of dwellings	Number of households	Surplus of dwellings over households	Surplus as a % of dwellings
Tyneside	299	282	17	6
West Yorkshire	641	629	12	2
Merseyside	430	402	28	7
South East Lancashire	871	846	25	3
West Midlands	821	799	22	3
Greater London	2,667	2,611	56	2
Central Clydeside	571	543	28	5
All conurbations	6,300	6,112	188	3
England and Wales	18,086	17,322	764	4
Scotland	1,907	1,753	154	8
Great Britain	19,993	19,075	918	5
Great Britain excluding conurbations	13,693	12,963	730	5

Source: Regional Statistics, 1977, HMSO.

If one is right to suggest that the falling off of population growth and of the rate of household formation in the conurbations means the re-direction of policy and management, the first question must be to decide the regime under which it should be done. As Table 2.16 has shown all the conurbations except London and South East Lancashire have percentages of local authority stock above the national average. In London the size of the private rented sector is large. All except South East Lancashire and West Yorkshire tend to have relatively low owner-occupied sectors. Much of the stock is currently managed by the public sector. How this is done and how much responsibility is devoted to occupiers will be major issues. The greater age of conurbation stock by comparison with the average elsewhere means that improvement will be a more pressing concern. Therefore while the policies suggested in the remainder of the chapter have a national relevance, their implementation is more immediately desirable in the conurbations.

The issues that most interest and disturb people are not the grand ones to do with the level and structure of housing subsidies, with allocative efficiency and equity, but the more immediate issues of mis-management and difficulties of access to housing. By their training economists incline to start at what they see as the top and work down because of the connection they expect between maladroit intervention in the housing market and the more immediate problems. But there is something to be said for starting with the more immediate problems if only because they may be susceptible to treatment without wide-ranging reform of housing finance; and in so far as this is true of some but not all, problems, we need to be clear about the 'scale' of the solution.

The tenants' right to repair

One of the most vexatious areas of dispute in housing is that of tenants' rights in the public sector. The rights themselves cover a number of points. Most councils still try to behave according to the lights of a traditional 'good' landlord, or hope that after a few years of labour shortages and public expenditure cuts they can return to such an image. They aim to maintain their property in good repair and decoration. Often they have built up large staffs for this. Once they could argue that if they did not take this on, many, even the majority, of their tenants would be unable financially to keep their housing in good order. There was a real risk of deterioration which would not be in the council's interest. Therefore good councils sent workmen round quickly in emergencies and kept to a schedule in routine maintenance, decoration and major overhauls. Usually tenants had little choice in what was done for them because standardisation was cheaper and often seemed fairer.

There must be comparatively few councils that find it easy to be good landlords in that sense now. The costs of repairs and maintenance have risen very rapidly over recent years, reflecting the labour intensity of the service and in some cases the effects of vandalism, rather than rising standards. To have maintained the old standards would have meant increases in rents which would have been politically unacceptable if not in some years contrary to national government prices and incomes policy. The same pressures have been at work in the owner-occupied sector. One aspect of the move to tenants' rights is to move away from the repairs and maintenance policy central to the ideal of the local authority as a good landlord towards giving the tenant more of the rights and responsibilities of an owner-occupier. But there is more to this than the gift of what is widely held to be a superior status. Owner-occupiers for the most part formerly used local builders and repairers and tried to adhere to repainting cycles; but there can be few who do so still because of rising costs. Instead they have done more and more of the work themselves, substituting their own unpriced labour for that of others. This raises the interesting questions of why tenants should be forced to pay for high labour costs through high rents, or why indeed national government or local ratepayers should be forced to subsidise high-cost repairs and maintenance?

A way out of the dilemma is surely to shift repairs and maintenance as far as possible from the council to the tenants and to reduce rents *pro rata*. The tenant then could choose how far to do the work himself or buy it from others. But this implies giving tenants more freedom. One could no longer require tenants to use standard colours or to redecorate at regulation frequency; or even to undertake minor repairs immediately. If they are to shoulder the cost, there is a presumption they should have as much right as owner-occupiers to vary their standards and indulge their tastes, including a taste, if they have it, to put off until tomorrow what could be done today. Moreover, once public housing was almost solely for the poor. Now there is a considerable range of household incomes and family circumstances in this sector. A consequence of having higher income is the ability not only to vary the level, but also the proportion of it, one devotes to housing upkeep. Higher real income means greater freedom of choice. Occupiers will want to vary more in the weight they give to such items as central heating, the modernisation of their kitchens and bathrooms, and building extensions to get more space. If a council tries to impose common standards they will become increasingly too uniform and low for the majority. The fear of so many concerned with the sector will be realised: it will become second-class housing suitable only for the underprivileged. Moreover the quality of the sector always lags behind the standards tenants want: councils persistently fall behind in their improvement programmes, even given these low standards.

An answer to all their problems would be to give tenants so far as possible the freedom to improve their dwellings as they please and at their own cost. What they do inside will be invisible except to themselves and their friends. No doubt they will break up the external uniformity of appearance of terraces and rows of similar housing; but there is no obvious reason why tenants should be more restricted in this than owner-occupiers, who are in practice only restricted by the planning law. Diversity will result because many studies have shown that most people like their homes to differ from their neighbours' even if in only quite trivial respects. Such freedom would undoubtedly increase council tenants' satisfaction with their homes as well as leading to a much higher average standard of upkeep than councils can now afford. Moreover it would be easy to harmonise subsidy arrangements with those now available to the owner-occupier. The mechanism already exists. All loans for the improvement of one's residence are eligible for interest relief.

There are various objections to such freedom. One is that while most tenants will maintain their property well, others will not; and that in particular there will be a tendency to skimp repairs when a tenancy is coming to an end, either because the tenants are old or do not care. Neglect often follows from the fact of tenancy. They have no interest in the property after they leave it because it is not theirs to hand on or sell. One solution to this would be to allow the councils to retain the responsibility for keeping the fabric of the property in a basic state of repair (and charging for this through the rent level), so that it does not decay. Thus the council might, for example, re-paint, re-roof, re-wire periodically, while leaving minor repairs, improvements and decorations to the tenant. (Some improvements might mean there is more basic maintenance for the council to do. Thus one might expect some rent increase to compensate councils, as for example when there is a home extension.)

A second objection is that tenants have no incentive to improve in so far as they merely pass on the benefit of what they do to the next tenant. Therefore they will spend less on improvement and maintenance than an owner-occupier would. However, the private leasehold sector has found a means for dealing with this. What is needed is a valuation for council and tenant of the value added or subtracted at the end of a tenancy. The tenant will get a lump sum reflecting an agreed estimate of any enhanced value through improvements he has made and the maintenance he has done. If his improvements are eyesores so that they are a deterrent to future tenants, or if the general state of the property has deteriorated below average, the outcome of the same valuation process could mean his paying a lump sum in dilapidations, itself an inducement to maintain the property in good order.

A third objection is that there are still tenants who cannot be expected to maintain the property in good order. They may be too poor, or physically incapable. Again there would seem to be an answer. A council could indeed decide – perhaps as part of its social services expenditure – to provide a service to help the elderly or disabled tenant, or single parent family, to maintain and decorate its home. Indeed given the reduction in the amount of general maintenance it had to do, it might find it easier to meet such special needs. Where the difficulty was purely financial it could provide material but not labour.

A rather different problem is whether a tenant could offer enough security to secure a loan for home improvement. But it is possible to exaggerate the problem. Most improvements will not cost very much and would require no more security than is needed for a personal loan from a bank or from a finance house. Where helpful it might also be possible to have a prior valuation of the enhancement likely to be achieved by the improvement and which would be reimbursable at the termination of a tenancy. Sometimes a local authority might itself provide security or indeed make a loan with repayment through the monthly rent bill. One way or another, and preferably through a diversity of sources and mechanisms it should be possible for creditworthy tenants to get the loans required.

A last objection arises with flats and maisonettes where some repairs, maintenance and improvement must be done in common. Yet again the private sector has devised a mechanism. Where there are leasehold flats in a multi-occupied building, the leases state what tenants cannot do and what they are obliged to do. There are provisions for raising money from them for annual repairs and maintenance and for any other service charges. In practice, the growth of such arrangements is leading to demands by leaseholders for some say in determining what is spent and how.

Tenants and self-management

There are other tenants' rights that could be granted. Security of tenure normally obtains in practice, but not as a right. More controversial is the right of self-management. Like repairs and maintenance, supervision and management are rapidly escalating items of cost. Both are labour-intensive. Councils that aim to be 'good' landlords feel the need to provide more supervisory and advisory services and for these to be decentralised. The cost must be met from subsidy or – as the general central government subsidy does not provide for this – from rents. Delegation of responsibilities to tenants, especially to committees on estates, should both increase tenant satisfaction and keep down costs by mobilising voluntary labour to provide supervision, management and advice. Those who believe in it argue it will mean more effective action to prevent vandalism, a better environment and more co-operation to help those in need. On the other hand, many tenants do not want it; and on occasion such management can be worse and more expensive because of dissension. But the economic arguments for considering such devolution of responsibility are very great and will increase.

An authority must stop short of full devolution of responsibility to tenants. It should expect any tenants' committee to keep careful accounts, obey any relevant contracts and behave democratically. It might also reasonably expect minimal standards of efficiency and reasonable cost control. American experience suggests that tenants' committees should not control access to public housing stock, as they will fill vacancies with kindred spirits. This sometimes leads to racial discrimination or discrimination against those in greatest housing need, or corruption where there is a housing shortage. A loss of political control over access could transform the nature and eventually the function of the public housing stock. If local authorities continue to allocate stock, there would remain a major difference between public rental and owner-occupied stock.

Tenants' rights in the private sector

Are there changes which would similarly improve consumer satisfaction and efficiency in the private rental sector? A possibility would be the extension of the tenants' charter so that private tenants could put their own money into repairs, maintenance or improvement, even where the landlord had no inducement to do or allow this. Virtually identical problems would have to be overcome. (1) Landlords could well have a right and duty to do basic maintenance to maintain the fabric and could be able to reflect the cost of doing this in the rent. (2) When a tenant left, a valuation might result in a tenant receiving a lump sum for betterment or paying for dilapidations. But there would be a problem if a poor landlord could not raise the money to pay for betterment; or even if he could, was unable to recoup it by raising the rent to the next tenant. One aspect of the difficulty could be met by the law on rent control expressly allowing landlords to recoup the cost of paying betterment to a leaving tenant by raising the rent to a new tenant. But a landlord could face a problem if he were unable to do this because there was not the demand for the improved property at a sufficient rent. Theoretically, it should not be a problem since the valuation of betterment figures should reflect the enhanced marketability of the property; but in practice a landlord could find he had paid out more than he could recoup over a reasonable time period. The only complete solution here would be if the risks in such cases could be underwritten by a local or some other body if the landlord could not take the risk, but it would have to reserve power of being able to let the property at the highest rent it could get, at least when any debt in relation to the improvement was unpaid; and there was a danger that the landlord was not securing the highest possible rent. (3) Very poor tenants could not be expected to maintain or improve their property, but they might become eligible for help to do this from the council or the Supplementary Benefits Commission. (4) A tenant here should have no greater difficulty in providing security for a loan than he would in the public sector. He might here also be eligible in some circumstances for a local authority loan or guarantee. (5) Many private landlords of blocks of flats are finding a need to come to terms with the desire for more tenant management.

Owner-occupation – the superior sector

If the direction of the changes suggested in the two rental tenures is to give occupants some of the freedoms of an owner-occupier, one alternative instrument is to encourage the sale of council houses in the public sector and comparable sales or municipalisation in the private rented sector. There would not necessarily be any inconsistency in encouraging those who can afford and wish to undertake the responsibilities of actual ownership to do so; while granting a tenants' charter to the rest. Such a charter would even benefit those who buy their public housing, since the value of property and the pleasantness of the environment depends on the standard to which their neighbours – many of whom will be tenants – maintain their property. Municipalisation is a change of ownership – that is, of landlord – not necessarily of occupation; and arguably a local authority tenant needs a tenants' charter as much as a private tenant does. At another level, there may still be a conflict between encouraging owner-occupation or municipalisation, and a tenants' charter. Some might oppose the charter because they believe tenants would be less likely to buy if they were free to maintain or improve as they please. At present, differences in the subsidy system for the tenures encourage the sale of council houses. If subsidy systems between tenures were harmonised – and here is a point where one cannot avoid a mention of the large issues of subsidy and equity – there should be no public finance reason for preferring sale to letting. While subsidy stays unharmonised one fears that one good – allowing tenants to buy their houses, will discourage some politicians from encouraging another – the introduction of more tenants' rights and duties in respect of their homes. Moreover, owner occupation can never be the solution for all local authority or private rental dwellings. As US and Australian experience has shown, there is both a poorer and also a more mobile population who must rent; as well as others who would prefer to rent rather than assume the burdens of ownership.

Are there corresponding problems in the owner-occupied sector soluble without fundamental reform of housing finance? A persistent problem is that of those without access to the sector because they cannot afford or for some other reason cannot get mortgages. While this could be remedied by larger subsidies in general or to marginal would-be owner-occupiers, another remedy would be to introduce more competition into the mortgage market. At present there are broadly two markets. There is the one operated by the building societies (and the insurance companies) which in general charges a single cartelised mortgage rate to all mortgagors it finds eligible. Then there is a second market of much higher interest rates for those unable to borrow from the building societies. In a competitive market, interest rates would vary with the risks presented by a particular borrower buying a particular dwelling. There would be low rates for those whose earnings expectations in relation to the value of the property seemed most secure and higher rates for those whose financial circumstances or dwelling presented the greater risks. The practical effect of ending the interest rate cartel would be that many more could and would get mortgages since even at higher interest rates, the benefits would outweigh the extra cost.

Though central government has at times tried to introduce more competitiveness into other parts of the financial system, it has not attempted this amongst the institutions providing housing finance. The Bank of England and the commercial banks are now more aware that the cartelised behaviour of the building society movement, responding slowly to changes in the money market, has a destabilising effect on the market and even indirectly on the balance of payments while, as they see it, providing unfair competition for the banks. To the building society movement itself the dangers entailed by growing central government interest, both economic and political, in the stability of the mortgage rate, are also evident. But the difficulty of introducing competition into a market which is so cartelised is also great, especially because of the long-run tendency for the mortgage market to be in disequilibrium: the demand for loans normally exceeds the supply so there are queues and managers ration mortgages. Because of this, it has proved difficult to persuade building societies to provide many low-start mortgages or to lend on much old dilapidated property (though on this last there has recently been some improvement). A local manager who must ration mortgages finds it commercially prudent to lend on the best properties to the most creditworthy clients. Yet the results are unfortunate. On the margin there are prospective buyers who are kept out of a market they could afford to be in; and in particular not only do they find it difficult to achieve home ownership, they are excluded from what is now the most important route to (subsidised) capital accumulation by the small saver.

Insurance and the lender

There is a relatively simple solution to the problem which would mean the least possible disruption to building societies. Mortgages would be issued still at one interest rate but purchasers would buy insurance to reflect their particular circumstances. Thus, to give the security a building society needs in a run-down inner-city area, a higher insurance premium would have to be paid. So might someone have to pay a high premium if, for example, their occupation meant their prospective earnings were particularly risky. To make this a meaningful concession, prospective mortgagors must be able to go to any reputable insurers of their choice and provided they pay the premium they must have a right to obtain a mortgage at the going interest rate. Most of the risks, in effect, would be transferred from the societies to the insurers. In order to prevent certain types of persons being subjected to what might seem unreasonably high premia, there could be an appeals procedure before which insurance companies might be expected to demonstrate that there was a sound actuarial basis for the premia they were charging; though if there were enough genuine competition, this should not be necessary. But this would be difficult to combine with a situation in which there was a permanent excess of demand over supply of funds. However, in a market where effective interest rates were so differentiated there would be less reason for building societies not lending to all borrowers whose demand was effective at the going interest-rate-plus-premium that was relevant for them. One would expect more lending for house purchase in aggregate as well as to the various kinds of persons now practically excluded from the system.

The supply of houses in the conurbations

Particularly in the conurbations, the supply of private housing might be constrained. One reason is that there are still councils reluctant to allow much private house-building – a difficult matter to resolve under the present planning law. A second applies especially in Central London where exceptionally high subsidies in the public sector make it difficult for the private sector to compete in buying land for house construction. The second could only be put right by changing the subsidy system, so as to make the public subsidy available in high-cost areas the same proportion of the value of the house as in the private sector.

There are often severe problems of access in conurbations because owner-occupation is likely to be a smaller proportion of the total and because the dying private rental sector, which is becoming almost closed to new entrants, is concentrated there.

But even when local authorities have vacant housing, some keep out classes of tenants who do not meet their criteria, not seeing it as their function to house the single, or the mobile, or those just released from a mental hospital or other institution who, in many cases, need support as well as housing. One could try to require local authorities to offer surplus property for rent to all in need.

Even without overall scarcity, there can be dissatisfaction because of immobility within the local authority sector. The location of jobs within the metropolis may alter, or particular workers may wish a change of job, but the sheer difficulty of effecting a housing transfer often means that people must travel further to work than they would choose. This will cause a reduction in their welfare and may encourage them to migrate from their conurbation. There seems no good reason why council tenants should not be free to exchange their homes with other tenants provided due compensation is paid as outlined above for any improvement or dilapidations. The council need have no right to prevent this as long as the new tenant could show he had paid his rent at his last address. Because tri-lateral or even more complicated exchanges might in the end produce the most satisfaction, Estate Agents might act as broker for these arrangements, as might local authorities.

What of the remaining areas where demand exceeds supply; or where as often happens there is a queue for homes even at the same time as there is a surplus of difficult-to-let property; or where the shortness of the housing waiting list is a consequence of the restrictiveness of the criteria for admission to it?

Ten to fifteen years ago preference was given on most local authority waiting lists to long-standing families of the neighbourhood with children. Then immigrants, and other new arrivals, single persons and childless couples who could not afford a mortgage, often found their homes in the private rented sector. Reaction built up against the poorest so often being housed in the worst and dearest housing conditions. Both Labour and Tory councils, particularly in the cities, were persuaded to alter their priorities and promote the homeless, the single parent families, the immigrant families and others in greatest housing need to the top of their housing lists. Though humane, it had some difficult consequences in many areas of scarcity. It has created concentrations of the economically inactive where traditional tenants were ageing and a high proportion of the adults in the new households for one reason or another were not in full-time employment. More important, the children of tenants who wanted to start a family and get a council dwelling found it more difficult to do so. The aspirations of their parents and indeed their own were different enough from those of earlier generations to make it less acceptable for them to spend the first years of marriage under their parents' roof. Many started their married life in the private rented sector but as entry to that has become more difficult more have migrated, especially from the conurbations, to areas where they could get council housing or private housing at prices they could afford. However, more recently because of the effects of this on the composition of an area and its political impact, some councils have been trying to alter their criteria to give such couples more weight; but to alter the point system does not in itself shorten the queue.

More recently, and especially since 1974, there are other groups who used to find poor and expensive homes in the private rental sector and whose housing needs are now pressing. Councils find it emotionally hard to give priority to such groups as long as there are families in 'genuine' housing need. Thus the problems of finding accommodation have increased for the single of all ages, including students, for the couples who have not and may never start families, for the mobile and those discharged from a variety of institutions. Where council housing is abundant such groups have sometimes been let in. But in many conurbations the areas where there is spare housing and the quality of that housing are often unattractive to people, many of whom are at a stage of life when they have their greatest purchasing power, or are highly dependent upon being in a good location to seek out job opportunities. There may also be economic consequences. It is difficult not to connect the shortage of secretaries and to some extent of nurses in London, at this stage of the recession, at least in part to the shortage of relevant housing, even when overall there may be a large enough housing stock.

The role of housing plans

Various attempts have been made to solve the problem through planning but often this merely dramatises the underlying differences in priorities. A succession of London housing plans has tried to locate substantial London overspill in the outer London Boroughs. By their actions and procrastination many boroughs have successfully avoided such overspill since it conflicted with their own priorities and plans. When the GLC was Labour controlled, it often countered with a demand that it should be given power to override the boroughs; or that a strategic housing authority should be set up able to impose its will; or that central government should do this. So far and despite repeated attempts it has proved almost impossible to force unwanted housing on resistant boroughs; and at present the GLC has more or less given up the attempt, divesting itself of its real powers in housing. In Scotland similar conflicts of view have arisen between regional and district housing planners, where, for example, Strathclyde is anxious to retain housing in central Glasgow and the outer districts believe – in their judgement realistically – that the demand for it will migrate out to them. As so often in such situations many of the disputes appear to be over forecasting, but may be difficult to disentangle from the different political aspirations of the various authorities. It is a common experience that the sum of the populations each hopes for is substantially in excess of the Registrar General's expectations for the whole area. Planning on such a basis of course would mean a substantial surplus of housing.

The new housing plans in Scotland and in England are meant to serve many purposes. One is to encourage local authorities to consider the total housing needs in their areas irrespective of whether they are to be served by public or private housing; and to plan the public sector contribution in the light of all those needs. A second implies the construction of careful forecasts which in the past has only been attempted in any detail by a relatively small number of authorities. Such an effort to think comprehensively about housing must make for more thoughtful planning and policy-making; but it is already clear that, in general, many local authorities have exaggerated beliefs in the growth prospects for their populations. Moreover, there can be strong differences of opinion over the extent that local authorities are planning satisfactorily for the needs of certain groups – particularly those for whom the sector has not provided traditionally but who cannot now easily get into either the rented or privately owned sector. In short, the production of more housing plans by various tiers of government may expose differences in policy though often they can be obscured by disagreements which are apparently technical. What planning cannot do is to make sure that housing is provided for all in need where there are different social and political priorities; and where increasingly a large proportion of new households – those who cannot own – are in the hands of one monopoly provider, the local authority.

New providers of housing

If planning in itself is no solution, another remedy is to increase the number of providers of rented accommodation. The two major initiatives have been those of the Housing Corporation and, in Scotland, of the Scottish Special Housing Association as well. Their activities have been growing rapidly. To satisfy those who find access to local authority housing difficult, ideally one might hope they would provide access to housing for the mobile and for those who are not given priority by local authorities. In effect, they would be providing a 'market' by seeking out tenants the local authorities do not want. Ideally one might hope for a very large number of independent housing associations, each catering for some special client groups and doing their best to make available such housing wherever it is needed.

But this presents two kinds of difficulty. The first is that many housing associations themselves started with the idea they were catering for the most deprived; and are often reluctant to alter their market when the local authority effort is diverted to the same priorities. The second is that many local authorities resent housing associations pursuing different priorities from their own; and, most unfortunately, this has led to a common policy of requiring housing associations to accept nominations for their stock which at its worst can mean that their priorities remain those of the local authorities and they are not providing for those the local authorities are not interested in. As the private rental sector declines, such a policy is bound to be almost disastrous if it means that there continue to be groups that are insufficiently provided for.

But there remains a problem in determining the accountability of housing associations. If they are seen as the creatures of central government, they will be resented by local government. If they are independent, to whom are they responsible? A more difficult alternative would be to revive the private rental market, but there would seem to be two pre-conditions for this. The first is that there would have to be some landlords' register or other safeguard to protect tenants from Rachmanism and the other evils of landlordism which have been resented more in Britain than possibly in any other nation – so that landlords would be 'sanitised' as the jargon puts it. The second is that they would require subsidies as good as those received by the housing associations if they are to be financially viable and be able to maintain their property in good condition. It would be far easier to imagine a viable and competitive market in which public and private agencies were providing subsidised housing if subsidies were paid to individuals who were then free to spend it on the housing they chose and which they could afford. But that would require a revolution in housing finance.

One fears the housing market will continue more or less as at present. Anomalies in provision and access will persist in various forms in different places. They will alter their character slightly when parties change nationally or locally. But there will always be a sizeable minority for whom rented housing is not available, with a distorting effect on the composition of the local population and on employment. Moreover, the most likely way of easing the pressure could be the provision of ever more public sector housing to the point where councils feel forced to open it to everyone. One fears the solution of the housing problem in many areas will only occur when there is vacant housing which cannot be filled; and that of course is only to create another problem. In that prospect there will be areas of dereliction and abandonment which in some neighbourhoods could have a snowball effect as it has had in some parts of New York, in encouraging out-migration.

Unless we have confidence in the ability of local authorities to plan the housing of all those not able to afford owner-occupation, the chances are sooner or later that we will be driven to find ways of subsidising other landlords to compete where local authorities are reluctant; and this will mean eventually at least some harmonisation of the subsidy system or, to be more efficient, the replacement of subsidies to providers of housing by subsidies to consumers – that is, a form of universal housing allowance. But the extra cost of that could be so great that one could be forced back to the economist's natural starting-point of raising the price of housing by reducing the subsidy as housing deficits disappear.

In the nineteenth century, and indeed until some 20 years or so ago, the arguments for heavy subsidisation of housing were evident. The affluent stood to gain from it. Slums bred epidemics and fire hazards which reached beyond the slums. To put this right required improvement of housing and a reduction in densities which would raise both housing and commuting costs for many beyond what they could afford. Moreover, bad housing and a slum environment stunted the growth of the young. That was not in the interests of industry or of defence; and was objectionable to many on humanitarian grounds. Further, the subsidisation of public housing when that began to be built in substantial quantities after the First World War could be defended on the grounds that it was housing for the poorest, though not all the poor were in it. Now the sector contains many other than the poorest. The minimum standard of housing in Britain is high by the standards of comparable countries abroad, while the proportion of income that goes in rent or mortgage payments is comparatively low. As is well known, the subsidisation of the owner-occupier sector through mortgage relief was never planned as a housing subsidy though the progressive elimination of other personal interest relief has now made it such. The question remains: how can one now justify such a high level of general housing subsidy to most households of all income levels, especially when an effect of it may be that the sheer magnitude of public money going to housing makes it difficult to find funds to house those still in real need, and drains funds from the social services where arguably the needs are greater?

References

Department of the Environment (1977) Housing Policy. Technical volume Part 1, pp. 1, 8, 76, 147, 156.

Chapter 7

Transport in the conurbations

The pattern of transport in the British conurbations, as in any geographical area, depends fundamentally on two factors. First, the distribution of people and of their activities – economic, social, cultural – which gives rise to the demand for transport, whether of people or of goods. Second, the available means of transportation – which incorporate both the fixed infrastructure, in the form of rail and roadbeds, and the available stock of vehicles to run on them.

Spatial structure and its effects

Superficially homogenised by the Census classification, the British conurbations have in fact very different spatial structures (Freeman, 1951; Hall, 1970). Greater London has least claim of the seven British conurbations to that title – at least as Geddes (1915) originally coined it: it grew outwards in roughly concentric rings, in the process swallowing villages and small market towns which however were in no sense equal to it. Central Clydeside comes perhaps closest to London in this category, though some of the towns enveloped in the growth of Glasgow – Paisley, Greenock – were stronger and more independent than Croydon or Ilford or Ealing. Liverpool too grew in concentric fashion, though necessarily as a hemisphere rather than a circle; and if the accident of the estuary is ignored there is indeed a roughly circular pattern. But the West Midlands, South East Lancashire, Tyneside and West Yorkshire all represent literal con-urbations – the last to such a degree that the Census does not recognise a centre.

These differences partly arose because of varied economic structures. London's concentric growth represents the dominance of its double-barrelled (City of London/City of Westminster) commercial and governing core. Other conurbations (Merseyside, South East Lancashire) also had important commercial functions, but never on London's national and international scale. Others (in particular the West Midlands, West Yorkshire, Tyneside) were based far more on manufacturing industry than on service industry. As already explained in Chapters 2 and 3, in comparison with Greater London no other conurbation has as high a proportion of its total workforce employed in service industry or in white-collar occupations. Thus all the other conurbations have far smaller central concentrations, in relation to their total employment, than does London. These areas (and indeed also London) are typified by an inner belt of employment in small factories and workshops and warehouses (and also in a variety of employments such as gas, electricity and water, and in transport) and outer concentrations of manufacturing developed generally in the period between the two world wars, and usually on a larger scale than the typical Victorian-era industry. Thus (Table 7.1) over 32 per cent of Greater London's workers found employment (in 1971) in the officially-defined central area; in no other conurbation did the proportion exceed 20 per cent, in the West Midlands it was less than 10 per cent, and the average for six conurbations (West Yorkshire excepted) was just over 20 per cent. Thus, while London is a strong-centre conurbation in Michael Thomson's terminology (Thomson 1977), the others are not.

The conurbation central areas were defined on the basis of fairly careful survey, albeit as long ago as the 1950s. In contrast the distinction between central city and conurbation remainder is an arbitrary one, as has recently been emphasised by researchers who have developed standard metropolitan area concepts (Hall et al. 1973; Department of the Environment, 1976; Hall and Hay, 1980). But to some extent the variations here do represent the realities of spatial structure (Table 7.1). Thus Merseyside and Clydeside do have higher proportions of people and employment in their central cities because these cities still dominate somewhat centralised conurbations; South East Lancashire and Tyneside stand out in contrast as very decentralised, with strong competing towns in the conurbation remainders; West Yorkshire is distinguished by extremely low densities both in its central cities and its remainders; London has an exceptionally high density of both people and jobs in its 'central city' (defined as the 14 so-called A Boroughs); overall, densities of population in central cities are nearly three times as high as in remainders, and densities of employment four times as great; overall, again, three in five of the people of the conurbations live outside central cities while just over one in two work in them; and – most striking imbalance – over 20 per cent work in the conurbation central areas though only just over 1 per cent live in these areas. Thus the daily movement in the British conurbations is still dominantly inward in the morning, outward at night.

Aggregate Census data thus give a convenient cartoon sketch of differences between the conurbations. For a closer look, it is possible to plot small zone data for population and employment, not available from the Census, from conurbation transportation studies made during the period 1960–65. Immediately evident (Fig. 7.1) is that London has far steeper gradients both for population and for employment than South East Lancashire or the West Midlands; this reflects the high densities of both residences and jobs in the innermost part of London,

Table 7.1. Resident and working populations, 1971

	Resident population			Working population		
		per ha	% total		per ha	% total
1. *Greater London*	*7,452,346*	*47.2*	*100.0*	*3,815,780*	*24.2*	*100.0*
Conurbation centre	230,008	100.0	3.6	1,241,000	460.1	32.5
Core cities	3,051,935	95.2	41.0	2,209,420	68.9	57.9
Remainder	4,400,411	35.0	59.0	1,606,360	12.8	42.1
2. *West Midlands*	*2,371,565*	*35.0*	*100.0*	*1,147,720*	*16.9*	*100.0*
Conurbation centre	5,768	14.5	0.2	103,910	261.1	9.1
Core city	1,014,670	48.6	42.8	565,140	27.1	49.2
Remainder	1,356,895	28.9	57.2	582,580	12.4	50.8
3. *S. E. Lancs.*	*2,392,993*	*24.3*	*100.0*	*1,066,180*	*10.8*	*100.0*
Conurbation centre	2,145	6.8	0.1	122,690	387.0	11.5
Core city	543,650	49.3	22.7	321,480	29.1	30.2
Remainder	1,849,343	21.2	77.3	744,700	8.5	69.8
4. *Merseyside*	*1,266,723*	*32.1*	*100.0*	*535,150*	*13.6*	*100.0*
Conurbation centre	6,525	17.2	0.3	91,540	240.9	17.1
Core city	610,113	54.2	48.2	312,310	27.8	58.4
Remainder	656,610	23.3	51.8	222,840	7.9	41.6
5. *West Yorkshire*	*1,728,251*	*13.8*	*100.0*	*777,810*	*6.2*	*100.0*
Conurbation centre	—	—	—	—	—	—
Core cities	790,186	29.5	45.7	384,920	14.4	49.5
Remainder	938,065	9.6	54.3	392,890	4.0	50.5

Table 7.1. Resident and working populations, 1971

	Resident population			Working population		
		per ha	% total		per ha	% total
6. Tyneside	805,434	34.3	100.0	363,420	15.5	100.0
Conurbation centre	2,774	7.0	0.3	66,710	167.2	18.4
Core city	222,709	49.6	27.7	148,020	33.0	40.7
Remainder	582,725	30.7	72.3	215,400	11.4	59.3
7. Central Clydeside	1,727,625	22.2	100.0	716,280	9.2	100.0
Conurbation centre	6,931	34.8	0.4	110,860	557.1	15.5
Core city	897,483	57.3	51.9	414,020	26.4	57.8
Remainder	830,142	13.4	48.1	302,260	4.9	42.2
All 7 Conurbations	17,744,937	30.1	100.0	8,422,340	15.3	100.0
Conurbation centre (6)	254,151	57.9	1.4	1,736,710	395.6	20.6
Core cities	7,130,746	58.4	40.2	4,355,310	35.7	51.7
Remainders	10,614,191	22.7	59.8	4,067,030	8.7	48.3
Great Britain	53,978,538	2.4	—	22,333,460	1.0	—

Source: Census, England and Wales, Scotland, 1971, Workplace Tables.

so that one-fifth of total employment occurs in areas with 150,000 or more workers per square mile (58,000/km²). The population density gradients are less steep than those for employment, though again London's is far steeper than the other two. The conclusion must be that London has a far higher degree of central attraction, both for employment and for residents, than the other two conurbations.

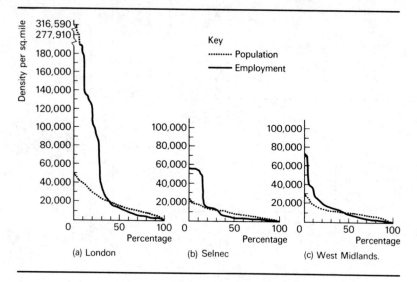

Fig. 7.1. Population and employment densities ca. 1965.

As already remarked in Chapter 3, however, centrality of employment in the conurbations is everywhere weakening (Table 7.2). Between 1961 and 1971 the seven conurbations lost jobs at over three times the rate of the national economy. The loss in the core cities was even greater, over four times the national average, and the conurbation central areas shed employment at almost the same rate. The overall loss was most drastic in London and in South East Lancashire; it was far less evident in the West Midlands, West Yorkshire or Tyneside. But the central city loss – and thus the rate of overall internal decentralisation of employment – was highest in South East Lancashire and Merseyside. Here Manchester lost close on 107,000 jobs in a decade: Merseyside over 88,000. Yet in absolute terms the decline in employment in London's A Boroughs – no less than 494,000 – represented more than half the total central city loss, and indeed more than 42 per cent of the total conurbation losses. Overall, the central cities contained over 55 per cent of conurbation jobs in 1961, less than 52 per cent a decade later (Table 7.3.). The shift was especially dramatic in South East Lancashire (35 to 30%) and on Merseyside (66 to 58%), on Tyneside (46 to 41%) and on Clydeside (62 to 58%). Merseyside also suffered a dramatic loss in central area employment – from 27 to 17 per cent in a single decade.

All this means that – for work journeys and also for shopping, entertainment and other journeys – centrifugal forces have been weakening. Jobs have been leaving the central areas and the inner cities; in the

Table 7.2 Employment changes, 1961–1971

	1961	**1971**	**Change**	**%**
Greater London	4,487,830	3,815,780	−672,050	−15.0
Conurbation centre	1,414,730	1,241,000	−173,730	−12.3
Core cities	2,703,790	2,209,420	−494,370	−18.3
Remainder	1,784,040	1,606,360	−177,680	−10.0
West Midlands	1,223,010	1,147,720	− 75,290	− 6.2
Conurbation centre	120,930	103,910	− 17,020	−14.1
Core city	655,080	565,140	− 89,940	−13.7
Remainder	567,930	523,580	+ 14,650	+ 2.6
S. E. Lancashire	1,223,750	1,066,180	−157,570	−12.9
Conurbation centre	157,290	122,690	− 34,600	−22.0
Core city	428,150	321,480	−106,670	−24.9
Remainder	795,600	744,700	− 50,900	− 6.4
Merseyside	607,700	535,150	− 72,600	−11.9
Conurbation centre	167,140	91,540	− 75,600	−45.2
Core city	400,880	312,310	− 88,570	−22.1
Remainder	206,820	222,840	+ 16,020	+ 7.7
West Yorkshire	856,530	777,810	− 78,820	− 9.2
Core cities	438,180	384,920	− 53,260	−12.2
Remainder	418,450	392,890	− 25,560	− 6.1
Tyneside	386,050	363,420	− 22,630	− 5.9
Conurbation centre	78,330	66,710	− 11,620	−14.8
Core cities	178,710	148,020	− 30,690	−17.2
Remainder	207,340	215,400	+ 8,060	+ 3.9
Central Clydeside	807,310	716,280	− 91,030	−11.9
Conurbation centre	139,300	110,860	− 28,440	−20.4
Core city	502,420	414,020	− 88,400	−17.6
Remainder	304,890	302,260	− 2,630	− 0.9
All 7 Conurbations	9,592,280	8,422,340	−1,169,940	−12.2
Conurbation centres (6)	2,007,720	1,736,710	−341,010	−16.4
Core cities	5,307,210	4,355,310	−951,900	−17.9
Remainders	4,285,070	4,067,030	−218,040	− 5.1
Great Britain	23,271,810	22,333,460	−938,350	− 4.0

Source: Census, England and Wales, Scotland, 1961, 1971, Workplace Tables.

Table 7.3 Distribution of employment 1961, 1971

| | Percentage of total employment | | | | | |
| | 1961 | | | 1971 | | |
	Centre	Core city/ies	Remainder	Centre	Core city/ies	Remainder
Greater London	31.5	60.2	39.8	32.5	57.9	42.1
West Midlands	9.9	53.6	46.4	9.1	49.2	50.8
S. E. Lancashire	12.9	35.0	65.0	11.5	30.2	69.8
Merseyside	27.5	66.0	34.0	17.1	58.4	41.6
West Yorkshire	–	51.2	48.8	–	49.5	50.5
Tyneside	20.3	46.3	53.7	18.4	40.7	59.3
Central Clydeside	17.3	62.2	37.8	15.5	57.8	42.2
All 7 Conurbations	21.7*	55.3	44.7	20.6*	51.7	48.3

*Excluding West Yorkshire.

Source: Census, England and Wales, Scotland, 1961, 1971, Workplace Tables.

conurbation remainders they have sometimes grown, sometimes shown a modest decline (Table 7.2.). While Liverpool lost nearly 89,000 jobs during the 1960s, the remainder of the conurbation gained 16,000 overall. While Newcastle lost 31,000 jobs, the rest of Tyneside gained 8,000. While Glasgow lost 88,000, the rest of Clydeside gained 2,600. This means that fewer journeys have been bound for the centre, more for the suburbs.

Infrastructure and vehicle stock

The conurbations also differ somewhat in the transport facilities they provide to their residents. In terms of fixed infrastructure, the road system is perhaps the most uniform as between one conurbation and another. After all, all of them have belonged to a single nation state, with considerable centralised uniformity of spending and administration, since 1707; and even before that, there has been considerable cultural homogeneity. South of Hadrian's Wall in some conurbations – notably London – the Roman roads provide an important part of the modern primary road network; medieval trade routes, upgraded and widened as appropriate, provide another; eighteenth-century turnpikes, swallowed up in the urban growth they helped promote, yet another. Most major cities embarked on ambitious schemes of central-area reconstruction towards the end of the nineteenth century, producing whole new streets which today form a vital part of central area circulation; thus Charing Cross Road, Shaftesbury Avenue and Kingsway in London, Corporation Street and New Street in Birmingham. In some areas developed for upper-middle-class occupancy – the

West Ends of London and Glasgow – the road system has a notable straightness and regularity missing from less socially prestigious areas. The twentieth century saw some stretches of bypass and arterial ring road constructed between the wars, together with new roads serving the peripheral municipal housing estates (Princess Road and Parkway in Manchester, Tyburn Road in Birmingham, Queen's Drive in Liverpool) and varying amounts of urban motorway in the period after 1960. By the late 1970s most British conurbations have at any rate partial ring motorways, which pass generally through the green belts that surround them, but which occasionally invade the built-up area (as the M63 in the Greater Manchester conurbation); in the West Midlands two national motorways, the M5 and M6, slice through the heart of the conurbation, as does the M8 soon to be linked up through the very centre of Glasgow. Only in Birmingham, Leeds and Glasgow does the national motorway system give direct access to the heart of the city, though in Newcastle it comes close to it.

The seven conurbations differ far more in their rail systems. All of them are of course served by rail, and all indeed form nodes of British Rail's inter-city system. But what differs is the extent of the suburban rail system. Here London is unique in its dense network of commuter lines, many of them developed specifically for this purpose as a vital agent in the outward spread of London, and supplemented by London Transport's underground system (Hall, 1964; White, 1965; Barker and Robbins, 1969, 1974). Indeed, in the area within 15 miles (24 km) of the centre of London, there are very few areas farther than fifteen minutes from a rail station. Elsewhere it is very different. Liverpool, Manchester, Newcastle and Glasgow have systems either specifically built for commuter traffic, or converted through electrification for the purpose: the Mersey Railway lines and the Ormskirk–Southport system in Liverpool, the Bury and Altrincham lines in Manchester, the North and South Tyne lines in Newcastle, and the Queen Street system in Glasgow. The Mersey Railway and the Glasgow underground were both Victorian underground lines, actually built some years before the bulk of London's tubes. But in none of these cities does the rail system provide the backbone of public transport as it does in central London. Rather – at any rate down to the present – it has provided a rather special supplementary system, serving one or two favoured radial directions with a longer-distance commuter service that takes middle-class white-collar commuters to favoured suburban areas such as the Wirral peninsula, or the north Cheshire suburbs of Manchester, or Bearsden and Milngavie to the north-west of Glasgow. Recent developments in the rail system are treated at the end of this chapter.

All the conurbations developed extensive public-transport systems from the last quarter of the nineteenth century onward. First based on the horse tram and bus, then on the electric tram, then on the motor bus, they were essentially road-based. Though private enterprise started some of these systems, by the First World War most were municipalised. The exception was London, where the bus system was controlled by a private company which eventually took over the underground rail system, but which competed with a large number of smaller operators. In London too, the trams were run by a mixture of municipal and private enterprise. This system was rationalised finally in 1933 by the creation of London Transport, an early model for nationalisation elsewhere. In many cities – Birmingham, Liverpool, Manchester, Leeds – the city authorities extended their tram systems into open countryside in the 1920s and 1930s, simultaneously developing large new housing estates and even satellite towns. But from 1927 the tramway mileage diminished year by year, and rapidly after the Second World War the bus replaced the tramcar as the standard means of public transport in the conurbations. What remained was the tradition of a dense, frequent and remarkably cheap public transport system, in which cross-subsidisation might be used to encourage decentralisation to more distant housing areas on the periphery of the conurbation. That was possible so long as the majority of travellers were captive to the buses – that is, roughly down to the present time.

For, as Table 2.22 shows, the British conurbations in the late twentieth century are very far from the age of universal private mobility that has long been predicted. Over all, at the 1971 Census, over 57 per cent of households there – as against 49 per cent in the country as a whole – did not own a car. This proportion was lowest, 51 per cent, in the West Midlands – Britain's Detroit – and, at just under 54 per cent, in Greater London. But it rose to 58 per cent in Greater Manchester, to 59 per cent in Merseyside, to close on 60 per cent in West Yorkshire, to 66 per cent on Tyneside and to 67 per cent in Central Clydeside. Even these figures conceal the true lack of cars in the conurbation central cities – where over-all two-thirds of households owned no car, the proportions ranging from just under 58 per cent in Birmingham to no less than 76 per cent in Glasgow. Outside these central cities, in the more suburbanised conurbation remainders, levels of car ownership were higher. But even here almost exactly half of all households lacked a car, and in all but London and the West Midlands the figure was well over half.

Even these figures do not tell the full story. For, as Mayer Hillman and his colleagues have reminded us, household car ownership is a very different thing from personal car availability. One of Hillman's studies, in 1971, looked at five representative contrasted areas ranging from rural, through suburban and new town, to inner urban. He found that in a typical ward of an inner London borough – 'Lonborough' – 57 per cent of respondents lived in households with no cars, as against only 41 per cent in all five study areas. But no less than 66 per cent of adults surveyed in Lonborough, as against 51 per cent in all five areas, had no driving licence (Table 7.4). When licence holdership was compared with car ownership, then only 26 per cent of Lonborough respondents (against 40% generally) both had licences and lived in car-owning households. A further 16 per cent (against 19%) had no licence though the household had a car. Altogether no less than 53 per cent of respondents in London, against 36 per cent in all five areas, had the lowest level of personal mobility: they had neither a licence nor a car in their household (Hillman, Henderson and Whalley, 1973, 1976). But this proportion was much higher for women (61 per cent in inner London) than for men (44%); and it was highest of all for old age pensioners, 91 per cent of whom in inner London had no licence and no car in the household.

Table 7.4 Car availability, 1971

	'Lonborough'	5 study areas
1. Car ownership		
No. of cars in household:	(%)	(%)
0	57	41
1	38	51
2 or more	5	8
Total	100	100
2. Licence-holding		
Adult has:	(%)	(%)
No driving licence	66	51
Provisional licence	3	4
Full licence	31	44
Total	100	100
3. Level of car access		
Respondent is:	(%)	(%)
Licence-holder in Car-owning household (Level 1)	26	40
Non-licence-holder in car-owning household (level 2)	16	19
Licence-holding in non-car-owning household (Level 3)	5	6
Non-licence-holder in non-car-owning household (Level 4)	53	36
Total	100	100

Source: Hillman *et al.*, 1973, 1976.

Car availability reflects both income and household structure. Income is the more important; it provides the main explanation why so few pensioners own cars, and also why fewer cars are owned or available in conurbation central cities. Density, already considered, is also closely (though inversely) related to income and car ownership. But household structure and life cycle are also important in explaining why, in a given household, a wife is less likely to hold a licence than her husband. Life cycle also provides part of the explanation for the low car availability of pensioners, since many of them reached maturity in decades when car ownership was the privilege of a small minority and when urban bus services were exceptionally well-developed and cheap; they simply never acquired the habit.

The pattern of journeys to work

In summary, then, the British conurbations are characterised by a variable but generally rather weak concentration of employment (except for London), and an even stronger dispersal of residential population; their typical citizen lives and works outside their central areas, and indeed lives outside their central cities. They are also characterised by rather low rates of car ownership: the same typical citizen, in the early 1970s, was more likely to belong to a household with no car than to a household with one, and even if the household did have a car he (or particularly she) might well not hold a driving licence, so that in all perhaps 60 per cent or more of conurbation adults had no immediate access to a car. In central cities, of course, the lack of access to a car was likely to be even more extreme.

The pattern of journeys to work is a response to these facts of life. As Table 7.5 shows, in 1971 only a small minority of work journeys were made into conurbation central areas. In London they amounted to over 30 per cent of the total, with most of these coming from the remainder of the 'central city' (the fourteen A boroughs) or the remainder of the conurbation, but with 6 per cent coming from further afield – that is, generally 15 miles each way. Elsewhere central journeys were less than 20 per cent of the total, and journeys to the centre from beyond the conurbation limits were never more than 5 per cent. Everywhere, including London, the biggest categories of journey were either wholly within the central city or wholly within the remainder of the conurbation (that is, the suburbs). In London these two categories totalled 52 per cent of all journeys, in the West Midlands 73 per cent, in South East Lancashire 72 per cent, on Merseyside 61 per cent, on Tyneside 58 per cent, and on Clydeside 64 per cent. In every area, the suburb-to-suburb journey is the most important single category, ranging from 32 per cent of the total in Clydeside to 60 per cent in South East Lancashire. Of course these figures partly reflect arbitrary definitions, but they also suggest that for the average conurbation dweller, the work journey may be relatively short.

The Census does not give information on actual journey length, either in terms of distance or in terms of time. But this may be gauged from National Travel Survey data. In 1975–6, 25 per cent of all journeys in London and 31 per cent of all work journeys in provincial conurbations were of less than 15 minutes duration; in all, 56 per cent in London, and 70 per cent in the provincial conurbations, were of less than 30 minutes duration. Even in London only 24 per cent of work journeys took 45 minutes or more; in the provinces the figure was as low as 10 per cent. The notion of the typical conurbation resident as a long-distance commuter is thus a myth (Department of Transport, 1978, p. 19).

The mode of travel used for the work journey shows significant differences, which again depend on socio-economic factors and on spatial structure (Table 7.6). Broadly, modes can be grouped into three main types: public transport, private motor transport and other modes (bicycle, walking and miscellaneous). The table shows that, over all in the conurbations, in 1971 public transport took 46 per cent of all work journeys, private motor transport another 31 per cent and other modes over 23 per cent. In practice each of these main groups is dominated by one mode: buses and private cars each carry nearly 30 per cent of all conurbation work trips, while walking accounts for 17 per cent. As compared with the country as a whole, people in the conurbations make much more use of public transport and decidedly less use either of private motor transport or of other modes. Particularly notable is the use of rail: it comes close on 15 per cent of all conurbation work journeys, against just over 6 per cent in the country as a whole.

However, these averages conceal important differences, both between and within conurbations. Public transport is much more important in central cities than in suburban remainders, and it is overwhelmingly important for journeys to conurbation centres where it accounts for more than three-quarters of all journeys. In the suburbs cars account for more than one-third of work journeys, while in central cities public transport carries nearly three in five. Rail, insignificant for journeys to suburban jobs, accounts for close on half all journeys to central area ones. However, this last figure is distorted by the size of London's central employment mass; here trains carry close on 63 per cent of all workers, and public transport as a whole nearly 80 per cent. In the other conurbation centres, the share of rail ranges from 21 per cent in Glasgow to a mere 8 per cent in Birmingham. Thus these centres are all bus-dominated, with between 40 and 55 per cent travelling by this mode. The centres outside London also manage to accommodate a much higher proportion of car commuters than does London: between 17 and 32 per cent, against 12 per cent. And this difference persists for the inner areas as a whole. Inner London's workers come overwhelmingly by public transport, with more than 41 per cent on rail and 19 per cent on the buses. Only Glasgow, with its extremely low car ownership, compares with these figures; elsewhere between 44 and 55 per cent come by public transport and between 40 and 50 per cent by bus. Over all, though the importance of rail to London's centre reflects the size and density of the employment mass there, public transport usage in the conurbations seems to have little relationship to their size – a point confirmed by White (1974).

Table 7.5 Journey-to-Work, 1971

| | Total Work force | Travelling from | | | | | | | |
| | | Conurbation centre | | Remainder central city | | Remainder conurbation | | Outside conurbation | |
	(000's)	(000's)	(%)	(000's)	(%)	(000's)	(%)	(000's)	(%)
Greater London	4,079.3								
Conurbation centre	1,250.0	97.6	2.4	473.1	11.5	418.7	10.3	260.6	6.4
Remainder central city	1,081.5	13.8	0.3	752.4	18.4	247.9	6.1	67.5	1.7
Remainder conurbation	1,747.8	3.7	0.1	145.2	3.6	1,388.1	34.0	210.7	5.2
West Midlands	1,197.6								
Conurbation centre	104.0	1.5	0.1	63.5	5.3	23.8	2.0	15.1	1.3
Remainder central city	482.3	1.0	0.1	357.1	29.8	71.1	5.9	53.1	4.4
Remainder conurbation	611.3	0.1	0.0	34.8	2.9	523.5	43.7	52.9	4.4
S. E. Lancashire	1,122.7								
Conurbation centre	122.8	0.6	0.1	46.1	4.1	64.0	5.7	12.1	1.1
Remainder central city	212.6	0.1	0.0	131.7	11.7	71.1	6.3	9.7	0.9
Remainder conurbation	787.3	0.1	0.0	49.9	4.4	676.5	60.3	60.8	5.4
Merseyside	561.7								
Conurbation centre	91.7	1.1	0.2	44.8	8.0	28.4	5.0	17.3	3.1
Remainder central city	233.2	0.8	0.1	159.0	28.3	35.4	6.4	37.6	6.7
Remainder conurbation	236.8	0.2	0.0	20.4	3.6	186.6	33.2	29.6	5.3

Table 7.5 Journey-to-Work, 1971

	Total Work force	Travelling from							
		Conurbation centre		Remainder central city		Remainder Conurbation		Outside conurbation	
	(000's)	(000's)	(%)	(000's)	(%)	(000's)	(%)	(000's)	(%)
West Yorks	801.7								
Central cities	400.7	—	—	310.0	38.1	61.5	7.6	29.2	3.6
Remainder conurbation	410.0	—	—	31.3	3.9	350.5	43.2	28.3	3.5
Tyneside	378.5								
Conurbation centre	66.8	0.7	0.2	23.9	6.3	26.3	6.9	15.9	4.2
Remainder central city	85.8	0.2	0.1	45.1	11.9	27.7	7.3	12.8	3.4
Remainder conurbation	225.9	0.1	0.0	17.4	4.6	173.0	45.7	35.4	9.4
Central Clydeside	740.1								
Conurbation centre	111.0	1.2	0.2	70.4	9.6	28.2	3.8	10.8	1.5
Remainder central city	315.4	1.1	0.1	236.4	31.9	57.3	7.7	20.6	2.8
Remainder conurbation	313.7	0.2	0.0	42.7	5.8	237.5	32.1	33.3	4.5

Source: Census 1971, England and Wales, Scotland, Workplace Tables.

Note: Totals do not agree with those in earlier tables, since they include persons failing to answer the Census question or answering 'no fixed place'; all these are treated as working at place of residence.

Table 7.6 Travel-to-work mode, 1971

	Total		Public transport				Private motor transport			Other modes			
	No.	(%)	Total (%)	Train (%)	Bus (%)	Other (%)	Total (%)	Car (%)	M/c (%)	Total (%)	Bike (%)	Walk/none (%)	Other n.s. (%)
Greater London	4,079,280	*100*	*49.8*	*27.8*	*20.5*	*1.5*	*28.5*	*27.4*	*1.1*	*21.7*	*2.0*	*15.2*	*4.5*
Centre	1,250,030	100	79.4	62.9	15.2	1.3	12.7	12.0	0.7	7.8	0.5	5.4	1.9
Core burghs	2,331,530	100	62.5	41.6	19.3	1.6	19.8	19.0	0.8	17.6	1.0	12.5	4.1
Remainder	1,747,750	100	33.0	9.4	22.2	1.4	40.0	38.6	1.4	27.1	3.3	18.7	5.1
West Midlands	1,197,560	*100*	*35.9*	*1.5*	*33.3*	*1.1*	*38.4*	*37.4*	*1.0*	*25.7*	*2.5*	*18.6*	*4.6*
Centre	103,990	100	60.7	8.0	50.7	2.0	33.2	32.5	0.7	6.1	0.3	4.5	1.3
Core city	586,310	100	44.0	2.4	40.1	1.5	36.9	36.0	0.9	19.2	1.2	13.7	4.3
Remainder	611,250	100	28.2	0.7	26.7	0.8	40.1	38.9	1.2	31.8	3.7	23.2	4.9
South East Lancs.	1,122,640	*100*	*40.0*	*3.4*	*35.4*	*1.2*	*32.9*	*32.1*	*0.8*	*27.2*	*2.0*	*20.1*	*5.1*
Centre	122,780	100	65.1	14.2	49.3	1.6	29.9	29.4	0.5	4.9	0.6	3.3	1.0
Core city	335,360	100	50.2	7.4	41.4	1.4	31.5	30.9	0.6	18.3	1.6	12.8	3.9
Remainder	787,280	100	35.5	1.6	32.8	1.1	33.5	32.6	0.9	31.0	2.2	23.2	5.6
Merseyside	561,680	*100*	*44.1*	*5.9*	*36.9*	*1.3*	*33.1*	*32.1*	*1.0*	*22.8*	*2.4*	*16.0*	*4.4*
Centre	91,680	100	65.1	16.5	47.2	1.4	27.1	26.5	0.6	7.7	0.7	5.1	1.9
Core city	324,840	100	52.4	7.5	43.4	1.5	28.5	27.7	0.8	19.1	1.4	14.1	3.6
Remainder	236,840	100	33.0	3.8	28.1	1.1	39.4	38.1	1.3	27.7	3.7	18.6	5.4
West Yorkshire	810,750	*100*	*42.5*	*1.0*	*40.3*	*1.2*	*32.0*	*31.1*	*0.9*	*25.6*	*0.8*	*20.0*	*4.8*
Core city	400,730	100	48.7	1.5	45.8	1.4	31.0	30.3	0.7	20.2	0.6	15.3	4.3
Remainder	410,020	100	36.4	0.4	35.0	1.0	33.0	31.8	1.2	40.7	11.0	24.4	5.3

Table 7.6 Travel-to-work mode, 1971

	Total		Public transport				Private motor transport			Other modes			
	No.	(%)	Total (%)	Train (%)	Bus (%)	Other (%)	Total (%)	Car (%)	M/c (%)	Total (%)	Bike (%)	Walk/none (%)	Other n.s. (%)
Tyneside	*378,540*	*100*	*46.5*	*4.1*	*41.4*	*1.0*	*29.7*	*29.0*	*0.7*	*23.8*	*1.3*	*19.1*	*3.4*
Centre	66,830	100	62.3	8.3	52.4	1.6	28.6	28.3	0.3	9.1	0.3	7.4	1.4
Core city	152,650	100	53.4	5.6	46.5	1.3	29.8	29.3	0.5	16.8	0.7	13.6	2.5
Remainder	225,890	100	41.9	3.1	38.0	0.8	29.8	28.9	0.9	28.4	1.7	22.8	3.9
Central Clydeside	*740,070*	*100*	*53.9*	*7.7*	*45.1*	*1.1*	*25.6*	*25.4*	*0.2*	*20.4*	*0.5*	*17.2*	*2.7*
Centre	110,950	100	76.8	21.4	53.9	1.5	17.5	17.4	0.1	5.7	0.1	4.4	1.2
Core city	426,330	100	61.5	11.0	49.2	1.3	22.7	22.5	0.2	15.8	0.3	13.1	2.4
Remainder	313,740	100	43.6	3.3	39.5	0.8	29.7	29.4	0.3	26.8	0.7	22.8	3.3
All 7 conurbations	*8,890,520*	*100*	*45.9*	*14.7*	*29.9*	*1.3*	*30.8*	*29.9*	*0.9*	*23.3*	*1.8*	*17.1*	*4.4*
Centres (6)	1,747,260	100	65.8	39.1	25.3	1.4	16.8	16.2	0.6	7.5	0.5	5.2	1.8
Core cities	4,557,750	100	56.9	24.0	31.4	1.5	25.1	24.4	0.7	18.0	1.0	13.1	3.9
Remainders	4,332,770	100	34.2	4.8	28.3	1.1	36.8	35.7	1.1	28.9	2.7	21.2	5.0
Great Britain	*23,213,420*	*100*	*31.9*	*6.2*	*24.8*	*0.9*	*37.3*	*35.8*	*1.5*	*30.6*	*4.2*	*20.2*	*6.2*

Note: Totals do not necessarily add exactly to 100 per cent because of rounding.

In the suburbs, in contrast, cars account for nearly 36 per cent of all journeys to work, the proportions ranging from 29 per cent in Clydeside and Tyneside to between 38 and 39 per cent in Greater London, the West Midlands and Merseyside. Bus is the next most important mode, and in the less affluent northern and Scottish conurbations it carries more commuters than the private car. But also notable is the importance of walking, which is responsible for 20 per cent of trips to all suburban jobs and for over 24 per cent in West Yorkshire. It is clear that many suburban work journeys must be extremely short. One explanation is that many of them are made by women whose family responsibilities may restrict them to work near their homes.

The overall journey pattern

The journey to work, however, represents a minority of all personal journeys in the typical British conurbation. Even in 1962, at the time of the first London transportation study, it accounted for only 47.5 per cent of total personal trips. The rest consisted of a variety of home-based non-work trips such as personal business, shopping, social and entertainment (in total 40.7%) and of non-home-based journeys (11.8%). What is important to notice is that even though work journeys are somewhat sensitive to car ownership – particularly through the ability of women to take jobs – non-work journeys are highly sensitive both to car ownership and to income. Table 7.7 shows that in London in 1962 the average car-owning household made 6.05 journeys a day while the average non-car-owning household made only 2.47. Even for work journeys the difference was significant: 2.34 against 1.50. But for personal business, for instance, it was 0.97 against 0.17. Even holding car ownership constant, however, higher incomes generate noticeably more trips, as Table 7.8 demonstrates.

It is a statement of the obvious that the extra trips in car-owning-households are made by car. Table 7.7 also shows that the difference in generation rates per household in London in 1962 – 6.06 minus 2.47, or 3.59 – is explicable entirely in terms of journeys by car drivers (3.23 minus 0.01, or 3.22) and by car passengers (0.88 minus 0.14, or 0.74); in fact, as might also be expected, car-owning households made fewer public transport trips than non-car-owning ones. Though all this is obvious, it is also a fact of profound importance for transportation planning in the conurbations. For, at the time of the major transportation studies – the early and middle 1960s – it indicated that as car ownership levels rose with income, then trip generation rates would also rise dramatically. The original forecasts of the London Transportation Study, made without any imposition of policy or capacity constraints, indicated that between 1962 and 1981 the trip generation rate of non-car-owning households would rise marginally from 2.47 to 2.73 and those for car-owning households from 6.06 to 6.56. But, because car-owning households would increase by almost 90 per cent in that period – from 1.12 million to 2.13 million – total personal journeys[1] would rise by more than 47 per cent. Within this total, work journeys would increase by 105 per cent, social trips by 74 per cent and convenience shopping trips by 90 per cent and trips to school by 123 per cent (Greater London Council 1966, pp. 50–51). Trips by car drivers would rise from 4.1 to nearly 9.0 million, while bus trips would fall from 3.9 to 2.7 million; and while work trips by drivers would increase by 74 per cent, from 1.5 to 2.7 million, non-work driver trips would increase by no less than 144 per cent, from 2.6 to 6.3 million (Greater London Council 1966, p. 87). Similar planning forecasts were made for other conurbations: thus in the West Midlands total person journeys were assumed to rise by 35 per cent between 1964 and 1981, with an increase in car journeys of 105 per cent and a decrease in public transport journeys of 33 per cent (Freeman Fox et al., 1968, p. 8).

Policy responses

Policy for transport in the conurbations has responded chiefly to the perception by policy-makers of the main problem needing solution. Until 1960, it can be said, transport was not seen as one of the priority problem-solving areas; housing and general urban renewal took a far higher place. Then, during most of the 1960s, it responded mainly to the fact of rapidly rising car ownership and increasing congestion on the roads. The result was a series of large-scale transportation studies, either carried out by American consultants or heavily influenced by the methods they had evolved in similar studies in the United States. Mathematical models demonstrated 'laws' of traffic generation, distribution and assignment, which showed that traffic in urban areas was a function of socio-economic characteristics, incomes, and activity patterns. Provided that these variables could be projected for the future – which in British urban areas seemed easy, given the control of planners' over many of the most important of them – then future traffic patterns could be forecast with confidence. The results, which depended heavily on assumptions of regularly rising car ownership, everywhere showed vastly increased traffic flows by the 1980s or 1990s, requiring large-scale new road construction in order to alleviate massive problems of congestion. Almost every urban area, by the late 1960s, had produced ambitious plans for urban motorway networks; the plan for London alone involved spending over £2,000 million on new highways over an approximate twenty-year period.

Very shortly these plans produced a counter-reaction. First, faced with the impossibility of paying for the programmes without an

Table 7.7 Internal trip generation rates, Greater London, 1962

Main mode of travel	A: Car-owning households				B: Non-car-owning households				C: All households			
	Number of trips	Percentage	Trips per person	Trips per household	Number of trips	Percentage	Trips per person	Trips per household	Number of trips	Percentage	Trips per person	Trips per household
Car driver	3,620,437	53.3	0.99	3.23	28,205	0.6	0.01	0.01	3,648,742	32.2	0.43	1.23
Car passenger	984,885	14.5	0.27	0.88	260,853	5.7	0.05	0.14	1,245,738	11.0	0.14	0.42
Cycle driver	134,937	2.0	0.04	0.12	335,409	7.4	0.07	0.18	470,356	4.2	0.05	0.16
Cycle passenger	11,387	0.2	0.00	0.01	35,173	0.8	0.01	0.02	46,560	0.4	0.01	0.02
Bus	1,198,049	17.6	0.33	1.07	2,692,249	59.4	0.55	1.47	3,890,298	34.3	0.46	1.32
Underground	419,902	6.2	0.12	0.37	658,012	14.5	0.13	0.36	1,077,914	9.5	0.13	0.36
British Rail	341,145	5.0	0.09	0.30	415,243	9.2	0.08	0.23	756,388	6.7	0.09	0.26
Taxi	34,252	0.5	0.01	0.03	35,491	0.8	0.01	0.02	69,743	0.6	0.01	0.02
Coach	29,924	0.4	0.01	0.03	25,860	0.6	0.01	0.01	55,784	0.5	0.00	0.02
Commercial vehicle passenger	23,327	0.3	0.01	0.02	47,425	1.0	0.01	0.03	70,752	0.6	0.01	0.02
Total	6,798,245	100.0	1.87	6.05	4,533,920	100.0	0.93	2.47	11,332,275	100.0	1.33	3.83

Table 7.7 Internal trip generation rates, Greater London, 1962

Basic trip purpose	A: Car-owning households				B: Non-car-owning households				C: All households			
	Number of trips	Percentage	Trips per person	Trips per household	Number of trips	Percentage	Trips per person	Trips per household	Number of trips	Percentage	Trips per person	Trips per household
Work	2,631,152	38.7	0.72	2.34	2,746,028	60.6	0.57	1.50	5,377,180	47.5	0.63	1.82
Employer's business	173,828	2.6	0.05	0.15	50,860	1.1	0.01	0.03	224,688	2.0	0.03	0.08
Personal business	1,083,861	15.9	0.30	0.97	299,863	6.6	0.06	0.17	1,383,724	12.2	0.16	0.47
Entertainment	360,082	5.3	0.10	0.32	243,736	5.4	0.05	0.13	603,818	5.3	0.07	0.20
Sport	62,478	0.9	0.02	0.06	42,797	0.9	0.01	0.02	105,275	0.9	0.01	0.04
Social	494,997	7.3	0.14	0.44	317,393	7.0	0.06	0.17	812,390	7.2	0.10	0.27
Shopping – convenience	367,191	5.4	0.10	0.33	292,482	6.5	0.06	0.16	659,673	5.8	0.08	0.22
Shopping – hard goods	149,684	2.2	0.04	0.13	126,335	2.8	0.03	0.07	276,019	2.4	0.03	0.09
School	398,228	5.9	0.11	0.35	151,390	3.3	0.03	0.08	549,728	4.9	0.06	0.19
Miscellaneous	1,076,744	15.8	0.29	0.96	263,036	5.8	0.05	0.14	1,339,780	11.8	0.16	0.45
Total	6,798,245	100.0	1.87	6.05	4,533,920	100.0	0.93	2.47	11,332,275	100.0	1.33	3.83

Source: Greater London Council, 1969, p. 33.

Table 7.8 Effect of income and car ownership on trip generation, Greater London 1962*

Income class	No car	1-car	2-car or more
Low income	2·06 —— [+1·99] —— 4·05		
	[+1·01]	[+1·24]	
Medium income	3·07 —— [+2·22] —— 5·29 —— [+2·32] —— 7·61		
		[+1·34]	[+3·34]
High income		6·63 —— [+4·32] —— 10·95	

* 24-hour average weekday rates for LTS area residents of households with one employed resident in areas of medium rail and bus accessibility

inconceivable increase in public expenditure on transport, and with new requirements to pay compensation for injurious effects after 1972, policy-makers questioned the unconstrained nature of the forecasts on which the original plans were based. The result was a series of constrained plans, which assumed a combination of traffic congestion and deliberate policy restraint on traffic growth – especially in the innermost, most highly congested areas of the conurbations. Second, even the constrained plans ran into grassroots political opposition in the areas which they would affect. In London this undoubtedly played a role in the 1973 Greater London Council elections, where Labour were returned on a platform of scrapping the whole programme (Hart, 1976). A year later the newly returned metropolitan county councils in many cases also undertook wholesale reviews of their road-building plans, abandoning a substantial proportion. Thus by 1977 Greater Manchester had scrapped schemes totalling over £450 million of its original £800 million programme, and further schemes were still in doubt.

Third, all this was fortified by a general shift in perception of the problem, associated with new emphases on resource conservation and the campaign against pollution. Gaining massive momentum from the 1972 publication of the Club of Rome report (Meadows et al., 1972), this got further support from local British work (Hillman, Henderson

Table 7.9 Transport Supplementary Grant (TSG), 1978–1979

| | Expenditure accepted for TSG | | Revenue support | | Other Current expenditure | Capital Expenditure | TSG awarded | |
| | Total | | To British Rail | For Bus, etc. | | | At Nov. 1976 prices | Revaluated to Nov. 1977 |
	(£m.)	(%)	(%)	(%)	(%)	(%)	(%)	(£m.)
At November 1976 prices								
Greater London	180,100	100	0.0	27.2	32.7	40.1	76,925	86,344
West Midlands	42,953	100	6.5	28.4	45.8	19.3	10,848	12,176
Greater Manchester	39,255	100	17.8	14.5	41.0	26.7	8,680	9,743
Merseyside	29,883	100	26.8	24.8	37.3	11.2	9,900	11,112
West Yorkshire	37,362	100	11.0	19.5	48.3	21.2	11,621	13,044
South Yorkshire	18,991	100	5.8	11.6	60.8	21.8	4,104	4,607
Tyne and Wear	69,441	100	3.0	10.8	13.2	73.0	40,353	45,294
Total conurbations	417,985	100	6.0	21.8	34.6	37.6	162,431	180,520
Total England	774,300	100	3.3	15.6	49.0	32.1	219,193	246,033

Source: Hansard, 16 November 1977.
Note: TSG does not apply to Scotland.

and Whalley, 1973, 1976) which focused attention on the still remaining majority of people – especially in inner conurbation areas – lacking access to a car. The result was a remarkable reversal of policy: away from massive road-building, towards traffic restraint and policies to maintain the quality of public transport. And, fourth, all this was aided by changes at national level. In 1968, for the first time, the government's Transport Act accepted the principle of national subsidy to local authorities for investment in public transport; previously only highway grants had been available. In 1975 came an even bigger change: specific government aid to local authorities for transport was rolled up in a single Transport Supplementary Grant (TSG), available for current expenditure as well as capital expenditure, and payable on approval of a Transport Policy and Programme (TPP) to be submitted annually by each local authority. This came just as the newly-formed metropolitan county councils were developing policies to meet their transport planning responsibilities, and it neatly accorded with a desire among a number of them to give greater support to public transport. Table 7.9 shows the pattern of expenditure by metropolitan counties in England approved for TSG in 1978–79. Over all, only 38 per cent went for capital expenditure, and this was distorted by the very large grant to Tyne and Wear for completion of the Tyne Metro system. Other current expenditure – especially road maintenance – received 35 per cent of the grant; revenue support for bus operations claimed another 22 per cent, and support for British Rail – almost exclusively in Greater Manchester and Merseyside – another 6 per cent.

The capital projects aided by TSG included a number of road schemes – part of a much truncated programme, and consisting chiefly of isolated improvements at junctions – together with traffic management schemes such as signal controls and bus priority improvements, plus developments like bus stations and bus garages. All these accorded neatly with a general emphasis on small-scale improvements, particularly with the aim of improving the quality of public transport. But they also allowed for some expenditure on major capital-intensive projects.

During the mid 1970s, in fact, four British cities have seen major urban rail development schemes serving their central areas – a development unparalleled since the early days of the twentieth century. In London the Jubilee line formerly, the Fleet Line, was opened after considerable delays in May 1979. For the most part it employs existing infrastructure dating from between 1880 and 1939, but for a short (3 km) stretch between Baker Street and Charing Cross it uses a new tunnel. Its main function is to relieve overloaded services for commuters and tourists in London's West End, but the GLC's plan is to extend it eastwards to form a central element in the revitalisation of London's docklands. In Liverpool the county council's Passenger Transport Authority and British Rail have co-operated in a £40 million scheme (originally £23 million) to link existing BR electrified tracks from north, south and west via a new loop and link lines under the city centre; 75 per cent of the cost was covered by government grants (Halsall, 1978). On Tyneside, similarly, 41 km of British Rail line are being joined by 12 km of new track, partly underground through central Newcastle, at an estimated (1975) cost of £161 million. Lastly, on Clydeside British Rail tracks have been upgraded while the archaic narrow-gauge subway system has been comprehensively modernised and linked to it to provide a distributor for the BR services, at a cost of £33 million. The Liverpool system opened in 1977; the Glasgow system opened in 1979, Tyneside follows in 1980 (Anon., 1978).

Already, however, an air of doubt hangs over these expensive investments. Three of them were intended in large measure to win traffic back to rail systems that had suffered massive passenger losses; the question must be how far, with falling employment totals in central areas, this objective can be secured. In Manchester a very similar city centre underground link between existing BR services – the so called Pic-Vic line – was postponed repeatedly from 1975 and now seems destined for oblivion; the Government have refused to support the Jubilee line extension through the London docklands on the ground that the cost-benefit ratio is said to be negative, though the GLC have countered by threatening to go it alone (and indeed have started but then abandoned the first 2 km with ratepayers' money). The experience of San Francisco, where the much vaunted BART system was only carrying 51 per cent of its forecast passengers (in 1976) and where each ride cost local taxpayers more than it cost the passenger, has been salutary here (Webber, 1976). For the future, it seems certain that the official government policy will be to support more modest, lower-cost, piecemeal improvements to the existing public transport services – particularly the bus system on which most British conurbations traditionally rely.

Behind the facts of the policy shift – first from road to rail, now from rail to more modest piecemeal improvements in public transport – lie a number of important unanswered questions concerning conurbation transport policy. One of the most important concerns transport as a means not so much of urban efficiency (though that must always be an important consideration) as of urban equity. In the past, and to some degree up to the present, inner-city dwellers were compensated for their relative lack of car ownership by the density of public transport and the relatively short distances they needed to ride on it in order to reach jobs, shops, schools, doctors and a host of other services. Now, however, these areas have lost many of their former jobs, while new jobs have been created in the suburbs often a considerable distance away. Merseyside for instance is estimated to have lost 80,000 inner-city jobs and to have gained 100,000 new jobs at the periphery – but these, in places like Runcorn and Ellesmere Port, may be outside the time and cost range of typical inner-city residents (Department of the

Environment, 1977, p. 5). The question is whether transport ought to be used as a means of public policy, perhaps by subsidising reverse commuting, or whether jobs can be re-created in the inner city (Chapters 3 and 12). Similarly, a question-mark hangs over developments like London's Jubilee line through the Docklands, which – as already seen – has a negative rate of return but which the Greater London Council claims is vital to increase job opportunities by extending local labour markets.

Closely associated with this is the question of how far the battle to improve public transport can ever be won in the face of rising car ownership. Though the rise in new registrations showed a distinct slowing-down in 1974 and 1975 after the oil crisis and during the recession, it seems again to be resuming its previous course and August 1978 – the start of the new registration year – set an absolute record for new registrations. Should economic growth begin again, the return to the previous trend is almost certain – especially since the real cost of petrol in 1978 is equal to what it was before 1973. On the other hand public transport, as a necessarily labour-intensive industry, finds it hard to avoid a cost curve that rises faster than the general earnings or cost-of-living curve. Though some conurbation authorities, notably South Yorkshire, have deliberately maintained high subsidies in order to keep fare levels down, they tend to run foul of the Department of Transport and risk a reduction in their TSG levels. In London, where the GLC are implementing a policy of raising fares and cutting costs in order to avoid a rise in subsidy, there is now a widespread impression that the high cost of commuting acts as an actual discouragement to the operation of the central area – and staff have threatened to strike over what they see as a reduction of service levels.

Behind this, again, is the question of how far the TPP-TSG system has really given freedom to local authorities. It has meant that they have greater freedom to divert spending from roads to public transport, and thereby from capital to revenue support. But this can be exercised only within the fairly narrow limits laid down by the Department of Transport, as the South Yorkshire example shows. It could be that for the future the conurbation authorities are given greater incentive to work out quite radically different approaches to their transport planning, with some giving heavy public subsidies while others encourage the use of the private car – perhaps with some official scheme of shared rides for the carless. For one point is certain: that as long as the dispersal of homes and jobs continues, so will conventional public transport fight a losing battle against the flexibility of the private car.

Note

1. Defined as 'internal basic journeys'. Journeys on foot were, somewhat remarkably, ignored.

References

Anon. (1978) 'Metrorails', *Town and Country Planning*, **46**, pp. 281–4.

Barker, T. and **Robbins, M.** (1969, 1974) *The History of London Transport* (2 vols). George Allen and Unwin, London.

Department of the Environment (1976) *British Cities: Urban Population and Employment Trends*, Research Report No. 10.

Department of the Environment (1977) *Inner Area Studies: Liverpool, Birmingham and Lambeth.* HMSO, London.

Department of Transport (1978) *Transport Statistics Great Britain 1966–1976.* HMSO, London.

Freeman, T.W. (1951) *The Conurbations of Great Britain.* Macmillan, London.

Freeman Fox, Wilbur Smith and Associates (1968) *West Midlands Transport Study*, vol. 1. Freeman Fox, London and Birmingham.

Geddes, P. (1915) *Cities in Evolution.* Williams and Norgate, London.

Greater London Council (1966) *London Traffic Survey Volume Two.* GLC, London.

Greater London Council (1969) *Movement in London.* GLC, London.

Hall, P. (1964) 'The development of communications' in Coppock, J.T., and Prince, H., *Greater London.* Faber and Faber, London.

Hall, P. (1970) 'Transportation', in Cowan, P. (ed.) *Developing Patterns of Urbanisation.* Oliver and Boyd, Edinburgh.

Hall, P., Gracey, H., Thomas, R. and **Drewett, R.** (1973) *The Containment of Urban England* (2 vols). George Allen and Unwin, London.

Hall, P. and **Hay, D.** (1980) *Growth Centres in the European Urban System.* (1980) Heinemann Education, London.

Halsall, D.A. (1978) 'Rapid transit on Merseyside', *Area* **10**, pp. 212–16.

Hart, D.A. (1976) *Strategic Planning in London: The Rise and Fall of the Primary Road Network.* Pergamon, Oxford.

Hillman, M., Henderson, I. and **Whalley, A.** (1973) *Personal Mobility and Transport Policy*, Broadsheet 542. Political and Economic Planning, London.

Hillman, M., Henderson, I. and **Whalley, A.** (1976) *Transport Realities and Planning Policy*, Broadsheet 567. Political and Economic Planning, London.

Meadows, D. et al. (1972) *The Limits to Growth: The Club of Rome Report.* Potomac Associates, London.

Sammons R. and **Hall, P.** (1974) *Urban Activity Patterns and Modal Split in the Journey to Work*, Geographical Papers 32. Department of Geography, The University, Reading.

Thomson, J.M. (1977) *Great Cities and their Traffic.* Gollancz, London.

Webber, M.M. (1976) *The BART Experience — What have we learned?*, Institute of Urban and Regional Development, Monograph No. 26. University of California, Berkeley, California.

White, H.P. (1965) *Greater London — A Regional Railway History of Great Britain*, vol. 3. David and Charles, Newton Abbot.

White, P.R. (1974) 'Use of public transport in towns and cities of Great Britain and Ireland', *Journal of Transport Economics and Policy*, **8**, pp. 26–39.

Chapter 8

Education and the British conurbations

Introduction

Although great schemes for compulsory State education are part of the history of educational thought (the most noticeable one in this context being Knox's plan for universal education for Scotland put forward in the sixteenth century), the development of the modern educational system in Britain, based essentially on State control, was due to the growth of urban areas. Indeed the two pieces of Victorian legislation on which the contemporary educational system is formed – the Education Act 1870 (England and Wales), and the Education (Scotland) Act 1872 – were, to a considerable extent, designed to meet an urban crisis. The Argyll Commission of the 1860s had reported that in Glasgow, for example, a substantial majority of children were without formal education of any kind, while the Newcastle Commission found a similar state of affairs in the large industrial towns of England which, like Glasgow, had mushroomed as a consequence of the Industrial Revolution. Here the Victorian educational crisis was perceived not only as a desperate need for an educational system which would fit scholars for an industrial environment but also for institutions capable of adequately socialising the young in circumstances where the failure of both the Church and the family appeared to be leading to a state of 'urban barbarism'.

As a consequence of the Victorian 'Great Debate', the Education (Scotland) Act 1872 established over 900 popularly elected School Boards based mainly on the parish as the unit of administration with a remit to build schools, to hire teachers, to raise money by property rates and borrowing, to receive government grant with its attendant inspection and to ensure attendance, between the ages of 5 and 13, of children whose parents were either unable or unwilling to ensure adequate education for them by other means. In Glasgow many of the schools built by the Boards still exist and generations of Glaswegians have been (and still are!) being educated in them. They were originally designed to instil discipline and to teach the basic skills – the 3 Rs. They were, to many, institutions which symbolised State compulsion, staffed by teachers not regarded as members of the local community but as agents of a higher, remote and alien authority.

After 1872 there ensued something of a 'battle for attendance' which was to all intents won by the State by the 1880s. The role of the attendance officer has been well (and humorously) described by Roxburgh:

> At least once a week a special operation was mounted against vagrant or truant children to be found in the streets, docks, fairs and markets.
>
> Disguised in plain clothes and deployed to districts in which they were not known, the officers swooped down on their prey in a Day Raid. They always got a good bag; 350 was an average figure in 1879. On another day 1,034 names were taken – twenty-three false addresses received! (1971, p. 172).

Throughout the whole country, of course, as E.G. West, for example, has pointed out (1965), State compulsion only appeared necessary for a minority of children. Few were then, or are now, in a position to make alternative provision for themselves, so that, although the law has never stated that all children must attend school, rather than receive a suitable education, it has and remains for the vast majority an irrelevant nicety.[1]

Compulsion has remained probably the major characteristic of British educational systems. Not only is it enshrined in the detailed procedures laid down in current legislation for ensuring attendance, with consequent penalties upon parents (and children) who fail to comply, it has been extended by the progressive raising of the minimum leaving age to its present 16 years. It has once again become a major issue for debate and doubt.

However, it is not the point of this chapter to outline the history of the development of British education; there are plenty of standard works on that. Nevertheless some of the current major characteristics may be indicated. The Victorian *ad hoc* boards have been replaced by large authorities responsible for a whole range of social services. For example, the Local Government (Scotland) Act 1973 established nine Regional (and three Island) Authorities with responsibility for a variety of essential services, including education. The 1970s also saw the reform of local government in England and Wales which stressed both the virtues of larger units of local administration and of corporate management approaches.

In the twentieth century the education service has evolved to include secondary education for all, a vastly expanded system of further and higher education, a school curriculum at both primary and secondary level of a breadth and complexity much greater than anything envisaged by the Victorians, a sophisticated system of external examinations and a strong emphasis on health and welfare. Apart from a succession of major Education Acts, many changes, especially in Scotland, were brought about by a powerful civil service, a strong Inspectorate, as well as by the initiative of the old School Boards and the Education Authorities which succeeded them. At the same time the teaching profession has increasingly demanded full professional status (another matter of direct relevance to the relationship between education and the conurbations), illustrated, for example, in the processes leading to the establishment of the General Teaching Council (Scotland) Act 1965. Both the 1944 Education Act which applied to England and Wales and the Education (Scotland) Act 1946 saw education as part of the Welfare State and, above all, demanded that education be provided not only in terms of a basic minimum for the majority but in terms of 'age, ability and aptitude' for all. Implicit in this goal and in the abolition of fees in State Schools (with a few exceptions in Scotland) was acceptance of the goal of equality of opportunity.

By the end of the Second World War there was optimism and confidence about the educational system which was seen as a major means of creating a better society. Education was regarded not only as a means to the good life but as a sound economic investment, an argument used by successive official reports (Central Advisory Council for Education, 1959 (Crowther Report); Committee on Higher Education, 1963 (Robbins Report)), to justify increased expenditure on the education service. Perhaps the most idealistic post-war report, parts of which make strange reading in the current climate of opinion, was the now generally accepted classic of its kind: 'Secondary Education' (Advisory Council on Education in Scotland, 1947). This brilliantly written report, in its determination that the horrors which Britain had so narrowly missed should never be repeated, is almost Knoxian in its belief in the capacity of formal education not only to develop the skills of the young, to socialise them into society, but to create the 'Good Life'. It refers to the need, through education, to build a 'Christian Democracy'. It points out that the 'grave weaknesses revealed by the evacuation scheme and by wartime stresses in general show clearly that the new generation needs as well as merits a fuller wiser schooling' (p. 3). To this end it postulated equal care for the education of all boys and girls up to eighteen years of age, whether through secondary schooling or compulsory day-release. Although the latter demand is contained in the Education Acts of 1918 and, along with the raising of the statutory leaving age to 16, was the major recommendation of the Crowther Report, it has never been implemented.

The post-war education debate has, until comparatively recently, tended to view the educational system as fulfilling many goals – spiritual, physical, social, economic and industrial. Discussion about education has tended to be in terms of broad aims rather than in terms of problems peculiar to specific areas. The question, therefore, to be asked is why has it come about that in recent years increasing attention has been paid, both in Britain and in other countries, to the relationship which exists between the educational system and the urban environment and even whether a theory of education with its own aims, related to that environment, is necessary.

The growth of interest in education and the conurbations

First of all it may be fairly claimed that the general post-war optimism and euphoria about the possible contribution which the educational system can make to society have to a large extent been dissipated.

In the 1940s the Harvard Report (Conant, 1946) had regarded education as a means of preserving a free society. However, by the 1960s many Americans were talking about the crisis of the cities and some were saying that not only had education failed to resolve the problem but was a major contributory factor. Thus one of the most significant publications of that time *The Politics of Urban Education* (Gittell and Hevesi, 1969) attributed much of the problem to the closed administrative bureaucracy characteristic of many American city educational systems. Gittell's study of New York City, for example, was highly critical of a self-interested and self-centred educational bureaucracy for its failure to adapt to or even appreciate the significance of the political pressures building up within New York City among hitherto deprived ethnic minorities for a right to participate in educational decision-making. She attributes the conflict between this demand, Mayor John Lindsay's attempt to support it and the reaction of the educational establishment, as one of the main causes of the longest and most bitter strikes of American teachers in their history.

Disillusion with educational systems can be found not only in the USA. One of the main academic 'inputs' into educational research in post-war Britain has undoubtedly come from sociologists, many of whom have argued that equality of opportunity has not been achieved, and indeed have led some of its most prominent proponents, such as A. H. Halsey, to argue that 'the essential fact of twentieth century educational history is that egalitarian policies have failed' (1972). Some of the evidence on which this argument is based is quoted later in this chapter. Other more radical voices have argued that formal schooling creates and promotes inequality. Others have sought, especially in an urban setting, much more radical alternatives to traditional patterns of schooling – including the free school, the community school and, amazingly, from both extreme political left and right, an emphasis on the voucher system.

Added to all this there have been the student riots of the 1960s leading to a disillusionment with higher education (from the right a source of dangerous left-wing malcontents, from the left a group of élitists out of touch with the working-class movement), a (to a large extent mythological) belief that educational 'standards' are falling, a distrust of progressive methods, especially in primary education, and a dislike of the effects of comprehensive schools in secondary education (most articulately and, from a propaganda point of view, most effectively expressed in the 'Black Papers'). Another persistent strand in these criticisms has been the concern with the acute deprivation suffered in particular areas of those receiving formal schooling. In the next section we look at the origin of this alleged deprivation and the reasons why urban deprivation has caused so much concern.

Equality of opportunity

One of the main reasons why educationalists have become interested in the conurbations, and indeed in the general social environment of the child, has been the research carried out by social scientists. Such research, of course, is not new; many examples of research into the influence of the home can be traced back to the nineteenth century. Nevertheless, it was only in the post Second World War period that social science in Britain began to have a major impact on educational thinking. During the inter-war years the main discipline which had influenced educational thought had been psychology, added to which was a general theory of education derived from philosophers such as Plato, and more recently, John Dewey. From the 1950s onwards there emerged a vast volume of socio-economic research indicating that the achievement of children in terms of academic attainment, staying on beyond the minimum leaving age, entering higher education, were all very closely related to the social and economic environment of the child. Thus Douglas *et al.* in *All our Future* (1968) argued that, 'Early leaving and role job aspirations make it probable that as many as 5% of the next generation of manual workers will be recruited from pupils, who in other circumstances might have qualified for administrative or professional occupations.'

He also argued that children from large families were likely to be handicapped. 'Children from large families make low scores in all attainment tests at all ages. The more young children there are in the family, when a child is learning to talk, the lower his score in the 8-year-old vocabulary test. This early deficiency in the understanding of words is not made up later' (Douglas, *et al.* Ch. XVII).

There is also some evidence that educational handicap deriving from social and environmental factors may occur very early in life. Thus: 'The chances of an unskilled manual worker child (Social Class V) being a poor reader at 7 years old are six times greater than those of a professional worker's child (Social Class I). The chances of a Social Class V being a non-reader at this stage are fifteen times greater than those of a Social Class I child' (Davie *et al.* 1972).

It did not seem clear from research in the 1950s and the 1960s that these forms of handicap had a spatial bias. However, although disadvantage was not found *exclusively* in inner-city areas, it seemed to occur most obviously there and in higher proportions and in greater number than elsewhere. Evidence we can cite, for example, is presented in the Plowden Report, *Children and their Primary Schools*

(Central Advisory Council, 1967); the Halsey Report (1972) and by the research of Eric Wilkinson in the ongoing Strathclyde Experiment in Education (1978, a and b).

More recent thinking has suggested that educational deprivation is a problem which is perhaps not specific to the conurbations but one which varies from area to area within cities, from city to city and which is to be found in non-urban areas. For example, we may quote Jessel from *Education and the Urban Crisis*: 'The criteria of definition should be flexible enough to embrace a wider variety of multiply-deprived districts; not just in city centres, but in economically declining urban areas, in redevelopment housing estates and in some rural areas' (Field, 1978, p. 56).

This is also illustrated in the Halsey Report which finds social deprivation is a consequence of a variety of factors and in rural areas as well as in cities. The problem of the spatial aspects of educational deprivation requires further research. Halsey indicates that most of the work indicating such a problem relevant to the conurbation was carried out not in Britain in the 1960s but in the United States where the relationship between deprivation and the movement of the urban population received considerable attention. In Britain, however, the full significance of the spatial dimension has yet to be fully explained although, as indicated elsewhere in this chapter, much important work in the field has been done and is currently in progress. One could indicate in Scotland, for example, the significant work being carried out at the moment, not only in inner-city areas but in the Western Isles, where nineteenth-century reports found deprivation equal to that to be found in the most deprived areas of our industrial cities. There is also the problem that disadvantage varies considerably with geographical location in a much more general sense than mentioned above. For example, we could quote the following:

> One child in sixteen was a proportion of disadvantaged among all children in Britain, but in individual regions the prevalence varied. In Southern England there was only one in 47 children. In Wales and in Northern England, on the other hand, there was one in every 12. The most disturbing proportion was found in Scotland, where one in every 10 children was disadvantaged (Wedge and Prosser, 1973).

We find, therefore, that there is a variation in the degree of deprivation, both within cities and throughout the regions of the country. For example, Wilkinson *et al.* indicate that there is a disproportionate degree of urban deprivation in Strathclyde (1978a). They also quote the work of Eric Midwinter to show that, at each stage of the schooling process, children living in disadvantaged circumstances perform at an inferior level when compared with their more privileged peers and their differentiation increases as children get older.

We are, therefore, faced with a number of issues and problems. It is clear that deprivation and its associated problems are not confined to the conurbations. It remains to be asked, however, whether or not the degree to which it is found in the conurbations elevates itself into a qualitative as well as a quantitative difference. We shall return to this later on. Let us look at some of the other reasons put forward for deprivation and some of the proposed solutions before discussing this fundamental issue at a later stage in this chapter.

There has been both here and in the United States a considerable debate as to the extent to which education can play any part in solving problems associated with deprivation, whether within the urban environment or not. It is clear, for example, that one of the major factors, if not the major factor, in deprivation is the role of the family. Countless studies have indicated that consistent parental encouragement is of vital importance in the attainment of children. This was found, for example, in the classic study by Professor Elizabeth Fraser in Aberdeen in the 1950s (1959) and can be seen in the work of Plowden, Halsey, Douglas and numerous others. It is also indicated very strongly in America, for example, in the results of the Coleman Report (1966). Fraser found that consistent parental encouragement was most important in providing incentive to effort that resulted in achievement at school. Such encouragement arose out of attitudes favourable to education. Attitudinal factors, of course, have not been the only indicators of poor achievement in schools. The work of J. B. Mays (1962) in inner-city Liverpool, for example, indicated that the school represented what he termed 'an alien culture'. And other studies have suggested that there can be circumstances in which the 'general culture' of the community is of crucial importance both in influencing the family and, therefore, the child in attitudes to education. This, of course, has led to the view by many educationalists that the school must take account of the environment and, of course, in our society this must include the environment of the major urban centres if it is to have any impact at all in the education of the majority of children.

The discussion about the effects of the culture of a local community on motivation to learn does not mean that the values of such communities are to be regarded as necessarily inferior to those held by schools. It has been argued by some that it is the culture of the school which must be changed in order to improve communication with the community. This argument has most clearly been put by writers like Halsey and Midwinter. In their study of 'Educational Priority Areas', established as a result of the recommendations of the Plowden Committee, they found that in areas of deprivation parents were not hostile to education, but they did find it difficult to communicate with schools. It has been increasingly stressed that the educational opportunities of deprived children can only be improved by better communications between school and home. Just how this can be achieved is one of the most important issues in the current educational debate.

The Plowden Report, for example, identified areas of multiple deprivation where schooling appeared irrelevant to the perceived needs of the child, either at his present stage or in the future. This has led to a number of debates as to what the curriculum of the school should be and how it should relate both to the culture of the community and to the industrial environment. This is a point to which we shall return.

Another set of factors, which may militate against the learning of children in inner cities, have demographic origins. Halsey, for example, gives figures for the high turnover of staff and the disturbing effects on classroom behaviour of rapid population shifts in inner city areas. However, once again, it must be pointed out that population reduction is not confined to inner city areas but is found, for example, in rural areas. Indeed population decline in many rural areas has been a problem for a period much longer than the course of the present century. But whatever the location, given the current over-supply of teachers in many subjects, the problem is likely to be less one of high turnover because of teachers' unwillingness to serve in 'difficult schools' and more one of the problem of maintaining staff morale and involvement in conditions of declining school rolls.

Of course we could take the line that the debate about culture and education is irrelevant and that the real problem is purely economic. Lord Vaizey, for example, has stated that the problem of deprivation is almost entirely one of low wages, and similar arguments will be found in contributions to *Education and the Urban Crisis* (Field, 1978). The debate is very fully argued out in the Halsey Report, where Halsey himself takes the line that both economic and cultural arguments have validity and that while the educational system cannot by itself improve the economy, it can improve training and aspirations. Halsey, in reviewing the 'culture of poverty' argument which he claims was very prevalent in America in the early 1960s, saw it based in its simplest form on the assumption 'that the poor are different, not primarily because of low income, but because they have been habituated to poverty and have developed a sub-culture of values adapted to these conditions which they then pass on to their children'.

His own conclusion is as follows:

> Out of this debate so far we must conclude that the 'poverties' to which urban industrial populations are prone must be understood to have their origins in both situational and cultural characteristics of those minorities which suffer disadvantage and discrimination and to have their cures in both economic and cultural reform, not only at the local or community level but also in the total structure of society (p. 17).

This now takes us on to a number of questions concerning policy with regard to education and the conurbation.

Compensatory education. The debate as to whether or not education, particularly in the pre-school years, can compensate for the various handicaps, whether they be cultural, motivational or economic, has raged fiercely both here and in the United States. The Halsey Report, having reviewed some of the rather depressing conclusions arrived at in America, for example in the 'Headstart Programme', concluded as follows: 'The Educational priority area, despite its difficulties of definition, is a socially administratively viable unit to which to apply the principle of positive discrimination.'

Some of the evidence provided by the Halsey Report indicates that children can maintain improvements in language and number given pre-schooling experience. However, Jessel, having reviewed the evidence both in Halsey and in America, came to the conclusion that 'the evidence is not compelling'. On the other hand Wilkinson, Director of the Strathclyde Experiment in Education, argues that: 'There is a considerable amount of evidence, not only showing that levels of attainment in disadvantaged areas are low, but that substantial improvements are feasible when there is overt co-operation between professional and parent' (1978b). He adds a cautious rider that 'although substantive results will not be available for some time, encouraging patterns do seem to be emerging'.

It appears, therefore, that so far as compensatory education is concerned, especially with regard to the pre-school child, the signs are hopeful, but not yet conclusive. Further comment on this will be made towards the end of this chapter.

The concept of community

For many years now a number of educationalists have been inclined to see the school, not as an isolated institution, but as part of a community. This attitude has taken a number of different forms. Pedley, for example, (1962) has seen the comprehensive school as a centre of community activity and, since his work, there have been many references to the term 'community school'. The community school, of course, can mean many things. It can mean a comprehensive school which draws its pupils from a particular type of community. If one thinks of this in terms of the conurbation, the community school may reflect the very different types of communities which exist within these conurbations. In the Glasgow area, for example, a community school in the East End would be rather different from some community schools in the South side in terms of social composition. Other people have seen the community school as an attempt to break down the boundaries of communities. Not so much to break down community barriers but to prevent inequality of provision and racial segregation.

This has led, in its most extreme form, to 'bussing', for example in the United States where a great deal of trouble, if not violence, has occurred as a result. Other views of the community school are to be found, for example, in the Plowden and Halsey recommendations that certain areas be designated as educational priority areas and given increased resources to overcome the handicaps which children suffer. Such reports, especially the Halsey Report and the work of Eric Midwinter (1973), wished to see the school much more involved in the community and the community in the school. They tend to see the community as a curriculum resource and, indeed, in Glasgow some interesting experiments have been done in this. Others see the school as a community centre where community facilities, such as swimming pools, libraries and evening classes are deliberately built into the school. Both of these approaches may pull in different directions. Thus we have the concept of the school going out into the community and the community becoming part of the school. There is, at the moment, interesting research being conducted into this, not only in the Glasgow experiments referred to already, but in the North East of Scotland under the direction of Professor John Nisbet. Certainly one of the aspects in which educational theorists concerned with the environment of the child appear to be in agreement, as indicated above, is that some means must be found to bring about a closer co-operation and understanding between parents, school and the teaching profession.

The labour market

The educational system has historically been associated with, but has had an uneasy relationship to the labour market and industry. It can be argued that the introduction of formal compulsory education was designed exclusively to meet the needs of industry in the nineteenth century. It can also be argued that there were moral, philosophical, religious and general arguments concerning socialisation which lay behind such policy. There has also been a tendency for many educationalists, who believe in a broad child-centred theory of education, which sees education as allowing the child to grow and develop his talents in all directions, artistic, physical, imaginative, and emotional, to regard industry as somehow a threat to the educational process. One can point, for example, in Scotland to the writings of former headmaster R. F. Mackenzie, who underlines this kind of distrust. Attempts have been made to overcome this distrust, which at times has become a conflict. There was introduced, for example, in Scotland in the 1960s, a programme called 'The Teacher in Industry Scheme' in which the present author participated, having spent some time working in Colvilles' Steel Works in order to gain industrial experience. In 1963 there appeared in Scotland 'The Brunton Report' which argued that many children of 'non-academic' bent could only be motivated into learning by school programmes related to the practical world of the adult, which meant the industrial world and, of course, in rural areas, the world of agriculture, fishing and forestry.

Most recently we have been faced with what the former Prime Minister Mr. Callaghan has described as the 'Great Debate'. This debate has come about partly as a result of disillusionment with the educational process. The argument by industrialists and politicians that the levels of literacy are falling, can be traced back to the mid nineteenth century. By and large, so far as Scotland is concerned, the notion that basic literacy and numeracy levels are falling is doubtful. The problem, however, remains with us and the need to relate the world of the child, particularly the adolescent, to the world of the industrial environment, which to him is the real world, and to his future job prospects, especially in a world and a society faced with a severe unemployment crisis, has become acute. It has become acute also because of the raising of the school-leaving age, but it has produced some very interesting work. One may refer, for example, to a recent publication *Glad to be Out?* (Weir and Nolan, 1977) which among its conclusions, states 'the manner in which young people are casually dropped into the adult world, and are left to find their own way with the minimum of preparation, is undoubtedly a contributory factor in creating the feelings of frustration which can be observed in the behaviour of young people both in and outside work'. The debate, therefore, as to how the schools relate to the world of work continues. If one reads, for example, the recently published Munn Report in Scotland (Scottish Education Department, 1977), which advocates a general curriculum plus a degree of choice for all children, one finds that the perennial educational debate between the need to provide general education in a democratic society and the need to relate to industry, particularly in an urban society, remains one of the central concerns of education.

Parental choice

One of the major debates in British education at the moment concerns the question of choice of school. In the past the argument in favour of parental choice has often been identified with the 'right wing' in politics; however, recently a much broader spectrum of opinion has taken the view that motivation, particularly among parents, may be related to the right to choose schools of their wish for their children. The administrative implications of such a policy, of course, goes beyond the scope of this present discussion. The main point, however, is to indicate that both writers from the right of politics, for example Dr Rhodes Boyson, and people of a more 'left-wing' disposition, for example many of the radical left in the United States, have argued in favour of a policy of giving parents vouchers to enable them to purchase education in the school of their choice. Some educationalists who do not identify themselves with any particular political view-point have argued that increased choice for parents would be of great benefit in areas of urban deprivation, because it would give them the opportunity to become much more involved in the educational process and much more likely to consider the impact of curriculum and methods on their children (Macbeth, 1974).

These ideas, of course, are being put out in a general way at the moment. There is a need to define the area of the professional competence of the teacher and the area where parents may have legitimate choice. On this some argue that teachers could be given a great deal of professional autonomy over content while parents were given choice over which type of school they wish their children to attend. There may also be areas of curriculum, for example moral education, where parents should have a more direct say than they would, for example, in the teaching of mathematics. There is, therefore, a possible conflict between some of the concepts of community-centred education, as indicated above, and those of choice. This will be a continuing debate within the conurbation with regard particularly to the traditional policy of zoning schools within catchment areas and, again, it is one which is of relevance not only to the educationalist. For example, were parents to be given more choice this might influence the level and the disposition of population within cities. In other words, many parents may choose their residential location in accordance with their ideas of good schooling. This may have contributed to the depopulation of the cities. It may be that the 'flight to the suburbs' is related to the type of schooling which is provided within the cities. It is clear to the present author that insufficient work and research has been carried out in this field and that social sciences generally, when discussing problems of urban depopulation, have paid insufficient attention to the relationship between schooling and the other social services. Indeed many parents may well perceive schools of traditional reputation, vigorous staff, extra-curricular activities and so on, as providing their major motivation in the choice of a new house.

Radical alternatives

There have recently been put forward in Britain various proposals which would radically alter the nature of schools as institutions. Once again these proposals apply not only to the conurbations but can be seen in a wider context, though one must point out that some of them arise particularly out of concern with the problem of the inner city. The latest radical proposal in England and Wales is found in the recently published Taylor Report (DES, 1977). This advocated that each school be controlled by a body consisting of representatives of the elected members, the teaching profession, the parents and the community. It proposes giving a considerable degree of power to such bodies. For example, it states: 'The governing body should be given by the local education authority, the responsibility for setting the aims of the school, for considering the means by which they are pursued, for keeping under review the school's progress towards them, and for deciding upon action to facilitate such progress' (Ch. 6). The Taylor Report is at the moment the subject of considerable debate in England and Wales, but were it to be recommended, it would involve a degree of parental and community involvement in school management unprecedented in the public sector in British educational history.

The second innovation to which one should refer emerges from the Local Government (Scotland) Act 1973 which set up bodies called School Councils. This Act gave the Scottish regions a very wide discretion as to the composition and powers which they might delegate to such councils. Such bodies may become of great relevance to the future development of the educational system and, again, although they exist in rural as well as urban areas, they may well have special significance in the major urban areas, particularly with regard to problems of deprivation, to parental choice and to the relationship between schools as institutions, the teaching profession and local community.

The opening part of this section stated that the first points made were the least radical. There are, of course, many other much more radical alternatives which have been put forward. One thinks, for example, of the work of Ivan Illich and others who have seen schools as institutions which themselves should be abolished and that education should be community-centred. Others have thought to find alternatives to schooling or to break down the barriers between schools and communities in more radical ways. One can point, for example, to the work of the Barrowfield School in Glasgow which has used very radical methods to educate children actually outside of the traditional system, given the child a vastly increased degree of choice over his own education, and sought to much more directly involve the parent and the community. Needless to say, such radical departures have received a great deal of both praise and criticism. It is therefore clear that, so far as education and the conurbation is concerned, there are numerous unresolved problems and issues far too extensive to be discussed in a short essay. The final section of this chapter is merely intended to indicate one or two areas which are likely to be on the agenda for future concern.

Concluding remarks

(a) Education and the falling urban population.

Other chapters of this book have indicated the fall in population which has taken place in all of the conurbations, particularly in the inner-city areas. The consequences of this fall for education have been very important and extremely complex. Indeed, its full impact has yet to be realised and worked out and the policy implications adequately understood. One of the first results, of course, has been an over-supply of teachers. On the other hand it can be argued that this over-supply of teachers combined with a fall in population, particularly in the inner-city areas, can in fact offer a solution to some of the problems which we have already indicated. For example, Halsey and others have pointed out that one of the main problems facing inner-city schools has been the rapid turnover of teaching staff, adding to a social situation already characterised in many respects by instability. Other authors have indicated both the problem of increased unit costs of education associated with the fall of population and the administrative uncertainty associated with the same development.

In looking at the whole picture, Newsam (in Field, 1978, pp. 75–6) has argued

> Against the one overriding benefit of more and perhaps better space for those who remain there are at least four problems that falling numbers bring. The first is financial. As numbers fall, unit costs tend to rise. London's experience of a fall of 12,000 in the primary school population is that the pro rata saving of £2.75 million that might have been expected in a full year will become an actual saving of £1.6 million in a full year. Schools with somewhat reduced rolls still have to be heated, the rates have to be paid, the roofs mended. In this situation, an education service cannot act abruptly. It cannot suddenly close down plant, as it were, in these participating days even if on educational or financial grounds it was thought desirable to do so. The second problem brought by falling numbers is its effect on the whole planning process; on the possibility of planning itself. The whole tradition in educational planning is based on rising numbers. Schools are built; they become full, and other schools have to be added. Always there is a programme, a looking ahead and a race not to be left too far behind. But the process cannot be reversed when numbers fall. Falling numbers mean a situation that is in principle unstable and to a large extent unpredictable. If it is known now that in five years numbers in an area will have fallen so far that one or more schools in bad premises could close, it ought to be possible, the planners think, to say so and plan accordingly. But life is not so simple. To discuss officially and in advance the closure of a school is like talking about devaluation. Either the discussion brings it about too soon, because there is a run on the currency or away from the school, or promises have to be made that it will never happen at all. So the drift continues until there is room to spare in several schools in the area and a growing uncertainty about what is to happen next.
>
> This uncertainty seems essentially an urban phenomenon.

Newsam continues:

> In the inner city, falling numbers reduce stress and provide new opportunities by improving spatial standards; but these other uncertainties are already arising and their force and effect make for structural instability.

It is, therefore, clear that falling population, both with regard to costs and educational policy, will remain a major educational and social issue for the policy-makers in coming years especially within the inner cities of the British conurbations.

(b) Some other considerations for the future

It may well be argued that the idealism which produced the current education system and which perhaps reached its peak towards the end and immediately after the Second World War, was a little overdone. But there is at the moment an even greater threat from a current mood of pessimism, doubt and uncertainty. It has already been argued strongly in this chapter that one of the purposes of this book must be to raise issues and ask questions with regard to the future of the British conurbation, rather than provide simple bland answers. It is the view of the present writer that, contrary to the views of the most extreme de-schoolers, schools remain essential institutions in our society, but that they must become much more adaptable, contain more variety and flexibility, and that there must be more parental and community involvement in their affairs, combined with more efficient management at both political and official levels. This is in no way to argue against the interests and future status of the teaching profession. On the contrary, the challenges presented by the problems of the British conurbations, offer the teaching profession a more diverse and, indeed, a more important rôle than in the past. It is the task not only of the educationalist, but of the policy-maker at all levels, to discuss fully the future rôle of the teacher, particularly in areas of policy-making where the teacher has a peculiar professional rôle to play and where he can help solve a wider range of problems than he has been expected to do in the past. This will place even greater demands on the profession, but there is no reason to believe that it is unequal to rising to these demands and that, when it does so, it should not receive the status and remuneration which it deserves as a consequence. It may also be seen that parental choice is not necessarily solely in the interests of the middle class but as many, both in America and in the United Kingdom, have argued, can also be in the interests of the poor. It would be necessary that schemes for parental and community involvement, both in Scotland and in England, as outlined, for example, in the Taylor Report and in the School Councils established by the Local Government (Scotland) Act 1973, should be looked at critically and closely and their future development be a matter both for widespread public debate and for research monitoring.

In all of this, however, there is a need for caution and balance. In spite of legitimate claims for the need to adapt the school curriculum to the local environment of the child, whether it be urban or rural, and to increase parental (and pupil) choice, both the Harvard Report and the recently published Munn Report (Scottish Education Department, 1977) are correct in arguing that a democratic society requires a centrally determined core curriculum, as well as a wide range of choice. This combination is needed to ensure the broad general education to which all children are entitled, and to underpin the increasingly complex decisions which participative democracy requires. This author, therefore, broadly endorses the recommendations of the Munn Report. Thus education can never be exclusively a question relating to urban areas alone but must remain fundamentally an issue for and about society as a whole.

On the other hand this author is clear that there *is* an urban problem, not because the problems are exclusive to urban communities but because of their sheer immensity and their apparent intractability. Education has a part to play in solving such problems. Schools and schoolteachers will become, as Shane argues (1977), more important in our society, although they may be required to change. This is not to argue, as some of the more extreme radicals do, that they must become involved in direct political activity at community level. Much of the impact of the Halsey Report was vitiated precisely because of the apparent political motivation of some of its contributors. On the contrary, change in accordance with the needs of a changing society ought to be careful and controlled. As the great Harvard Report argued, general education and a free society depends both on *Heritage* and *Change*. We are at one with Halsey when he argues that whilst educationalists cannot solve the economic and political problems of the country, they can, not only by teaching young people how to learn, and go on learning all their lives, *make a contribution* both to the health of the individual and to the society in which he lives. The current pessimism is misplaced. The education system has become more, not less, important.

Note

1. Of course the great nineteenth century theoretical debate on compulsion which exercised the minds of Parliamentarians and philosophers, at its most classic in J. S. Mill's essay 'On Liberty', had never been of the same concern to the Scots. Knox, after all, in the 'First Book of Discipline' (1561) had stated that 'no father shall use his child at his own fantasie' and had put forward the superior rights of the theocratic state (with effects on Scottish culture which last to this day). Nevertheless, in the new urban environment consequent upon industrialisation, schools appeared to some, especially to the urban deprived, as alien and unwelcome intrusions. This is in no way to deny the long-standing respect for education among working people, described, for example, in the important work of writers such as Richard Hoggart and Raymond Wlliams.

References

Advisory Council of Education in Scotland (1947). HMSO.

Central Advisory Council for Education (England) (1959) *15 to 18* (Crowther Report). HMSO.

Central Advisory Council for Education (England) (1967). *Children and their Primary Schools* (Plowden Report). HMSO.

Coleman, J.S. (1966) *Equality of Educational Opportunity*. United States Publication Office.

Committee on Higher Education (1963) *Higher Education*. Report of the Committee appointed by the Prime Minister under the Chairmanship of Lord Robbins 1961–63, Cmnd. 2154. HMSO.

Conant, J.B. (ed.) (1946) *General Education in a Free Society*. Harvard University Press, Cambridge, Mass.

Davie, R. *et al.* (1972) *From Birth to Seven*. National Children's Bureau. Longman, London.

Department of Education and Science, Welsh Office (1977) *A New Partnership for our Schools*. Report by a Committee of Enquiry appointed by the Secretary of State for Education and Science and the Secretary of State for Wales under the Chairmanship of Mr Tom Taylor C.B.E. HMSO.

Douglas, J.W.B. *et al.* (1968) *All our Future*. Peter Davies, London.

Field, F. (ed.) (1978) *Education and the Urban Crisis*. Routledge and Kegan Paul, London.

Fraser, E. (1959) *Home Environment and the School*. Scottish Council for Research in Education, Edinburgh.

Gittell, M. and **Hevesi, A.G.** (eds) (1969) *The Politics of Urban Education*. Praeger, New York.

Halsey, A.H. (ed.) (1972) *Educational Priority, E.P.A. Problems and Policies*, vol. I. Report of a research project sponsored by the Department of Education and Science and the Social Science Research Council. HMSO.

Macbeth, A.M. (1974) 'Parents have rights too', *The Times Educational Supplement*, 16 August.

Mays, J.B. (1962) *Education and the Urban Child*. Liverpool University Press.

Midwinter, E.C. (1973) *Patterns of Community Education*. Ward Lock International, London.

Pedley, R. (1962) *The Comprehensive School*. Penguin Books, Harmondsworth.

Roxburgh, J.M. (1971) *The School Board of Glasgow, 1813–1919*. University of London Press.

Scottish Education Department (1977) *The Structure of the Curriculum in the Third and Fourth Years of the Scottish Secondary School* (The Munn Report). HMSO.

Shane, H.G. (1977) *Curriculum Change Towards the 21st Century*. National Education Association of the United States. Washington D.C.

Wedge, P. and **Prosser, H.** (1973) *Born to Fail?* Arrow Books in association with the National Children's Bureau, London.

Weir, A.D. and **Nolan, F.J.** *Glad to be Out?* Scottish Council for Research in Education, Edinburgh.

West, E.G. (1965) *Education and the State*. Institute for Economic Affairs, London.

Wilkinson, E., *et al.* (1978a) *Strathclyde Experiment in Education*. Govan Project. Strathclyde Regional Council and University of Glasgow, Department of Education.

Wilkinson, E. (1978b) 'The Strathclyde Experiment in Education, (Moorpark Scheme)'. University of Glasgow Newsletter.

Chapter 9

Poverty and the conurbations

Introduction

The first problem which has to be faced at the beginning of any discussion of poverty is what is actually meant by poverty. Do we define it in some absolute sense, in that, say, those whose incomes only allow them to live at or below some subsistence level are 'in poverty' or do we define it in a relative sense, in that, say, the poor are those whose incomes are less than a certain proportion of the average income or, alternatively, those whose incomes are at or near the level which society deems to be poor in some sense (in Britain this will usually be the supplementary benefit scale rate)? The earliest work on the subject by Seebohm Rowntree at the turn of the century used an absolute standard of poverty but most recent research has used a relative standard. This method can be used to show what progress there may have been in the gradual elimination of poverty with economic progress. The disadvantage of the second method is that 'the poor are always with us' because they are thus defined, even though the poor in a developed economy may, as Harrington (1962) puts it, be better off than medieval knights on the one hand, or Asian peasants on the other. If, however, one is concerned with the characteristics and situation of those who are the poorest in a society at any one time, then, obviously one has to define poverty in a relative sense and so that is what we shall do here.

The characteristics of the poor

The use of relative standards for the identification of poverty allows the identification of the characteristics of those who are likely to be poor at any time and a comparison of the characteristics of the poor at earlier dates. One of the most recent studies of poverty shows that over half the low-income households in the United Kingdom were pensioners. As Table 9.1 shows, no other household type accounted for so

The author is indebted to Madelaine Drake, Bert Nicholson, David Eversley and others for their helpful discussion on the subject of this paper; of course they do not necessarily agree with the views expressed here.

Table 9.1 Distribution of low-income households and prevalence of low income in the United Kingdom: by household type, 1975

Household type	Proportion of all low-income households (%)	Prevalence of low-income households (low-income households as a percentage of all households)
Single pensioner	34	50
Married couple pensioner	21	41
Single person	5	15
Two adults	7	7
Other households without children	3	6
Single parent families	6	51
Two adults, 1, 2 children	12	10
Two adults, 3 or more children	9	26
Other households with children	4	9

Source: Van Slooten and Coverdale (1977).

Note: In the study quoted, low-income households are the 20 per cent of all households which have the lowest 'equivalent income', that is the lowest income on a basis which adjusts for the size and composition of households. The incomes of these households are, approximately, 'at or below the long-term supplementary benefit scale rate (including an allowance for average housing costs) plus 20 per cent' (Van Slooten and Coverdale, 1977, p. 30).

many poor households. Moreover as the second column of the Table shows this is not solely due to there being now a large number of pensioners; 50 per cent of households consisting of a single pensioner are poor, and over 40 per cent of married pensioners. The only other household type with a similar probability of being poor is the single-parent family of which over 50 per cent are poor. The household type with the next highest probability of being poor is the large family – over a quarter of two-parent families with three or more children were poor. Of the 45 per cent of the non-pensioner households which were poor, in 47 per cent of these households the heads were not in work, either through sickness or unemployment (i.e. 21 per cent of the total number of poor households).

Table 9.2 shows the way in which the relative importance of different types of poor households has changed over time. Whilst at the turn of the century the aged accounted for less than 10 per cent of poor households, the proportion has risen consistently since then to 55 per cent now, largely of course for demographic reasons as the number of people living well beyond retirement age has increased. On the other hand the relative importance of households which are poor even though the head of the household is at work has declined considerably, from over three-quarters of poor households in 1899 to less than one-fifth in 1975.

In one way, however, the situation has not changed so much over the years. Still only a small proportion of the poor are poor because of

Table 9.2 Immediate causes of poverty in Britain, 1899–1975

	Proportion of people in poverty (%)					
	1899	1936	1953–54	1960	1972	1975
Old age	} 10	15	49	33	55	55
Sickness		4	7	10	11	} 21
Unemployment	2	29	5	7	11	
Family with man in work:						
4 or fewer children	55	37	} 38	32	} 14	} 18
5 or more children	22	5		8		
Single-parent family	11	10		10	–	6

Sources: Data for 1975 are derived from Van Slooten and Coverdale (1977) and relate to households: the remainder of the Table is derived from Atkinson (1975). Single parent families were not distinguished separately in the source for 1972; it includes a further unclassified group.

'exceptional circumstances', i.e. unemployment, sickness or the absence of one parent; most poverty is related to the life cycle, the child-rearing stage in 1899 and old age now.

Yet another way of looking at these figures is to ask the question, 'Is the poverty of the household likely to be transitory or is it likely to be permanent?' Obviously to the household it makes a great deal of difference whether the situation is completely black or whether some light can be seen at the end of the tunnel. From this point of view the poverty of the aged is worst because it is completely permanent; there is no end but death. The poverty of the single-parent family is the next worst; it is likely to persist until the children have started to earn, or until the parent re-marries.

For the rest, we must distinguish between the sick and the healthy. A study of multiple deprivation in Lambeth showed that the job record of the disabled 'was often unstable – either they had a lot of time off work or they changed jobs often – and in any case they were usually in low-paid work. So their incomes were low' (Shankland Cox *et al.*, 1977, p. 32). And of course one reason why the disabled are in low-paid work is that their education will often have been interrupted because of their disability, and the interruptions to their work record will have hindered them from acquiring skills or responsibility on the job. Thus to a large extent their poverty is also likely to be permanent.

The situation of the healthy is different. In most parts of the country their poverty is likely to be transitory. In his pioneering study Rowntree noted the trough in the family cycle when children were being reared, and the man had to support the household on his earnings alone. This trough still exists. But as the consultants observed in the first report in the Lambeth Inner Area Study, now that many, if not most, wives go back to work (usually part-time) when their youngest child is at school, the trough of family poverty lasts less long that it used to. We might add what has obviously always been true, that it lasts longer the larger the family, and that the fall in family size over the last century has worked in the same direction as that other major change it has helped facilitate – the greater participation of wives in the labour force (Shankland Cox *et al.*, 1975, p. 20).

So, as the consultants observe in their second report, 'in families with children, the wife's earnings were often crucial in determining whether the household was deprived or not. As couples themselves recognised, when the wife is able to go out to work, even part-time, this immediately lifts the family out of income poverty (Shankland Cox *et al.*, 1977, p. 33). Thus for the young and healthy, poverty may be relatively short-term. For example, in one recent empirical study it was found that 'less than half of those who were in the lowest tenth of the [individual earnings] distribution in April 1970 were still in the lowest tenth in both April 1971 and April 1972' (Thatcher, 1974; quoted in Shankland Cox *et al.*, 1975, p. 19).

It should be noted that the reports referred to above relate to Lambeth in Inner London. Although much has been written about the deterioration of the economies of the inner cities in recent years it remains true that the general employment situation in London is better than in most other British cities, particularly those in the Assisted Areas. Thus in London, as against say Newcastle or Liverpool, any period of unemployment is likely to be shorter, earnings in any job are likely to be higher, and the wife is more likely to be able to find a job, whether part-time or full-time, when she wishes to return to work. It follows that in the development areas poverty because of unemployment, or poverty because of the child-rearing stage of the family cycle, is likely to last longer, and so to be qualitatively worse than in the more prosperous areas of the Midlands and Southern England.

As a digression we may wonder whether it would ever be possible to eliminate, solely by fiscal means, the child-rearing stage of the family cycle as a cause of *relative* poverty. Any fiscal policy, such as increasing child benefits, must also benefit the families with older children in which the wife goes out to work; thus relative inequality will be maintained. The only way of eliminating it would be by ensuring that children are not looked after during the day by their mothers, but in crêches and nurseries, as appears to be the policy in the countries of Eastern Europe.

Another factor which is important in determining the 'quality' of poverty is the existence of resources, and once again this is related to the degree of permanence of poverty. A household which has been able to build up a stock of resources, though poor in terms of income, will be able to survive a period of poverty without getting into difficulties. A family which has not will find the situation more difficult than one which has. Thus a worker who has been in employment all his life will find retirement on an old-age pension easier than one with similar skills who has been periodically out of work, either because of sickness, disablement or unemployment. (Moreover because of earnings-related benefits his pension will be higher.) The couple aged seventeen or so who marry with a baby on the way do not have a chance to acquire even a stock of domestic equipment before the husband has to support wife and children on his income alone. A couple having children later have had an opportunity to acquire furniture and domestic equipment and maybe other assets. Again, a period of unemployment will be easier to bear financially if it has not been preceded by similar periods of unemployment since the household is more likely to have resources to fall back on.[1]

Poverty and deprivation

The above discussion leads into the subject of deprivation. Whilst most economic discussion of poverty focuses almost exclusively on the level of income (Atkinson, 1975, Ch. 10), other studies have discussed the concept of deprivation. Thus Holtermann identifies areas of 'urban deprivation' and the Lambeth Inner Area Study Consultants report on 'Poverty and Multiple Deprivation' in their first and 'Multiple Deprivation' alone in their second report. To what extent is this distinction useful or meaningful? The problem which arises here is that to most people a 'deprived urban area' would be thought to be an area inhabited mainly by people who are poor. But if deprivation and poverty can be distinguished, then this is not necessarily so.

As we have shown above, certain kinds of households are more likely to be poor than others – the elderly, the disabled or those suffering from ill-health, those frequently unemployed, the single-parent family. To the extent that these count as deprivations, and it is obvious that at least disablement and ill-health can, then it is clear that people can be deprived and yet *not* be poor, since not all the disabled have very low incomes. The Lambeth study shows, however, that if different kinds of deprivation are measured in a large number of families, then many are associated together. In their study they found that absence of leisure activities, no holidays, few evenings out, were all, for fairly obvious reasons, associated with low incomes. Low income can also lead to a lack of social contact; it's no use going to the local pub if you can't afford to buy your round. This lack of contact with 'the outside world' explains why it is a mistake to regard the presence of a television set as indicating that a home is not poor. Television provides the cheapest way of compensating for the lack of social contact and leisure activities, and poor families will rightly fight to retain it. The Lambeth study (Shankland Cox et al., 1975, p. 23) found three major types of deprivation – income deprivation, in which, as already mentioned, lack of income was associated with lack of social contact; disablement which was associated not only to some extent with lack of income but also with other problems (as assessed in interviews); and housing deprivation – the quality of housing, the presence or absence of household amenities such as bath, w.c., and the ownership or lack of household accessories such as cooker, refrigerator, washing machine and so on. At first sight the most striking finding of the consultants is that in the study area there was an almost complete lack of correlation between income deprivation and housing deprivation. Within this area of central Lambeth people with higher incomes were not necessarily any better housed than people with lower incomes. Similar studies carried out in Camden in Inner North London and in Small Heath in the inner area of Birmingham obtained similar results (Shankland Cox *et al.*, 1977, p. 38). Whilst it would be wise to recognise that the higher incomes in these areas are not very high, and that a national study would be more likely to find a greater correlation between income levels and housing, the surprising fact remains that in the bottom half of the income distribution the correlation is minimal. Why should this be? The explanation put forward by the consultants is that in these areas the impact of local authority housing construction and allocation had been such as to completely break the link between the quality of housing and income.

Let us show why this should be so. Suppose that there was some correlation between income and housing in the past, before the large-scale construction of council housing. Then those with the lowest incomes would tend to live in the worst housing, in the slums. If the local authority now engages in a programme of slum clearance, the poorest families will mostly be rehoused in council housing, which, though it may not be of the very highest quality, will be of an adequate standard and will include all the basic amenities. Thus the process of slum clearance will in itself tend to break the link between income and housing quality. Moreover, once a stock of local authority housing is in existence, local authority allocation procedures will also tend to break the link, for in any waiting list the authority will give extra points to, and therefore preference to, households with the kind of characteristics which make them likely to be poor, i.e. single-parent families, large families, the disabled, the aged; additionally the aged are more likely to be in local authority housing simply because they are older and have therefore had more chance of being allocated a dwelling at an earlier stage of life. These allocation procedures make the finding of almost no relationship between 'income deprivation' and 'housing deprivation' in Lambeth not so surprising as it appears at first sight. It should however be stressed once again that in areas such as Lambeth one is considering a situation where almost everyone rents, there is not much owner-occupation, and where almost all household incomes are less than average. A similar investigation carried out on a national or even an urban scale would be more likely to find some correlation between income and the quality of housing.

Given that we can distinguish between income deprivation, which is what is generally understood as poverty, and housing deprivation, and that on the basis of both theoretical reasoning and empirical evidence we would expect the two kinds of deprivation not to be highly correlated in low-income areas, it follows that the use of housing indicators to identify areas of urban deprivation may, indeed must, identify areas of housing deprivation rather than areas of income deprivation. We have no reason to believe that because the majority of the population in an area are badly housed, the majority of the population are also poor. They may have lower than average incomes but they are not necessarily at or near the Supplementary Benefit level. Unfortunately, the British Census collects a lot of information on housing but none on incomes and relatively little on income-related variables. As a result housing variables tend to dominate other data in any attempt to identify areas of urban deprivation. In the study of urban deprivation by Holtermann (1975) one method of finding areas (actually Census Enumeration Districts or EDs) was to find those EDs which were in the worst 1 per cent of EDs on at least one of 11 indicators. Of these indicators, eight were indicators of housing conditions, and the others were male unemployment, female unemployment and households with no car. Only these three are likely to be indicators of income deprivation, with the last having the strongest relationship to income.

An alternative method of identifying deprived areas, indeed the major method used by Holtermann, was to find those which are 'multiply deprived' in that the ED is in the worst 5 per cent on one indicator and in the worst 5 per cent of EDs on some other, or others. Once again, however, housing conditions in one form or another always provide one of the indicators, with male unemployment being the only clearly income-related variable.

The difficulty with this kind of area-based approach is that the population who are poor cannot necessarily be identified from the Census, and even if they can be, they are not necessarily concentrated into particular small areas. Thus the Census does not collect information on the disabled or on single-parent families, and anyway there is no reason to suppose that they would be spatially concentrated. Information is collected about age and this shows that the elderly, whom we have shown will probably be poor, are very dispersed compared with bad housing conditions. Thus if we take the 5 per cent of EDs with the highest concentrations of pensioner households in the country, only 9 per cent of the pensioner households in the country are in these EDs. On the other hand, if we take the 5 per cent of EDs with the worst housing conditions, over 50 per cent of households sharing accommodation live in these EDs; similarly, 30 per cent of the households which lack a bath live in the 5 per cent of the worst EDs.

The three income-related variables used by Holtermann are also not so spatially concentrated as bad housing conditions. Only 7 per cent of the households not having a car live in the 5 per cent of EDs in which car ownership is least, and only 16 per cent of unemployed males and 12 per cent of unemployed females live in the 5 per cent of EDs which come out worst on these indicators. Thus not only will this kind of analysis be better at identifying areas of housing deprivation than income deprivation, but also, if it is used to identify areas of income deprivation, the difference between these areas and 'non-deprived' areas will not in fact be very great. The vast majority of those living in poverty will live outside these areas. This will not be so true of those suffering from housing deprivation.

Areas of urban deprivation

For what they are worth, given the problems outlined above, Table 9.3 sets out the geographical distribution of the EDs which could be described as areas of multiple deprivation in that they are among the worst 15 per cent of EDs on two or three indicators. What stands out from the table is, firstly, that London and Clydeside have far more than their share of the worst areas, and that the other conurbations, though to a lesser extent, also have more than their share. Table 9.4 shows that within these conurbations the vast majority of the areas of urban deprivation are located in the inner areas. We should, however, be wary of drawing any conclusions from these statistics about the norma-tive significance of this concentration of deprived urban areas in the inner cities of the conurbations. In one of the first ever studies in urban economics, R. M. Haig (1927), talking about New York, commented that 'the magnitude of the metropolis . . . operates like a Bunsen flame under a test tube' to ensure the spatial separation of different economic activities which would 'not become explicit in small places where the pressure for space is not great'. Even if the population were randomly distributed within any urban area, since Enumeration Districts are fairly constant in size, one would expect to find that, in the smallest town, each of the few EDs would contain a random assortment of the population. In the larger cities, however, purely as a matter of chance some EDs would be bound to contain a disproportionate number of the poor and a disproportionate number of the wealthy. In fact, of course, the distribution of the population is not random and various economic forces lead to the social segregation of the population (Evans, 1975) and also lead to the lower-income groups locating in the inner areas of the city (Evans, 1973). Obviously the number of people in any particular income group will be larger the larger the city, so that the contiguous areas occupied by any income group or displaying any particular kind of housing condition will also be larger the larger the city. As a result, if EDs do not vary in size with city size, not only will the *number* of EDs dominated by any characteristic increase with city

Table 9.3 Geographical distribution of EDs with levels of two or more kinds of deprivation (among the worst 15% of EDs on two or three indicators)

Area	All EDs in Great Britain	1. Households over-crowded (>1.5 p.p.r.*) 2. Male unemployment	1. Households over-crowded (>1.5 p.p.r.) 2. Lack excl. use of all basic amenities	1. Male unemployment 2. Lack excl. use of all basic amenities	1. Households over-crowded (>1.5 p.p.r.) 2. Male unemployment 3. Lack excl. use of all basic amenities
Conurbation					
Inner London	8.6	11.7	37.1	12.0	18.1
Rest of Greater London	10.4	1.1	6.7	1.2	1.4
Tyneside	2.0	4.6	1.8	4.6	3.2
West Yorkshire	4.3	4.4	4.1	4.5	5.9
Merseyside	2.7	5.2	1.4	6.7	2.9
South East Lancs.	5.8	5.4	4.4	8.9	6.7
West Midlands	4.8	5.6	7.4	5.6	8.4
Clydeside	4.3	28.6	14.9	14.2	26.6
Region					
Rest of South East	14.9	2.5	3.3	3.2	2.9
Rest of Northern	4.1	4.4	2.2	6.6	3.6
Rest of Yorkshire and Humberside	5.0	1.4	1.1	5.6	1.2
Rest of North West	5.4	2.5	1.3	4.5	1.7
Rest of West Midlands	4.2	0.1	1.3	1.9	1.4
East Midlands	5.0	2.2	3.2	5.0	4.2
East Anglia	2.0	0.4	0.3	1.2	0.4
South West	5.3	1.6	0.9	1.7	1.3
Rest of Scotland	6.8	15.1	8.0	6.2	9.0

* persons per room
Source: Holtermann (1975).

Table 9.4 The worst 5 per cent of each conurbation's EDs on individual indicators – proportion in core local authorities

Indicator	Greater London	Tyneside	Merseyside	South East Lancashire	West Midlands	Clydeside	Greater Nottingham Area
Overcrowded households (>1.5 persons per room)	81	63	81	66	89	97	98
Lack excl. use all basic amenities	94	55	92	72	77	94	98
Males unemployed, but seeking work or sick	86	65	82	73	89	90	100
Females unemployed, but seeking work or sick	73	46	75	56	81	69	74
Per cent of conurbation's EDs in core local authorities	47	41	53	29	59	55	45

Source: Holtermann (1975).

Note: The central cores of the conurbations were defined as follows – Greater London: the area of Inner London Education Authority excluding Greenwich and including Newham; Tyneside: Newcastle upon Tyne and Gateshead; Merseyside: Liverpool and Bootle; S.E. Lancs.: Manchester and Salford; West Midlands: Birmingham, Walsall, and West Bromwich; Clydeside: Glasgow; Greater Nottingham: Nottingham. The remainder of the Greater Nottingham Area comprised Arnold, Beeston, Stampleford, Carlton, Hucknall, Long Eaton, West Bridford, Basford, Bingham.

size but also the *proportion* which are dominated will increase. It should not be at all surprising therefore to find that the conurbations, and London in particular, contain a disproportionate number of the worst 5 per cent of EDs with particular kinds of deprivation; we should also expect to find that the conurbations, and London in particular, would contain a disproportionate number of the best EDs, from any study of urban 'non-deprivation' to be carried out.

The more important question from a welfare point of view is not 'In what parts of the country are there the largest contiguous areas populated by the poor?', but 'In what parts of the country is there the largest proportion of poor households?'. Table 9.5 gives an answer to this

Table 9.5 Distribution of low-income households and prevalence of low income: by standard region, 1975.

Area	Low-income households as a percentage of all households in the same region	Percentage of all low-income households
England:		
North	23	7
Yorkshire and Humberside	24	11
East Midlands	22	7
East Anglia	25	5
Greater London	15	9
South East (except Greater London)	13	11
South West	19	7
West Midlands	20	9
North West	23	13
Wales	24	6
Scotland	21	10
Northern Ireland	43	4

Source: Van Slooten and Coverdale (1977).

question. Clearly Northern Ireland is the most deprived region in the United Kingdom (it is unfortunate perhaps that its urban areas were not included in Holtermann's study of urban deprivation). Apart from this region the others are not very different from each other. Low-income households account for 25 per cent of the households in East Anglia, the highest proportion in Great Britain, and 13 per cent in the South East excluding London, the lowest. It is interesting to see that despite the large number of areas of urban deprivation in Greater London the proportion of low-income households is the second lowest, a clear indication of the importance of separating the problem of areas from the problem of proportions. Moreover, even Scotland does not have a large proportion of low-income households, an indication that the bad housing conditions which are used as indicators of urban deprivation, particularly in Glasgow, are not necessarily indicators of poverty in the strict sense.[2]

A further question which could be asked instead of 'In what parts of the country is there the largest proportion of poor households?' is 'Where is there the largest number of poor households?'. Once again, we get different answers. From Table 9.5 it can be seen that the largest number of low-income households in any region is in fact in the South East (if Greater London is included). Thus the most prosperous region has the most low-income households, but solely because it is anyway the largest region in terms of population. Northern Ireland, because it is the smallest region, has the fewest low-income households even though 43 per cent of the households in the province have low incomes, a far higher proportion than in any region of Great Britain.

The answers to this last question seem the least relevant of the answers to the three questions relating to area, proportion or numbers. The question of proportion seems to me to be the relevant question from a welfare point of view. There is no doubt, however, that the question of area, or perhaps one could say mass or concentration, is important in determining whether or not poverty in a region is considered to be an important political problem. A large area entirely populated by people with below-average incomes, with a high proportion in poverty, is more likely to get political attention even when the situation occurs in a large city and the surrounding suburbs have above-average incomes, than the same number of the poor living scattered among the same number of the better-off in a region of small industrial and commuter towns and seaside resorts like the South East. Partly this is a result of the electoral system in Britain. Where representatives are elected from single-member constituencies both to Parliament and to the councils of local government, any representative will be aware of the problems of the majority in his area, and less aware of the problems of the minority. Thus if the poor, or any other group, are scattered they are less likely to be well represented than if they are concentrated. The other reason why greater political attention will be paid to concentrations of the poor, or any other group, is simply that when concentrated they become more *visible*. Poverty which could be ignored when scattered becomes difficult to ignore if the poor dominate a district.

Possibly this tendency for areas or concentrations of poverty to attract greater political attention than scattered poverty would be unimportant were it not that concern over areas leads to attempts to provide solutions for areas. As a result various area-based policies and experiments have been developed and tried out over the last ten years.[3] The first of these, the Urban Aid Programme, was introduced in 1968. About £4 million per year was spent under this programme and used to support a variety of projects – nursery schools, family and housing advice centres, family planning projects – all of which were to be in 'localised districts which bore the marks of multiple deprivation'.

Next, in 1969, came the National Community Development Project. Under this scheme twelve local Community Development Projects were set up, to last for five years; later an Information and Intelligence Unit was created to evaluate and co-ordinate the work of the twelve CDPs which were supposed to find new ways of meeting the needs of people living in areas of high social deprivation.

In 1971 the Community Programmes Department of the Home Office was set up to co-ordinate the various policies and itself set up Neighbourhood Schemes, 'to observe and test the effects of coordinating £150,000 worth of capital resources going into an area of special social need'. Although it was intended that there should be ten such schemes, in fact only two were set up.

The Inner Area Studies were set up in 1973, to be carried out by consultants in Small Heath in Birmingham, central Lambeth in London, and Liverpool 8, with the aim of investigating conditions in these areas and ways in which these conditions could be improved.

Even before these reports had been published yet another co-ordinating body was set up in the Home Office, the Urban Deprivation Unit. In 1974 this proposed that there should be Comprehensive Community Programmes. The CCPs were based on a policy of finding areas of intense urban deprivation and then directing existing resources into them – no additional resources were to be provided. Most of the energy behind this approach has gone into trying to identify the areas (it is from this research that the work by Holtermann quoted earlier derives) and in arranging for the setting up of trial CCPs, the first in Motherwell and the second in Gateshead, 'to test the applicability of the approach and to develop a framework for the development of CCPs in other areas'.

The common themes which run through these various policy initiatives, apart from the obvious one that they are all based, in one way or another, on the idea of areas of deprivation, are the ideas of investigation and experiment to find out what should and can be done, and of economising on resources by only spending money on areas where deprivation could be proved, whilst, if possible, diverting this expenditure from other areas. Since the policies in fact rarely got beyond the experimental stage, one may note, somewhat cynically, that a double economy was achieved; very little was actually spent on areas of urban deprivation because all the effort over the last 10 years has gone into actually identifying the areas or trying to find out what would be the best thing to do if they could be identified. Presumably this economy is not deliberate; governments have meant to do something rather than merely put off doing anything. The main result has been that the Government has put up what is, by the standards of the social sciences (if not the pure sciences), a large sum of money for research into the problems of the inner areas. But, as we have attempted to show, poverty is not area-based – most of the poor live outside areas of urban deprivation however defined – so it is difficult to formulate satisfactory area-based policies. Thus the research and investigation which was carried out on the premise that area-based policies would work, the only question being to identify the right policies, in fact showed that areal policies were unlikely to work and therefore that the initial premise was incorrect. Two responses from policy-oriented researchers may be noted. Holtermann (1978) has argued that poverty may not be area-related but area-based policies might be more efficient than national policies. Since, as we show at the end of the paper, national policies can be conceived which are probably more efficient than area-based policies, this view seems incorrect.

In the work of the CDP the combination of factors outlined above resulted in a neo-Marxian interpretation of the situation, set out for example in the CDP's (1977) *Gilding the Ghetto*, one of the final reports from the project. The fact that governments appeared unwilling to actually *do* anything about the conditions found in the CDP areas other than set up investigatory teams to undertake palliative measures at minimal cost was taken as confirming the view that the state is run by and for Capital (cf. Marx's remark to the effect that the government of a capitalist state is a committee for managing the common affairs of the bourgeoisie), so that the palliative measures taken were merely measures of social control to ensure that the working class didn't get too restive. The fact that poverty and deprivation were not areally concentrated so that there was little that could be done in particular areas to remedy the situation was taken as confirming the view that poverty and deprivation are endemic in the capitalist system so that nothing could be done without changing that system.

Cumulative deprivation?

As we have shown most poverty would be remediable with adequate social security benefits. Only a small section of the population of households with low incomes seems to suffer from low income as a result of low wages and/or prolonged unemployment. For obvious reasons, however, areas where high proportions of the population suffered from this kind of poverty are precisely the areas where Community Development Projects were likely to be set up – areas in which the local industries employed mainly unskilled labour and were declining.

As we have already shown, it is in precisely these areas where the impact of poverty on any household may be greatest since households will have been unable to build up resources to survive a short period on low incomes and also because any period of unemployment is likely to be longer rather than shorter, thus eating into any resources which the household may have. Obviously this kind of poverty is hard to live with and it is most likely to occur in the less prosperous regions of the country, the development areas. But the problems of these areas affect the individual household, and would still affect it even if there were no concentration and it were the only poor household in the area – i.e. it affects the chances of employment of those seeking work in the house-hold and their past job chances. This still leaves unanswered the question as to whether any concentration of poverty is peculiarly bad. In general in this discussion we have assumed that a number of poor households concentrated in one place are no better off and no worse off than similar households dispersed amongst the higher-income households.

It is often implied that this is not so, though it is difficult to track down explicit statements, let alone any empirical evidence to support the view that concentration makes the poor worse off. As an example I quote at length below from a paper given by Edwin Brooks at a symposium conducted by the Royal Geographical Society in 1975 to discuss the problems of the inner cities. He said:

> The inner cities of post-war Britain have experienced deprivations of a cumulative and multiple nature, which now threaten social and political stability no less than the depressed regions of that earlier period.
>
> However inadvertently, Government has facilitated a spatial sifting policy which was the geographical expression of the rise of those *elites* collectively termed the meritocracy. Employment objectives sprang from a background of upward social mobility and rising economic affluence among various strata of the working class, and this vertical movement has been translated via a combination of local authority housing policies and locational preferences by owner-occupiers into horizontal geographical displacement. Meanwhile, back in the drained poverty ghettos ... of the inner city, the ranks of the future employables are recruited from the ROSLA (raising of the school leaving age) truants, the educationally sub-normal coloureds, and the heterogeneous social cripples who make up the obverse of meritocracy. (p. 356).

The clear implication of this passage is that concentration makes poverty worse but there is no explicit statement to this effect. Again the CDP said in 1977 that in the areas where they were sited 'there was a higher proportion of people in such places eligible for state support [and] the ways in which they had formerly cared for each other were breaking down, and when family and neighbour support failed they were going to the social services or social security' (p. 38). Another view often expressed with respect to the inner city is that the out-migration of the skilled from these areas worsens the position of those who are left. Thus the Secretary of State for the Environment stated that 'the causes of inner city decline lie primarily in their relative economic decline, in a major migration of people, often the most skilled, and in a massive reduction in the number of jobs which are left' (Peter Shore, 17 September 1976). Once again it is hinted, but not stated, that the outward movement makes those who remain worse off.

The problem is to establish from these hints the way in which the poor are thought to be made worse off by concentration. There is a possible confusion here. Suppose that there is a mix of skilled and unskilled workers living in an area and that the skilled workers leave. It is clear that the average income level in the area must fall, the average unemployment rate will probably increase and the proportion in poverty will increase. Thus in one sense the area is in decline and the population of the area is worse off than it was before. In this sense the migration of the skilled can be a cause of an area's decline. But this out-migration does not necessarily mean that the unskilled who remain in the area are any worse off or any better off than they were before. The average may have changed but the condition of each individual household has not necessarily changed.

It seems to me that many speakers on this subject may have made this confusion, and of course we come up against the fact that while the condition of the poor may not have changed, as we have already remarked, their situation will have become more visible and more likely to be seen as a political problem.

Is there any way in which concentration will make the poor really worse off? If the skilled leave an area will the situation of the less skilled who remain be altered for the worse, or even, of course, for the better? Possible answers to the question are discussed below.

1. One possibility is hinted at in the remark quoted above about 'systems of mutual support breaking down'. If only some of the population are poor at any one time, then the rest of the population is more likely to be able to help them if they are not themselves poor. Within the extended family, clothes, toys and other things may be passed on to those who are poor because of their stage in the life cycle or because of unemployment, or both. Children in work are more likely to be able to help their elderly parents. Shops are more likely to sell 'on tick' to those who it is known will only be in difficulties for a short time but will soon get another job. But if all are poor, then each is in need and each is unable to help any other. Obviously this point relates to our earlier discussion of the importance of the existence of resources and the problems created by long periods of unemployment. A situation in which some of the people are unemployed for some of the time is a great deal better than one in which most of the people are unemployed for most of the time.

2. The point is sometimes made, particularly with reference to the problems of the inner city, that the movement of industry, particularly its decentralisation, is leading to a similar movement by the skilled workers who follow, and are encouraged to follow, their jobs to other areas. The selective character of the movement may be exacerbated by the unskilled finding it more difficult to move house because of the tenure restrictions controlling movement into and out of local authority housing. Nor are the unskilled likely to be offered favourable terms in new towns or development areas to acquire housing since they will

not be 'essential' workers. The skilled workers, it is said, are likely to be more articulate, the natural leaders of the working-class community. If they leave, so the argument seems to run, those who remain will be worse off both because they will lack anyone to lead any community action which might become necessary and because they will lack people to explain or interpret the rights of those who remain. Even if this argument is correct, it seems unlikely that market forces will lead to complete areas being denuded of the skilled and/or articulate to the extent hypothesised.

3. However, whilst it is unlikely that market forces will lead to the sort of situation which is implied, it is clear that government action can, and does, ensure that the least able of the poor are brought together in one place and discussion with social workers and tenants suggests that their situation is thereby made worse. Local authorities have a statutory duty to provide housing for the population of their area. Obviously some households may be bad tenants, either because they are bad rent payers or because they cause damage to the property or because they disrupt the social climate in any estate that they live in. If this is so, the local authority may fulfil its statutory duty by putting these tenants into its least desirable estate. As a result this estate will become even less desirable and tenants who are able to choose will move out of the estate and will not move to it. The result will be an estate marked by social problems of all kinds. Since families with social problems, almost by definition, create problems for those in contact with them socially, the situation of those families, who, because of their own problems, are sent to the estate, must be worsened because they will have to bear the brunt of the social problems created by the others. Moreover, the selection procedure of the local authority leads inevitably to such an estate lacking people with initiative, able to organise or lead any community organisation or action group, or able to explain or interpret either their own rights or the rights of others.

In the end, of course, the unwillingness of any household with any choice to go to such an estate is likely to lead to it increasingly consisting of empty vandalised dwellings which eventually have to be demolished. For descriptions of such a situation see the papers by John English on Ferguslie Park (1974) and on another unnamed but strikingly similar estate (1976), and also the paper by Alan McGregor (1977) on the labour market for residents of Ferguslie Park.

4. Apart from the above, one effect which an increase in the poverty of an area, through market forces, may have is in demoralising the population and leading to their alienation. If upward mobility within an area is limited, because of the shortage of skilled jobs, so that upward mobility must therefore mean leaving the area, and if the number of jobs available is decreasing, then this is likely to lead to the demoralisation or alienation of the population, who may feel both neglected

within a hostile environment and with little incentive, because of pessimism about the future, to do anything for themselves. If anything, activity will be against the outside world, in the form of sit-ins and other community action.

Conclusions

If one can draw any conclusion from the above discussion it is that poverty is not usually an areal problem. Even if one can identify areas in which a large proportion of the population are poor, there is little ground for believing that such a concentration makes them worse off except in the case of some local authority housing estates. The majority of the population in any area will usually not be poor and the vast majority of the poor in the nation do not live in large concentrations of poverty. Moreover, though it is easy to identify areas in which housing is bad, because of the type of information collected in the British Census, there is no necessary correlation between housing and income, so that areas which are identified as areas of urban deprivation using Census statistics, may not be areas of poverty but areas of bad housing. For all these reasons we must conclude that area-based policies present no easy way of solving the problem of poverty. Nor will they necessarily be more economically efficient, as Holtermann (1978) has argued. National policies can be conceived which are both relatively cheap and will affect selectively a large number of the poor. The substitution of Child Benefit for each child, paid in cash to the parents, for an income tax allowance for each child, which of necessity only benefited those families whose income was high enough for them to pay tax, results in deliberate transfer of income to those on low incomes with large families. The payment of an extra benefit to the first child in a single-parent family is also a deliberate transfer of income to a group with a high incidence of poverty. Both these policies, which are only recent, will have the effect of removing a high proportion of the families with children out of the poverty group at a fairly small cost to the exchequer. As a result, however, as a glance at Table 9.1 will confirm, the group who are poor will increasingly consist of the elderly, and to do anything for this group can be very costly. In the long run the recent improvements in pensions schemes may have some effect but only after many years, and those who always earn very low incomes will still only be entitled to the minimum basic pension which is likely still to be below the then Supplementary Benefit level. Probably the only cheap way to approach this problem would be to find out among which groups of the elderly the incidence of poverty is highest; it is probable for example that the probability of poverty increases with age, so that an increase in the, at present tiny, additional amount paid to those of seventy-five or eighty-five or so, with graded increases for different age groups might be one possible, cheap non-spatial policy.

Notes

1. It may, however, be less easy to bear psychologically, just as in an area of high unemployment there may be less psychological strain in being unemployed than in an area where few other people are unemployed.
2. The causes of the legacy of housing problems in Glasgow are difficult to establish for certain; for the most convincing explanation see the recently published history of the city in the nineteenth century by Sydney Checkland (1976).
3. The Community Development Project publication *Gilding the Ghetto* (1977) gives a brief history of these policies.

References

Atkinson, A.B. (1975) *The Economics of Inequality*. Oxford University Press.

Brooks, E. (1975) 'Development problems of the inner city', *Geographical Journal* **141**(3), Nov., pp. 355–62.

Checkland, S.G. (1976), *The Upas Tree, Glasgow 1875–1975. A Study in Growth and Contraction*. Glasgow University Press.

Community Development Project (1977) *Gilding the Ghetto*. Home Office, London.

English, J. (1974) 'Ferguslie Park: profile of a deprived community', Paisley Community Development Project Research Team, *mimeo*.

English, J. (1976) 'Housing allocation and a deprived Scottish estate', *Urban Studies* **13**(3), Oct., pp. 319–24.

Evans, A. (1973) *The Economics of Residential Location*. Macmillan, London.

Evans, A. (1975) 'Economic influences of social mix', *Urban Studies* **13**(3), Oct., pp. 247–60.

Haig, R. M. (1927) *Regional Survey of New York and its Environs*. City Plan Commission, New York.

Harrington, M. (1962) *The Other America*, Macmillan, London, and Penguin, Harmondsworth.

Holtermann, S. E. (1975) 'Areas of urban deprivation in Great Britain: an analysis of 1971 census data', *Social Trends* **6**, pp. 33–47.

Holtermann, S. E. (1978) 'The welfare economics of priority area policies', *Journal of Social Policy* **7**(1), Jan., pp. 23–40.

McGregor, A. (1977) 'Intra-urban variations in unemployment duration: a case study', *Urban Studies* **14**(3), Oct., pp. 303–14.

Shankland Cox Partnership in association with the Institute of Community Studies (1975) 'Poverty and multiple deprivation'. Department of the Environment, London.

Shankland Cox Partnership in association with the Institute of Community Studies (1977) 'Second report on multiple deprivation'. Department of the Environment, London.

Thatcher, A. R. (1974) 'The new earnings survey and the distribution of earnings'. Paper to the Royal Economic Society Conference, July.

Van Slooten, R. and **Coverdale, A.H.** (1977) 'The characteristics of low income households', *Social Trends* **8**, pp. 26–39.

Chapter 10

Unemployment and the labour market

In this chapter we concentrate on the labour market problems, and in particular on the problem of unemployment, that conurbations have experienced or are expected to experience in the future. We will examine the condition of, and recent changes in, the labour markets of the conurbations to see whether it can reasonably be concluded that they have distinctive problems. In the light of this discussion we will then evaluate some labour market policy initiatives that have been advocated for the conurbations.

It is commonly said that there are three types of unemployment. First, there is frictional unemployment, which is an inevitable consequence of people moving, either voluntarily or not, from job to job in search of better conditions. Second, there is unemployment that results from a deficiency of aggregate demand in the economy. Third, there is structural unemployment, resulting from a too rapid change in the economic structure of an area or from too much inertia in the face of change.

The British conurbations, in common with other areas, experience each of these types of unemployment. As regards frictional unemployment it is not clear whether they have more or less than do other areas. The theory on this point is ambiguous and no reliable empirical work has been reported. Whatever the precise facts, however, there are unlikely to be substantial differences in the amount of frictional unemployment between conurbations and other areas.

As regards deficient demand unemployment, there is no doubt that some conurbations suffer from persistent difficulties. Clydeside is an obvious example here. These difficulties, however, normally reflect wider regional problems rather than a specially conurbation one, and it is clearly not the case that British conurbations in general have suffered from a lack of aggregate demand.

To the extent that there is a distinctive problem of unemployment in the conurbations it must reflect structural difficulties. In nineteenth-century Britain such difficulties were associated with a rapid growth of population and economic activity, as they are today in the large cities of many underdeveloped countries. Currently in Britain they are more likely to be seen as a product of the reverse phenomenon, that is, of the rapid decline in the conurbations both of population and of work-places.

For a number of reasons many, if not all, of the conurbations have tended to lose their appeal as work-place centres. The reasons here include technical advances of many kinds, transport and communication developments, changing factor prices and certain public policies, notably planning policies (see Ch. 3). A consequence of these developments is that the number of jobs located in the conurbations has fallen. Taken by itself this fall in job opportunities would imply a rise in unemployment, particularly among less mobile and more vulnerable groups in the labour force. The high unemployment might show up either as a rise in the number on the unemployment register or as a fall in activity rates, as discouraged workers withdrew from the labour force. In addition to this rise in unemployment there would probably be some consequential net out-migration of population and some fall in net inward commuting. These latter changes would reduce the rise in unemployment that would otherwise occur.

It is this pattern of work-place decline and unemployment increase that has probably been perceived by many observers as the major development in British conurbations in recent years. It is, however, a very one-sided view. It overlooks the largely simultaneous reductions in population and resident labour force that have occurred for reasons that are often independent of those causing the decline in work-places. The most important influences here are rising incomes, housing market changes and transport developments, particularly the growth of car ownership.

Again, taken by itself, a fall in the resident labour force would tend to reduce unemployment rates in the conurbations, by reducing the supply of workers relative to the demand for them. The reduction in unemployment would not be the same for all of those remaining behind because the out-migration would tend to be concentrated among certain types of labour, for example among skilled manual workers. Nevertheless, all workers remaining are likely to witness some improvement in their job opportunities. As with work-place migration, population migration is likely to generate consequential movements. Thus, some firms in the conurbations might close down or move out in search of labour, and there might be some increase in net inward commuting. Both of these developments would reduce the fall in unemployment.

A balanced assessment of the structural changes in the conurbations requires an investigation of both work-place loss and population loss taken together. Until this is done, the likely change in the unemployment rates in the conurbations must remain an open question.

Some facts on unemployment in the conurbations

In April 1971, according to the Census of Population, the unemployment rates for males in the conurbations were: Central Clydeside 8.7

per cent, Greater London 3.7 per cent, Merseyside 7.8 per cent, South East Lancashire 4.4 per cent, Tyneside 7.8 per cent, West Midlands 4.0 per cent and West Yorkshire 4.5 per cent. These rates refer to males in the labour force who were out of employment and not sick. The question is, with what should they be compared in order to assess the unemployment position in the conurbations?

One possibility is to compare each conurbation with its surrounding region. If this is done for 1971 the results show that unemployment rates in the conurbations were relatively high, except in West Yorkshire, where they were the same. In comparison to the surrounding region, they were particularly high in Clydeside, Merseyside and Tyneside. This pattern, however, is typical of large urban areas and is not confined to the conurbations. For example, a comparison of the male unemployment rates in 1971 in 13 of the largest county boroughs of England and Wales with those in their associated counties shows a similar relationship. Except for Plymouth and Sheffield, unemployment rates in the county boroughs were everywhere higher than those in the surrounding counties. It is also clear that county boroughs had higher unemployment rates than the conurbations of which they were the cores. For example, Liverpool county borough had an unemployment rate of 9.6 per cent, as compared with 7.8 per cent for the Merseyside conurbation; similarly, Newcastle had an unemployment rate of 9.3 per cent compared to Tyneside's 7.8 per cent. This hints at inner-city problems, to which we return below.

Given that conurbations had relatively high unemployment rates in 1971, the next question to be considered is, has the pattern always been that way? Unfortunately, it is not possible to estimate the relative position of the conurbations in 1961, the date of the previous full Census, because the basic data are not available for the relevant areas. We can, however, compare the county boroughs with their associated counties. As before, with the exception of Plymouth and Sheffield, the county boroughs had higher unemployment rates than did their associated counties. Over the decade there was an improvement in the position of some county boroughs, relative to their counties, and a deterioration in the position of others. Thus Plymouth, Liverpool, Nottingham and Stoke-on-Trent improved their relative position, while Bristol, Manchester and Sheffield suffered a relative decline. Over all, however, there was no clear trend. The same is true for those county boroughs that are constituent parts of the conurbations. Manchester has a relatively sharp deterioration, while Bradford and Leeds each had small ones; Liverpool had a very sharp relative improvement, while Birmingham and Newcastle each had very small ones. Over all, for these county boroughs, there was no clear trend of deterioration or improvement in relation to their associated counties.

However, a different comparison suggests that the conurbations might well have suffered a deterioration in their relative unemployment position between 1961 and 1971. The Department of Employment has provided estimates of the male unemployment rates in the conurbations for 1961 and 1971 (DOE, 1977, p. 82). These estimates include those who were out of employment but sick. If these estimates are compared to the corresponding figures for Great Britain, the picture that emerges is that only in Merseyside was there a slower growth of unemployment than in the nation as a whole. Of the other conurbations, West Yorkshire and the West Midlands had particularly large relative increases in unemployment.

The two sets of evidence cannot easily be reconciled. It is possible, however, that the deterioration in the conurbations, relative to Great Britain, is more a reflection of regional trends than of developments in the conurbations as such. Alternatively, there may be peculiarities in the spatial distribution of the out-of-work sick.

Direct comparisons can be made between the conurbations and their associated regions for 1966, from the 10 per cent sample Census. These show that in 1966, in contrast to 1971, there was no definite pattern of the conurbations having a higher unemployment rate than their surrounding regions. Given the 1971 pattern, this implies that between 1966 and 1971 unemployment rose somewhat faster in the conurbations than in their surrounding regions. A similar tendency is evident in the corresponding figures comparing county boroughs with their counties.

For the years after 1971 we must rely on a different source of information, the monthly count of registered unemployed issued by the Department of Employment. This source does not permit us to make comparisons between conurbations and their associated regions, but we can make rough estimates for the conurbations and compare these with national figures. In doing this we cannot compare unemployment rates, because annual estimates of the resident labour force are not available for the conurbations. Instead, we must compare the changes in the absolute numbers on the register. It should be noted that when the labour force is changing rapidly these comparisons can be misleading.

The comparisons for the period 1966–71 confirm the results from the Census data. Over the five-year period, the percentage of national male unemployment registered in the conurbations rose from 32 to 35. However, virtually all of this increase was associated with the rapid rise in unemployment late in 1966 and early in 1967, and was particularly marked in Birmingham and Greater London. Since 1971 there has been no tendency for the conurbations as a group to have a faster increase in unemployment than the nation as a whole – indeed, after reaching a peak in 1973, their share has tended to fall. This conclusion must be qualified to take into account the falls in population and labour force in the conurbations that have probably continued after 1971. The implication is that relative unemployment there might have risen slightly.

Within this over all picture since 1971, the conurbations have not had similar experiences. Greater London has had a relatively large rise in unemployment, but only since 1975. Over the whole period, Glasgow has not had as rapid a rise as has Britain, but more recently it has begun to cacth up. Liverpool and Manchester have both had a faster growth in unemployment since 1971 than the national average; Tyneside has had the reverse. Birmingham, too, although subject to sharp fluctuations, has done somewhat better than the national average, as has, to a lesser extent, West Yorkshire.

The monthly register data can also be used to examine the average duration of unemployment. The significance of this is that a given unemployment rate can be the result either of a small number of workers each being unemployed for a long time or of a large number of workers each being unemployed briefly. Policy-makers, and others, may not be indifferent between these two combinations. Greater London is the only conurbation for which duration figures are published regularly, and we will report comparisons between it and the rest of the south-east region. In April 1978 the average duration on the register for males was virtually the same in the two areas. However, before 1973 there was a small but distinct difference between them, with Greater London having proportionately fewer long-duration men on the register. This says that average unemployment duration in London has tended to rise somewhat relative to that in the surrounding region. We do not know whether this development is common to the other conurbations.

From all of these data there emerges a fairly consistent pattern of male unemployment in the conurbations. In common with most concentrations of population, conurbations tend at all times to have somewhat higher male unemployment rates than do their associated hinterlands. There is some slight evidence that the relative unemployment position of the conurbations has deteriorated somewhat over the period 1961–78, but this conclusion is by no means clearly established. A more balanced conclusion would probably be that there has been no marked change either way. Within the period there do seem to have been shorter-run changes but their significance is not yet established. Finally, individual conurbations have had their own developments and it may be quite inappropriate when considering policy advice to group them together.

In many respects, the unemployment patterns of females in conurbations are similar to those of males. One difference is that in 1971 female unemployment rates in the conurbations were roughly the same as those in the surrounding regions, for both married and unmarried females. In addition, there was a distinct tendency for a higher proportion of the female population to be in the labour force in the conurbations than in the surrounding regions. This might well be evidence that job opportunities were relatively good in the conurbations and that there was extensive hidden female unemployment outside the conurbations. (An alternative view is that women, particularly wives, might be under more pressure to work in the conurbations to offset higher prices, e.g. for housing.)

Comparing counties and county boroughs in 1971 gives a similar result, with only Liverpool county borough having a distinctly high unemployment rate in comparison with its associated county. Over the period 1961–71 there was little change in structure, although unemployment rates everywhere rose substantially. However, in 1966 the conurbations generally had lower female unemployment rates than did their associated regions. After 1971 the conurbations fully shared in the extraordinary rise in female unemployment, but there was no clear tendency for conurbations as a group to suffer more than the national average. Manchester and London, and to a lesser extent Liverpool and Birmingham, have suffered a greater increase, while the rest have suffered somewhat less.

These figures suggest that, in contrast to males, female workers in conurbations are not on average prone to more unemployment than are females elsewhere. However, over the last 20 years as a whole, in common with males, they have probably experienced no marked change in their position relative to workers outside the conurbations; within the 20-year period, there have been fluctuations.

The last factual question to be considered is the pattern of unemployment within the conurbations. In some respects this is the most important question of all because it is the high rates of unemployment in certain parts of the conurbations that have been the focus of much recent public discussion. Over the years observers have become increasingly aware of the fact that the older, inner parts of the larger cities have very high average rates of unemployment. Even in Greater London, an area of much lower unemployment than the national average, there are parts with higher unemployment rates than those typically found in the development and special development areas.

There is no doubt that parts of most inner areas have high average unemployment rates. One indication of this comes from a study by Holtermann (1975) which divided the conurbations into very small areas, census enumeration districts, and calculated the unemployment rates in each for 1971. From this work it is at once apparent that the inner areas of each of the conurbations have a disproportionately large share of the enumeration districts with high unemployment rates. To take an extreme example, the inner area of the South East Lancashire conurbation contains 29 per cent of all enumeration districts in the conurbation, but 73 per cent of its high male unemployment rate districts; the inner West Midlands contains 64 per cent of the conurbation's enumeration districts but 89 per cent of its high male unemployment rate districts and 81 per cent of its high female unemployment rate districts.

Although it is clear that unemployment is distributed very unevenly within the conurbations, it is not clear that the patterns have changed appreciably over the years. In particular, it is certainly not well established that the inner areas are tending to increase their shares of the total. The fact is that there are insufficient data available that allow a judgement to be made on this question. One piece of evidence that is available concerns Greater London, where male unemployment (including the sick) is estimated by the Department of Employment (DOE, 1977, p. 82) to have increased from 2.4 per cent in 1961 to 4.7 per cent in 1971, an increase of 96 per cent. The corresponding figures for the inner London boroughs mostly show a somewhat slower rate of increase, although in all cases both the absolute unemployment rate and the absolute increase in the unemployment rate was greater in the inner boroughs.

Alternatively, an examination of unpublished data for the Greater London employment office areas suggests that the recent increase in unemployment, for example from 1971 to 1977, is not disproportionately associated with the inner areas. Further, and this is also evident from the Census figures for the period 1961–71, the various inner areas in Greater London have had a considerable variety of experience.

On summary, it is probable that those parts of the conurbations which currently have high average unemployment rates have been similarly disadvantaged for many years. Whether they have generally suffered a recent deterioration is not known.

Explaining unemployment in the conurbations

So far, when comparing unemployment rates in different areas, we have concentrated on average unemployment rates. This implicitly assumes that the average worker is the same in the different areas, because if they were not, the unemployment rates would not be directly comparable. Therefore, one explanation of the differences in average unemployment rates across areas might be that workers in the different areas are not the same.

Workers differ in many characteristics, some of which are positively or negatively associated with unemployment. We do not have data on all the characteristics thought to be so associated, but we are able to consider age, race, skill, family size and marital status. When an employer is faced with two applicants for a job and cannot easily vary wages according to his estimate of their individual productivity, he is likely to offer the job to the applicant he believes is more productive, more stable or less costly to train. From this argument, the demand for labour within a labour market is likely to be lower, and unemployment higher, for workers that are old, unskilled, single or non-white. There are further arguments on the supply side. In particular, there is some evidence to suggest that young workers have high unemployment rates in part because they change jobs so frequently. In addition, workers with large families are thought to have high unemployment rates in part because they have to look a relatively long time to get a wage offer that is appreciably above their transfer payment from the State while they are unemployed.

We can now consider whether these arguments might explain unemployment patterns, first in conurbations relative to their surrounding regions, and second within conurbations. For the first comparison the above arguments probably have less force. The demand-side arguments are only powerful when the different types of workers are in direct competition with one another, i.e. when they operate in the same labour market. It may be stretching things to assume that a conurbation and its surrounding region form a single labour market, and if they do not the demand-side arguments lose force. To the extent that they do form a single labour market, however, and to the extent that conurbations have relatively many old, unskilled, single or non-white workers in their labour force, we would expect conurbations to have higher unemployment rates. Similarly, to the extent that conurbations have relatively many young workers or workers with many dependants, we would expect them to have higher unemployment rates.

In fact, conurbations do tend to have high proportions of all these 'unemployment prone' workers. In comparison to their surrounding regions, all of the conurbations in 1971 had high fractions of very young and very old workers; only Merseyside had a lower proportion of non-whites; only West Yorkshire had a lower proportion of unskilled workers; all conurbations had a high proportion of single men and families with many dependants. It is not easy to go further than this qualitative result and calculate the degree to which these compositional differences explain the relatively high rates of unemployment in the conurbations. Put another way, one cannot with assurance say whether conurbations have high unemployment rates for comparable workers.

On the basis of published data, one step that can be taken is to examine unemployment rates by age. Even though this ignores the other influences on unemployment rates, the analysis is revealing. In comparison with their associated regions, the conurbations have particularly high unemployment rates for 'prime-age' males, i.e. males aged between 25–50. More precisely, unemployment rates in the conurbations tend to be higher for most ages, but they are especially high for the 25–50-year-old group. For 60–64-year-old workers, however, unemployment rates tend to be lower in the conurbations.

These findings for the age structure of unemployment suggest that if other characteristics were taken into account, the unemployment picture in the conurbations might be quite complex. It is unlikely that all the conurbations would have the same patterns. Further, it is probable that for certain groups unemployment would be lower in the conurbation than outside, while for other groups the reverse would be true.

The above analysis can also be applied to the different parts of a given conurbation. Here it is more obviously relevant because the extensive commuting that is observed within conurbations makes it more reasonable to assume that we are dealing with a single labour market, in the sense that workers in one part of the conurbation are in pretty direct competition with workers in the other parts.

Empirical work on this question has been carried out for Greater London using the Census data for 1971 (Metcalf & Richardson, 1976). From this it seems that a great part of the variation in unemployment rates across Greater London can be explained by localised concentrations of different types of workers. In particular, there are high unemployment rates in those parts of London where unskilled workers tend to live. In addition to skill, the age and racial composition, the marriage patterns and the family structure are important in explaining unemployment patterns. Another way of expressing this is to say that there seems to be a considerable uniformity across Greater London in the unemployment rates of given types of workers. Unskilled workers in the outer areas have broadly the same unemployment rates as unskilled workers in the inner areas (Evans and Russell, 1979). Because unskilled workers generally have high unemployment rates, however, average unemployment rates will be high in those areas where unskilled workers are concentrated.

It would certainly not be true to say that this kind of analysis provides a complete explanation for the patterns of unemployment within conurbations. The assumption that each conurbation forms a single labour market is surely too strong, and it is undoubtedly true that some areas have persistently high unemployment rates even when the characteristics of the local labour force have been fully taken into account. Nevertheless, the approach has considerable value in cautioning us against using unstandardised, or unqualified, average unemployment rates when comparing the situation in different areas.

So far we have demonstrated the existence of an association between the composition of the labour force and the unemployment rate of an area. This is at least qualitatively clear for the conurbations in comparison with their surrounding areas and is quantitatively of substantial importance for the different parts of Greater London. However, an association does not by itself tell us anything about causation. The suggestion made here, most strongly for the patterns within a conurbation, is that labour-force composition has caused the unemployment pattern. This requires us to say something about what causes the composition of the labour force, e.g. why do some areas have high proportions of unskilled workers?

The most powerful determinants of residential choice within an urban area are probably the characteristics of the housing market. Unskilled manual workers tend to go to certain types of housing, skilled non-manuals to others. Once this process has started, it is reinforced by consequential neighbourhood effects, class perceptions, the perceived quality of the local schools and so on. In this context very local job opportunities are probably of minor importance in influencing residential choice. If this is true, the composition of the labour force is logically prior to, i.e. helps to cause, the observed patterns of unemployment.

Some observers might not agree with this analysis. They might argue that a shortage of local jobs causes local unemployment, and that this in turn affects the composition of the local labour force to produce the observed association. This is a plausible argument for some spatial comparisons, but much weaker for others. If we were comparing strictly separate labour markets it is clearly possible, indeed probable, that migration patterns could validate this second interpretation. For example, it is generally true that immigrant workers in Britain do not tend to settle in the depressed regions, a clear case of unemployment causing a particular composition of the labour force. It is also true that skilled workers are much more likely to migrate away from depressed areas than are unskilled workers.

However, if we are comparing parts of an integrated labour market the argument is much less powerful because of the ease of commuting and the importance of local housing conditions as a determinant of residential choice. A crucial test of whether an area is an integrated labour market is the uniformity of the unemployment rates for similar workers within the area. They seem to be roughly uniform within conurbations but they clearly vary across towns in different parts of the country. As a result we are probably safe in interpreting the direction of causation within conurbations as running from labour-force composition to unemployment patterns.

Apart from work investigating the composition of the labour force there has not been much empirical analysis seeking to explain unemployment patterns within the conurbations. Some work by McGregor (1978) suggests that certain parts of Paisley, near Glasgow, have distinctly high unemployment rates even after the composition of the labour force has been taken into account. Other work, so far unpublished, suggests that the eastern parts of London have somewhat higher unemployment rates, and the western parts somewhat lower rates, than can be explained purely by the characteristics of the local labour forces. It is important to note here that the areas with high standardised unemployment rates are not necessarily the areas with high average unemployment rates; nor are they necessarily to be found in the inner areas; nor do all, or even most, inner areas suffer from high standardised unemployment rates. These conclusions are very important for policy, to which we now turn.

Unemployment in the conurbations and policy

In the above sections we have described some spatial unemployment patterns and discussed explanations of some of them. The general tenor of the analysis has been that conurbations are not typically suffering from a marked unemployment problem, that much of the pattern of unemployment within the conurbations can be explained by local concentrations of different types of workers, and that different areas, even those with superficially similar characteristics, should not lightly be lumped together for policy purposes.

In contrast, perhaps, to the above there has been a growing disquiet about unemployment in, and within, the conurbations. This has led, over the last two years, to explicit public action in response to what is evidently seen as a major social and economic problem. In this section we wish to consider the various policy possibilities facing the authorities when they seek to change an uneven distribution of unemployment. We are therefore not considering policies which seek to reduce total unemployment, but policies which change its distribution between areas.

The authorities may seek to reduce unemployment in a particular area by changing either conditions of supply or conditions of demand. For either of these, the authorities might wish to focus on the whole labour force or on its composition.

Traditionally, in regional policy, governments have concentrated on altering the demand conditions in different areas. This may be attempted directly by financial incentives of many kinds or by a relaxation in particular areas of some of the rules and regulations affecting business activity. For example, it has recently been suggested that the operation of the Employment Protection Act might be relaxed for small firms setting up in the inner areas of large cities. Alternatively, the authorities might indirectly seek to raise the demand for labour in certain areas, by inhibiting, or even preventing, expansion in other areas, for example by planning controls. All of these policies can be tailored to affect the demand for labour generally or the demand for specific types of labour.

The success of these policies in reducing an uneven distribution of unemployment clearly depends on the causes of the unemployment. They are likely to be most successful, in the limited sense of evening out unemployment, when the areas in question are isolated from one another and when migration is sluggish. This is not to say that even when they are 'successful' these policies are necessarily worth while, because their introduction may involve larger inefficiencies elsewhere in the system, but they may then be effective in reducing unemployment disparities.

Where the areas in question are parts of highly integrated labour markets, these demand-focused policies are much less likely to be effective. If the authorities suceed in increasing the number of jobs available in, say, the inner areas of large cities, and even if these extra jobs are relevant for the local residents, there is still the problem of spill over. That is, these extra jobs will also attract similar workers in adjacent areas. The more integrated is the labour market the more completely will the extra job opportunities be diffused to the residents of adjacent areas.

To see this important point more clearly, consider a concrete example of the authorities designating a part of the inner area of a particular city as its target area. Assume that the authorities succeed in raising the number of jobs in the target area and that the jobs in question relate well to the particular characteristics of the labour force there. Most of these extra jobs would, in the absence of the policy initiative, have been located elsewhere (we shall ignore the complicated questions of whether the policy causes the total number of jobs to rise or fall and whether the composition of all jobs has been altered). Many of the extra jobs might well have been located in areas adjacent to the target area and have had their precise location moved slightly in order to qualify for whatever benefits or inducements the authorities were offering to make the target area more attractive. To give a point of reference, we may assume that in harmony with the increase in jobs in the target area there has been an equal fall in the number of jobs that would have been available in adjacent areas.

If the labour market of the target area is well integrated with those of the adjacent areas, will the re-location of jobs lead to a more even pattern of unemployment across areas? The answer clearly depends on the degree of integration. If the target area were very small and integration complete we could expect no enduring impact on unemployment patterns. If the target area were large and the degree of integration small, we would be back to considering regional policy.

It must be concluded that demand-side policies seeking to change unemployment patterns within the conurbations must satisfy stringent conditions before they are likely to be effective. They must first succeed in relocating jobs; secondly, they must relocate jobs that local residents can fill; thirdly, the labour markets of the target areas must not be highly integrated with those of the rest of the conurbations, i.e. unemployment rates must be relatively high for comparable workers. An effective policy would thus require a refined procedure for choosing appropriate target areas and sophisticated inducement mechanisms for securing the right mix of jobs for the local workers.

The alternative strand of anti-unemployment policy emphasises the supply of labour. It recognises that given the state of demand, certain types of workers face poorer job opportunities. If the authorities wish to make job opportunities more equal between people, or groups of people, they might seek to alter those characteristics which lead to unemployment. Most of the discussion here focuses on skill and training programmes, but one could equally consider action to change employers' attitudes, e.g. to immigrants or old workers, or to change the relative cost of particular types of workers (e.g. subsidies on young workers).

These various supply-based policies have one common difficulty. A programme that reaches only part of a disadvantaged group can make things worse for the others in the group. If, for example, some of the unskilled are given training and, on the strength of that training, get jobs, the remaining unskilled workers may well find it even more difficult to get any work at all. This displacement effect would not be important if those who received training relieved what would otherwise be a labour market bottleneck, an acute shortage of a particular type of labour. In this case, the trainees would not be competing with the still unskilled and the latter would face less competition for the available jobs. Generally, however, these bottlenecks are not large in number and are not easily predicted by public training programmes. As a rule, the trainees will still compete with the unskilled for the available jobs, whose number has not been increased by the policy, but will now compete more successfully. Therefore, it is not clear that a supply-side policy will even be effective in reducing the unevenness in unemployment. If it is not pursued with very great vigour it may do the reverse.

We must therefore conclude that it is not easy to affect the uneven distribution of unemployment. Given the over all level of demand there will inevitably be substantial variations in unemployment from person to person and area to area. Relocating jobs is likely to be effective only in certain circumstances, and changing people's characteristics may merely compound the problems facing other disadvantaged workers.

It is now appropriate to consider recent policy initiatives by the Government, and in particular to consider the White Paper *Policy for the Inner Cities* (Cmnd. 6845, 1977). In this context, unemployment patterns are only part of the story because the White Paper is deeply concerned with the complex interaction between economic decline, poverty, social problems and environmental deprivation. Nevertheless, unemployment is a very important focus of the White Paper and it is worth quoting the relevant passages in full.

> The decline in the economic fortunes of the inner areas often lies at the heart of the problem. Compared with their own conurbations, the inner areas of the big cities suffer from higher unemployment at all stages of the economic cycle. In inner areas generally there has developed a mismatch between the skills of the people and the kinds of job available. In some cities such as Glasgow and Liverpool, there is a general lack of demand for labour which affects the whole conurbation but is particularly severe in the inner areas.
>
> The inner areas have long had more than the national proportions of unskilled and semi-skilled workers, the groups among whom unemployment is highest. In 1971, for example, unskilled and semi-skilled men accounted for 38% of the labour force in inner Birmingham, 35% in inner Manchester and 34% in inner Glasgow, compared to 23% nationally. The loss from the cities of a higher proportion of skilled than less skilled workers has made unemployment worse. Between 1966–71 only 15% of net migrants from Birmingham comprised semi-skilled and unskilled workers; from Manchester it was only 16%. Most of those who left were skilled and managerial people.

This description echoes some parts of ours, but not others, and suggests some things not mentioned above. It is no surprise that inner areas have high average unemployment rates. When the White Paper talks of a mismatch, however, the implication must be that inner areas generally have rather more structural unemployment than do other areas. It is important to see that this is suggested to be the case for inner areas generally, as opposed to outer areas generally. There is also a hint, in the word 'developed', that there has been a growing divergence in this respect between the inner and outer areas.

As is indicated above, none of this is clear from the published data. To repeat, inner areas have not obviously suffered a relative increase in unemployment; comparable workers in inner areas generally do not seem to have high unemployment rates; and those areas where such unemployment rates are high are by no means always found in inner areas. Some very limited confirmation of these points can be found in the report issued by the Department of Employment, which provides unemployment rates by socio-economic groups for component parts of the conurbations in 1971 (Department of Employment, 1977, pp. 88–92). Unfortunately these data are for males and females together, but it is still clear that inner areas by no means generally have high unemployment rates, particularly for unskilled workers, whose average unemployment rates are four or five times greater than those of other workers. For example, in the West Midlands, where the unemployment rate for the unskilled averaged 18 per cent, the corresponding rates in two wealthy suburbs were 21 per cent in Solihull and 23 per cent in Sutton Coldfield. Similarly, in Tyneside, the outer area of Whitley Bay had a 26 per cent unemployment rate for the unskilled as compared to 22 per cent for the conurbation average. Again, in Greater London, inner-area boroughs like Camden, Islington, Tower Hamlets and Westminster all had lower unemployment rates for the unskilled than did the conurbation as a whole.

The White Paper recognises that the labour force resident in the inner areas has an untypical skill composition. It is unfortunate that the recognition does not lead to a qualification in the arguments based on simple average unemployment rates. The White Paper then asserts that differential migration patterns have made unemployment worse. This, however, is a very unsatisfactory summary of a very complex process.

For simplicity let us assume that unskilled workers do not migrate, while skilled workers do. What is the impact of migration on those who remain? Given any rate of workplace loss, labour migration clearly improves the labour market position of those who stay. Unskilled and skilled workers are not perfect substitutes but in reality a reduction in the number of skilled workers would be met by some upgrading of less skilled workers and, hence, some improvement in their total job opportunities. Thus, while those not migrating would suffer from a reduction in work-places, in practice they must gain from the migration of other workers. The migration of the skilled can only damage the employment position of the less skilled if there is a more than proportional outflow of work-places as a reaction to the migration of the skilled. This is highly unlikely and is not suggested by the available evidence.

It is true that the migration of the skilled can lead to a rise in an area's unemployment rate, but this would be a trivial arithmetic consequence, not one of substance. To see this, assume there are three people, two of whom earn £5,000, while the third earns £11,000; average earnings are £7,000. If the third person leaves, average earnings fall to £5,000, but no one is worse off. So it is with unemployment rates, unless the exodus of the skilled actually harms the unskilled. In fact, as has been suggested above, the reverse is more likely.

It must be concluded that the White Paper has not perceived the subtlety of the unemployment patterns within the conurbations. It focuses too much on average unemployment rates and makes some ambiguous statements, the natural inferences from which are not supported by the available data.

It could be argued that in spite of these weaknesses the analysis of the White Paper should still be supported because concentrations of unemployment, whatever their cause, are a legitimate focus of concern and policy. But this is to argue that a given number of unemployed workers living fairly close to one another deserve more attention than the same number of identical unemployed workers who are dispersed. This is a difficult case to argue and its basis in efficiency or fairness is not obviously strong.

It could also be argued that the policy initiatives associated with the White Paper might be supported on labour-market criteria other than unemployment patterns. For example, the run-down of work-places in the conurbations, even if it has not been accompanied by higher unemployment, might have resulted in less desirable jobs. There might have been reductions in earnings, lower status levels, inferior working conditions or longer journeys to work. These possible adverse effects might well be spatially concentrated, for example in the inner areas. All this might support some initiative to bring jobs, of certain kinds, to the inner areas. However, all these possibilities remain conjectures. Even if they have occurred they may have been more than offset by advantages elsewhere. Further, it is by no means clear that they have occurred, nor that they have been concentrated spatially. In short, the case is a possible one but it is a long way from being demonstrated.

In conclusion, we may say that the complex labour-market patterns involving unemployment in the conurbations are not fully understood. What is known about them, however, casts some doubt on the overall wisdom of the analysis in the White Paper. Certainly the notion of partnership areas, or target areas as they were labelled above, must be viewed with some scepticism until the basis of their selection and the details of their operation are made public.

References

Cmnd. 6845 (1977) *Policy for the Inner City*. Department of the Environment, White Paper, June. HMSO.

Department of Employment (1977) *Employment in Metropolitan Areas*. Project Report by the Unit for Manpower Studies.

Evans, A. and **Russell, L.** (1980) 'A portrait of the London labour market' in Evans, A.W., and Eversley, D.E.C. (eds), *The Inner City: Employment and Industry*. Heinemann, London.

Holtermann, S.E. (1975) 'Areas of urban deprivation in Great Britain: an analysis of 1971 census data', *Social Trends* **6**, pp. 33–47.

McGregor, A. (1978) 'Family size and unemployment in a multiply deprived urban area', *Regional Studies* **12** (3) pp. 232–30.

Metcalf, D. and **Richardson, R.** (1976) 'Unemployment in London', in Worswick, G.D.M. (ed.), *The Concept and Measurement of Involuntary Unemployment*. Allen and Unwin, London.

Chapter 11

The socio-economic impact of urban renewal

Introduction

Both in the US and in the UK urban renewal has been a controversial programme. New housing and urban motorway systems have been hungry in their demands for land whilst existing inner-city land-use patterns were outdated in terms of the demands of a modern economy. In order to redress the disequilibrium urban planners tore out the heart of the blighted inner city replacing it with high-rise housing, urban motorways or just vacant lots as city councils ran out of resources. However, the effects of urban renewal can immediately be seen which means that attention can readily be drawn to any deficiencies in the policy. Those who criticise the 'federal bulldozer' policies highlight the destruction of inner-city business areas, the elimination of neighbourhoods, the reduction of low-cost housing and the social problems caused by high-rise living.

An appraisal of urban renewal policies, therefore, requires a balancing up of the costs and benefits imposed upon the residents of the inner city redevelopment area. The costs of renewal include losses imposed upon residential households by displacement itself, the losses imposed by uncertainties and delays, and losses imposed on those not directly displaced but located in surrounding areas. Against these costs are weighed the benefits of improved housing and employment prospects and compensation paid. But do things work out as planned? Is the compensation paid adequate, does it reflect the costs actually borne; and are employment opportunities improved? These are amongst the issues which will be examined in this chapter.

This kind of cost-benefit approach is somewhat unusual. Indeed one commentator has remarked of the urban planning process and the policy instrument used that, 'although many planning decisions closely influence the wellbeing of groups or individuals, most British planning machinery is not conceived in terms of a delivery system serving social welfare objectives ... planners have not defined their profession in terms of the creation of explicit benefits for people. Instead they have thought in terms of land and physical development standards for private and public development' (Harrison, 1975, p. 273).[1]

The other complicating factor is that urban renewal attempts to deal with a problem which is part physical, part economic, part social and part political. In common with metropolitan areas throughout the world many parts of British conurbations contain areas of severe deprivation; areas in which unemployment, poverty, poor housing and low quality public services exist on a much greater scale relative to other parts of the region. These areas are frequently referred to as ghettoes, slums, blighted areas or areas of social stress. More recently in the UK they have been designated as areas of *multiple deprivation*.

Whilst not confined solely to city regions, many of the worst areas of multiple deprivation are to be found located within the older cities, especially in those parts which are closest to the core or the inner city. These are the zones of the city which have long since passed their zenith of economic prosperity. In most cases they were the former middle-class areas of the city but, as national economic conditions changed, the decline and out-migration of the area's industries took with them the middle classes and opportunities for employment. The result was the creation of a lower-price housing area into which the poorer income groups moved. The ghettoes were born.

What we have described above is, of course, a stereotype, but one which most will recognise as a reasonable description of parts of most cities, although the precise conditions and processes of decline will vary from case to case. For the purposes of this chapter, therefore, we concentrate upon one particular dimension of the problem, that is, the issue of urban blight and the policies of urban renewal in older areas of the conurbations.

What is urban renewal?

In order to discuss the impact of urban renewal policies it is essential that we know precisely what is meant by the term. The recent White Paper, *Policy for the Inner City*,[2] has given an inner-city dimension to almost all aspects of the Government's socio-economic policies. Thus, employment, housing, income maintenance and education policies, etc., are all thought to be a contribution towards the problems of inner-city decay. Such a comprehensive and integrated approach to the problem seems reasonable but it claims everything and yet at the same time says very little. Urban renewal is one element in the catalogue of policies directed towards urban regeneration.

According to Richardson (1971) urban renewal has come to refer to three types of programme: *rehabilitation*, i.e. bringing substandard structures up to a prescribed standard; *conservation*, involving both rehabilitation and spot clearance in order to upgrade an area; and *redevelopment*, the demolition, clearance and reconstruction of an entire area. Urban renewal is, therefore, an improvement in the physical environment of an area within an urban region, usually close to the centre, and a rearrangement of land-use patterns therein.

In the UK during the 1950s and 1960s urban renewal became synonymous with comprehensive development. Comprehensive urban renewal, as compared to a more piecemeal approach, refers to area-wide land-use planning and as such is more than just slum clearance. By means of voluntary market transactions or through compulsory purchases the local authority within a city region acquires the property rights to the blighted areas surrounding the central core of cities. After clearing the site the whole area is rebuilt with new housing, new industrial locations and new transport networks. In many instances redevelopment and changes in land-use patterns have been initiated by the city's roadbuilding programme[3] which required the clearance of large areas of the inner city, rather than by the housebuilding programme.

Why urban renewal policy?

In a market economy urban renewal would be a fully anticipated process resulting from the rise and fall of product and factor markets. Why then does the State involve itself in urban renewal, producing urban renewal policies and instruments such as subsidies, and comprehensive development plans? A brief examination of the answer to this question is necessary if we are to provide an adequate appraisal of renewal policies.[4]

Why do slums and blighted areas develop and persist? To answer this question we shall view the problem of urban decay from an economic perspective.

Assume that urban land is owned privately and, moreover, it is held in small packets of land. Further assume that housing, again privately owned, is erected on this land and that housing has reached the stage of its economic life when it requires repairs and maintenance to be done before it begins to deteriorate. The decision whether or not to incur the expense of repairs depends on weighing up the costs of the repairs against the likely financial returns. If the discounted present value of the costs exceed the present value of the future revenues then it would be rational for the individual property owner to allow the property to deteriorate.

When calculating the likely future revenue from the property we need to consider how the value of the property is determined. In addition to the value of the consumption benefits embodied in the housing stock, the value of the property is also a function of the neighbourhood within which it is located.[5] These *neighbourhood effects* on the valuation of housing (property) services play a key role in understanding the process of urban decay.

Consider two individual property owners. Both own adjacent properties and both are trying to decide whether or not an additional investment will alter the return which can be expected from their property services. Moreover, given the externality (neighbourhood effect) of the investment decision, by making a contribution to the improvement of the neighbourhood the owner of the adjacent property receives an external benefit. Assume that individual 2 is making a similar decision with respect to renovation of his property. In the absence of communication between the two individuals it is likely that the following arguments would be considered by each: if I invest in upgrading my property the increased rate of return I can expect (due to charging higher rents) will depend on whether or not my neighbour improves his property. If he doesn't the neighbourhood isn't too good so I cannot charge a rent sufficiently high to cover the costs of the investment in maintenance expenditure. The neighbourhood will decline and the process will reinforce itself. [6]

This simplified example is presented to illustrate the point that in the absence of coordination between the decision-makers the result will be a less than optimal supply of housing renovation and maintenance expenditure. Like David Hume's example of the *tragedy of the commons* the pursuit of uncoordinated self-interest by each individual results in an outcome which is less than optimal for the group as a whole. In other words, the externalities created by the interdependence of the decisions brings about a failure in the market to allocate resources efficiently. This situation calls for collective action; either public collective action or private collective action. For a small number of individuals the transactions costs of organising private collective action is less than that for a larger number of individuals. Moreover, as the number of individuals in the group increases it becomes easier for each person to adopt some form of strategic behaviour like that of the *free rider*, thereby destroying any incentive for potential private collective action.

The Tenth Report of the House of Commons Expenditure Committee (HMSO, 1973) had recognised this problem in its discussion of housing improvement grants: 'almost all the evidence submitted to us suggests that the introduction of the proposals will result in a very limited role for the private landlord in voluntary improvement' (HC349, para. 55). Moreover, Paris's (1977) account of the voluntary take-up of improvement grants in Birmingham reinforces this conclusion.

Given the presence of the negative externalities described above, government intervention via urban renewal policy is usually necessary. Neighbourhood externalities are not the sole argument which can be used to justify public collective action in urban renewal. Increasing returns in manufacturing and commerce also require the development of a large area of continuous land under single ownership. Suppose a private developer was to plan to buy up a large area of land in order to reap the benefits of increasing returns to scale, then if each supplier (seller) of every small piece of land realised the strategy of the developer they would actively bargain to appropriate as large a share of the surplus which the developer would hope to make. The degree of success of each seller in gaining a share of the surplus might, in the end, produce the result that the private development is no longer profitable. In this case the redevelopment of the area would not take place by the private sector since insufficient incentive exists. A development gap, therefore, exists to be filled by the public sector. The public sector, by employing compulsory purchase orders, offers the suppliers a fair price. Clearly then one key problem is that of establishing a *fair price*.

Finally, government through its urban renewal policy attempts to pursue a regulatory and coordinating role on urban land use. A market solution to optimal land use is unlikely to exist in so far as such a process is piecemeal depending upon the sequence in which land comes onto the market. Moreover, from the point of view of maximising the net social benefits from land use, as compared to the more limited maximisation of private interests, government acts as a referee in the land market. Government intervenes in the urban development process especially at the stage of site acquisition and overall land-use planning because no single private individual would be in a position to internalise all the social benefits.

In summary, government's urban renewal policy is aimed at the elimination of blighted areas caused by externalities and market failure in the urban land market.

The UK's urban renewal programme

The UK does not have a national coordinated urban renewal prog-ramme. Instead urban renewal is initiated at the local level either by private enterprise, as in the case of many non-residential schemes, or by local governments. It is, however, true that a great deal of co-operation does exist between local and central levels of government in carrying out renewal programmes especially in terms of the provision of resources.

Urban renewal is generally associated with the post-war period but it should be remembered that slum clearances on a substantial scale did take place in the 1930s. Much of the foundation to the urban renewal policies is to be found in the successive post-war housing acts and the Town and Country Planning Acts. [7] These acts established the rights of compulsory purchase powers of the local authorities and also made provision for central government to provide long-term loan and grant finance to local government for the purpose of acquiring development land, especially for residential renewal.

During the 1950s and 1960s comprehensive development was the main instrument of urban renewal. Whole sites were demolished and rebuilt. However, later in the 1960s rehabilitation or improvement of existing dwellings came to be favoured as the more appropriate means of urban renewal where previously redevelopment would have been automatically pursued. There have been many reasons for this change in thinking regarding urban renewal policy. First, it is generally thought that rehabilitation is cheaper in resource terms compared to re-development. After the 1967 devaluation of Sterling and successive public expenditure cuts, reductions in the housing programme have threatened the achievement of its original objective. Cheaper means were therefore sought. Second, 20 years of experience with com-prehensive urban redevelopment has caused many, not least those who have been directly affected by the policies, to reconsider whether or not redevelopment is a socially preferred means of proceeding. The destruction of social communities and the social costs produced by redevelopment are considered by many to be too high a price to pay. These considerations of rehabilitation vs. redevelopment are consi-dered in greater detail below.

This change in preference for rehabilitation instead of redevelop-ment can be traced back to official thinking in the mid 1960s. If we examine the views of Richard Crossman when he was Minister of Housing we can see a change in his attitudes. In November 1964 he wrote:

> I am pretty clear that the decision means comprehensive urban renewal. We
> have to concentrate upon six or seven places, Liverpool, Manchester,
> Birmingham, Glasgow, London, where the problem of housing is so bad
> that the local authorities simply can't grapple with the job . . . . A Labour
> Minister should impose central leadership, large scale state intervention, in
> those blighted areas of cities, the twilight areas which were once genteelly
> respectable and are now rotting away where Commonwealth citizens settle
> and where there are racial problems (Crossman, 1975, p. 44).

Then in January 1965 he advocated: 'It is far better to give thirty years more life to some of this existing central property than to let it become a slum and then have to pull it down. In Salford I found that for £200 they were making people happy. Since I don't like the idea of people having to live in huge blocks of high rise housing, I found the Salford efforts extremely attractive' (Crossman, 1975, p. 124).

Changes in the local urban renewal policies of Birmingham City Council have been reviewed by Paris (1977). In 1973 Birmingham announced a new policy of phasing out comprehensive development and concentrating instead upon a programme of house and area improvements. Under this policy 75,000 houses in the city's inner ring were involved over a 10-year programme; 68 general improvement areas (GIA) were declared, containing 60,000 houses, with a further 26 potential 'renewal areas' for a mixed policy of clearance and improvement. On the launching of the new programme an official statement from the City of Birmingham Council announced,

> the urban renewal problem has now reached a new threshold. Today the
> task is to prevent dwellings becoming slums . . . the old slums were so worn

out and outmoded that the only solution was to demolish the houses whilst the preventive measures necessary today to arrest the social and physical decline of dwellings and large areas of the City call for a different technique. Unless these dwellings and areas are dealt with in the next decade . . . they will become slums. The cost to the City, the destruction of communities and the hardship to individuals would be unacceptable (Paris, 1977, pp. 118–19).

In 1973 the Department of the Environment produced the document *Better Homes The Next Priorities* which was the foundation for the 1974 Housing Act. The new housing act provided emphasis on improvement rather than redevelopment, introducing Housing Action Areas (HAAs) defined in terms of the physical conditions of housing (i.e. whether or not they lacked standard amenities) and social conditions such as the degree of shared facilities. The objective of the Act was to obtain an improvement of the living conditions in the HAAs in five years. In order to achieve this the policy instruments which the Act introduced were 75 per cent house renovation grants (90 per cent in the case of hardship). Also the Act gave powers to the local authority to initiate the compulsory improvement of some tenanted dwellings. If a tenanted house is sold within seven years of receiving such a grant then the grant is repaid with compound interest.

Optimal urban renewal policy is therefore now viewed to be an appropriate mix of rehabilitation and renewal.[8] What seems, however, to be lacking from the discussion is how policy-makers might go about deciding upon what constitutes an optimal mix of the two means of urban renewal and what information and analysis is required by them to aid their decision-making. For example, which zones are better suited for redevelopment and which for improvement and under what conditions?

An evaluation of urban renewal

The urban renewal programme has not passed without critical comment. Such criticism has generally been directed at the means or the policy instruments rather than at the policy objectives, although as we will see, more recent commentary has questioned the latter. The slow speed at which the programme has moved has been the focus of many critiques. This has been due in part to an inadequate allocation of funds to allow the realisation of targets more quickly but is also due to the slow-moving bureaucratic planning machinery which has resulted in long delays in granting planning approvals. Not only does it take time to reach agreement amongst the various parties to a comprehensive redevelopment but such schemes also tend to be very long-term (10 to 20 years) and inflexible, taking little account of changing conditions and the need for modification of the plan.[9]

Reactions against specific urban renewal schemes have increased both in frequency and in strength and gave birth in the 1960s to a new kind of local pressure group, particularly at the level of the neighbourhood (Paris, 1977, and Clark, 1970). Those groups attacked and questioned many aspects of the urban renewal schemes which have been adopted throughout the UK. They have attacked the aesthetics of the high-rise blocks which replaced traditional low-level housing, they have reacted against the loss of community values and the social consequences of urban renewal, and they have sought to find out who benefits from such programmes, the displaced or the private property developers who have enjoyed the economic rent created by local government planning delays.

A catalogue of complaints against urban renewal schemes might be instructive but by itself it is of very little value. Whilst neighbourhood pressure groups reveal their preferences for one scheme as opposed to another they do not necessarily represent the preferences of all relevant parties and interests. To evaluate urban renewal schemes it is essential to do so within a framework which will enable us to weigh up the benefits and the costs associated with each policy and to enquire further about the incidence of these benefits and costs across different sections of the population.

In this section we will consider briefly the evaluation framework that we will adopt and then we will proceed to review a number of economic studies of renewal schemes. It should be emphasised that our approach is one of economic evaluation. This means that many other dimensions, especially the political, are ignored.[10]

The cost-benefit framework

Cost-benefit analysis is normally used as an *ex-ante* investment appraisal technique to assist in the choice between alternative public sector capital projects. It can, however, be used *ex-post* in retrospective evaluation studies of previous decisions. In both cases care has to be exercised in using the analysis but attention is drawn particularly to its latter use. An *ex-post* evaluation of the benefits and costs of a project will reveal whether or not the project turned out to be 'profitable' on economic efficiency grounds and which groups benefited most on distributional grounds. The project may, therefore, be judged to be good or bad relative to a set of external criteria. It is not, however, possible to evaluate the earlier *decision* as being good or bad relative to its outcome without additional information about the objective function of the decision-makers (i.e. the weights they assigned to efficiency and distributional objectives) and the data (social benefits, costs, and discount rate) available at the time of the decision.

Economic efficiency. The relative weights attached to efficiency and distributional objectives when deciding upon the form of public policy is an extremely controversial issue which lies at the heart of discussions about the design of optimal policies. Whilst we cannot expand upon that debate in this essay we should recognise the essence of the problem when evaluating policies such as that of urban renewal. The efficiency objective recognises that all public policies have a resource opportunity cost associated with them. Thus resources allocated to urban renewal could have been used otherwise in the private sector or for other public sector projects. Given a resource constraint and assuming that there exist alternative renewal schemes that might achieve the policy objective, efficiency requires that resources be allocated so as to maximise the present value of net social benefits.[11]

Distribution of welfare. Efficiency, however, is not the only criterion against which public expenditure programmes may be judged. If certain public expenditures are to be justified on the grounds that they represent efficient investments, should such expenditures be made when they are not efficient? For example, assume that public health expenditures have a high net present value of net benefits. Would they continue to be 'profitable' if such services were provided for the health of the aged? Because the aged are normally retired and, therefore, contribute little to the current and future output of the community, it is clear that expenditures on their behalf would not be shown to be efficient. Does it follow, therefore, that there should be no public expenditures devoted to the health of retired people?

Public expenditures may be made on the expectation that they will increase productivity and the rate of growth of output of the economy or they may be made for entirely different reasons such as to ensure an improvement in the welfare or the well-being of some particular under-privileged group in society. Thus, resources will be allocated to the aged irrespective of whether or not the output of the economy increases. Resources will be allocated to improving housing, better physical and social environments, social services and all kinds of education and training for those in greatest need regardless of whether or not the productive potential of the economy rises. In these cases it is necessary to be aware of the possibility that investments in human resources (as the urban renewal programme is in part) may not always be as efficient in raising the rate of economic growth as are alternative instruments. We may, never the less, make investments in human resources anyway.[12]

Distributional questions do, however, raise a number of methodological and technical problems. This means that an *ex-post* evaluation of urban renewal policies is not a trivial exercise and indeed a complete evaluation which takes account of economic efficiency and distributional (social) issues awaits to be done.[13] For example, what are the *a priori* distributional criteria which are to be used in judging whether or not a welfare gain by one group relative to that of another is deemed desirable or not?[14] How is the change in welfare to be measured; are we concerned with net benefit incidence or public expenditure incidence?[15]

In considering optimal policy-making either *a priori* or in an *ex-post* evaluation of policies, the end point chosen on the efficiency/distribution trade-off is interesting in so far as it reveals the price, in terms of lost output, that has been paid to obtain a redistribution of welfare. Moreover, *ex post* evaluations of the distribution of net benefits forces us to check upon the actual incidence of net benefits so that we may know whether or not social legislation in practice turns out to be pro-rich instead of pro-poor as intended!

Finally, as with all pieces of social legislation, there is a real danger, when discussing urban renewal policies, to refer to the welfare of an abstract organism such as the city. Policies are frequently thought of as renewing the city rather than serving the welfare of the individuals who live in the city. One prevalent general view is that of regarding benefits as being attached to a piece of land: an improvement in the value of the land or on the value of the buildings placed on it, or in some instances in its aesthetics, may be thought to have conferred benefits upon the community. This approach ignores the effect on these individuals (usually the low-income groups) who previously lived in the area and who now face increased competition for housing space.

Urban renewal evaluated

We will approach the question of evaluating urban renewal in a number of ways. First, we will review the pros and cons of alternative policy instruments, especially rehabilitation as compared to renewal. Second, a review will be made of studies which have examined the urban renewal process in alternative contexts. Third, the debate will be opened up in order to consider whether or not discriminatory area-specific policies are the most appropriate.

Rehabilitation vs. renewal

It will be recalled from the earlier discussion that urban renewal may be achieved either through comprehensive redevelopment of a complete area or by means of rehabilitating the blighted area or a mixture of both. The 1969 and 1974 Housing Acts and the revealed preferences of neighbourhood pressure groups have moved current thinking closer towards policies designed to improve older homes. The appropriateness of either policy is a complex issue whose resolution depends upon a careful specification of the objective of the renewal policy along with the cost of the over-all scheme in relation to the resource constraint. However, in judging between the two policy instruments a number of specific questions can be answered: (a) does it cost more or less to rehabilitate an area as compared to redevelopment; (b) what is the incidence of the benefits and the costs of the two schemes?

One of the clearest accounts of the problem involved in choosing between rehabilitation and renewal is to be found in the debate between Needleman (1965, 1968, and 1969) and Sigsworth and Wilkinson (1967). Because rehabilitation and renewal are not perfect substitutes, choosing between the two tends to be a complex process of weighing up many diffferent factors. Consider the following trade-offs which face the decision-maker:

1. Renewal is more expensive than rehabilitation. Therefore in times of capital shortage for the economy as a whole an unconstrained pursuit of the renewal policy will contribute to a rise in general interest rates[16] which will then feed back into the next round of decisions resulting in the abandonment of many renewal projects that would have been efficient at the previous lower rates of interest. If capital is constrained for renewal projects then the speed at which the policy is executed is greatly reduced.

2. Whilst modernisation (rehabilitation) is cheaper new dwellings are more likely to last longer. Moreover, the maintenance costs of new buildings will be lower.

3. New buildings are constructed to new densities. In some cases, as in the case of high-rise buildings, these densities increase. This makes the decision extremely complex since the problem facing the tenants is how they value a modern house of high quality compared to lower densities.[17]

4. Non-housing benefits arise from redevelopment since such a policy allows a review of total land use in the area. These non-housing benefits will include accessibility to shopping and transport facilities, changes in travel-to-work patterns and more open spaces.

5. Modernisation produces less social disturbance than replacement and redevelopment. Neighbourhood and kinship ties tend to be unbroken. There have been many sociological studies of urban renewal such as the well-known Bethnal Green study carried out by Willmott and Young (1957) which have emphasised the social value of preserving existing neighbourhoods and communities but, as Sigsworth and Wilkinson (1967) have pointed out, many individuals do have a strong preference to leave these areas and to move to new areas offering clean surroundings, open space, greater privacy, and access to better social goods which will provide greater opportunities for them and their children.

6. One of Needleman's (1968) arguments was that modernisation would be more able to be carried out by small building firms within the local areas, thereby generating income and employment within the area. This is of course true, but only over certain phases of the building cycle. In the case of Birmingham it was found that there was a limited

availability of contracting firms and labour to carry out modernisation work.[18]

7. The administrative processes involved in rehabilitation and redevelopment should also be compared. Frequently it is argued that rehabilitation is less time-consuming than large-scale redevelopment. Cullingworth (1973, p. 73) has said of slum clearance and redevelopment that: 'the lengthy nature of the whole process results from the inherent complexities, the multiplicities of departments involved, the time taken for objections to be made by owners and for these to be considered by the local authority and... the time taken in arranging, holding and deciding upon a public inquiry'. But whilst the administrative costs of renewal are identified very few people check out the hypothesis against the administrative costs of rehabilitation. Needleman (1968) was one of the earliest to point out that large-scale modernisation takes time also. In the case of Birmingham it was argued by the City's Housing Department that housing improvement requires an increase in housing department staff in order to inspect housing conditions before and after improvement.

8. Redevelopment of one area can induce decay and blight in neighbouring areas. Moreover, it has often been the experience that cities have bought up large areas of the inner core of the city as they have become available to the market. Such purchases are often well in advance of building plans for housing, motorways or redevelopment. Such sites create uncertainties for those in neighbouring areas, thus causing accelerated blight. In other instances cities have cleared sites just to discover that they are unable to build on them. This may occur because of public expenditure cut-backs, or because loan sanctions do not cover expenditure on social facilities that should accompany redevelopment. Sometimes, too, Department of Environment building-cost yardsticks are too low, thus making it impossible for local councils to fulfil contracts for new building and redevelopment. Finally, deferred demolition and patching up is an unsatisfactory compromise between rehabilitation and full scale redevelopment. In this case a local council purchases property in a development area well in advance and then patches up (i.e. improves to an extent) these houses. But the uncertainty caused thereby (i.e. not knowing when demolition will actually take place) speeds up the decline of the area. Such areas become characterised by a rapid turnover in their population, a high immigrant population, and have in some instances been used by councils to house their *problem families*.

It will, therefore be appreciated from a consideration of the above list that the choice between rehabilitation and redevelopment is no mean task. One in-depth study which has attempted to analyse the costs and benefits of improving older homes is the Dundee study which was carried out by members of the Scottish Development Department and is presented in Grant, Thomson, Dible, and Randall (1976), with an extension by Randall (1976).

The Dundee Study sets out to compare the costs and benefits, and where possible their incidence, of the improvement of older homes against their replacement. These costs and benefits are summarised as:

1. *Improvement*
  (i) *costs*: demolition costs, annual repair and maintenance costs, the cost of replacing any displacement of existing dwellings;
  (ii) *benefits*: provision of relatively cheap centrally-placed housing for younger, more mobile households, i.e. newly married couples, students and single people; a means of securing a public-sector house for families and elderly households; preservation of existing communities, shopping centres, etc., and hence reduced costs of learning about a new environment.
2. *Replacement*
  (i) *costs*: costs of demolition and replacement, annual repairs and maintenance, cost of additional land for housing in those cases where redevelopment results in lower densities;
  (ii) *benefits*: new building, new environment, etc.

Clearly the benefits from improvement are not the same as the benefits from a new home as is revealed in individuals' preferences and willingness to pay. Magnitudes such as gross annual values and the sale price are lower for improved houses than for new. The Dundee study is by no means exhaustive but what it does achieve is a careful specification of the problems involved in identifying and measuring these benefits and costs as set out above. Randall (1976, p. 347) in his conclusion argues that, 'the choice between improving or redeveloping older housing is a complex one which cannot be resolved by the mechanical applications of a quantitative formula'. That this is the case can be seen when we consider the problems of changing the conditions in which the replacement/renovation decision has to be made. For example, will the decision change if we consider the choice between replacement/renovation for a small area as compared to a large area? In the case of the latter, large area renewal and replacement brings about different standards of density and space, i.e. benefits which are less likely to enter as key decision-variables for small-area renewal.

Consequences of urban renewal

The choice between alternative means of urban renewal, rehabilitation vs. renewal, is an example of *ex-ante* evaluation. In *ex-post* evaluation we are interested in tracing out the actual consequences of renewal policies on a number of spheres of economic activity. Urban renewal affects a number of markets. The redevelopment of an entire area changes land-use patterns and therefore affects the location of industrial, commercial and service establishments which, in turn, affect employment opportunities, travel-to-work patterns, shopping patterns and so on. Urban renewal also directly affects urban housing markets.

In *ex-post* evaluations we are interested ultimately in the well-being of the individual. Thus such evaluations trace out the consequences of renewal policies first upon the value of the goods finally consumed by each individual, and second upon the prices of these goods. For any single individual an improvement results from urban renewal if there is a net increase in the consumption benefits.[19] Finally, we try to record who benefits from the policy by analysing the incidence of net benefits.

We will examine the consequences of urban renewal under the following headings: (a) impact on the individual; (b) impact on the housing market; (c) impact on industrial location and employment.

Urban renewal and the individual

The only comprehensive evaluation of urban renewal policy which has been conducted at the level of the individual in the UK is that which was carried out by Flowerdew and Rodriguez (1977). Their study concentrates on a renewal scheme in London over the late 1960s and early 1970s. A complete area was cleared and redeveloped with the last of the original residents moving out in 1969 and the new residents arriving in 1972. The area was replaced with council housing and the number of residential properties fell from 156 to 108, whilst the population of the area increased from 515 to 586.

Flowerdew and Rodriguez divided their sample survey into two identifiable groups with the intention of examining the effects of the renewal scheme upon the different sub-groups. The first group were the displaced residents (D), i.e. those who moved out of the redeveloped area, and the second group were the new residents (N) who moved into the area after renewal.[20] Each group were asked a series of questions relating to the effect of the policy. The main results can be summarised as:

1. *Housing Conditions* were compared before and after the renewal. For group D; 89.3 per cent thought that the internal conditions of their new home were good or very good. Prior to the move 30.8 per cent thought that the internal conditions of their original home were good or very good. For group N the corresponding figures were 87 per cent and 40 per cent respectively. Therefore, over all, both groups in the main preferred their new home. This was due to improvements in dwelling amenities, space and the condition of the house. Members in group D mentioned conditions and amenities most frequently whereas those in group N made most frequent references to space and amenities. Those in N also liked their new home because it was a house rather than a flat, because it had a garden and because it was well designed.

2. *Location Factors*. Most members of D and N were at least no

worse off as a result of the move and a significant number were much better off. Both groups experienced improvements in access to public transport. Members of group N expressed benefits from better access to a greater variety of shops, to doctors and to parks, whereas those in D were slightly worse off with respect to access to shops.

Journey to work did not change dramatically since households moved relatively short distances in this renewal scheme. For D, 50 per cent moved less than one mile from their original home and less than 10 per cent moved more than five miles. Those in N had moved greater distances but in most cases they had moved closer to their place of work.

3. *Social Ties*. The result of this part of the study are tentative. For N and D more than two-thirds had no relatives living in their pre-renewal area. The majority of households in both groups generally found the post-renewal areas to be less friendly and for those in D this appeared to be especially so since the D group move was an involuntary move away from friends compared to the N group which was more a voluntary move. The problem with this part of the study is that such feelings may be initial and short-lived.

4. *Housing Costs* increased for both groups. The rents faced by those in group D increased from an average of £2.54 per week to £4.55. For group N the average rent paid rose from £4.87 on average to £6.90. Other housing costs brought about at the time of the move were divided into avoidable costs such as the purchase of new furniture (those were ignored) and unavoidable costs which included decorating and the installation of household appliances. For group D the costs of the move averaged £206, whereas for N it was £333.

The fuel bills for both groups were also found to have increased (allowing for temperature and weather variations). In the case of D fuel bills were up by 52.7 per cent, i.e. 50 pence per week, and for N by 77.1 per cent or 75 pence per week.

Taking all factors together Table 11.1 provides a summary.

Table 11.1 How the move turned out over-all

	Group D (%)	Group N (%)
Very good	24.7	27.1
Good	37.7	57.1
Neither good nor bad	16.1	8.6
Bad	14.0	2.9
Very bad	7.5	4.3
Observations	93/94	70/70

Source: Flowerdew and Rodriguez (1977, Table 17).

Urban renewal and the housing market

A number of questions have been asked about the nature of the benefits and costs which follow from urban renewal. To these we now add a further one. Does the elimination of slum property automatically improve the welfare of low-income groups?

Earlier we stated that the conditions for an improvement of the welfare of those affected by the renewal policies were that the final consumption benefits should increase *ceteris paribus*. If, however, the increase in final consumption benefits is accompanied by an increase in their price without a corresponding improvement in the individual's real income, then such a change will not lead to a welfare improvement. This rather obvious remark is frequently ignored in those studies which only concentrate upon final consumption benefits.

When considering the relationship between slum clearance and the welfare of low-income groups it is necessary to begin by distinguishing clearly between slum dwellings and low-income housing, since frequently the two concepts are confused. At any moment in time there is a demand for housing units of a low quality from low-income groups. Slum dwellings on the other hand represent a concentration of low-quality housing on such a scale that neighbourhood effects and other negative externalities result in a deterioration and decay of the area.

Low-income housing is generally supplied through a *filtering down* of the existing housing stock from middle- to lower-income groups. Like a motor car, housing is a durable consumption good which depreciates over time. The more depreciated it becomes, the more likely it will be consumed by lower-income groups. Filtering of the housing stock is initiated by higher- and middle-income groups who release property by purchasing new constructions. A stock of old, worn-out housing is the market's efficient way of providing housing for the poor. So long as there exist poor families the existence of a significant supply of low-quality housing units might represent an optimal use of resources in the market. If this is so, then we must consider the implications of reducing the supply of low-income housing through urban renewal policies.

If low-income housing is demolished then the relative price of such housing units will rise. Thus the displaced low-income families now face higher prices (rents) for housing which makes them worse off. Moreover, given the demand for low-income housing, it becomes profitable for higher-income groups to divide their housing into smaller units and allow it to filter down. This creates the conditions for a concentration of low-income housing or, in other words, it creates the basic conditions for another set of slums in the future.

The timing and phasing of demolition, redevelopment and rebuilding is, therefore, of crucial importance if these effects of temporary disequilibrium at the lower-income end of the housing market are to be avoided. The problem is that we do not know how long the temporary disequilibrium might be. To eliminate these consequences slum clearance must be accompanied by the production of low-income housing at a price that these households can afford. This would probably mean that slums would be replaced by public-sector housing rather than private development, up-grading of housing and subsidisation.

The elimination of slums is, therefore, a necessary but not a sufficient condition for helping the poor.

One of the questions which we asked in the previous section was what happens to the pattern of land use following slum clearance? Clearly the answer to this question is crucial to the discussion of welfare distribution. Unless the poor are moved to new low-income housing estates, replacement of slums by higher-income housing or by manufacturing or commercial properties is going to have the same effect as that described above. A reduction in the supply of low-income housing will make the poor worse off. The rich who move back into the city will vacate their property and a reshuffling will take place in the housing market with higher-quality housing filtering down to the poor but at higher relative prices.

Urban renewal is not a once-and-for-all event and the dynamics of urban housing markets must be understood in order to prevent the coalescing of conditions which will end up as slums. Housing standards and expectations are continually rising which means: first the product of earlier renewal programmes becomes obsolete, and second, there is a continuous process of filtering in the housing market. To ensure the existence of a dynamic equilibrium requires conditions that will hasten retirements from the housing market, accelerate filtering and increase supply. An increase in the supply of high-quality low-income housing would also assist in reducing general immobility of labour as too would subsidies to the costs of mobility.

Slum clearance and replacement may not be automatically optimal as we have seen. But, obviously, no one is suggesting that we preserve slum areas. Given the choice of a slum environment to an alternative with higher price-tags on it, in terms of higher rents and disruption costs, as in the Flowerdew and Rodriguez study, individuals would be likely to choose the latter. What we have done is to explore the possible consequences of slum clearance in an attempt to be informed.

Some insight into this kind of problem is found in Mason's (1977) analysis of the operation of a Housing Action Area (HAA) in Manchester. The HAA was found to serve two principal housing functions. First, it provided cheap, furnished rented accommodation (i.e. low rent, low amenities) for low-income tenants. In 48 per cent of the households studied, 20 per cent of their take-home pay or social security benefit or pension was going into rent. Second, it provided first-time owner-occupied housing for several minority groups. Mason's observation was that 'the big task facing any improvement action programme in this area would be to facilitate physical improvement of dwellings while sustaining the two housing functions' (p. 23).

Department of Environment circulars frequently warn local authorities against improving their housing to unrealistically high standards because low-income families will be unable to pay the new rent.

Urban renewal, industrial location and employment

Comprehensive redevelopment of inner-city areas brings about changes in land-use patterns. Industries and services which once provided employment opportunities relocate, which could result in reduced employment and increased costs of journey to work. Two studies of the effects of comprehensive redevelopment in Glasgow have examined the impact upon industrial location and employment of renewal policies. These studies are described in Cameron and Johnson (1969) and McKean (1975).

The Cameron and Johnson study examines the net costs of urban renewal which confront the manufacturing establishments in the comprehensive development area. For a firm the costs of renewal will include removal costs, a loss of goodwill which is embodied in the site location, writing off plant, and higher rents (per floor area) in the new location, whereas the benefits to be gained from relocation are increased productivity from a more efficient new plant, and a reduction in diseconomies such as traffic congestion, environmental pollution and non-optimal land use.

In weighing up the benefits and costs of relocation one important element in the calculation is the valuation placed upon a central site location by affected firms. Some firms have a high demand for central locations because of the benefits which arise such as easy access to labour and other factor markets, access to final-product markets and networks of distribution. For such firms a central location, post renewal, would be a high priority. Cameron and Johnson's study, however, shows that for many firms a demand for central locations no longer existed. Changes in communications and in methods and costs of transport had altered firms' demand for central sites. Moreover, non-central sites were cheaper in rent and site preparation, whilst increases in car ownership meant that labour was willing to travel further to work.

The conclusion of the Cameron and Johnson study was that 'whilst it is often assumed that compulsory powers of acquisition are used by redevelopment authorities in an indiscriminate manner, with the dispossessed the unfortunate victims of coercion in the guise of the public interest', an examination of the manufacturers in the Glasgow sample showed that this was not the case. Why was this so? First, few of the manufacturers were actually displaced; second, those who were acquired by compulsory purchase were protected by rights of appeal; third, some small firms who considered redevelopment their death knell would have died despite redevelopment given their other circumstances, e.g. declining product market and liquidity. Finally, whilst the demands for centrality are important, the relocation requirements of industry are varied, which means that an optimal renewal policy must accommodate such variability.

McKean's (1975) study was wider in its scope. Examining the impact of urban renewal in seven redevelopment areas in Glasgow over the period 1958 to 1968 the hypothesis to be tested was, has the urban renewal process failed to take account of the deleterious effects upon the structure and the performance of the inner city?

Some of the consequences of urban renewal are set out schematically in Table 11.2.

Table 11.2

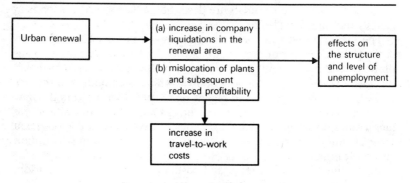

Each linkage in Table 11.2 represents a hypothesis which is capable of being tested. Using control groups elsewhere within the Glasgow city boundary McKean set about testing whether or not urban renewal had brought about an increase in the rate of liquidation in the seven redevelopment areas. He found that 43.5 per cent of all recorded closures in the study group were due to renewal. Such firms were typically small, employing less than 25 people. The remaining closures were due to non-renewal factors such as firm size, poor management, and contracting product-markets.

Many small firms in the redevelopment areas had depended upon the low rents afforded by such locations. A large number of these firms had relocated within Glasgow to areas which were designated for future redevelopment. Thus firms had kept their local markets whilst keeping their rent costs down. Of the firms who relocated only 3.3 per cent subsequently closed down, indicating that relocation did not have an adverse effect on industrial performance in this sense.

The loss of low-price centrally-sited property might have been thought to be a disadvantage since such areas are the seed-bed for the growth of firms. But as Cameron and Johnson had previously demonstrated, central location is no longer of such importance. McKean's analysis proved that following renewal there was no perceptible change in the birth-rate of firms.

What was the net effect of these changes upon employment prospects within the area? McKean's conclusions were that 'while urban renewal has affected the outmigration rate there is little evidence to suggest that this dislocation has resulted in any more than a redistribution of employment over space (p. 11) . . . . urban renewal did not cause absolute employment decline as much as it resulted in a spatial redistribution of the demand for labour away from the inner city' (p. 14).

Finally, McKean also examined the effect of population decline and property redevelopment on the quantity, function and organisation of service activity in the development areas. For example, many shops were placed on the market either for rent or for sale whilst others were used for purposes other than retailing, such as storage. Did this reduction in the number of shops cause inconvenience to shoppers? From the community viewpoint it was found that the loss of the small corner shop did result in an added cost which was borne in terms of loss of convenience. Even those areas which had gained the multiple stores had experienced important changes since the small corner shop frequently granted credit and provided the customer with quantities smaller than the standard amount. However, it should be realised that competition from the multiple stores would probably, in the absence of redevelopment of the area, have resulted in the liquidation of the small corner shop. It is therefore difficult to blame urban renewal.

Urban renewal and welfare distribution

The question of who bears the net benefits and who the net costs of urban renewal is of particular interest for the design of optimal policies, and yet it is an area that we know very little about. Questions about the infringement of property rights has been central to the debate (Clark, 1970). But in order to sort out the problem we would need to clearly separate normative issues from positive ones. We need to decide *a priori* upon who should benefit and by how much, i.e., should it be the children of the family, the landlord, the tenants, owner–occupier, building society, the building industry, housing officials, or who? There are potentially many who could benefit but who does in practice? Are those who are dispossessed during the urban renewal process adequately compensated? Are funds such as improvement grants equitably allocated amongst local governments?

There are very many questions which could be asked but far fewer which have actually been answered.

Kirwan and Martin (1972), for example, found that the diversion of public expenditure from new housing to the improvement of old housing during the late 1960s had resulted in a switch of real income from the poor to the rich and from older to younger householders (see also Mason, 1977). Resources had also been redistributed spatially from the suburbs to the inner-city areas.

Kasper (1971) showed that many of the families rehoused in peripheral estates from some of the worst inner-city housing conditions ended up, in cash terms, worse off than when they started once account was taken of the earnings of all members of the family, their travel costs, and the loss of earnings during periods of unemployment in the course of transition. The male unemployment rate was found to increase after compulsory residential relocation. Moreover, the activity rates of females declined due to the reduced number of employment opportunities. Also, as in the Flowerdew and Rodriguez study, the rates and rents of the new houses were higher because the houses were larger and of a better quality.

In a study of US urban renewal experiences, Downs (1970, p. 219) found that it was the poor who bore the bulk of the uncompensated costs of urban renewal. 'These households are the least able to pay such costs, derive the least benefits from the projects concerned, and are already unfairly compelled by society to bear heavy burdens resulting from racial discrimination and segregation'.

Downs's estimate of the uncompensated costs from urban highway and urban renewal programmes between 1964 and 1972 were

at least $156.2 to $230.2 million per year upon approximately 237,200 displaced persons and at least another 237,200 non-displaced persons. In my opinion, this represents injustice on a massive scale. It amounts to an uncompensated loss averaging from $812 to $1194 per household for each of the estimated 192,800 households involved. The median income of these households is probably around $4000 per year. Therefore, the average uncompensated loss which each is compelled to suffer amounts to confiscation of from 20 to 30 per cent of one year's income (p. 223).

The above estimates are, however, in contradiction to those made earlier by Rothenberg (1967, p. 190) who tentatively concluded that 'the dislocates were not hurt much, if at all, by relocation (except for their attachment to their original dwellings). It will be assumed, therefore, that in this particular situation, the development projects had no important adverse distributional effects to offset advantages to those who eventually moved into the new units (in the long run)'.

Yet another US study, this time by Anderson (1964) found that there was a strong tendency for renewal programmes to subsidise higher-income groups and to penalise those at the lower end of the income distribution. Replacement housing was frequently designed for those with higher incomes. This resulted in a contraction in the supply of housing to lower-income groups which caused the price/rents of low-income housing to rise.

The results of these US studies are clearly inconclusive. This is primarily due to the major conceptual and empirical problems which such studies face. Despite this inconclusiveness, urban renewal policies continue: what we cannot be sure of is who benefits from such policies?

Can public policies make a difference to the urban crisis?

A number of people have come to question whether or not the Government can, through its urban renewal programme and other area-based policies, effect a cure to the urban problems.

In the USA Banfield (1970) has argued that there is very little that the existing members of society can do about urban poverty and deprivation. Urban renewal policies will always be frustrated and our expectations will not be fulfilled. For Banfield the urban poor are 'enmeshed in a culture of poverty which virtually guarantees the failure of positive action programmes'.

Bateman and Hochman (1971, p. 343) place their emphasis on the failure of urban renewal on the political majority. 'It is the political majority that has failed by not adopting the essential reforms in social and economic institutions...our belief is that responsibility for the urban crisis stems neither from the lower classes nor from market failure, but from the deficiencies of the process of government itself and the systems of rights it sanctions'.

Thus, before any social policies can hope to succeed there must be fundamental structural reforms in society's economic, social and political institutions. If these reforms do not take place then planners may put their fingers in dykes but their doing so will not make any perceptible difference in the long run.

Urban renewal is but one example of the more general class of area-specific or area-based policies which make a positive discrimination between areas in terms of special needs. Area-based policy recommendations were popular in the 1960s. For example the Plowden Committee Report (1967) recommended education priority areas, the Seebohm Report (1968) which examined personal social services designated areas of special need, the Milner Holland Report (1965) argued similarly for housing and the Home Office's first circular, which launched the urban aid programme in 1968, defined areas of special social need to get resources for welfare services, day nurseries, and education.

However, there are advocates for and against area-based policies. Amongst those who favour them is Holtermann (1978), who argues that their advantages are, first, that they assist in resource savings since they make it possible to help more deprived people from a given level of resources, and second, that they help in achieving a possible higher take-up rate of special assistance.

Those who argue against area-based discrimination include Benington (1973), Donnison (1974), and Townsend (1976). They point out that an exclusive focus on small neighbourhoods of concentrated multiple deprivation may prove to be misleading. Many of the critical social problems are not inherent or specific to the neighbourhood but are instead manifestations of wider processes in society. Most of the deprived in practice live outside the boundaries of area policies. Thus many of society's most severe social problems will be helped more effectively by national policies aimed at individuals. The fundamental causes of inequality (either class causes or life-cycle causes) are found at the national level of the economy.

Clearly the choice between area-specific policies and national-level personal-income transfers, including in-kind transfers through public service provision, is not an either/or decision. These policies are not perfect substitutes. Instead the challenge to policy-makers is to find the appropriate mix of policies.

Conclusion

To summarise the above discussion would be an impossible task. What this chapter has attempted to do is to take stock of what we know about the urban renewal process and to review the problems of implementing renewal policies. The choices which have to be made between alternative policy instruments are complex and turn out to depend upon local circumstances. Not until we have more case-study material covering a greater variety of local conditions can we be confident in our expectations of the outcome of urban renewal.

Until recently urban planning and renewal has tackled the physical problem directly. But we need to return and ask once again what is the problem which renewal policy is supposed to be solving? Regeneration of the physical environment in terms of improved housing, new amenities, new communications networks, obviously have positive advantages and bring welfare gains. Indirectly the policy of renewal reduces negative externalities and other neighbourhood spill-overs such as high delivery costs. But it does not solve the problems of poverty and unemployment. Indeed as we have seen in some cases the policy might unwittingly contribute to these problems.

Urban renewal policy requires to be harnessed to other social policies both at the national and at the local level and integrated so as to improve economic efficiency whilst achieving an improvement in distribution. 'To attain efficiency along with justice and fairness, what is needed is a broad moral consensus, founded in a heighted perception of human interdependence and an understanding that a just and free society are the stakes of a game which must be played within a viable time frame' (Bateman and Hochman, 1971). Urban renewal by replacing or renewing the physical environment cannot hope by itself to eliminate poverty. Poverty is the result of the distribution of power in society and this distribution of power (or property rights) is protected by powerful interest groups. The elimination of poverty, therefore, necessitates the abdication of some power by the affluent majority in favour of the poor minority. Instead, 'urban renewal should be seen as a way of dealing with the processes which force people into slums: land use studies are becoming less relevant as planners concern themselves with the provision and the use of social services and the economic and political consequences of the policies they recommend' (Pahl, 1969, p. 122).

Notes

1. See also Donnison (1977).
2. See, Cmnd. 6845, *Policy for the Inner City* (HMSO, 1977). The annex to this White Paper provides an extensive description of the socio-economic environment of UK cities. Readers should also consult *Inner Area Studies* (Department of the Environment, 1977).
3. Especially that for urban motorways and expressways.
4. A more complete explanation can be found in Richardson (1971), Flowerdew and Rodriguez (1977), and Davis and Whinston (1961).
5. Neighbourhood effects can be traced back to Marshall (1920 p. 445). See also Oates (1969).
6. This decision problem has been set out formally in terms of game theory by Davis and Whinston (1961) as an example of the Prisoner's Dilemma.
7. These started off with the *Town and Country Planning Act* of 1944. Also the 1959 *House Purchase and Housing Act* introduced grants to cover 50 per cent of the cost of providing standard amenities such as w.c., bath, hot water, ventilated foodstore, etc.
8. See Spencer and Cherry (1970) and Duncan (1974).
9. The inflexibility inherent in many long-term projects is discussed in Friend and Jessop (1969).
10. Readers wishing to follow up the other dimensions will gain a useful introduction from the essays contained in Harloe (1977) and Pahl (1969).
11. The basis of these statements are fully discussed in Prest and Turvey (1965). The time profile of social rather than private benefits and costs are set out and discounted. This means that any employment multiplier effects, etc. generated by the project are included. The appropriate set of prices, including the interest rate, which is used in the evaluation is the subject of debate.
12. Musgrave (1958, p. 13) discusses this in the context of merit goods.
13. Rothenberg (1967) and Flowerdew and Rodriguez (1977) recognise the problem of distribution but given their data set are unable to take the analysis very far in that direction.
14. In welfare analysis we have a number of alternative welfare criteria to choose from. For example, the Paretian criterion, and the Kaldor /Hicks compensation principle require that a change in policy make no one in the society worse off, whereas the Rawlsian maximin criterion seeks to maximise the welfare of the least well off member of society irrespective of the change in welfare at upper reaches of the income scale, and of course utilitarians seek to maximise aggregate welfare irrespective of its distribution.
15. These issues are developed in Aaron and McGuire (1970) and reviewed in Brown and Jackson (1978, Ch. 20).
16. Some readers will recognise this as a crowding out argument.

17. Questions of this type are considered by Flowerdew and Rodriguez (1977) and are dealt with below.
18. See Paris (1977, p. 151).
19. More formally; for individual i

$$\max U^i (X, G) \text{ subject to } p_x X + p_G G \leqq M_i$$

where U^i is the individual's semi-strictly quasi concave utility function dependent upon consumption of the private goods vector X and the vector of publicly supplied goods G with prices p_x and p_G respectively. The individual's real income is M_i. Renewal policy will result in a welfare improvement for the individual if (*ceteris paribus*) X and G increase (assuming normal goods) or if p_x and /or p_G fall. If employment opportunities fall, e.g., then M_i falls; if prices, e.g. of housing, etc. rise, then the individual is made worse off.

20. Those in group D were older and contained more retired people. They had also been compelled to move because of the renewal. Group N were younger and had either volunteered to move into the new area or had been on the council's housing waiting list.

References

Aaron, H. and **McGuire, M.** (1970) 'Public goods and income distribution', *Econometrica* **38**.

Anderson, M. (1964) *The Federal Bulldozer: A Critical Analysis of Urban Renewal.* M.I.T. Press, Cambridge, Mass.

Banfield, E.C. (1970) *The Unheavenly City.* Little Brown, Boston.

Bateman, W. and **Hochman, H.M.** (1971) 'Social problems and the urban crisis', *American Economic Review*, Papers and Proceedings, May.

Benington, J. (1973) 'Focus on Government', *Municipal Journal* **81**(4), 26 Jan., pp. 114–18.

Brown, C. V. and **Jackson, P. M.** (1978) *Public Sector Economics.* Martin Robertson, London.

Cameron, G.C. and **Johnson, K. M.** (1969) 'Comprehensive urban renewal and industrial location: the Glasgow case', in Orr, S. C., and Cullingworth, J. B. (eds), *Regional and Urban Studies.* Allen and Unwin, London.

Clark, G., (1970) 'The lesson of Ackam road', *New Statesman*, 7 Aug., pp. 139–40.

Crossman, R. (1975) *The Diaries of a Cabinet Minister*, Vol. 1. Hamilton Cape, London.

Cullingworth, J. B. (1973) *Slum Clearance and Improvement: Problems of an Urban Society.* Allen and Unwin, London.

Davis, O. A. and **Whinston, A. B.** (1961) 'The economics of urban renewal', *Law and Contemporary Problems* **26**, pp. 105–17.

Department of the Environment (1973) *Better Homes The Next Priorities*, Cmnd. 5339. HMSO.

Department of the Environment (1977) *Inner Area Studies.* HMSO.

Donnison, D. (1974) 'Policies for priority areas', *Journal of Social Policy* **3**(2), pp. 127–35.

Donnison, D. (1977) 'Urban development and social policies', *Social and Economic Administration* **11**(3).

Downs, A. (1970) *Urban Problems and Prospects.* Markham, Chicago.

Duncan, T. (1974) *Housing Improvement Policies in England and Wales.* Centre for Urban and Regional Studies, Birmingham University, Research Memorandum No. 24.

Flowerdew, A. J. and **Rodriguez, F.** (1977) *A Retrospective Economic Evaluation of Physical Planning*, mimeo, Centre for Environmental Studies, London.

Friend, J. K. and **Jessop W. N.** (1969) *Local Government and Strategic Choice.* Tavistock, London.

Grant, R. A., Thomson, B. W., Dible, J. K. and Randall, J. N. (1976) *Local Housing Needs and Strategies: A Case Study of the Dundee Sub-Region*. Scottish Development Department, HMSO.

Harloe, M. (1977) *Urban Change and Conflict*. CES Conference York, Conference Series 19.

Harrison, M. L. (1975) 'British town planning ideology and the welfare state', *Journal of Social Policy* 4(3), pp. 259–74.

HMSO (1977) *Policy for the Inner City*. Cmnd. 6845.

HMSO (1973) *Tenth Report of the Expenditure Committee, Housing Improvement Grants*. HC 349, Session 1972–73, Vol. 1.

Holtermann, S. (1978) 'The welfare economics of priority area policies', *Journal of Social Policy* 7(1), pp. 23–40.

Kasper, H. (1971) *Measuring the Labour Market Costs of Housing Dislocation*. Discussion Paper No. 4, Urban and Regional Studies Discussion Papers, University of Glasgow.

Kirwan, R. and Martin, D. B. (1972) *The Economics of Urban Residential Renewal and Improvement*. Centre for Environmental Studies, Working Paper 77.

McKean, R. (1975) *The Impact of Comprehensive Development Area Policies in Glasgow*. Discussion Paper No. 15, Urban and Regional Studies Discussion Papers, University of Glasgow.

Marshall, A. (1920) *Principle of Economics*, 8th ed. Macmillan, London.

Mason, T. (1977) 'Intention and implication in housing policy: a study of recent developments in urban renewal', *Journal of Social Policy* 6(1), pp. 17–30.

Milner Holland Report (1965) *Housing in Greater London*, Cmnd. 2605. HMSO.

Musgrave, R. A. (1958) *The Theory of Public Finance*. McGraw Hill.

Needleman, L. (1965) *The Economics of Housing*. Staples Press, London.

Needleman, L. (1968) 'Rebuilding or renovation: a reply', *Urban Studies* 5, pp. 86–90.

Needleman, L. (1969) 'The comparative economics of improvement and new building', *Urban Studies* 6, pp. 196–209.

Oates, W. E. (1969) 'The effects of property taxes and local spending on property values: an empirical study of tax capitalization and the Tiebout hypothesis', *Journal of Political Economy* 77, pp. 957–71.

Pahl, R. (1969) 'Whose City?', *New Society* 13 (330), pp. 120–2.

Paris, C. (1977) 'Policy change: ideological consensus and conflict', in Harloe, M. (ed.), *Urban Change and Conflict*. CES Conference York, Conference Series 19.

Plowden Committee Report (1967) *Children and Their Primary Schools*. Report of the Central Advisory Council for Education (England). HMSO.

Prest, A. R. and Turvey, R. (1965) 'Cost benefit analysis: a survey', *Economic Journal* 75, pp. 683–735.

Randall, J. N. (1976) 'The costs and benefits of improving older homes', *Urban Studies* 13, pp. 345–7.

Richardson, H. W. (1971) *Urban Economics*. Penguin, Harmondsworth.

Rothenberg, J. (1967) *Economic Evaluation of Urban Renewal*. The Brookings Institution, Washington D.C.

Seebohm Committee Report (1968) *Report of the Committee on Local Authority and Allied Personal Social Services*, Cmnd. 3703. HMSO.

Sigsworth, E. M. and Wilkinson R. K. (1967) 'Rebuilding or Renovation', *Urban Studies* 4(2).

Spencer, K. and Cherry, G. (1970) *Residential Rehabilitation: A Review of Research*. Centre for Urban and Regional Studies, Birmingham University, Research Memorandum No. 5.

Townsend, P. (1976) 'Area deprivation policies', *New Statesman*, 6 Aug.

Willmott, P. and Young M. (1957) *Family and Kinship in East London*. Penguin, Harmondsworth.

Chapter 12

Economic policies for the conurbations

The concept of conurbation policy

One of the recognised and accepted phenomena of applied economics is the existence of a series of lags or time-intervals between the emergence of an unfavourable trend in an economy and the implementation of policy measures designed to counteract the developments that are deemed to be undesirable. It is usually the case that the inception of an adverse movement in an economy's rate of growth or pattern of development can only be identified retrospectively, and thus there is always a period of time before its existence is recognised. Yet further periods of time will then pass whilst the magnitude, speed and structure of the new trend is measured; the nature of its causes isolated and analysed; the impact and the effect of its continued existence predicted; and whilst policies designed to counteract undesirable features of the change are formulated, put into practice, and finally take effect. It is also widely recognised that the longer the over-all lag between the first and last stages of the above process, the less likely it will be that the policy instruments normally encountered in a mixed economy will be able to moderate or reverse the changes that are taking place.

The existence of such lags is one of the more important problems that regularly have to be overcome by those engaged in the formulation of economic policy, and an inability or refusal to recognise their nature and substance can have a critical impact on the effectiveness of any policies that are devised. This fact, while important in all areas of economic policy, perhaps assumes an even greater degree of prominence in the context of a policy issue as complex as the encouragement of the long-term growth of the British conurbations. As will become clear in this chapter, a sense of historical perspective is a fundamental prerequisite for anyone involved in attempting to shape their future.

It is clear that, at least in aggregate terms, the economies of the seven British conurbations have been diverging away from the national growth performance for some considerable time, although it is not easy to measure this divergence with any accuracy. Throughout most of the post-war period the most visible aspect of this comparative decline has been the contraction in the proportion of the British population that lived in the conurbations (see Ch. 2) but there are indications that these major metropolitan areas may have begun to lose ground as seen through other more directly economic measures (see Ch. 3).

One interesting illustration of this decline can be seen if the share of the conurbations in the UK's personal net income (PNY) is examined (Table 12.1), with attention being focused on the most recent seven-year period for which data is available. The conurbations' share of the personal net income of the nation's taxpayers has fallen from 39.7 to 36.4 per cent, but closer inspection indicates that all this decline is attributable to the relatively large fall in the PNY of taxpayers in Greater London: a further confirmation of the capital's unique position. Indeed, if London is excluded, the other six conurbations managed to push their share up from 18.5 per cent in 1967/68 to over 20 per cent by 1974/75. The explanations for these changes are complex, and outside the scope of this chapter, but this topic would seem to justify further research and analysis.

A more marked decline can be seen to emerge if the average PNY per tax case (an admittedly crude but simple measure) in each of the conurbations is examined (Table 12.1). With the exception of Clydeside and West Yorkshire – two interesting exclusions – the average incomes fell compared to the UK average during the seven-year period to 1974/75. Whereas in 1967/68 the average PNY per tax case was 5 per cent higher than the national average, by 1974/75 it had fallen to a mere 0.5 per cent above, and it may well have fallen below the national average in the ensuing period. The heaviest proportional declines have taken place in Manchester (−5.6%), Greater London (−4.6%) and the West Midlands (−3.5%): the three traditionally affluent conurbations. The reasons for these declines are complex, and reflect a number of changes such as the distribution of incomes within the conurbations; the changing residence (though not necessarily the work-place) of affluent taxpayers; the impact of fiscal legislation; the workings of Gibrat's Law; and the changing composition of personal incomes. Little is known about the relative importance of each of these factors, but the overall broad picture does seem to be that the relative levels of personal incomes in the conurbations are growing at a slower rate than those for the nation as a whole. This does indicate a further dimension to the over-all decline outlined elsewhere in this volume.

What is perhaps more important is that the conurbations have come to contain a share of the major economic and social problems that is greater than their relative populations would indicate. This is true for a large number of issues, ranging from sub-standard and decaying infra-structure to unemployment and low-income households and individuals. It is this concentration of the nation's problems that represents the fundamental policy issue of the conurbations, and which has led to the emergence of the present perceived aggregate decline. The forces and factors that have been responsible for this aggregate decline are, as yet, inadequately understood, but they have continued, largely unnoticed and unchecked, for perhaps the last quarter of a century; and, in the cases of Clydeside, Merseyside and Tyneside, for a much longer period. The interesting question that confronts both economic

Table 12.1 Personal net incomes and net incomes per tax case in the British conurbations, 1967/68 and 1974/75

Conurbation	Personal net income				Personal net income per tax case			
	1967/68		1974/75		1967/68		1974/75	
	Total (£m.)	% of UK	Total (£m.)	% of UK	Per tax case £	% of UK	per tax case £	% of UK
Central Clydeside	718.7	2.9	1,640.9	2.9	1,082	94.0	2,544	95.6
Tyneside	323.8	1.3	1,117.8	1.9	1,099	95.2	2,501	93.9
West Yorkshire	748.2	3.0	2,028.8	3.5	1,122	97.2	2,614	98.2
South East Lancashire	1,077.8	4.3	2,399.1	4.2	1,102	95.0	2,441	91.7
Merseyside	548.7	2.2	1,455.3	2.5	1,103	96.0	2,479	93.1
West Midlands	1,223.5	4.9	2,995.3	5.2	1,175	101.8	2,614	98.2
Greater London	5,322.1	21.2	9,228.1	16.1	1,305	113.1	2,872	107.9
All conurbations	9,962.8	39.7	20,865.3	36.4	1,212	105.0	2,676	100.5
United Kingdom	25,080.6	100.0	57,339.4	100.0	1,154	100.0	2,661	100.0

Sources: 1967/68: Board of Inland Revenue, *Inland Revenue Statistics, 1970: Survey of Personal Incomes* (BIR, 1970).
1974/75: Board of Inland Revenue, *Inland Revenue Statistics, 1977: Survey of Personal Incomes* (BIR, 1978).

Notes: The figures above relate to personal net incomes of taxpayers covered by the surveys, and thus exclude the incomes of non-taxpayers, the proportion of which may vary between conurbations. As they are residence-based, changes in levels over the period may reflect changes in residence but not necessarily in place of work. The figures are in current prices, and thus may exclude the effects of differential rates of inter-conurbational price inflation. They should therefore be treated with caution.

historians and political scientists as well as economists is why a historical trend reached such proportions before it came to be recognised and perceived as a national problem.

It is both instructive and important to briefly review the reasons why the comparative decline of the conurbations went unnoticed, for this will provide some of the components of the historical background that are essential inputs into any consideration of future policy initiatives. There can be little doubt that the minds of the national economic policy-makers were not really focused on the 'micro-spatial' aspects of economic development, and certainly the idea of having any concern for the problems of individual large urban areas was something which would have been regarded as faintly ludicrous by Treasury mandarins in the 1950s. The broad Keynesian view of the economy as a series of national aggregates that could be manipulated by government expenditure, monetary policy and taxation, left little room for an urban dimension. Indeed, even regional policy was largely seen, until the mid 1960s, as a means of contributing to a more efficient national growth performance, by improving the distribution and utilisation of factors of production.

In retrospect, there was also an element of confusion inherent in regional policy throughout much of the post-war period. The main focus of spatial planning of the British economy was directed towards regional economic development objectives, and the most important of such objectives was that relating to the need to provide more employment opportunities for the unemployed in the declining regions. The Keynesian orthodoxy that lay behind many UK economic policies in the late 1950s and 1960s saw the existence of regional differences in employment opportunities as an issue that could be tackled by policies and programmes that were essentially demand orientated, and thus the intention of most of the regional incentives was to encourage mobile industry to move from the affluent areas to the regions where job shortages existed. Within this perspective, the southern conurbations were seen as affluent, fast-growing and economically over-heated areas that were able to act as major sources of new industries and new employment opportunities for the declining regions without harming their own long-term economic potential. In retrospect, this belief seems naive, but it was often reinforced by the misplaced self-confidence in these conurbations that was engendered by the continuous national economic growth climate that characterised much of the post-war period.[1]

Simultaneously, the main policy objectives in the northern conurbations were dominated by physical planning considerations that assumed that national regional policy would ensure sufficient mobile industry being made available, and thus the requirements in such as Clydeside and Tyneside were to provide the essential infrastructure needed to attract mobile industry. Indeed, the main preoccupation of the physical planners throughout much of the post-war period in the northern conurbations has been to tackle the problems of the over-crowded urban areas, which were seen as socially undesirable slums containing populations far in excess of what was considered proper, and which thus needed to be demolished. There was little understand-ing or concern for the real problems of the urban economies, but merely a single-minded desire to tackle housing problems, which usu-ally required that inner-city populations be dispersed to new peripheral housing estates or to the new towns that were established in the twenty years after the end of the Second World War. Such a simplistic view of the planning of the conurbations also existed in the southern conurba-tions, but to a lesser degree, and in none of their cases did it reach the level of commitment that was achieved in Clydeside, where, for exam-ple, the City of Glasgow – which now expresses serious and justified concern about its population decline – paid local authorities and new towns to take the families that were moved out of the city because of urban renewal schemes (Slaven, 1975).

In all the conurbations, the real economic issues and areas for con-cern were substantially more complex than realised. The nature of the decline that was beginning to develop in all seven was essentially the same, although revealed in different ways and over different time periods. It is only with the emergence of urban economics as a major academic and practical discipline in Britain in the 1970s that the rela-tionships between regional and urban growth and changes have been recognised (Hughes, 1979), and it is in the analysis of the experience of the conurbations that the essential unity of regional and urban development has become apparent.

The final reason why the decline of the conurbations largely escaped attention was that the economic and social indicators that would have pointed to the divergence were largely absent. The poor quantity, quality and timeliness of statistics for the regions, conurbations and urban areas of Britain have long been recognised to be an extremely serious handicap for both analysis and policy. The lags outlined earlier have thus been stretched to the point where policy-formulation that is intended to tackle current economic problems may in fact be more relevant to the constraints and opportunities that existed in an earlier period for which data, information and statistics are available. The critical importance of this problem has been recognised (House of Commons, 1974; Swales, 1976), and its resolution must form an important part of any long-term development strategy for the conurba-tions.

Despite these and other factors which delayed the emergence of the conurbations' decline as an issue of concern, the real situation in these major metropolitan areas became visible in the period after 1973, when for the first time in recent history the international recession had a proportionately greater impact on the more affluent areas like the South East and the West Midlands than on the traditional declining industrial areas of the periphery. The downturn in economic activity, which was most marked in the manufacturing sectors, compounded the decline which had already got under way in the inner areas of large cities such as Birmingham, Leeds, London and Manchester, with the result that in a relatively brief period of time the established wisdom about the existing nature and ranking of urban and regional problems in Britain was challenged and largely destroyed. The old conception of rich and poor regions, and growing and decaying cities was seen no longer to be valid.

The reappraisal of the spatial distribution of economic problems should not be underestimated for it may well have fundamental long-term implications for the British economic and political systems. Two recent developments which have played major parts in this reappraisal, and which are important in the context of future policy formulation for the conurbations, are the growing rôle of economists in urban and regional analysis, and the associated evolution of modern regional and sub-regional economic and industrial development plans. The gradual introduction of economists into the physical and policy planning departments of the larger regional and metropolitan authorities in the 1970s has introduced a capability for analysing and evaluating economic changes from a local perspective which was previously totally absent. The results of their work can be seen in the increasing sophistication of the political demands made by local authorities for special attention to be paid by central government to their own specific economic and industrial problems, which in effect is beginning to force central government to take account of the spatial impact of national policies.

The major regional studies that were undertaken in the 1970s have also had an important impact on the evolution of the new perspective on Britain's regional and urban system. Perhaps the most influential of these regional studies are those that have been undertaken for West Central Scotland (1974) and for the Northern Region (1977), and the latest version of the strategy for the South East (1976); although other important studies have been undertaken for the North West (1974) and the West Midlands (1975). The first three regional studies mentioned have all had a large element of central government participation, which has ensured that their conclusions have been taken especially seriously; have all had a primary focus on the economic and industrial problems and potential of the areas studied; and have produced strategic plans that give a high degree of priority to economic policies and programmes rather than physical plans. Further, all have identified the conurbations as the principal locus of the regional problems that were detected and that these problems were especially severe in the cities that dominated each of the conurbations. Most important of all they all concluded that future economic growth and development must increasingly be sought in the local economies rather than imported from other areas.

Thus by the mid 1970s the British conurbations could be seen as forming an increasingly important source of political demands for policies and resources to tackle fundamental economic and industrial problems, and the formation of major metropolitan authorities based on the conurbations following the reorganisation of local government has provided an informed and powerful set of new participants in the national economic policy forum (see Ch. 14). There can be no doubt that in the future there will be a growing emphasis on the formulation and implementation of decentralised economic and industrial policies in the UK, and that the conurbations will be the most important and perhaps the most logical points of coordination for such policies and programmes. In the remainder of this chapter the possibilities of such a development will be examined. In order to do this, it will be necessary first of all to briefly review the present state of knowledge about the nature of the conurbation economies and the causes of their problems; then look at the broad context in which policies will be formulated; discuss the objectives that programmes should seek to achieve; and finally look at the various levels of economic policy in the UK to determine where and what type of initiatives can be taken to improve the long-term performance of the conurbations. What does emerge from such a perspective can be clearly stated now, namely that there is no certain or easily available set of policies that will return these large local economies to the supposedly golden age of the second half of the nineteenth century. Rather, what is needed is a whole series of measures that can perhaps be implemented and coordinated most successfully at the level of the individual conurbation or metropolitan authority and which aims at fostering local economic enterprise.

Economic problems in the conurbations

The effectiveness of any economic policy depends critically upon the existence of a logical link between the problems that exist and the objectives that planners wish to see achieved. This in turn implies that the bundle of constraints, inefficiencies, and those market forces that are deemed undesirable, are capable of being identified with some precision and certainty. In the case of the conurbations, it is far from obvious to economists that the real underlying causal factors responsible for their comparatively poorer economic performance have been identified, despite the increasing sophistication of much of the urban and regional research that has been undertaken in Britain during the past decade. If this seems a harsh judgement, then it is worth pausing momentarily to review what is known about the problems that are assumed to exist in the conurbations.

Earlier chapters have looked at the structure and changes that have taken place in the economies of the conurbations, and have begun to point towards the nature of the problems that are thought to exist. The picture is one of aggregate decline, and the main features of this are well known by now: a contraction in the labour forces resident in the conurbations; the faster fall in the size and share of their manufacturing sectors; the sharp switch of population from the inner-city areas to the suburban areas; and a modest comparative deterioration in their unemployment and activity rates (Corkindale, 1977). There are, of course, other indicators of underperformance that could be used, such as the low birth-rates of new enterprises, but it is possible to regard the economic problems of the conurbations as having two main dimensions, namely, an aggravated deterioration in their inner-city areas; and a broader lack of efficiency in the manufacturing sectors, which traditionally have been the main export bases of the over-all conurbation economies. This latter aspect is hard to distinguish from the inner-city problem, and indeed it is accepted by now that many of the real problems are so interrelated that it is difficult and unrealistic to allocate them to any category, but for the purposes of analysis here a cavalier approach will have to be taken. Thus, let us look briefly at each of these two sets of problems.

The decline in the economies of the large British metropolitan areas has now become a major area for both research and policy, and concern about the economic condition of inner cities has evolved into *the* spatial policy issue of the 1970s. The components, rates, and structures of inner-city decline in the conurbations has been reviewed elsewhere (Keeble, 1978), and the main feature seems to be that the loss of establishments and employment in the central cores of larger cities has been due principally to the closure of enterprises in these areas, rather than to the migration of plants to suburban or rural locations. Further, the effects of these high death rates seem to have been compounded by low birth-rates of new firms and other new establishments in inner urban areas, and thus the combination of these two factors has led to a continued contraction in the stock of manufacturing plants in the centres of the conurbations. In most conurbations the shortage of modern industrial premises has meant that the few large new manufacturing plants that have opened in the past two decades have been on peripheral industrial estates, and this has had important economic implications for the functioning of the local factor markets, especially in relation to labour. The little evidence that exists so far for non-manufacturing sectors suggests that the same mix of components may also have been at work with the same results, but it is really far too early to draw any firm conclusion, except for the obvious one that it is strange that so few academic and government economists are currently engaged on research into those sectors of the national economy that account for over 60 per cent of employment.

The reasons for the well-documented decline in inner-city manufacturing are still far from clear. Part of the contraction is due to the industrial structure of inner cities, through the location in these areas of industries which are in industrial decline: what might be termed the 'industrial dendrochronology of urban decline' (Firn, 1976). Part is probably a consequence of the organisational structure of the firms located close to the city centres, and reflects the difficulty that small, independent, old-established businesses had in competing with the larger, multi-regional and multi-national plants that have emerged as a result of post-war mergers, take-overs, and inward investment.

Part of the inner city decline may reflect, as pointed out in an earlier chapter (see Ch. 3), marked changes in the locational economies and general economic environment of the central cities of the conurbations that have not been conducive to the growth, or indeed the survival, of business enterprises. Most economists who have looked at the impact of these locational factors have their individual list of crucial ingredients usually based on intuitive, anecdotal or generalised evidence, but common to most lists are transportation inefficiencies; the lack of modern and cheap industrial premises; the effect of a visibly deteriorating environment; vandalism; the sale and use of land for non-industrial purposes; and the impact of uninformed and uncaring physical planners who have no understanding of the nature or needs of industrial enterprises. It is exceptionally difficult in practice to attribute decline in inner cities to any particular mix of the above factors, and in practice all that can be done is to assume that all have been present to a greater or lesser degree, and thus all should be borne in mind when framing policies.

The second general feature of the conurbations has been the poor performance of their manufacturing sectors in the recent past, although it has to be stated at the outset that the evidence on this broad point is somewhat contradictory. Certainly between 1961 and 1971 the percentage decline in employment in the manufacturing sectors of the conurbations as a whole was greater than that for the rest of Great Britain, with the exception of Merseyside, Tyneside and the West Midlands (Corkindale, 1977, p. 1200), but more recent evidence indicates that between 1972 and 1975 this earlier decline has halted, and it may even since 1975 have shown an opposite favourable trend (Business Statistics Office, 1975, 1978). Further, given the switch that has been taking place between labour and capital, it may not in fact be sensible to use employment change as a measure of decline if gross output has risen, and if net value-added has increased. There seems to be a reluctance by many urban and regional economists to consider such possibilities, and thus it is possible for them to employ the use of such 'indicative' techniques as shift-share analysis to identify components of decline without any real conception of what the results are meant to show. Indeed, if conurbations' or regions' manufacturing industries are over-manned in comparison with other regions or, perhaps more importantly, with other nations, and the area concerned then proceeds to raise its efficiency through the shedding of surplus labour, a poor shift-share performance on an employment basis may be something which requires praise and emulation! However, the absence of regular and timely output figures on a conurbation basis means that this particular possibility will have to remain untested at present.

If the long-term decline in employment in manufacturing in the conurbations is taken as indicative of some genuine underperformance of the manufacturing enterprises in these areas – and Britain's national industrial performance in the world market does strongly suggest that this has been the case, then it is essential to identify the causes of this if we wish to formulate policies to improve the position. The main economic studies undertaken involving the conurbations have indicated that a whole range of factors are involved, not all of which may be responsive to public policy.

The West Central Scotland Plan in 1974 concluded that the reasons for the industrial decline of Clydeside were a combination of a poor industrial structure; low labour-productivity and high unit-labour costs; high levels of external ownership and control in the region's enterprises; a poor quality environment; a low rate of new firm formation; inadequate availability of business finance; dismal industrial relations; and poor quality local management (West Central Scotland Plan, 1974). The Northern Region Strategy Team found most of these problems in existence in Tyneside as well, but also showed concern about the relative absence of small firms in the region's economy, which was seen as acting as a real constraint on long-term growth.[2] (Northern Region Strategy Team, 1977).

So far, detailed economic studies of the other conurbations that contain an analytical examination of the reasons for the poor performance of the local industrial sector have been conspicuous by their absence, although partial recognition of the problems does exist. The North West Industrial Development Association, in their comments on the Strategic Plan for the North West (1974) criticised the superficial nature of much of the 'official' analysis that has been undertaken, and concluded that the types of studies used had ignored such '... important factors as the (organisational) status and size of plants, technology levels, the amount and quality of capital equipment and buildings employed by companies, and the suitability and competitiveness of products to markets', all of which the Association obviously regarded as being the locus of the region's poor performance.[3] More recently, Liggins concluded that the marked slow-down in the performance of the West Midlands local economy had been building up for some time before it became visible in the post-1973 period.[4] He attributed the main problems to the negative impact that physical planning had had on industrial development; the effect that the high level of post-war mergers in British industry had on the region; the constraints on industrial efficiency imposed by the growth of trade union membership and the influence of shop stewards; comparatively high labour costs; the Government's continued use of the car industry as a national (macro) economic regulator; the static industrial structure of the region during the 1940s, 1950s and 1960s, and the consequent absence of diversification; and finally, the adverse effect on an exporting region that resulted from the loss of much of Britain's share of world trade (Liggins, 1977).

The case of Greater London is more complex, and in many ways it is difficult to consider its problems in the same context as the other six conurbations, for they are of a totally different scale and of a completely different nature – even though many of the symptoms of industrial decline are similar. For instance, although Greater London's manufacturing employment has been declining and especially in the inner city, the conurbation's control over the nation's total industrial resources has been increasing. Thus at least part of its manufacturing decline has been matched by the growth in corporate headquarters staffs in London in the 1960s and 1970s. The fact remains, however, that the nation's largest and most important conurbation is by far the least studied and understood, and the special nature of its economy does mean that its economic problems will probably require a unique policy framework and set of operational programmes. It is necessary to bear this special caveat in mind when discussing actual policy possiblities below.

Despite the range of regional and sub-regional studies that have been undertaken, and the more reflective and analytical view that has recently been taken of the factors causing the perceived poor performance of the conurbations, there is still much that we do not know about the real nature of the problems. The relative contribution of international, national, regional and urban influences to the over-all problems of any one of the conurbations has not yet been determined with any accuracy; and little is known about the political, institutional and socio-cultural influences on economic growth and efficiency at the level of the conurbation: these are all assumed to be residuals in the stark modern calculus of regional and urban economics. It is obvious also that many of the problems that are assumed to be contributors to the decline of the major metropolitan areas turn out to be symptoms upon closer inspection: for example, the identification of 'bad management' as an explanation for the poor performance of an area's industrial sector tells us precisely nothing of any use for policy formulation. Indeed, many of the earlier examinations of the state of particular regional and sub-regional economies probably reached nearer to a grasp of essential problems than whole teams of econometrically-inspired regional and urban analysts.[5]

There is, however, one general and very important conclusion that can be drawn from the few studies that have been undertaken on the economies of the British conurbations, namely that the comparative decline that has taken place in their economic influence has been principally due to long-term inefficiencies developing and becoming entrenched within the manufacturing (and presumably within the service) enterprises located in a region.[6] No longer do the old explanations of demand deficiency and simple structural disadvantage seem credible, and the renewed interest in industrial economics, and especially in micro-based industrial policy, has led to regional and urban economists becoming, of necessity, involved with the factors and conditions that determine the competitiveness and success of the individual firm in its market environment.

This changing perception of the main locus of the problems of the conurbations as lying principally on the supply side does not, of course, exclude the necessity of being aware of demand factors. Indeed, one of the main factors that determines the success of any firm is its ability to forecast likely changes in the demand for its products, and to respond to these effectively and efficiently, even to the extent of diversifying production if the demand seems to be set on an irreversibly downwards course. Thus, more complex issues and variables such as information; technology; management quality; supply capability and continuity; linkages; and organisational structure become important factors that have to be examined in any policy analysis.

It is obvious too that the conurbations and large metropolitan areas may suffer from constraints and inefficiencies that are not related to the under-performance of their industrial sectors, but to other factors: inappropriate fiscal policies, misconceived local welfare schemes and operations, and general or specific malfunctioning of a range of bureaucracies and markets. Unless some understanding of these other issues is achieved and corrective actions taken (if required), the policies aimed at improving the general competitiveness of a conurbation through those sectors producing marketable output may well be totally ineffective. Other contributors to this book have examined some of these other policy areas, and the remainder of this chapter is devoted to the objectives and strategies that may be employed to further the long-term economic development of the conurbations.

Policy objectives for the conurbations

Before possible economic policies for the conurbations are discussed, it is worth briefly looking at the framework within which policy objectives should be set. The decision to produce a comprehensive strategic plan for a conurbation contains within it a number of judgements. There is the recognition that problems exist; have been identified; and are capable of resolution by those responsible for planning the disposition of the relevant resources and other planning instruments. As has become clear in this chapter, however, it is not possible to state with strong conviction that the factors causing their relatively poor performance have been identified with the degree of precision necessary for effective policies to be formulated. However, in practice, the fact that an economy is not behaving as expected or desired is normally sufficient to result in a decision to intervene.

This desire for intervention is normally allowed to proceed unquestioned, but it is interesting to occasionally reflect that there is always the option of non-intervention available, and the question 'why intervene in the development of the British conurbations?' does seem worth considering. It could be that the relative decline of the conurbations, and the associated changes that are taking place in their economic, social and spatial structures, are part of a long-term dynamic growth process which is common to all large metropolitan areas at some time in their history. There is no reason to assume that either the growth or the continued pre-eminence of the conurbations is immutable, enduring, or even desirable, especially given the changes in life-style that are presently under way. The possibility of the eventual decline of large cities has been recognised by some of our modern prophets, and one of the most perceptive of these was H.G. Wells, who wrote in 1901 that:

> the belief in the inevitableness of yet denser and more multitudinous agglomerations in the future is so widely diffused, that at first sight it will be thought that no other motive than a wish to startle can dictate the proposition that not only will many of these railway-begotten 'giant cities' reach their maximum in the coming century, but that in all probability they ... are destined to such a process of dissection and diffusion as to amount almost to obliteration, so far, at least, as the blot on the map goes, within a measurable further space of years.[7]

The marked redistribution of population and employment within all the UK conurbations, which can be seen most vividly in the long-term reduction of the slope of their density gradients, gives some support to Wells's prediction, but it would seem that their total disappearance is not a likely outcome of future changes as currently understood. Because of this, conurbations will be there and will invite policy intervention, but it is also true to state that no argued or reasoned case for such intervention seems to have been made, although the underlying assumption seems to have been implicitly and universally accepted.

In practice the construction of a fully documented case for policy intervention to shape the future development of any single conurbation (let alone all seven) would be a task far beyond this chapter. It would have to discuss the rationale for policy, and this would presumably involve a number of theoretical components including such mainline economic ones as market failure;[8] the distribution of costs and benefits; the delineation of leading and lagging sectors; the integration of infrastructural utilisation and industrial development; and many other similar factors. Almost certainly these would have to be built round some central prescriptive political view of objectives, and equally certainly past evidence seems to show that any such argument would have a large element of a subconscious desire to recapture past comparative levels of economic development and economic growth. This last point is crucially important, because if policy is built upon a basis of a future dominated by images of the past, it may well result in objectives, programmes and goals that combine to work *against* future change, and this in turn can fossilise cities into increasingly less competitive entities. Thus it should be remembered that there is no *a priori* reason for assuming that future conurbations will, or should, resemble those that presently exist.

There is one other issue of importance here, and that concerns the most appropriate and effective point for intervention to achieve policy goals that are specified.[9] For some specific objectives national (and increasingly, international) policies and legislation will prove the optimum means to effect and direct change, whilst others can be best achieved at a regional or a conurbational level. One of the most complex planning problems is the coordination of all the various points and types of intervention, and it has to be accepted that in practice many instruments and programmes will partly or fully cancel each other's effectiveness. A large measure of administrative and legislative devolution to major coherent areas like the UK conurbations (or their encompassing regions) does offer one possible compromise to this particular planning difficulty, although in the UK the brief experience of local government reorganisation seems to indicate that it is very difficult indeed for large metropolitan areas to influence national policies to achieve their own objectives.

There is, however, another important implied judgement in any decision to produce a strategic plan for a conurbation, and this is that a consensus exists about the broad goals that should be sought. It is obvious that any discussion of these will be complicated by the recognition that it is impossible to exclude the political beliefs and influences that play a major role in shaping broad policy objectives in the UK. But in the case of the conurbations, it is made easier by virtue of the existence of broad agreement amongst most economic and political advisers to local and national political parties in Britain about the need to become actively involved in the future economic development of the conurbations, although it has not as yet been the subject of any substantive debate.

In terms of the longer-term goals for the conurbations, and in the light of the earlier analysis about the changing perception of the nature of their economic problems towards supply-side inefficiencies, it is clear that a fundamental objective for the conurbations must be the achievement of a greater degree of economic self-sufficiency. It should be stated at once that this does not imply an inward-looking, autarkic approach to policy formation: rather the opposite, namely that policies and programmes should be designed to assist the local economy to become more competitive and flexible in its response to changes in national and international economic conditions. Enterprises and individuals in both the local private and public sectors should be encouraged to accept change as a normal constituent of economic development,[10] and thus policies should be framed in such a way as to allow them to respond more positively to change than has been possible in the past. Indeed, an efficient and competitive local economy will, through the improvement of existing products, and the development of new products, services and technologies, be able to create its own demand influences.

There are a number of interesting implications that stem from the above primary objective for conurbation policies. First, the concept of increased economic independence, at least as defined above, forces consideration of the possible costs and benefits of the alternative objective, namely an increased integration of the conurbations into the national economy, and a reduction in their ability to determine their own futures. Whilst it is possible to argue in favour of increased centralisation, the current evidence is strongly supportive of the view that the UK's economy (and indeed its political system) has become too centralised. Second, if individual conurbations do consciously aim at being more competitive, it implies that there will be greater competition between the conurbations, not merely for markets or for resources or scarce factors of production, but for influence. It is conceivable that this may in turn improve the utilisation of resources, and thus the over-all national economic performance. One very intriguing area of analysis and debate that is currently little explored by regional economists in the UK concerns this very issue, namely the effect on national economic growth of operating regional development policies that aim at reducing the inter-regional disparities that exist: so far it has not been conclusively demonstrated that the reductions in regional differences in such as wages, incomes, unemployment rates, and industrial structures have been the result of regional as distinct from national policies.

Third, an improvement in an economy's ability to become more self-reliant of necessity forces detailed attention to be paid to the supply capability of the local economy, not just in terms of products and services, but also from the viewpoint of entrepreneurship; education; training; housing; transport; and the myriad other factors that comprise the local economy. It also requires that national policies be more closely examined to see whether their impact will have a beneficial or harmful effect on the local supply response. Fourth, it is also important to realise that the utilisation of resources (financial and otherwise) at a conurbation level does have implications for the local area's competitiveness, and thus the current local authority philosophy that 'welfare-orientated' expenditure is unrelated to and conceptually distinct from economic development expenditure, requires to be challenged. Finally, increased self-reliance does not require that no consideration should be given to assisting flows of factors between the conurbations, or between the conurbations and the other parts of the UK. Indeed, if we take the longer perspective of Wells and others, there may be merit in assisting inefficient or constrained markets to redistribute factors to where they are most required, and where they can make the highest long-term contribution to the nation's economic development. This in turn may mean smaller, leaner, but more efficient conurbations and central cities.

However, in the short term there is likely to be a need for more central government intervention and assistance while areas like the conurbations are weaned from their increasing dependence on centrally determined subsidies, which in some cases appear to have become almost addictive. This is not so much an 'infant industry' argument as one that parallels the provision of short-term subsidies and grants to enable industrial enterprises to re-equip and restructure themselves in order to improve their efficiency.

Whilst there may well be other strategic objectives of a generally accepted kind applicable to the conurbations, such as a desire to improve the over-all level of welfare of the area's inhabitants; to expand the opportunities for individuals to participate fully in the area's development; and to enable the economy to make the most productive use of its resources, these should all be orientated towards supporting the primary strategic economic policy objective outlined above. However, these broad strategic goals can only be achieved through the deployment of resources in specific, detailed, coordinated programmes, which are framed in such a way as to be capable of both effective implementation and evaluation. This in turn requires that programmes be given definite time-scales and, more importantly, relatively specific targets for goal achievement.

The imposition or adoption of specific quantified targets for policy programmes has never been popular in British government (although it is accepted as essential by most corporate planners in industry), principally because the existence of targets gives a visible yardstick to measure performance, and non-achievement can bring political retribution. However, realistic planning requires that any specific goals or targets be monitored, evaluated and, if necessary, re-specified regularly as part of an ongoing process where plans are up-dated and adjusted in the light of changing circumstances. The days of one-off plans for regions and conurbations should, in this light, be ended.[11]

Before looking at a range of possible economic policy initiatives that could be employed to achieve the longer-term strategic goals that have been outlined above, there is one final and critically important issue that requires to be briefly discussed, namely, the likely future economic environment within which the conurbations will be operating, and within which they will have to undertake their strategic planning.

The future economic environment

Policy-making for the conurbations would obviously be easiest in an economic environment where the major forces and influences were similar to those that have existed in the past or at present. However, it is certain that the general economic climate facing the conurbations and their economies will be subject to substantial changes in the coming decades, not all of which are predictable, and many of which are not capable of being influenced by policies or programmes.

Perhaps the most important influence in the foreseeable future is the shape of changes that are already taking place within the conurbations themselves, and of these the most evident and economically influential is that of the future level, structure and distribution of the population in the conurbations. At the national level, present demographic trends indicate that total population will grow very slowly between now and the end of the century, and that its composition will change towards older age-groups with a consequent rise in the number of dependants and a fall in the population of working age, although this latter phenomenon may well be desirable given the growing concern about the ability of many developed nations to generate employment opportunities at a rate sufficient to absorb the workforce.

However, the most interesting feature of future trends is that it appears likely that the British conurbations' share of the national population will decline (Table 12.2) quite sharply during the period up to 1991 if present assumptions about birth-rates and migration prove to be accurate. Projections made in 1977–78 show that the population in the six metropolitan counties and Clydeside which approximate to the old conurbation areas could fall by 9.3 per cent from 19.2 million in 1975 to around 17.5 million by 1991, against a national population growth that is estimated to be around 2.4 per cent over the same period. Thus, there is the prospect that in the immediate future these major metropolitan areas will be losing population at an annual rate of over 112,000, a prospect that has exceptionally important implications for the economies of the conurbations. It appears that very little consideration has been given to the consequences of this continued population decline, yet it cannot be doubted that the effect on, for example, the structure of local labour markets and on the financial structure of the conurbations will be substantial.

Further, it appears that the decline will be proportionately greatest in Greater London, Clydeside and Merseyside, but it is also clear that the decline of the central cities lying at the core of the conurbations will be even heavier (Table 12.2). Some of the forecasts are positively daunting for those faced with the task of framing programmes to regenerate the inner cities: Glasgow's population may fall by nearly one-third by 1991; Manchester's by 23 per cent; Liverpool's by 21 per cent; and Newcastle's by 14 per cent, whilst the population of Inner London is also expected to decline sharply although no figures have been made available so far. The population forecasts for the relevant regions show a more stable picture, and thus the inference to be drawn is that of a continued transfer of population from the central cities to suburban and other urban areas around the conurbations, with consequent increased travel-to-work flows and also fiscal imbalances between core cities and their hinterlands. The ability of the conurbations to alter these forecasts of population decline, at least over the next decade, appear to be slight, and thus one important parameter to their

Table 12.2 Projected population changes, 1975–1991, for Metropolitan counties plus Clydeside, their standard regions, and core cities

Metropolitan Areas*	Standard region		Metropolitan Areas		Core city‡	
	# (000's)	% change	# (000's)	% change	# (000's)	% change
Clydeside†	−169	−6.8	−234	−13.0	−271	−31.6
Tyne and Wear	–	–	− 69	− 5.8	− 42	−14.0
West Yorkshire	+ 40	+0.8	+ 14	+ 0.7	+ 3	+ 0.2
Greater Manchester			− 75	− 2.8	−118	−23.4
	− 77	−1.2				
Merseyside			−176	−11.1	−120	−21.8
West Midlands	+104	+2.0	−126	− 4.5	− 95	− 8.8
Greater London	− 43	−0.3	−1,132	−15.9	n.a.	n.a.

Sources: Office of Population Census and Surveys, OPCS Monitor PP3 77/1: *Population Projections mid-1975 based* (OPCS, December 1977); General Register Office for Scotland, *Projected Home Population: 1976 Based* (GROS, November 1977).

* These are all Metropolitan Counties with the exception of Clydeside, which is an aggregate comprising Glasgow District and eight adjacent Districts. It approximates to the old Central Clydeside Conurbation. On this definition these areas are not exactly comparable to the pre-1974 definition of conurbations. Figures on this 'older' definition are given in Tables 2.2 and Appendix Table A2.1.

† The figures for Scotland, Clydeside and Glasgow District are based on 1976 population estimates, and the projection for Glasgow District for 1991 was a personal projection using a log model on the published 1976–86 population estimates. It is, therefore, to be treated with some caution.

‡ The core cities are based on the Local Authority Districts.

(# = numbers change between 1975–91; % change = percentage change between 1975–91).

planning possibilities appears to be relatively immutable, although, as noted earlier, it has not yet been made clear why major attempts to change this decline should be made.

Within the national economy, it is clear that the switch away from manufacturing towards the service sectors will continue to be a dominant feature of industrial change, as will the adoption of increasingly sophisticated production technologies. It is hard to predict the likely impact of such changes upon individuals, especially in relation to their employment prospects; except that recent research has indicated that there may well be increasing (rather than decreasing) mismatches between labour supply and demand, despite the growing intervention of the government of the developed nations in their labour markets (Freedman, 1978). These imbalances have begun to surface in the conurbations, and their reduction represents an important policy area during the next few years when the world employment situation can be expected to be exceedingly difficult. The degree of pessimism which policy-makers should adopt depends, to some extent, on how convinced they are that attitudes to employment as being a necessity can be changed.[12]

There are other continuing developments that will work against any desire of the conurbations to become more self-reliant. There can be little doubt that the involvement of central government in the national economy will continue by both direct (via state ownership of productive resources) and indirect (subsidies, legislation, etc.) means, and thus on a whole range of issues that critically affect the conurbations, decisions will continue to be made as a result of political bargaining rather than as a natural outcome of market forces. It seems likely that, despite the renewed interest in the small firm sector (see below), concentration of ownership and control in all sectors of industry will continue to grow. Recent evidence suggests that the regional implications of such organisational changes can be a major determinant of any region's long-term economic development (Keeble and McDermott, 1978). It appears that, for instance, the experience of recent acquisition activity in British manufacturing industry has effectively worked towards integrating the regions of the UK, with control shifting towards the South East, which is 'becoming more of a head office and control region with enhanced external economies of service supply, but with a lower rate of factory expansion' (Leigh and North, 1978, p. 244). This development has been seen to have an adverse effect on the provincial regions where the short-term benefits that result from an external acquisition may be countered by the long-term drawbacks, 'in particular the capacity for self-generated industrial growth may be hindered by the economic readjustments that typically follow' (ibid., p. 244). This conclusion makes the need for a concentration of policy effort on raising self-reliance in the conurbations all the more vital.

Other possible changes that could be crucial for future planning efforts in the conurbations include for instance radical shifts in relative energy prices and the effect that these might have on the price elasticity of distance; major developments in communications and transport technologies which might make decentralised industrial and service activities more feasible; and, hardest of all to predict, substantial changes in general attitudes towards urban areas and towards the desirability of maintaining the conurbations as distinct and important entities in the national economic system.

Economic policies for the conurbations

The discussion in this chapter of the economic problems of the conurbations has already pointed to the conclusion that the main focus for policy formulation specifically to assist and encourage the conurbations must lie at the level of the conurbation and its larger region. However, the current and future degree of national integration in the UK, together with the nature of the economies of the conurbations, effectively ensure that a prior condition for any growth in the conurbations is a higher real rate of national economic growth. It is inconceivable that the seven areas could collectively flourish whilst the rest of the UK stagnated or declined, and the obverse is equally true, although the fact that these major metropolitan areas contain many of the leading national sectors means that an improved growth performance by them is an essential component of any national economic advance. Thus, national and local policies that assist the conurbation economies to become more effective and efficient partners in the national economy have an importance sufficient to demand attention by central and local government.

It is also important to remember that each conurbation's potential and problems are unique, and require an individual approach to policy formulation, but there are a number of national and local initiatives that can be taken to assist the conurbations achieve the strategic objectives that they may set in future planning activities.

National economic policies

Political scientists have shown that in hierarchical administrative systems, innovations in policies can often be made most easily at the national level, where the broader requirements are more readily grasped and where resources are relatively easier to command and deploy. At lower levels, such as in the conurbations, political pressures tend to be conservative, and often directed to the lower risk maintenance of existing industrial and spatial structures in the local economy, rather than towards more uncertain but potentially higher yielding innovations in policy. This is an important consideration, for if it is decided that the conurbation economics should be encouraged to become more competitive and self-reliant, the initiatives required to begin such a development lie firmly with central government.

At a national level the single most productive policy innovation is a greater awareness by government and administrators of the spatial consequences of national economic and industrial programmes. At present most policies are conceived, framed and implemented on the (subconscious) assumption that all parts of the nation will be equally affected by any changes that ensue. This is simply not so, as can be seen by considering the case of the car and shipbuilding industries. In both these industries the success or failure of national, and increasingly international, strategies designed to restructure their productive capacity will impact themselves very heavily upon the conurbations, where much of the shipbuilding and automotive engineering is concentrated.

The spatial impact of these national policies is so marked as to be obvious to central government even in the unlikely absence of strong political pressures from the areas affected, but this is not so in the case of other major national economic issues such as monopoly and mergers; technology and R & D; foreign trade and overseas investment; and wages and prices legislation. Much benefit would be gained if central government consciously built a spatial element into all of the main areas of economic and industrial policy, and if all of these separate spatial parameters were brought regularly together for evaluation.

A start has been made towards incorporating such a spatial component in the national industrial strategy that has been coordinated by NEDO since 1975. The individual sectoral working parties that are charged with examining the problems, opportunities, and policy requirements of specific industries have been instructed in their terms of reference to take account of the regional implications of any of their recommendations. There has been no evaluation so far of the effectiveness of this instruction, and there may well be a case for a separate industrial strategy working-party which would integrate the regional implications made by the individual SWPs into a spatial impact strategy. This would ensure that important areas such as the conurbations were fully appraised of the likely influence upon their future development of the implementation of detailed sectoral strategies.

It is difficult to imagine any national policies specifically designed to assist the conurbations, especially in the continued absence of any reasoned argument as to why such a policy would be desirable, or how it could operate, or what it might achieve. But there are some national developments which go a little way towards such a focus, and two of the most important current ones are the administrative devolution of financial assistance to industry, and the formation of regional subsidiaries of the National Enterprise Board.

Since the passing of the 1972 Industry Act, the United Kingdom has had a comprehensive range of financial and other forms of assistance to make available to industrial enterprises to help them modernise and expand their operations.[13] Although most of the administrative decisions relating to the financial powers of the Act remain the responsibility of the Department of Industry in London, from July 1975 Ministerial responsibility for regional selective assistance in Scotland and Wales under Section 7 of the Act was transferred to the Secretaries of State for Scotland and Wales. Simultaneously the regional offices of the Department of Industry in England with the assistance of their local Industrial Development Boards were given discretion to decide on Section 7 applications: up to a level of £2 million in the North West, Northern, and Yorkshire and Humberside regions, and to a lower level in the remaining regions. One important innovation of the 1972 Act was that it made financial assistance available to existing industry in the regions as well as mobile industry, and this, together with the administrative devolution outlined above, has meant that the local offices of the UK's main industrial ministry have begun to become more directly involved with supporting and encouraging the industrial enterprises in their area. As all the conurbations have such offices, they have begun to benefit from the more responsive attitudes of the local representatives of central government, who are now seen as allies who will speak in support of them to central government. The importance of improving the competitiveness and efficiency of their conurbations, and of supporting and retaining key local sectors, is a major development in policy for the conurbations.

The second innovation that may offer long-term opportunities for the conurbations is the establishment by the National Enterprise Board of regional offices and of venture capital schemes designed to build up the locally-based existing and potential enterprises. This gain is one, as yet small, step towards preserving the indigenous sector, and of trying to improve the ability of the local economy to provide the entrepreneurs and finance needed to make itself more self-reliant. In the longer term, it may be that these subsidiaries, and the future ones that will be formed by the NEB in other regions, will develop into more comprehensive and independent institutions on the lines of the existing Scottish and Welsh Development Agencies. With command over sufficient powers and resources to formulate and implement detailed industrial strategies geared to the needs, abilities and objectives of the conurbations, and with the co-operation of the local private sector, such agencies could be a major and fundamentally important means of encouraging the development of the conurbations.

One other national economic event of the 1970s that has relevance for the conurbations' long-term future is the renewed commitment to encouraging and supporting the small-firm sector, especially in manufacturing. The reason for the importance of this development is that it is through small firms that the conurbations will have to look for much of their long-term indigenous generation of employment opportunities, output, and new technologies and products. So far, the measures introduced nationally to encourage small firms have been mainly advisory and exhortatory, together with an attempt by central government to reduce the administrative and taxation burdens that fall on small businessmen. However, in Wales, and especially in Scotland, the two Development Agencies have begun to implement comprehensive long-term development strategies for small firms based on a coordinated package of financial assistance; advisory services; and specially designed premises. As over 40 per cent of Britain's manufacturing units employing less than 200 (the standard statistical definition of a small firm)[14] are located in the conurbations, there can be little doubt how influential a successful national small-firm sector could be on the future conurbation economies.

Finally, at a national level, it could also be argued, especially in the light of the possible population changes outlined earlier, that Britain is beginning to require a national settlement strategy which would attempt to ensure a reasonable balance between population growth and industrial development. Such a strategy, which would aim at a closer integration of long-term spatial and sectoral changes, would not be easy to formulate, but it would provide a framework within which the existing and future regional plans could be integrated and the long-term consequences examined. Thus rapid changes in the relative position of the conurbations would, under a settlement strategy, be made clear, and there would be a more informed view about the extent and direction of policy intervention that might be required. Despite the fact that there is as yet no national spatial planning in the UK, there is a growing recognition that 'the geographical distribution of jobs and people is too important to be left any longer to chance' (Sundquist, 1978, p. 5).

Conurbation level policies

One of the main conclusions of this chapter is that because of the uniqueness of each of the conurbation economies, the prime focus for policy must be at the conurbation level, but under the current British system of government there are few influential economic and industrial development powers available to the relevant conurbational or regional authorities except the normal powers of local authority expenditure and the more recent Inner City aid. However, this does not mean that conurbations are powerless to influence their own future development.

One of the most important means for improving their economic performance is by becoming better informed about the structure and the competitiveness of the local economies, and by relating this knowledge to a more incisive understanding of national and international economic trends. This means that the relevant local authorities must further enhance their capability for economic analysis, especially in relation to their leading industrial sectors. This, in turn, will require the establishment of close working relationships with the leading local enterprises in their areas; the local offices of the central government departments and ministries with responsibilities for economic and industrial affairs; with representatives of the employers and trade unions organisations; and with the other sectors of the local economy that have influential rôles to play in shaping long-term economic development. This closer coordination does not mean a continuation of the ineffectual talking-shops graced with the titles of Regional Economic Planning Councils, but rather the formation of action-orientated, committed coalitions within the conurbations which can work for economic development and social betterment, on the lines of those that have helped to begin the process of rebuilding North American cities such as Chicago.[15]

An important rôle in developing an improved understanding of the local conurbation economies, especially in terms of being able to identify the emergence of significant opportunities or constraints affecting or likely to affect local enterprises, can be played by the universities and colleges. So far, relatively few of the economists, business management experts, or technologists seem to have become involved in studying their conurbation economies, or of helping local firms understand the implications of wider international trends, which is in distinct contrast to medical schools, whose personnel are normally actively involved with improving the local physical health of the population.

One issue where more direct innovations require to be taken to improve local economic performance in the conurbations is that concerned with achieving a quantum improvement in the relationship between physical planning and economic development, and principally in ensuring that such planning furthers economic growth and efficiency rather than hinders or destroys it. In retrospect, the 1950s and 1960s were a period when the rigid and arrogant planning schemes undertaken in the larger cities played havoc with the complex mix of industries that had developed in the nineteenth and early twentieth centuries. There can be little doubt that the confused notions about urban economies and industrial economics held by architect planners have materially contributed to the inner-city decline and to the poor performance of the conurbations in the 1970s. In the 1980s, physical planners must seek ways of positively assisting local industries, even if it means radical alterations to their current zoning proposals, and the acceptance of a closer mix of housing and industries in the future: after all, technological advances now seem to indicate that the old style and structure of cities may no longer be relevant or efficient. An especially important issue is that concerning the relationship between housing and employment. Indeed, minimisation of travel-to-work flows and maximisation of potential employment opportunities should be more important goals for planners than preservation of coloured areas on their maps.

Within the conurbations, local authorities, either alone or in conjunction with other public and private sector corporations can do much to help and encourage the more efficient functioning of the local economy, especially the small-firm sector. Small factory units located in inner-city areas are now seen to be in big demand, especially if made available on letting terms that encourage new enterprises. Local authorities can ensure that their education systems recognise the importance and needs of local industry, and that links are developed with the main training and retraining agencies to ensure that sufficient skills of the required type are available when required. Further, most conurbations could benefit by the introduction of industrial development divisions within local authorities that were given sufficient status and powers to ensure that other departments could not undertake policies that were likely to work against the local industrial sectors.

But, having made the above suggestions, how much further can the conurbations go in developing economic policies that can positively assist their long-term economic performance? Unfortunately, there are no easy or simple policy initiatives lying hidden away that can be unveiled, and which will substantially improve the competitiveness of local economies overnight. What is required is the ability to undertake a myriad of small, marginal improvements and innovations over a long period of time in the context of a harsh and uncertain economic environment. The construction of a long-term strategy of the type outlined above, and the coordination within it of all the national and conurbation level policy possibilities discussed here, can mark the beginning of a slow but certain improvement in the economic performance of the British conurbations, and thus of the national economy itself. But it will not be easy, and will require ingenuity, determination and persistence if the goals that are set are to be achieved: the encouraging factor is that it was precisely these qualities that made the conurbations the powerhouses of the national economy in the first place.

Notes

1. It has been estimated that between 1966 and 1971 the West Midlands Region, which is dominated by the conurbation centered on the City of Birmingham, had over 4,000 manufacturing jobs per annum diverted to other parts of the UK by national regional policy (Crompton and Penketh, 1977, p. 119). During the same period the creation of employment opportunities in new enterprises in the West Midlands Conurbation was relatively low (Firn and Swales, 1978), and thus the long-term effect of UK regional policy on this supposedly affluent area may well prove to have been adverse. It is certainly an issue that requires further research.
2. However, Keeble points out that an interesting statistical relationship exists that shows a highly significant rank correlation between the mean factory size in each conurbation in 1972(as measured by employment) and the rate of growth of manufacturing employment between 1959 and 1971 (Keeble, 1978, pp. 106–7). He acknowledged the problems involved in such a simple relationship, but it might indicate that a high level of small firms in a conurbation is no guarantee in itself of long-term economic success.
3. The Association was very unhappy with the study, and it did 'not accept the Team's bland statement that the performance of industry rather than the structure of industry in the North West ... is the main cause of poor employment growth. We fear that the Team's very limited use of the term "structural" (although correct in terms of the growth components technique) will become established in the minds of decision-makers and thus hinder the identification of suitable solutions to the Region's employment problems' (ibid., p. 6).
4. Perhaps the West Midlands also suffered as a result of its complacency. I remember attending a major conference in Birmingham in mid 1973 when the region's leading industrialists, trade unionists, and local and central government officials all concluded (a) that there was no need for any diversification away from the car industry, and (b) that the region could easily continue to supply mobile industry for the regions.
5. Two examples of such earlier studies that bear re-examination are the 1946 Clyde Valley Plan, and the 1948 'Conurbation' study of the West Midlands Group.
6. For a discussion of the concept of supply-side failure, see Segal (1979).

7. H. G. Wells, *Anticipations of the Reaction to Mechanical and Scientific Progress upon Human Life and Thought*, quoted in James S. Coleman, 'Can we revitalize our cities?', *Challenge* **9**, Nov.–Dec. 1977, p. 27.

8. There are four main sets of factors than can, individually or in combination, produce market failure: high transactions costs; high degrees of uncertainty; heavy information costs; and the complex 'free rider' problem. A stimulating discussion of these can be found in Charles L. Shultz, 'The public use of private interest', *Regulation* **1**, Sept.–Oct. 1977, pp. 10–14.

9. One of the best illustrations of the difficulties involved in deciding how and where to intervene concerns the development of UK policy for the inner city. Unfortunately it is still not clear whether or not there is a specific set of inner-city problems that can be distinguished from other national economic and industrial problems. See A. J. Harrison and C. M. E. Whitehead, 'Is there an inner city problem?', *Three Banks Review* **119**, Sept. 1978, pp. 31–46.

10. Individuals and enterprises may of course decide to opt out of future changes, but they should then bear the costs that they incur for so choosing. This includes the support of local industries that are no longer viable.

11. The production of one-off plans for areas is now known as 'thud-rate' planning: large volumes thud onto officials desk and then no longer rate any attention!

12. Freedman suggests that 'the time may be right to look to new horizons: to seek to change attitudes, to develop alternatives to present work patterns and life-styles, to move in the direction of new concepts of social well-being' (Freedman, 1978, p. 20). This may also be true for the conurbations, namely that their future role in the nation's development should be substantially different from their past contributions.

13. It is interesting to note that the selective financial assistance under sections 7 and 8 of the 1972 Industry Act effectively makes 'regional type' assistance available to non-development areas.

14. Unfortunately UK statistics on small firms as distinct from small establishments are not available in Britain. In a large 1977 survey of small manufacturing establishments in Scotland undertaken by the Small Business Division of the Scottish Development Agency, it was found that less than 80 per cent of units employing under 200 workers was a true small firm, which might indicate that the sector is smaller than supposed.

15. For an interesting discussion of the means by which one city in the United States is starting to restructure its economic base, see Dick Griffin, 'The Chicago coalition is still holding together', *Fortune* **98**, 11 Sept. 1978, pp. 74–80.

References

Business Statistics Office (1975, 1978) *Analyses of United Kingdom manufacturing (local) units by employment size. 1972; 1975. Business Monitor PA1003*. HMSO.

Clyde Valley Regional Advisory Group (1946) *Clyde Valley Plan*. HMSO.

Corkindale, J. (1977) 'The decline of employment in metropolitan areas', *Department of Employment Gazette* **84**, pp. 1199–1202.

Crompton, D and **Penketh, L.** (1977) 'Industrial and employment change' in Joyce, F (ed), *Metropolitan Development and Change. The West Midlands: A Policy Review*. University of Aston for the British Association, Birmingham.

Firn, J.R. (1976) 'Economics microdata analysis and urban-regional change: the experience of GURIE' in Swales, J.K. (ed), *Establishment-Based Research: Proceedings of a Conference held at the University of Glasgow, April 1976*. University of Glasgow, Urban and Regional Studies Discussion Papers, 22.

Firn, J.R. and **Swales, J.K.** (1978) 'The formation of new manufacturing establishments in the Central Clydeside and West Midlands conurbations 1963–1972: a comparative analysis', *Regional Studies* **12**, pp. 199–214.

Freedman, D.H. (1978) 'Employment perspectives in industrialised market economy countries', *International Labour Review* **117**, Jan.–Feb. 1978, pp. 1–20.

House of Commons (1974) *Regional Development Incentives,* Report by the Trade and Industry Sub-Committee of the Expenditure Committee, HC 85–I. HMSO.

Hughes, J.T. (1979) 'An urban approach to regional problems' in Maclennan, D., and Parr, J.B. (eds), *Regional Policy: Past Experience and New Directions*, Martin Robertson, London.

Keeble, D. (1978) 'Industrial decline in the inner city and conurbation', *Transactions of the Institute of British Geographers* **3**, pp. 101–14.

Keeble, D. and **McDermott, P.** (eds) (1978) 'Organisation and industrial location in the United Kingdom', *Regional Studies* **12**, pp. 139–266.

Leigh, R. and **North, D.J.** (1978) 'Regional aspects of acquisition activity in British manufacturing industry', *Regional Studies* **12**, pp. 227–46.

Liggins, D. (1977) 'The Changing role of the West Midlands economy' in F. Joyce (ed) *Metropolitan Development and Change — the West Midlands*. Saxon House, London.

North West Industrial Development Association (1974) *Strategic Plan for the North West: Comments of the North West Industrial Development Association.* Mimeo. NWIDA, Manchester.

North West Joint Planning Team (1974) *Strategic Plan for the North West*. HMSO.

Northern Region Strategy Team (1977) *Strategic Plan for the Northern Region. Vol 1 Main Report*. Northern Region Strategy Team, Newcastle.

Segal, N. (1979) 'The limits and means of "self-reliant" regional economic growth' in Maclennan, D., and Parr, J.B. (eds), *Regional Policy: Past Experience and New Directions*. Martin Robertson, London.

Slaven, A. (1975) *The Development of the West of Scotland: 1750—1960*. Routledge and Kegan Paul, London.

South East Joint Planning Team (1976) *Strategy for the South East*. HMSO for the Department of the Environment, London.

Sundquist, J.L. (1978) 'Needed: A national growth policy', *The Brookings Bulletin* **14**, Winter–Spring, pp. 1–5.

Swales, J.K. (ed.) (1976) *Establishment-Based Research: Proceedings of a Conference held at the University of Glasgow, April 1976.* University of Glasgow, Urban and Regional Studies Discussion Papers, 22.

West Central Scotland Plan (1974) *West Central Scotland Plan: Supplementary Report 1: The Regional Economy*. West Central Scotland Plan Team.

West Midlands Group on Post War Reconstruction and Planning (1948) *Conurbation*. Architectural Press, London.

West Midlands Regional Study (1976) *A Developing Strategy for the West Midlands*. HMSO.

Chapter 13

Central/local relationships in the British conurbations

Although one of the principal elements in the central /local relationship has been the debate over local government reorganisation and the position of the conurbations in the local government structure, this is dealt with elsewhere and the present chapter confines itself to relationships under the form of local government in existence at any given time.

The historical phases

To place these in perspective, it may be useful to summarise, in broadly chronological order, the main events and the principal policies in the conurbations in the last 20 to 30 years which are relevant to the topic:

1. The adoption of the New Towns programme after the Second World War, and later of the expanded towns programme, which involved massive Government investment and subsidies to local authorities to encourage overspill.
2. The contemporaneous programmes of comprehensive redevelopment in congested urban areas, largely made possible by the building of new towns and out-of-town estates to receive the overspill.
3. The adoption of General Grant, and later Rate Support Grant, as the main source of Government financial contribution, apart from housing subsidies, to local authorities.
4. The introduction of the urban programme in 1969, as a means of giving special encouragement and financial support to deprived areas in towns.
5. The reports on local government reorganisation and the enactment of the new structure with the creation of local authorities which would need less Government tutelage as one of its main objects.
6. The commissioning of studies by consultants on 'the total approach' to managing the urban environment and later the inner-area studies.

The views expressed are personal to the author.

7. The introduction of the housing action area policy, and more generous grants and loans to housing associations with emphasis on rehabilitation and the reduction of overspill.
8. The Layfield Report on Local Government Finance and the Government's Green Papers of 1977 in response to it.
9. The Inner Cities White Paper of 1977 and the subsequent Inner Urban Areas Bill.

These events have led to far-reaching changes in the relationships between central and local government, which will now be examined first in their structural and then in their financial aspects.

The structural relationship

The structural relationship between central and local government – that is the nexus of powers, duties and avenues of communication between the two levels of government – has been regarded as a matter of cardinal importance in all studies of local government. The Redcliffe-Maud Commission (Cmnd. 4040, 1969) said that the right relationship did not exist; what was wrong was partly that

> central government tries itself to do some of the things that belong properly to local government, and partly that local authorities are not given enough freedom to go their own way.... Central government should not intervene in what a local authority chooses to do unless some clear national interest is involved or there are local objections which must be heard.... Another unsatisfactory feature of the relationship between central and local government is that the two parties sometimes seem to be at arm's length.... Sometimes decisions are handed down – or proposals are sent up – without any previous discussion or effort to reach agreement or at least understanding (pp. 30 and 31).

One of the main themes of the Layfield Committee on Local Government Finance (Cmnd. 6453, 1976) was that the structural relationship between central and local government determined the financial relationship as much as the reverse, and one of the sections of the Report which attracted most attention is its discussion of alternative systems of central/local relationship, which posed a choice between central responsibility and local responsibility. (The reservations by Day A. L. and Cameron G. C. chiefly related to their inability to accept that these extreme solutions were the only ones, but this further emphasises the point.) The Green Paper of May 1977 on Local Government Finance (Cmnd. 6813) and the similar Green Paper on Local Government Finance in Scotland (Cmnd. 6811) thought it right to seek a middle way, but could not envisage one which 'reduced the whole relationship between central and local government to a simply-defined form of allocation of responsibilities' (Cmnd. 6813, p. 5). The Government saw the duties and responsibilities involved in the provision of local public services as being 'shared on a partnership basis between central and local government'. The Central Policy Review Staff (CPRS) Report *Relations between Central Government and Local Authorities* (1977) said however that the relationship was a confused one: 'there is uncertainty not only about the precise role and responsibilities of central government but also following from this about how local authorities are meant to respond to many of its messages' (p. 46).

The implications of some of these statements will be discussed later in this chapter, but they share two assumptions which are questionable. The first is that the nature of the central/local relationship is virtually determined wholly by central government. In constitutional terms this is, of course, true, since the ability to legislate on this, as on other matters, rests with central government. But Parliament is not always prepared to do what the Executive wishes it to do, and it is by no means axiomatic that even the Executive is single-minded about the matter. Moreover, the policies of central government are to a large extent determined by pressures from the localities, not only from local authorities themselves, but from Members of Parliament whose attitudes are firmly rooted in the views held in their constituencies.

The second assumption is that local pressures are generally directed to obtaining more freedom of action for local authorities. But this is far from being the case. A substantial part of the time of Ministers and Departments concerned with local government services is devoted to rebutting attempts to make them intervene in matters which are a local government responsibility. Members of Parliament complain to Ministers if local authorities pursue courses which are unsatisfactory to them or their constituents; pressure groups complain about the failure of local authorities to do things which they ought to have done or about their doing things which they ought not to have done; and it is by no means unknown for dissatisfied councillors to try to get a Government Department to reverse the decision of their own local authority. The question of who and what is right is not at issue here; the point is that many people are not prepared to accept that responsibility can stop at a local authority. There seems to be a fairly general belief that central government ought to have and has power to intervene in many spheres where it has in fact abandoned powers of detailed control. The CPRS said (p. 46) that 'what is required is severe self-restraint on the part of Ministers and officials in trying to enforce centrally defined standards and values'; if this self-restraint is exercised it is often against the wishes of many individuals and groups.

It is, of course, proper that people should express their views strongly about local as about central government, and central government may rightly decide that the strength of opinion is such that something must be done to respond to it. The Layfield Committee was appointed largely in response to what they themselves described as the crisis about rates that occurred in 1974, producing 'a huge volume of complaint about increases in rate demands' and bringing to a head 'many of the reservations and dissatisfactions with the operation of local government finance' (p. 3). Similarly Dobry, appointed to consider whether the development control system under the Town and Country Planning Acts met current needs, submitted an interim report in a matter of three months (Dec. 1972) because of the concern felt about delays over planning applications and appeals. These examples of reviews could be multiplied, and all tend to illustrate the fact that the central government is under constant pressure to modify the central/ local relationship, and often in the direction of more central control.

Although these considerations apply to local government as a whole, the nature of the central/local relationship is of particular concern with regard to the conurbations because of the weight of population and the fact that social problems there are generally more acute and too big to be handled except in concert. Planning policies, housing policies and social policies have been largely determined by what the Government and large sections of public opinion saw as the needs of the conurbations – a matter of some complaint to the rest of the country, but not one to be dealt with here. Let us therefore look briefly at the changes in central/local relationships in two fields of special importance in the conurbations.

Transport

In the field of transport the adoption of the system of transport policies and programmes (TPPs) was due largely to dissatisfaction with the effects of massive roadbuilding programmes within the conurbations, and the growing belief that both central and local government must look at the means of transport as a whole. Leaving aside the national rail service, this meant that local authorities should look at local needs not only for road construction, but for the support of urban and suburban buses, as regards both capital investment and operational subsidies, and the support of the local rail system. The system also, however, represented an attempt, which has been largely successful, for the central government to dissociate itself from small-scale local decisions and to seek instead the preparation of comprehensive plans which could be examined and approved as a whole. The CPRS (1977, p. 48) thought that it allowed local authorities less latitude than originally envisaged. But there are also complaints in the opposite sense from those who feel they are disadvantaged by local authorities' policies and programmes and do not recognise that central government claims to stand aside from them.

Planning

In the field of planning, the replacement of development plans by the system of structure and local plans is a further exercise in central disengagement. The ultimate responsibility of the Government for national affairs has caused it to reserve the rights to approve structure plans and to determine planning applications of national importance. It is significant that the exercise of these rights rarely attracts criticism; local authorities seem prepared to accept it, and objectors tend to welcome it. The system, however, would benefit by a better definition of the circumstances in which planning decisions should be reserved to the central government. The national planning guidelines being issued in Scotland are starting to do this: they define the circumstances (by geographical area, and size or type of application, or a mixture of both) where *prima facie* a national interest may be said to arise, and require local authorities to notify the Scottish Office so that a decision may be taken whether or not to call in the application. Over a wide range of applications this frees local authorities from the need to notify central government, still less to obtain its approval. But obviously it can never be possible to classify all planning applications by means of a formula of this kind, since the most important ones are likely to be the only ones of their kind, and not amenable to classification.

An experiment in relationships in the planning field which has attracted much interest is the regional report which regional councils in Scotland have submitted to the Secretary of State for Scotland under section 173 of the Local Government (Scotland) Act 1973. The reports have ranged far beyond land-use planning, and are assessments of needs and policies across the whole of the authorities' responsibilities. They are not approved by the Secretary of State, but he comments on them, and his comments, which are published, have to be taken into account by planning authorities. As an illustration of this in practice, the Strathclyde report concentrated on the Central Clydeside conurbation, and not unexpectedly identified the high level of unemployment and the severity of urban deprivation as the key problems (Strathclyde Regional Council, 1976). The Secretary of State accepted this analysis, but much of his response was concerned with discussion of the likely change of distribution of population between Inner Glasgow and the rest of the region, and its consequences in terms of housing and other services. He accepted the council's target of 788,500 for Glasgow by 1981 as a reasonable goal, but pointed out that it could be achieved only if the annual net loss of population could be significantly reduced, and suggested that it would be prudent for services to be planned on the assumption that 750,000 or 760,000 was by no means unlikely.

National and local policies

The CPRS Report *Relations between Central Government and Local Authorities* accepted as a principle that there is a major part for central government to play in local policy, although local authorities should be allowed a large measure of discretion (p. 9). It rejected the views that central government often issues 'spectacularly' inconsistent advice or instructions to local authorities and that local authorities are far ahead of central government in developing sophisticated corporate planning, but found that central government departments still acted too much in isolation from each other. They instanced, as an example of the uncertainty about the respective responsibilities of central and local government, the practice of Ministers and Departments giving local authorities advice, guidance and encouragement about policies which are within local authorities' discretion. This is difficult to understand; whatever may be said about the quality of specific government decisions, the opportunities which Ministers and Departments have to see the functioning of local authorities over the whole country, their contacts with MPs and their ability to employ specialists on a scale which is difficult for local authorities, put them in the position to form opinions about the best ways of dealing with different services which it would be wrong to keep quiet about. Indeed the CPRS recognised that local authorities seek published guidance, if only to help them in making unpopular expenditure decisions – and their requests for guidance are by no means confined to such circumstances. Handbooks, memoranda and circulars have an essential role to play, provided they make clear the distinction between advice and direction, and in a complex society they must themselves be complex.

The demands on central government to restrain itself from interfering in local authority business, combined with the adoption of non-specific forms of financial assistance (discussed below) are, of course, not easily reconciled with the desire of governments to shape policies which are a vital part of their programmes as a whole, even though local authorities must be the instruments of carrying them out. An earlier CPRS Report, *A Joint Framework for Social Policies* (1975), argued that 'the trend towards giving greater discretion to local authorities... could not easily be reconciled with continuing attempts by central government to ensure that specific social problems are given high priority' (p. 5) and it is noteworthy that the first role of central government, as defined in the Green Paper of Local Government Finance is 'to ensure that the local services... reflect national priorities and national policies' (Cmnd. 6813 p. 3). It is inconceivable, for example that governments will be prepared to forego broad control over services so vital to the nation as a whole and so liable to arouse political passions, as education and housing. Reconciling local autonomy with what central government sees as its essential duty involves a continuous tension which is generally creative but occasionally erupts into bitter disputes in which local authorities resort to the courts and the central government seeks to trump their ace by additional legislation.

Inner city policy

The problems of reconciling Government initiatives with local autonomy are well illustrated by the development of the inner-city policy. This policy was formally introduced in the statement on Government aid to urban programmes on 22 July 1968, which said that in spite of large and expanding programmes there remained areas of severe social deprivation in cities, which required special help to meet their social needs and bring their physical services up to an adequate level. This led to the Local Government Grants (Social Needs) Act 1969, whose financial aspects are discussed below. But apart from providing a specific grant, the Act did not envisage any change in the structural relationship between the Government and local authorities. Signs of a change towards a partnership philosophy appeared with the commissioning by the Department of the Environment, in association with the local authorities, of the studies which were published in the series 'Making Towns Better', and later in the commissioning, on a similar basis, of the Inner Area Studies of Liverpool, Birmingham and Lambeth. The partnership concept for certain inner areas was specifically advocated in the White Paper on *Policy for the Inner Cities* of June 1977 (Cmnd. 6845) and had earlier been adopted, though not so called, in Scotland, for the Glasgow Eastern Area Renewal scheme. This latter was also of interest in that a quasi-government body, the Scottish Development Agency, was appointed as co-ordinator. The SDA, and also the Scottish Special Housing Association, were to devote extra resources to the area under their normal powers, and were included in the management machinery.

The White Paper showed how carefully the Government had to tread to obtain the implementation of a policy which was a main plank in its own programme but had to be carried out, in the main, by local authorities. The Government made its own views quite plain, namely that 'the time has now come to give the inner areas an explicit priority in social and economic policy, even at a time of particular stringency in public resources' (p. 1). Local authorities were recognised as the natural agencies to tackle inner-area problems, and the White Paper acknowledged that in large measure it is their resources which will need to be called upon. But the Government could only ask for a specific commitment on the part of local government to this policy, warning that both local and central government would be judged by their willingness to implement new priorities and make funds available.

The Government was therefore calling upon local authorities to adopt the policy it recommended but to secure this it had to proceed by way of persuasion and advice coupled with the offer of special partnerships to a limited number of authorities in inner-city areas, which would then benefit from increased access to urban programme grants (which were extended to cover industrial, environmental and recreational projects as well as social projects) and a bigger allocation of capital resources or authorisations. Programmes were to be agreed through the partnership machinery, consisting of a small team to analyse inner area needs, to draw up the programme and to oversee its implementation, together with steering machinery including both Ministers and local councillors. The participation of Ministers in committees set up to deal with the problems of particular areas was a significant development, and clearly recognised that full co-operation with local authorities could not be secured on the standard basis of communications between local and central officials, supplemented by deputations to Ministers when things seemed to be going wrong. To concentrate resources, partnerships in England were limited to Liverpool, Birmingham, Manchester/Salford, and Lambeth and the docklands in London, but in view of the demand from other areas for preferential treatment, it was announced that authorities which undertook inner-area programmes or comprehensive community programmes would be given preference in the allocation of the expanded urban programme after the partnership authorities. A substantial list of 'programme districts' was later announced.

A similar pattern of graded assistance was shown in the promise of increased powers for inner-area authorities to assist industry. The partnership area authorities were promised power to offer initial rent-free periods in the letting of factories and to help with the cost of site preparation in the inner areas. They were also to be empowered to make loans for land purchase and industrial buildings and to carry out or help in the conversion of buildings for more employment, better access or improved amenities. Other authorities than the partnerships were to be given only to the latter group of powers. Quite a high proportion of the districts to benefit from the new powers were outside the Assisted Areas under regional policy. In general where assistance to industry is given on a geographical basis, it is available only within the Assisted Areas, but it seemed that for the sake of the inner cities the Government was prepared to see some modification of this principle. The proceedings on the Inner Urban Areas Bill, which gave effect to the industrial proposals in the White Paper, illustrated very clearly the tension between MPs representing Assisted Areas and MPs for other areas, with the former suspecting a substantial dilution of regional policy.

A similar tension had long existed between the representatives of new and expanding towns and the representatives of the older towns. The Government had reviewed the rôle of the New Towns before the publication of the Inner Cities White Paper; some had been abandoned and in other cases long-term population targets were reduced, but the White Paper announced that the momentum of new town development would be maintained at the new level, and new towns would be expected to do more to relieve stress in the inner cities by taking more of the retired and chronically sick or disabled and unskilled or unemployed workers whose prospects of employment would not be worsened by moving. This modification of new towns policy was clearly intended to reconcile it better with the new explicit emphasis on the needs of inner cities.

It remains to be seen how the partnership concept will work out; so far it can be said that although there has been some restiveness on the part of some local authorities lest their responsibilities and powers are eroded, the outlook seems promising. It might be thought that local authorities would be at a disadvantage, in view of the specific controls still exercised by Government, and the *ultra vires* doctrine, but Government, to an increasing extent, operates only within powers specified in statute.

The financial relationship

Financial arrangements are an important factor in any relationship and the substantial degree of dependence of local authorities on central/ local government grants is therefore of great significance. While the tendency over the past 20 years has been to generalise government grants to local authorities, and reduce the number of specific grants and authorisations, there are voices raised that this process has gone far enough, and in one area at least a new specific grant – the urban aid grant – has been created.

In the 1950s the Government decided to replace a number of specific grants to local authorities, given to them on a percentage basis in relation to their approved expenditure on particular services, by the General Grant, which in particular embraced the former specific grant on Education. This process was carried further in the 1960s, when Rate Support Grant was devised, sweeping up not only General Grant, but the former Exchequer Equalisation Grant, which had played an essential part in equalising the very disparate rate resources of different parts of the country, and the new domestic element, a special subvention to reduce householders' rate poundages. With the exception of the police grant and housing subsidies, the remaining specific grants were relatively small in size. The amount of RSG to each authority was not determined by its individual expenditure, but by the results of a complicated distribution formula intended broadly to equalise the cost of providing equal services, and the object was explicitly to leave local authorities free to determine their own policies on current expenditure; the Government would not use grants as a means of influencing the level of expenditure by individual authorities. The Layfield Committee, referring to the guidance given to local authorities as a whole in the RSG determinations, said that this 'is being used as a means of directly controlling both the level and pattern of expenditure' (Cmnd. 6453, p. 42); but this ignores the fact that the Government cannot use the RSG machinery to make local authorities use their grants in any particular way. It remained clear, however, that the Government would resort to specific grants, either to give help towards local problems, as in the case of the 'Section 11' grants to assist local authorities with financial problems arising from numerous immigrants, or in order to secure the readier acceptance of Government policies. Mr Callaghan, as Home Secretary, introducing the Bill which initiated the urban programme (2 December 1968), said significantly that 'taking into account the need for the programme to be quickly effective and the need for co-operation between local authorities and the central government' there would be a specific grant at the exceptional rate of 75 per cent. He made the point that the new grant would not be 'all wrapped up and submerged in Rate Support Grant'. Since then the urban programme grant has clearly emerged as one of the main ways of moulding policies in the conurbations and the inner-city White Paper enhanced its role in this respect.

It was for long accepted without question, apparently on both sides, that assistance to housing should be given by way of subsidies on specific expenditure and this has involved detailed scrutiny, from both the financial and the technical point of view, of local authority proposals. The Green Papers on housing of June 1977 (Cmnd 6851) contained proposals which would radically alter this relationship, by modifying the housing-cost yardstick and the central scrutiny which it involves, and by replacing subsidies on approved capital works by a general deficit subsidy which would bridge the gap between housing costs and what the local authority could reasonably obtain from rent and rates. The central government's supervision would be much more in terms of a general review of local needs, based on comprehensive plans prepared by each authority, than of approval of specific projects. (An early exception was made to this in 1978 when in order to promote economy in the use of energy additional resources were allocated to housing authorities on condition that they were used for improvement to council house heat insulation.) It is to be hoped that special problems of high cost and land prices do not prevent the system being fully applied in the conurbations.

The financial relationship would obviously be substantially changed if local authorities were given additional tax-raising powers which would lower their dependence on government grants. The possibility of this was of course examined in detail by the Layfield Committee but the only survivor of the local taxes reviewed was Local Income Tax, and this was rejected by the Government (*Local Government Finance*, 1977, Cmnd. 6813, p. 18) because the rate of tax would have to be controlled for national economic reasons, because there would have to be equalisation arrangements between rich and poor areas, and because the local tax element in PAYE woud not effectively discipline local authorities' expenditure decisions. In the case of Scotland and Wales any local tax thought to be practicable would probably be claimed by the devolved administrations. The basic financial relationship between Government and local authorities is therefore likely to remain unchanged.

The other main financial tool in the hands of the central government is the granting or withholding of consent to borrow, or consent (in Scotland) to incur capital expenditure. The Layfield Report said that loan sanction had been developed beyond its original purpose: 'it is also one of the means by which Ministers secure the execution of the policies they favour' (Cmnd. 6453, p. 242). It remains, however, a very imprecise control simply because it operates only on matters for which borrowing or capital investment is necessary and has correspondingly less effect on local authorities in regard to staff-intensive services such as education and social work. Control over capital investment or borrowing operates at one remove, and a fairly distant remove at that, from the regulation of local authorities' immediate activities. It is notable that English local authorities decided in April 1978 not to accept the Government's proposal to replace borrowing approval for individual projects by block approvals of capital expenditure, such as were adopted in Scotland the previous year. It would have restricted their freedom to finance capital expenditure out of revenue, and they apparently felt the price was not worth paying.

Local government as a whole also operates under pressure from the centre as regards current expenditure, because the total amount of grant is determined by central government and excess expenditure is not subsidised, but the ability to raise revenue by rates puts a weighty counter in the hands of local government. Central government is increasingly concerned to ensure that local expenditure fits in with its plans for national resource control and the management of the economy, and the annual white papers on rate support grant reveal hard negotiation on both sides as to the amount of recognisable expenditure. Nevertheless Governments have refrained from seeking power to control directly the budgets of individual local authorities. A centralist approach, which would involve central government in direct control on both revenue and capital spending of local authorities was explicitly rejected in the Green Papers on Local Government Finance. The policy advocated was that 'the duties and responsibilities involved in the provision of local public services [would be] shared on a partnership basis between central and local government' (Cmnd. 6813). The partnership concept was thus as much in evidence as in the White Paper on Inner Cities.

Conclusions

To summarise this discussion of the central/local relationship, it is clearly one which fluctuates over the years in response to changing needs and policies, but neither side is single-mindedly in pursuit of more power for itself. There have been significant reductions of central control in the detailed financing of local government, in transport, and in planning, and the aim is to achieve it in housing. At the same time it is difficult for central government to relax control in matters which are of cardinal importance in government policies. Governments have rejected extreme policies of central control on the one hand and local independence on the other. Adopting the middle course leaves government to rely, in most cases, on persuasion and the weight of expertise it can bring to bear, supplemented by the introduction of specific grants, notably in two subjects of particular importance in the conurbations, namely immigrant-related problems and problems of urban deprivation. New tax-raising powers which would reduce dependence on central government funds have been rejected, but the budgetary independence of local authorities and their control of the yield from rates means that they are far from being clay in the hands of the potter. Governments have increasingly emphasised their desire to achieve a partnership with local authorities. It is possible that the local authorities may look on this as the partnership of the lion and the lamb, but there is at the least a good deal of evidence of their willingness to lie down together.

Postscript

The Government elected in May 1979 announced policies which may substantially affect the working relations between central and local government, but (so far as can be seen) without fundamentally altering the basic relationship described above. The Government intends to reduce the number of controls over local authorities, but it has announced its intention to introduce a new grants system which would assess the expenditure needs of each local authority in order to discourage excessive expenditure. It has also proposed the creation of Urban Development Corporations to promote the development of inner city areas presenting particularly intractable problems. Working in cooperation with the local authorities, whose powers would broadly speaking be unaffected except that the Corporations would have planning and building control powers (normally restricted to their own projects) these Corporations would supplement the activities of local authorities and other public bodies in the fields of land preparation, industrial promotion, housing, roads and transport. Dockland areas of London and Merseyside have been mentioned as possible contexts for such Corporations. The response of local authorities and other bodies to these proposals is not at present clear.

References

Central Policy Review Staff (1975) *A Joint Framework for Social Policies.* HMSO.
Central Policy Review Staff (1977) *Relations between Central Government and Local Authorities.* HMSO.
Cmnd. 4040 (1969) *The Royal Commission on Local Government in England and Wales*, Chairman, Lord Redcliffe-Maud. HMSO.
Cmnd. 6453 (1976) *Local Government Finance*, Committee of Enquiry under F. Layfield. HMSO.
Cmnd. 6811 (1977) *Local Government Finance in Scotland,* Scottish Office. HMSO.
Cmnd. 6813 (1977) *Local Government Finance*, Government's Response to Layfield Enquiry. HMSO.
Cmnd. 6845 (1977) *Policy for the Inner City.* HMSO.
Cmnd. 6851 (1977) *Housing Policy: a Consultative Document.* HMSO.
Strathclyde Regional Council (1976) *Strathclyde Regional Report.* Glasgow.

Chapter 14

The governance of the conurbations

The scope of urban government

It is natural when one speaks of the governance of the conurbations to think first of local government. Any adequate consideration of urban government must however consider far more than local government. The study of urban governance is the study of how our urban areas are governed irrespective of the particular agency responsible for that government: it is defined by that which is governed rather than by that which governs. Such a study takes one far beyond local government. It obviously includes health authorities and water authorities, but a whole range of other agencies such as the Manpower Services Commission, and that complex of government departments that govern the urban area.

In one sense that is the whole of government. However, it makes a nonsense of the study of urban governance if it is merely a study of the total national system of government under another term. It is, however, something else. It is a study of a system of government in terms of how it affects particular areas – the conurbations. That perspective gives the study of urban government its particular flavour.

It involves a study of how government responds to and of how government creates difference between different urban areas. It is a study of how different agencies of government interact to sustain and to change particular patterns of urban life. It is a study of how differing needs, demands and pressures are mediated and transformed by the complex patterning of urban government.

If one asks how a conurbation is governed, or how an inner city's problems are dealt with, it is a nonsense to consider merely the functions which at a particular moment of time happen to be held by local authorities. It would be a nonsense to consider the system of urban government without, for example, considering the operation of industrial development certificates, the work of the Supplementary Benefits Commission and the impact of the Manpower Services Commission.

There are three distinctive areas of concern for the study of urban governance. The first is how the system of government responds to and creates difference – it is about the government of difference. The second is how the elements in the system of a government interrelate in action or impact on a particular area – it is about the government of locality. The third is how those who live in a particular area control and influence the various agencies that affect the area.

The justification for a concentration on local government in any study of urban governance is not that it is the whole of urban government but that it plays or can play a critical part in these three distinctive areas of concern. But although that may be a justification for a concentration, local government must be seen in the context of urban government.

A diversity of systems of urban government

The last few years have brought major changes to the government of the principal urban centres of both Scotland and England. The reorganisation of local government in England and Wales in 1974 was only one element in what was in effect a triple reorganisation of the system of community government throughout the country creating new health and water authorities, as well as new local authorities. The Scottish reorganisation of local government took place in 1975 after the reorganisation of health authorities. Only in London has the main pattern of local government remained unchanged for at least the last decade, although even there the effect of the triple reorganisation of 1974 was felt in water and health service reorganisation.

The effect of these changes – Scottish reorganisation, English and Welsh reorganisation, added to an existing London reorganisation – has been to introduce three different systems of conurbation government in this country:

- the Scottish system which includes the Glasgow conurbation (Strathclyde Region);
- the London system for the Greater London conurbation;
- the Metropolitan County system which includes the other main English conurbations (Tyne and Wear, West Yorkshire, Merseyside, Greater Manchester and West Midlands, as well as including South Yorkshire).

There are further systems of government in other urban areas in England and Wales where non-metropolitan counties have similar functions to the Scottish regions. This chapter will concentrate however on the Metropolitan County system as the main system of conurbation government in England.

The three systems have certain features in common. Each of the three systems divides local government from the government of health. Each of the three systems divides the functions of local government between two sets of authority (Tables 14.1 and 14.2). One authority (region, metropolitan county, Greater London Council) governs an area at least as wide as the conurbation. The other authorities (district or London Borough) govern a more limited area within the conurba-

Table 14.1 Functions of local authorities in England and Wales

Function	Metropolitan County	Metropolitan District	Non-Metropolitan County	Non-Metropolitan District	Greater London Council	London Borough
Allotments (a)		X		X(z)		X
Arts and recreation:						
Art and crafts	X	X	X	X	X	X
Art galleries	X	X	X	X	X	X
Libraries		X	X	X(y)		X
Museums	X	X	X	X	X	X
Recreation (e.g. parks, playing fields, swimming baths)	X	X	X	X	X	X
Tourism	X	X	X	X	X	X
Cemeteries and crematoria		X		X		X
Consumer protection:						
Food and drugs (composition)	X		X	X(y)		X
Trade description	X		X			X
Weights and measures	X		X	X(y)		X
Education (b)		X	X	(c)		X(c)(d)
Environmental health:						
Building regulations		X		X		X
Clean air		X		X		X
Control of communicable disease		X		X		X
Food safety and hygiene		X		X		X
Home safety		X		X		X
Litter control	X	X	X	X	X	X
Refuse collection		X		X		X
Refuse disposal	X		X(w)	X(w)	X	
Rodent control		X		X		X
Street cleansing		X		X		X
Fire Service	X		X		X	
Footpaths and bridleways:						
Creation, diversion and extinguishment	X	X	X	X		X
Maintenance	X		X			X
Protection	X	X	X	X		X
Signposting	X		X			X
Surveys	X		X			X
Housing	(e)	X	(e)	X	X(f)	X(f)
Local licence duties:						
Collection (e.g. dog and game licences) (g)		X		X		X
Markets and fairs		X		X		X
Planning:						
Advertisement control		X		X		X
Building preservation notices	X	X	X	X	X	X
Conservation areas	X	X	X	X	X	X
Country parks	X	X	X	X		
Derelict land	X	X	X	X	X	X

Table 14.1 Functions of local authorities in England and Wales

Function	Metropolitan County	Metropolitan District	Non-Metropolitan County	Non-Metropolitan District	Greater London Council	London Borough
Development control (processing of planning applications) (h)		X		X		X
Development plan schemes	X		X		X	
Listed building control		X		X		X
Local plans		X	X			X
National parks (b)	X(j)		X(j)			
Structure plans (b)	X		X		X	
Police (b)	X		X		(k)	(k)
Rate collection (l)		X		X		X
Smallholdings	X		X		X	
Social Services (b)		X	X			X
Traffic, Transport and Highways:						
Driver and vehicle licensing	(m)	(m)	(m)	(m)	(m)	
Highways (n)	X	(o)	X	(o)	X(p)	X(p)
Lighting:						
Footway	X	X	X	X	X	X
Highway	X		X		X(q)	X(q)
Parking:						
Off-street	X	X(r)	X	X(r)	X(s)	X
On-street	X		X	X(x)	X(t)	
Public transport	X(u)		X(v)	(v)	X(u)	
Road safety	X		X		X	
Traffic regulation	X		X		X	
Transportation planning	X		X		X	

Source: Local Government Finance (1976), Chairman F. Layfield, Cmnd. 6453.

Notes:
(a) In areas where there is a parish council that authority will be responsible.
(b) Agency arrangements not permissible.
(c) The councils of non-metropolitan districts and inner London boroughs whose areas serve primary schools are minor authorities for the purpose of appointing managers of these schools except in areas where there is a parish or community council (or, in England, a parish meeting) which can act as minor authority. Where the area serving the school comprises two or more of the authorities mentioned above they act jointly as a minor authority.
(d) Education is a borough function in outer London. In inner London education is provided by the Inner London Education Authority which is a special independent committee of the Greater London Council.
(e) County councils have certain reserve powers to provide housing subject to a request by a district council and/or the approval of the Secretary of State.
(f) The London boroughs are responsible for the provision of housing. The Greater London Council maintains a stock of housing which it inherited from the former London County Council and also has a strategic role (e.g. aiding the slum clearance

programme of the inner London boroughs, provision of housing for Londoners outside London, re-housing GLC and London borough tenants whose accommodation needs change and providing accommodation through a nominations scheme for people on the borough waiting lists for housing).

(g) Most local authorities collect local licence duties through the agency of the Post Office.

(h) Some matters are reserved to the county councils but the district councils receive all planning applications initially.

(j) Two joint planning boards have been set up to administer national park functions in the Lake District National Park and the Peak National Park. For other national parks these functions are administered by a special committee of the county council mainly concerned which may include representatives of the other county councils and the district councils for the area of the national park.

(k) Greater London (except the City of London) and certain areas immediately adjacent are policed by the Metropolitan Police force. This force is responsible directly to the Home Secretary.

(l) Rate demands issued by the district councils include precepts from county and parish councils; those issued by the London borough councils and the City of London include precepts from the Greater London Council.

(m) The function of licensing vehicles and drivers is now vested in the Secretary of State for the Environment. The issuing of licences is being centralised, but for the time being local authorities act as the Secretary of State's agents. For Greater London the local authority is the Greater London Council. Elsewhere, the agent authority may be either a county or district council.

(n) The Secretary of State for the Environment is highway authority for trunk roads.

(o) District councils may claim the right to maintain unclassified roads in urban areas (this power is distinct from the powers to act under agency agreements).

(p) The Greater London Council is highway authority for all principal roads in London other than trunk roads (this is, the main strategic road network) while the London boroughs are highway authorities for non-principal roads.

(q) Highway lighting responsibilities in Greater London are divided on the same basis as highway responsibilities.

(r) Subject to the consent of the county council.

(s) Subject to the consent of the appropriate London borough council.

(t) On the application of the appropriate London borough council.

(u) The metropolitan county councils and the Greater London Council are the passenger transport authorities and there are passenger transport executives responsible for day to day administration.

(v) Non-metropolitan county councils are responsible for the coordination of public transport in their areas but in some cases district councils run transport undertakings.

(w) Welsh district councils have refuse disposal functions (including the disposal of abandoned vehicles) as well as refuse collection functions; in England refuse disposal is a county council function.

(x) Welsh district councils are able to provide on-street and off-street car parks, subject to the consent of the county council; in England district councils may only provide off-street car parks.

(y) Welsh district councils may be designated exceptionally to exercise libraries, weights and measures and food and drugs authority functions; they may also be designated to exercise functions relating to cold and chemical storing of eggs, enforcement of statutory provisions relating to fertilisers and feeding stuffs and the enforcement of certain provisions made by or under the Medicines Act 1968.

(z) In Wales, Allotments Acts powers are exercisable concurrently by district and community councils; in England the parish councils and meetings are the allotments authorities.

Table 14.2 Functions of local authorities in Scotland

Function	Regional Council	District Council	Islands Council
Allotments		X	X
Building control	X(a)	X(a)	X
Burial and cremation		X	X
Civic restaurants		X	X
Coast protection	X		X
Community centres	X	X	X
Deposit of poisonous waste		X	X
Diseases of animals and plant health	X		X
Education	X		X
Employment of young persons		X	X
Environmental health, including clean air and noise abatement		X	X
Fire services	X		X
Flood prevention and flood warning	X		X
Housing		X	X
Inspection of offices, shops, etc.		X	X
Markets and slaughterhouses		X	X
Miscellaneous regulation and licensing		X	X
Museums and art galleries	X	X	X
Planning:			
Local planning	X(a)	X(a)	X
Strategic planning	X		X
Police	X		X
Public libraries	X(a)	X(a)	X
Public parks and recreation	X	X	X
Refuse collection and disposal		X	X
Registration of births, deaths and marriages	X		X
Registration of electors	X		X
River purification (b)			X
Roads	X		X
Sewerage	X		X
Social work	X		X
Transport, including harbours, piers, ferries and aerodromes	X		X
Vaulation and rating	X		X
Water	X(c)		X
Weights and measures	X		X

Source: Local Government Finance (1976), Chairman F. Layfield, Cmnd. 6453.

Notes:
(a) Responsibility is with the district council, except in Highland, Borders and Dumfries and Galloway regions, where responsibility is with the regional council.
(b) Except in the islands areas, river purification is a function of *ad hoc* boards drawn from regional and district councils and other interests.
(c) Functions of the regional water boards, established in 1968, were transferred to regional councils and islands councils in 1975. The Central Scotland Water Development Board continues to exist, as hitherto controlling certain sources of supply such as Loch Lomond and Loch Turret, but not supplying water direct to consumers.

tion – often based on a previous authority. In all three systems the conurbation authority has a responsibility for strategic planning and transportation while the lower-tier authority has responsibility for the main housing functions, for local planning and for environmental health.

The three systems differ in the distribution of other functions. Thus in the Glasgow conurbation social service is the function of the conurbation authority, while in the English conurbations (including London) it is a function of the lower-tier authority. Similar differences exist between England and Scotland in education, except that in Inner London education is governed by the Inner London Education Authority. Consumer protection is a conurbation function in Scotland and the English metropolitan areas, but not in London.

The systems of conurbation government differ not merely in the way that the functions of local government are divided, but also as to the functions which are regarded as part of local government. In England (including London) Regional Water Authorities were set up with overall responsibility for water resource management in its widest sense, while in Scotland the new regional local authorities were able to assume many of these functions because their boundaries fitted better the needs of water resource management.

In all three systems the government of health was separated off from the main system of conurbation government represented by local authorities. However, the relationship between the government of health and local government differs in the three systems.

In Scotland the government of health was made the responsibility of Health Boards and the main authority of relevance to this chapter is the Greater Glasgow Authority, which although covering the main conurbation area covers an area significantly less than the Strathclyde Region. In England the government of health is divided between regional authorities and area authorities. In the metropolitan areas, each metropolitan county lies within a larger regional health authority area while the boundaries of area health authorities are made co-terminous with those of the metropolitan districts on the grounds that they were the main social service and education authorities. In London, on the other hand, the area of the Greater London Council does not lie within one Regional Health Authority, but is divided between four such authorities. Moreover in London the area health authorities are not co-terminuous with the London Boroughs.

Major differences are not confined to functions. In some conurbation areas the boundaries of the conurbation authority have been drawn close to the contiguous built-up area. In other cases the boundaries of the conurbation area have been drawn much more widely. Table 14.3 below illustrates these differences. It shows that the boundaries of Strathclyde and to a lesser extent West Yorkshire are set on a very different basis from those of the other conurbation areas.

Table 14.3 Greater London, Metropolitan Counties and Strathclyde

	Population (000's) (mid 1978)	1977 (hectares)	Population per 1,000 hectares
Strathclyde*	2,466.4	1,353,698	1,822
Tyne and Wear	1,167.6	54,221	21,534
West Yorkshire	2,091.9	203,911	10,259
South Yorkshire†	1,311.9	156,046	8,407
Merseyside	1,583.8	65,060	24,344
Greater Manchester	2,693.7	128,676	20,934
West Midlands	2,734.6	89,943	30,404
Greater London	6,956.0	157,950	44,039

* Strathclyde population at mid 1977.

† South Yorkshire is not a conurbation as defined by the Census of Population. It is included here as a metropolitan county.

There are thus three different systems of conurbation government in Britain. The differences are of great importance. The upper tier of conurbation government in the Glasgow area is clearly very different from the upper tier in, for example, the West Midlands. Its *per capita* level of expenditure is several times that of the West Midlands authority because its range of functions is much wider. Though differences are great the rationale for the differences remains uncertain and obscure.

Unity in diversity

Yet despite these obvious differences it is still important to consider conurbation government as a whole, for the three systems are products of processes of institutional change which were broadly similar in origin and in objectives.

Thus both the Scottish and the English reorganisations of 1974/5 represent a change in the basic structure of urban local government. Until then the major cities and many of the towns of Great Britain were governed by a unitary local authority. A single authority – be it a county borough in England or a county of a city in Scotland – was responsible for all the functions of local government. It was a powerful concept corresponding to a certain image of urban government as being the government of the free-standing town. It appealed to a deep-rooted tradition, which widespreading urban development had challenged.

Nevertheless it had led to a system of urban government that had strengths in action because of its capacity to bring together many functions in dealing with urban problems. The Royal Commission on Local Government in England (Cmnd. 4040, 1969, p. 68) described the strengths of the county borough as a unitary authority:

There is a great strength in the all-purpose authority; and this has been shown in the county borough councils. Not all of them have exploited their potential strength to the full, partly because their areas have been inadequate, partly because their organisation has been fragmented. But where a county borough council under strong leadership has coordinated its services and set out to achieve objectives through the use of all its powers, it has been the most effective local government unit we have known.

It was this tradition of urban government and its parallel strengths that was breached by the reorganisations of 1974/5. In all of the conurbations local government functions were divided between a conurbation-wide authority (or wider) and a district authority often corresponding to a previous all-purpose authority. The effect was to bring all other conurbations into line with London, where at least the inner London area had had two tiers of local government (London County Council and Metropolitan Boroughs) for the whole of the century.

Institutions of government reflect images of urban reality established within the system of government. The county borough reflected the image of the free-standing town. The institutional walls built so powerfully around the all-purpose local authority matched very old traditions of the walled city, isolated from its surrounding areas. New images of urban reality gained force and the institutions now built reflected that image. The new image of urban reality was the conurbation. The conurbation as a continuous built-up area: merging previous towns and cities was the image of urban reality reflected in the new system of government.

The image of urban reality represented by the conurbation was powerful in government. It was, however, not all-powerful, nor was it necessarily seen so clearly outside the world of local and central government and the academic world. To many who lived and worked in the conurbation it did not appear as reality at all. The older image of realities represented by Birmingham, Glasgow, and Manchester was still powerful.

This was recognised in government. The district represented that image in the new structure, but not as a free-standing authority, rather as an element within the wider conurbation. Thus the system of government reflected a dual perception of urban reality. It reflected acceptance of the reality of the conurbation as an entity requiring separate government. The West Midlands, Strathclyde and Merseyside were seen as realities as London had long been seen as a reality. Yet the old areas, although merged in the conurbation, were not overwhelmed by it and were also recognised in the system of government, although the weight given to that level varied between the systems. A new governmental representation of urban reality had been established. It had, however, been established at a cost in the loss of that strength that had been represented by the former county borough or county of a city. To achieve the new governmental representation of urban reality the functions of local government had had to be divided.

This division, although it made possible the new representation of one image of urban reality, ran contrary to another image of urban reality represented by such phrases as the total approach to urban problems.[1] The problems of the urban area are interrelated. Lines of division drawn across governmental functions in the urban area deny the representation of the urban area as a complex of interacting issues and problems. The new structures emphasised different levels of urban government at a cost to the interrelationships within the fabric of urban government.

The fragmentation of government

However, to tell the story of reorganisation solely in terms of the functions currently held by local government is to miss one of its important aspects. In England the functions of local authorities were divided not between two authorities alone – county and district – but between four: the two tiers of local government, the health authorities and the regional water authorities. In Scotland only the new health authorities drew functions from local government.

The changes in the government of health and water have to be seen as changes separate and apart from the changes in local government (which were influenced, as we have seen, by one perception of urban reality). They gave no recognition to the needs or concerns of urban government. The image which underlay those reorganisations was a different image. It was only a convenience that in England brought the reorganisation of health, water resources and local government at the same moment of time. It was not a result of the consideration of urban government in its complexity.

For the image that underlay the reorganisation of health and water services was a functional image. It was of the integrated management of the health services in England, as it was of the integrated management of water resources within the river basin. The functional image was also powerful in the consideration of local government. It meant that there was no split in certain functions (education and social services for example), but it was an image that was only one influence amongst other influences. The functional ideal of a separate functional authority was avoided for local government services.

The functional ideal is established at a cost. The integrated government of health is a reasonable aim, but if that integration is achieved by separating off virtually all aspects of the government of health from other aspects of community government, it is a divisive integration. That division was probably inevitable, given that the government of health was the subject of a separate review and the product of a separate design. Charged with looking at health alone, one looks at health alone and produces a solution for health alone.

The fundamental principle of the health service reorganisation was that the health services should be governed separately from other community services, including services such as housing, education, leisure and recreation, and social services, which are critical to the government of health if not always to the government of health services.

At every point and in every way the structure of the health service was differentiated from the structure of local government which controlled these other community services. An appointed board was set up rather than an elected board. Health authorities were totally dependent on government grant while local government had its own source of revenue. A hierarchical system of health regions and areas in England had no parallels in local government. Each of those differentiating principles made collaboration between health services and other services more difficult. Each created its own organisational environment. The structures failed to build a shared organisational environment for collaboration between related services. Perhaps no principle of the health service reorganisation made collaboration with local authorities more difficult than the principle that all doctors engaged in community services would be employed by the health authorities. The medical profession was removed from local government and concentrated in the health authorities. Yet a professional has the art of communication to fellow professionals. He can speak across organisational boundaries. The change reinforced the barrier to communication made by organisational boundaries. It removed from local authorities those who could communicate most easily to health authorities. It was necessary to the functional principle, but a barrier was built in the system of urban government.

The functional emphasis on the government of health is merely a symbol of a wider problem that has to be faced in discussion of urban government. For the functional principle is one of the dominant principles of our system of government. Problems are defined by functional departments in terms of those functions. Departments at the level of central government communicate to their parallel functional departments at local level.

Yet the very title of the chapter represents a different perspective. Urban governance is concerned not merely with functions but with how those functions interrelate in the government of an urban area. It is a perspective that can easily be lost because of the dominance of the functional perspective in our system of government. It is the perspective that is currently given expression in the Inner City Partnerships designed to bring together, in meeting inner-city problems, various agencies of government, some of which were separated in that fragmentation of urban government which the reorganisations of 1974 and 1975 brought about.

Institutional instability

The tragedy is that the massive reorganisations of 1974 and 1975 settled so little. At the time the hope was to remove the question of reorganisation from the political agenda for several decades – but this was not to be. The change has failed to achieve this, the least of what it was expected to do. Further reorganisation of health and local government is again on the political agenda.

The tragedy is the tragedy of institutional instability. Debate and argument about institutions can distract from debate and argument about problems. Institutional instability follows from the pursuit of the institutional fallacy – the belief that one solves problems by changing institutions, rather than changing institutions only because problem-solving has shown the necessity. The institutional fallacy can lead to institutional instability where new sets of institutions create new problems and the answer is again seen in institutional terms.

The creation of new health authorities and new local authorities led to new problems of collaboration. One could almost say the structures were designed to do so. The authors of the new health service structures saw the solution in further institution-building – the creation of new joint consultative committees (Norton and Rogers, 1977). That piece of structure failed because it was an institution externally imposed rather than worked out in the urban situation as a solution to real problems. It failed because it had no base at the local level. But institutional failure led on to further initiatives in institution-building.

Alternatively, consider the government of Glasgow. Only a brief period ago Glasgow was governed by two tiers of elected government. Now it is governed by six tiers:

- Community Councils
- District Council
- Regional Council
- House of Commons
- European Parliament

A sixth tier was proposed – the Scottish Assembly. It was a recipe for institutional instability, since each institution must inevitably struggle for its own existence – each expecting and seeking institutional change in its own interest.

One is drawn then to the tragic prophecy that further reorganisation is likely. If this comes then perhaps one can at least hope that the process considers the needs of urban government as well as the particular needs of particular functions.

The required characteristics of urban government

One should not expect that the creation of institutions will itself solve problems, but seek that within institutions problems can be solved.

That requires from our governing institutions that they have characteristics that enable them to perceive and to resolve the problems of urban governance. It would be an unnecessary assumption that those characteristics must be built through institutional change alone. Institutional change should neither be assumed to be necessary nor unnecessary.

Institutional change appears easy, if costly: its costs only imperfectly understood and rarely measured – for they are the costs of redirected administrative and political effort as attention is directed to institutional change rather than to the problems and issues with which the institutions are concerned. But at least in form, if not in reality, institutions can be changed simply by decisions.

More difficult to change are the governing principles which set the patterning of governmental behaviour within our institutions. These can be used to describe the very characteristics of our system of administration as it affects urban government. Thus we have

- the principle of functionalism or the necessary division of complex organisations into parts or elements with distinctive tasks;
- the principle of uniformity which requires the uniform application of rules for action and which could be argued to be one of the fundamental principles of bureaucratic organisation;
- the principle of organisational hierarchy leading to powerful traditions of administrative loyalty.

In these very general terms one is describing the way government at all levels conducts its business in our society. One is almost describing the meaning to our society of the word administration. Indeed one is describing not bad administration but the very principles of sound administration.

Such principles are important. Complex governmental organisations have to divide their business according to specified functions. All cannot consider all. Specialisation is necessary for effective action. That is the necessity of the functional principle.

Fair administration and even legal and political necessity require a uniform application of rules. Administration must not be seen to discriminate unless the principle of discrimination can be clearly stated, thus creating a new basis for the principle of uniformity.

Hierarchy is written into our administrative structures and it is written in by the requirements of political control and the necessities of public accountability. These require clear lines of responsibility. The principle of organisational hierarchy is powerfully supported.

These principles must be recognised to be vital to the functioning of our system of government – not least in urban areas. They are positive factors in securing the effectiveness of urban government. Yet these organisational principles have other effects. Although the principles support and are necessary to many of the rôles of urban government, they do not support and may even harm the fulfilment of other rôles.

Government in our conurbations and in our cities and towns plays many rôles. The urban area cannot be thought of separately from the process of government. The urban area is the creation of government as government is the creation of the urban area. Government and the fact of government maintains the urban area, patterns its ordering, changes and is changed by it.

Government maintains many services whose operation is essential to the functioning of the urban area. It provides a fire service, maintains roads and educates children. The physical and social infra-structure supported by government is essential to the urban areas. The *maintenance* function is one of the rôles of urban government.

Conflict is endemic in the urban area. Government has a rôle in imposing solutions on the conflicts that the very conditions of urban areas make inevitable. Order is set not merely and obviously by the police but by development control, by health regulations and by a wide variety of licensing and inspection functions. *Ordering* the urban area is one of the rôles of government.

Government helps the urban area to change. Economic growth and decline and social change require a variety of responses in the urban area, demanding new facilities and changed educational provision and creating new social problems. Government has a key *responsive* rôle in assisting change in the urban area.

Government may not be merely responsive to change. It can be more than the passive instrument recording requirements and providing them. It can itself be an initiator of change. This is the *directive* rôle of government, purposively changing the form of urban life by, for example, creating a new rôle for the inner city.

These four rôles may all be required of a system of urban government. There is a need to maintain the existing social and physical fabric of urban life. There is a need to impose solutions on conflicts if urban life is to be maintained. Perhaps this latter need is in reality also a part of the maintenance function.

But urban government must be concerned not merely with the maintenance function but with change. To a degree there is a choice between a responsive and a directive mode. An adequate system of urban government should have the capacity for both. Both are part of the change function.

The maintenance of functions of government are well sustained in the organising principles of functionalism, uniformity and hierarchy. Given a clear and defined task to be carried out, effective action can be achieved through functional specialism. The principles on which the task is to be carried out can be defined in clear rules to be applied throughout the area of the authority. The organisation is structured hierarchically to secure clear lines of accountability. A clear defined structure meets few problems in carrying out a clear defined task.

It is change that creates the problem. An organisation that is adapted to the maintenance function is not necessarily so well adapted to respond to or to direct change. Responsiveness requires the capacity to see problems that are not part of the defined task. It requires the capacity to see problems that do not fit easily into existing functional divisions and problems that may require for their handling a willingness to depart from the application of established rules. Responsiveness may also require the capacity to learn, and this may be lost in the infertile soil of the administrative hierarchy. Thus the softer information marking worry and concern gets lost as it passes through the tiers of the administration.

Directed change too creates its own requirements. It requires a capacity to bring together and re-order different functions, be it at conurbation, district or neighbourhood level. Existing functional principles and established hierarchies may be barriers to such changes. It may require experiment and the readiness to learn quickly, thus implying variety rather than uniformity. Traditional structures are unlikely to meet the requirements of directed change.

A system of urban government must have the capacity both for the maintenance functions and for the change functions. It must maintain the urban fabric, but must also enable it to change. The dominant organising principles of our system of urban government may be too centred on the maintenance rôle to carry out the change rôle.

Urban government must have the capacity for the maintenance functions, but it must have other capacities. The mistake may be to build a system of urban government on one set of organising principles. The system of urban government must give recognition to the organising principles of change as well as maintenance. It will require the capacity

- to detect and to deal with problems and issues across the functions of government;
- to recognise and to deal with diversity by allowing and encouraging differences in services provided;
- to create many and varied channels of communication and action to and from the urban environment.

On this basis a critique can be built of the present system of urban government.

The fragmentation of urban government

The list of major governmental agencies upon whom the conurbation depends has grown. The British system of urban government has traditionally been regarded as a relatively unitary system. The comparatively small number of local authorities even before reorganisation when compared with other countries, the comparative lack of special purpose agencies that are so important in the American system, and the lack of an intermediate state or provincial tier, combined to give the impression of a concentrated system of urban government.

It was, of course, an illusion perpetuated by the tendency to see urban government as synonymous with the local authority. The 1974/75 reorganisation has destroyed the illusion. By adding to the existing agencies it has made obvious the fragmentation of urban government. To describe the pattern of urban government in terms of agencies which operate directly at the urban level one has to encompass amongst major authorities in England:

- Metropolitan Counties
- Metropolitan Districts
- Regional Health Authorities
- Area Health Authorities
- Manpower Services Commission
- Regional Water Authorities
- Department of Health and Social Security

Leaving on one side the impact of nationalised industries and the range of other central government departments as well as organisations such as the Housing Corporation, the Commission for Racial Equality and the Sports Council, the major agencies whose functions are clearly critical for the planning of the urban environment and for urban life represent a new fragmented structure of urban government.

The growth of such agencies is the natural and immediate reaction of national government to a newly perceived problem. A special-purpose agency is seen as the proper instrument for effective action. That action is seen as directly under central government control precisely because those in charge of the agency are appointed, not elected, and the agency has limited purposes, rather than many purposes.

Each individual decision to create such an agency has a logic and a justification. This chapter is not however concerned with the justification of each particular decision, but the cumulative effect of a series of such decisions, an effect which may be imperfectly taken into account when each particular decision is taken. The particular decisions are made to meet immediate problems. The long-term effects can easily be neglected, and these have been increasing fragmentation.

Of course it is inevitable that there should be divisions in a system of urban government. It may well be argued that local authorities themselves have been divided by departmentalism, backed by separate committee structure. This was the critique in the long series of management reports (Maud, 1967; Bains, 1972; Paterson, 1973), and some would argue that critique could still be made in many authorities. Some division is inevitable. Any large and complex organisation divides itself to carry out its business. The issue is how deep are the divisions. It may not be so much that division in itself is important; rather it is the capacity to link together the various elements when joint action is required. A local authority ultimately has the capacity to make decisions binding on the elements.

It may be however that fragmentation between agencies creates no problems if the various agencies coordinate their activities. Indeed it could be argued that often the cooperation between independent agencies may be more effective in achieving action than formal decision in a local authority. The growth of agencies has certainly been matched by a growth of coordinating and consultative committees, designed to link in cooperation the fragmented elements. As well as the formal systems, there are also informal networks linking together different agencies (Friend, Power and Yewlett, 1974). Yet such systems of coordination and communication are far more likely to be effective within a single organisation than between agencies.

Organisational boundaries matter. It is no idle or indifferent debate that goes into the shaping of institutional change. Within the boundaries of organisations there is a basis for authoritative decision-making but also a shared organisational environment. Thus those who work in an urban local authority share an environment shaped by such elements as elected member control, political party conflict, a shared source of finance including an independent source of finance, a common geographical area, the conflicts of a multi-purpose organisation. None of these would be shared by those working for most other agencies.

It is not easy to coordinate and communicate across major organisational boundaries from one organisational environment to another. The occasional meeting of a coordinating committee may be adequate in dealing with an already perceived problem. To that extent the coordinating system may be adequate in resolving problems deriving from the maintenance function. But the creation of the shared understanding required for change is the more difficult to achieve through the occasional meeting of committees.

The informal networks can play a more important rôle. Nevertheless, there are administrative and political costs involved in bridging the fragmented system. It can be done, but at a cost.

The more fragmented the structure of urban government the more difficult it is to achieve significant directed change because that will involve many agencies and impose significant costs in achieving shared understanding and securing joint action. A fragmented structure can achieve disjointed incremental change and if that is appropriate to urban problems then that may be adequate. But if the scale of urban problems requires significant re-direction of urban policies, common strategies become the more difficult to achieve, because there is both the lack of a clear point of decision and control and because shared understanding is the more difficult to achieve.

Responsiveness, too, may be the more difficult to achieve if problems and the perception of problems are fragmented. Drawn across the conurbation are a diversity of boundaries as each agency or department within an agency draws boundaries for its own purpose. These boundaries reflect the fragmentation of urban government.[2]

Finally, control of urban government itself is the more difficult to achieve if urban government is divided between different bodies, some appointed, some directly elected and some directly responsible to ministers – each with their own lines of accountability. No one organisation has a clear responsibility for the quality of urban life. Accountability is lost in the fragments.

The dominance of functionalism

Fragmentation can take different forms. Urban government can be, at least in theory, fragmented geographically. But dominant in our society is the functional perspective. The special agencies reflect it. Sir Geoffrey Vickers has drawn a distinction between the choices before functional organisations and general organisations (1972, p. 134).

> Multiple criteria of success are inherent in the government of any political or social unit, however small. For the multiple needs and diverse standards of expectation of people bring together in a place, interact with and limit each other in ways which cannot be ignored. Functional organisation can ignore problems which they set for each other; and when in doubt they can simplify their choices by referring to their function as defining their primary responsibility. But general organisations, even the smallest, have no built in priorities to guide them in their multi-valued choices. They must decide not only what to do but what to want – more exactly what to value most in the concrete situation of every decision. They must define and redefine the unacceptable, not in one dimension alone but in many.

I have commented elsewhere:

> Central and local government have the capacity – even if not always realised in practice – for a wide-ranging concern across functions, a concern for place, be it country-wide or local. They are general organisations. A general organisation has the capacity to reach solutions critically different from a single functioned organisation.
>
> It faces choice between major functions and values. The multi-functioned organisation cannot avoid choices between the values placed upon different functions – even though it may not always face those choices explicitly. Those concerned with many functions have to set values upon those functions. The local authority is concerned not merely with education, with social services, with roads, with leisure and recreation considered as separate services, it is concerned with choice between them. It must make a multi-valued choice (Stewart, 1974, p. 135–6).

The danger in our system of conurbation government is a weakening in its capacity to make the multi-valued choice, implied by the change rôle. Such a multi-valued choice is required by the marked changes in population structure to be faced in the 1980s (Solace, 1978). This raises major issues as to the extent to which resources can and should be changed within and between the different functions in the conurbation, following for example the marked decline in the number of schoolchildren and the increase in the elderly. The choice may not be faced in our system of conurbation government. With functions divided between, for example, health authorities and local authorities, there is not the capacity in the system of urban government to make such a choice (Marshall, 1978).

It is not merely that the multi-valued choice will not be made, but that the need for the choice will not always be seen. The emphasis of the system of conurbation governance is on the functional problem and on the particular issues that can easily be identified and dealt with in that perspective. Problems that cut across the functions or problems that do not fit easily into the particular functional departments or organisations are less easily perceived, never mind dealt with. Governmental organisation constituted on functional lines sees what it is designed to see.

The challenge of the inner city or perhaps the whole challenge of conurbation government may require a perspective that goes beyond the functional. The problems of race relations, of economic decay and of endemic unemployment, of urban deprivation and of changing energy patterns are all problems which vary in type and character from urban area to urban area. They require a different response in different areas. They are at the heart of urban government. They cannot be dealt with by national action alone. Each requires a new response at the urban level and a response that goes beyond the functional.

Functions interrelate in the urban environment. The point has been made and will be re-made. A decaying inner city or a growing area has not merely a series of separate problems. They interrelate. The general organisation has the capacity to achieve a different type of solution than a complex of functional organisations.

There is, however, another reason why the multi-functioned organisation will achieve different solutions and this applies with most force where the various functions share a common factor – which in the local authority is the factor of place. The multi-functioned organisation can achieve integrative solutions which may be of higher value than the solutions which would be attained by an aggregation of the choices made by single-functioned organisations. The multi-functioned local authority may be able to achieve more for education in a deprived area by concern for housing, social services, libraries and parks as well as concern for education than organisations concerned only with the separate functions can achieve. The multi-functioned organisation can search for synergy (Stewart, 1974, p. 136).

None of this is to deny the rôle of the functional. To assert the need for another perspective is not to deny the rôle of the functional perspective. To assert the need for a new type of choice does not deny that there are also functional choices. It is not a question of all or nothing. Rather it is to argue for the need for counter-working forces in government. It is to argue that if the organising principle of government is functional, then within that system of government there should also be the capacity to look across functions and the capacity to deal with the problems seen.

This was the driving force of the movement to corporate management in local government. It was an attempt to improve the capacity of local government to look across functions. It was not an attempt to replace the functional perspective but to supplement it. However, the introduction of corporate management in local government, even where successful, is limited in its capacity to introduce such a perspective because of the fragmentation of the system of urban government. *Ad hoc* attempts such as the partnership arrangements for inner-city areas are then the only possibility in our existing structure of urban government.

It may be argued that the perspective that looks across functions can be supplied at the level of national government and that it is unnecessary to replicate that perspective at the level of urban problems. That argument might be supported if urban problems did not vary in character and in quality from area to area. They require approaches that vary from conurbation to conurbation. The problems should be defined differently and the multi-valued choice should be made differently in different areas. The general perspective at national level is not enough.

Besides, if the instruments at the urban level reflect the functional perspective, that reinforces the tendency for the functional perspective to dominate. Functional agencies and functional central departments reinforce each other. If the pressures on central government only come from functional organisations the general perspective is difficult to sustain. The general perspective requires to be sustained at more than one level. Other societies have recognised this. The prefect and the state government in other countries are each in their own way a recognition of the need for another perspective – a need that may be most critical in conurbation government.

To cast central government as the only general organisation concerned with conurbation government is to cast it for an impossible task. It would place a burden of choice upon it which it could only deal with by recognising, as it has, functional entities.

The limitations of uniformity

Formal uniformity faces the diversity of the city. Formal uniformity can lead to a failure to meet real and varying needs. The problems of the ethnic minority have highlighted the dilemmas of formal uniformity. Where needs vary, uniformity fails, unless and until it can be redefined. But that requires learning and learning comes from diversity. From a period when the emphasis of approaches to minority groups was on uniform policies fairly applied to all races, awareness has grown that real equality may require difference in policies.

Formal uniformity can lead to actual inequity. The local authority distributes its resources across the city by clear rules. Yet such distribution can and often does lead the local authority to distribute more of its resources to the prosperous areas than to the deprived areas. One reason is that it is in the prosperous areas that many services provided are most fully used. Children stay on at school, more library books are used. The prosperous area has better access and a greater capacity to demand. Uniformity may often be uniformity in relation to demand. Positive discrimination is called for in deprived areas, but if that implies those areas should should have an additional share of resources, then it underestimates the case. Deprived areas would achieve a major advance if they received a proportionate share of resources (Department of the Environment, 1976). Yet few authorities know how resources are distributed within their area. Uniformity is assumed to justify itself.

Within our system of government stand impressive barriers against varying the quality or type of service provided according to variation in needs or wants. National standards and standards of good professional practice stand as powerful barriers to the recognition of differing needs and as powerful barriers therefore against experiment.

The diversity of the conurbation calls for a diversity of response. It is not easy within the national system of government to justify a diversity of response to local circumstance. A local response can be justified by local elected authority responding to needs felt and values held at local level. Different local authorities in different urban areas can legitimately pursue different policies within the scope of their powers.

It is legitimacy that is conferred in society by elections that permit difference in response and which can provide the driving force for such differentiation.

Yet diversity and difference of both needs and wants lie also within the boundaries of these authorities. The dilemma is how the need for difference of response can be perceived and how it can be justified. The answer does not seem to be in some new extraneous tier of elected government, be they called community councils, neighbourhood councils or urban parish councils – or at least not alone in that. The answer may lie better within the authority which is beginning tentatively and occasionally to recognise that they have an under-used resource: a councillor elected to represent the needs of an area. Area management is designed to break up the uniformity of the authority but within a framework that is the authority (Horn, 1977; Mason 1977).

Area managment takes different forms in the local authorities that are developing this approach. In some the emphasis is upon the area committee of councillors discussing the problems of particular areas. In others the emphasis may be on area co-ordination of services. Yet in others it may be upon new forms of community involvement. Finally, in Newcastle it is concerned with increased resource allocation to stress areas.

The various approaches are linked by an awareness that within the urban area are diverse needs and that the local authority must be capable of responding to that diversity.

The disillusion of hierarchy

The long chains of accountability that lead from the field-worker to the formal points of decision-making in our public authorities are a result of the principle of organisational hierarchy. They are justified in terms of accountability and control. Clearly they have a rôle, but the long chains create problems as they separate teacher from education committee or social worker from social services committee – never mind from central ministries.

The hierarchies create but few problems for the uniform administration of predetermined policies. Indeed in their enforcement lies their justification. They create no problems therefore for the maintenance function of government. The change function requires learning and it is easy for the many levels set in the hierarchies of government to become barriers to learning.

The assumption is that much learning occurs at the field-worker level – at the point of contact between government and its environment. It is there that many of the problems involved in the maintenance of existing policies are encountered and the need for change in those problems identified. Yet the problem for the hierarchical organisation is how it can learn at the centre what is seen and felt and known in the field.

For the information obtained in the field will be rich and various. As the information passes up the hierarchy there is the danger that its variety is reduced because the reducing number of points in the hierarchy do not have the capacity to communicate it.

The dilemma is great. It is not easy to arrange routines to handle information one does not know about or to devise statistical returns on problems one still has to learn about. The administrative procedures required within the hierarchy for the handling of information for the maintenance rôle of government are not easily adapted for the responsive mode or for the learning required even in directed change. Variety is inevitably reduced by such procedures. Yet in the reduction of variety the very sensitivity of government to emerging problems, or to the misfit between policy and need, is lost.

A closed system

These forces continue to create a system of urban government that is curiously closed to the external environment or rather to those parts of the environment that cannot easily be fitted within the system.

Not least it is closed to many who live and work in the urban environment. The dominance of the maintenance function means that the system is closed to pressures for change. The fragmentation of the system has reduced its comprehensibility. The removal of important elements (health authorities; Manpower Services Commission) from the political process tends to closure. The length of an administrative hierarchy from field-worker to chief officer is itself a barrier.

The way ahead

Whether one seeks a massive new reorganisation or whether one seeks change and adaptation within the existing structure, this chapter has argued that our present structure of urban government is adequate for the maintenance functions, but requires strengthening in carrying out the change functions of urban government.

Our urban areas face many major problems which can only be adequately dealt with at the urban level of government. These are the problems that vary in quality and in quantity from area to area. That variation is why they are best dealt with at the urban level. They require differing responses in differing urban areas – albeit within a framework of national policy.

As these problems – problems of transportation, of pollution, of race relations, of industrial stagnation and so on – are examined, it is clear that the change function of government – be it in either the responsive or the directed mode – is critical, for these problems change rapidly and significantly over time.

What is required then is a strengthening of the organising principles that support the change function. This does not mean the destruction of the organising principles that support the maintenance function of government, but increasing the capacity for change while sustaining the capacity for the maintenance function. The aim is to establish countervailing principles in the system of urban government. The principles can be expressed in broad approaches to the problems of urban government which can guide either gradual change or massive reorganisation.

1. A reduction in fragmentation

The growth of many agencies of government, appointed and controlled in a variety of ways, reduces rather than increases the capacity of urban government to effect significant change. To bring many such authorities within the main structure of urban government would increase its capacity to respond. Local government would then be built on, rather than fragmented.

2. An emphasis on the general as well as the functional

There is the need to strengthen the capacity in our system of government to look and to act across functions. This could be achieved by widening the responsibility of local authorities, if necessary by widening their concern beyond the functions they directly administer – giving the duty, for example, to report on the activities of other agencies in their area to the public and to national government and giving them powers to influence the action of such an agency. Local authorities have not always aspired to this wider rôle in the past. Many have too often been content with the administration of a series of services rather than aspired to the local government of an area within a national framework. They have not been encouraged in the wider conception of their rôle by a central government, itself dominated by the functional perspective. Powers given, or the guidance suggested, has been defined in functional terms. A wider rôle is possible.

3. The development of difference within government

The retreat from uniformity is not easily achieved. One has to find the means to legitimate difference. Answers have been given in terms of the urban parish or neighbourhood council. They may have a rôle, but they remain external to the main process of government. To recognise within the main structure of government that there is a need for difference, may be the more important task. The move to area management can in the end be the more fruitful step.

4. Differentiation and discrimination

The most difficult task is to discriminate what is appropriate to each level of urban government. Certain issues pervade the conurbation and can only be dealt with effectively at that level. Others do not require action at that level and difference can be permitted – nay, more, should be encouraged. To know in government when to permit difference is the most difficult and yet, perhaps, in urban government, the most important task.

5. An open system

The hierarchies and the administrative rules of the maintenance function stand as barriers to the public. Special purpose agencies imperfectly understood can be remote from general pressure. The functional perspective is closed to those whose problems cannot be defined in existing functional terms. Over and above the steps already suggested, one may be in an era where new political initiatives are possible. Neighbourhood councils, tenant control of estates, the local referenda, the paid local councillor, changes in local electoral patterns, the area management development, new forms of community action are all present or discussed. New forms of urban politics are emerging. Others are possible.

Yet what do these principles mean for re-organisation in practice? In what scenario will they be developed? It still remains possible that we face another re-organisation. Under the present Conservative Government changes are taking place which could be argued to be a re-organisation of central/local relations and the rôle of local authorities. Change is proposed in the government of health which will increase the fragmentation of urban government in England, by drawing yet new boundaries. We cannot assume that the devolution issue is settled. Indeed, the very failure to resolve it may mean that regionalism will gain force. Regional government may come to England, setting conurbation government within its region and leaving the most-purpose urban authority beneath.

Perhaps the greatest need is to build up the authority and comprehensibility of general purpose elected government as a counter-balance to functionalism. Perhaps there could even be devolution to local government itself. Perhaps local government could become urban government – if it were allowed to.

Notes

1. See for example the terms of reference given by the Department of the Environment to the Urban Guidelines Studies set up in Oldham, Rotherham and Sunderland: 'to formulate guidelines to help local authorities in developing a "total approach" to the urban environment...'.
2. The point was well illustrated by the maps on p. 139 of *Another Chance for Cities*, SNAP 69/73, Liverpool Shelter Neighbourhood Action Project 1972, Shelter, London.

References

Bains, H. (1972) *The New Local Authorities — Management and Structure*. HMSO.
Department of the Environment (1976) *Inner Area Study — Liverpool*, Area Resource Analysis, District D Tables for 1973–1974. HMSO.
Cmnd. 4040 (1969) *The Royal Commission on Local Government in England and Wales*, Chairman, Lord Redcliffe-Maud. HMSO.
Friend, J.K., Power J.M. and **Yewlett C.J.L.** (1974) *Public Planning: the Inter-corporate Dimension*. Tavistock, London
Horn, C.J. et al. (1977) *Area Management: Objectives and Structure*. Institute of Local Government Studies, University of Birmingham.
Marshall, Sir F. (1978) *Report to the Greater London Council*. London.

Mason, T. et al. (1977) *Tackling Urban Deprivation: the Contribution of Area Based Management.* Institute of Local Government, University of Birmingham.

Maud, Sir J. (1967) *Report of the Committee of Management in Local Government,* vol. 1. HMSO.

Norton, A.L. and **Rogers, S.** (1977) Interim Report to the Nuffield Hospital Provincial Trust on Collaboration between local authorities and health authorities. Institute of Local Government Studies, University of Birmingham.

Paterson, J. (1973) *The New Scottish Local Authorities: Organisation and Management Structures.* HMSO.

Solace, (1978) *Population Change and Local Authorities.* Society of Local Authority Chief Executives

Stewart, J.D. (1974) *The Responsive Local Authority.* Charles Knight, London.

Vickers, Sir G. (1972) *Freedom in a Rocking Boat.* Penguin Books, Harmondsworth.

Chapter 15

The future of the conurbations

The nineteenth century spectator typically saw little reason for anything other than optimism about the continued growth of the world's giant cities. Conversely many recent commentators have been certain that the collapse of the older cities of the western world was inevitable. Each prognostication was and is wrong. Certainly many of the major cities of the western world have declined relative to other urban centres and, in Britain, this decline has been an absolute one as well. But as we have shown, the crucial considerations are the level of *per capita welfare*, the relative changes in this level and changes in inequality, and here the recent evidence for British conurbations is reassuring. Concurrently, too, their economic structures have adapted, central governments have aided their physical transformation and geographical enlargement typically has resulted in service delivery areas which make better economic, political and strategic sense.

And yet, despite this apparently successful process of adaptation the future of the British conurbations is shot through with uncertainties. In common with all portions of national space, the principal forces which will mould the future of the conurbations are external and only subject to marginal modification by the conurbations themselves. Thus the economic factors which favoured the growth of large urban centres in the nineteenth and early twentieth centuries have greatly weakened. The conurbations' advantages for manufacturing: diverse communication linkages, a large and varied labour supply, a heterogeneous collection of economic activities suitable for the support of unstandardised production – all of these are still powerful attracting factors for many activities. But taken as a set we see every reason to predict an increasing *proportion* of investment decisions favouring non-conurbation locations. Thus more and more alternative locations have adequate and varied communication facilities; the growth of privately-owned vehicles has increased the possibilities of assembling labour complements from relatively low-density residential locations; input/output linkages are increasingly controlled by internal corporate strategies rather than by geographical proximity, and investment decisions are more and more likely to favour those high-quality living environments which do not suffer the diseconomies and physical ugliness often associated with large urban scale.

The obvious outcome is a continuation in the *relative* decline of conurbation manufacturing activity. The corollary is that the future employment performance of the conurbations will be shaped increasingly by their success in creating comparative advantages for tertiary activity. So far the evidence on this is reasonably comforting with the big centres appearing to have particular attractions for corporate headquarters. But the other source of rapid tertiary growth has been in those services, especially educational, health and public administration, which draw their support principally from central government funds. Whether a continuance of a high level of support for local authority services is likely is something we address shortly, but first we must consider whether the predicted decline in the relative (and absolute) level of conurbation economic activity will be accompanied by a *per capita* deterioration in relative personal welfare. As long as governments go on actively *supplementing market forces* which automatically adjust local economic structures, bring local labour demand into balance with local labour supply, and channel investible funds to profitable local opportunities, we see no reason why the conurbations, with their economic structures increasingly like that of the nation, should not continue to generate *per capita income* growth at, or around, the national average. However, we see no current evidence to suggest that three conurbations – Clydeside, Tyneside, and Merseyside – will move to a fuller level of employment. Indeed the emergence of national policies with their emphases upon the growth of competitive industries and companies *wherever* they are located, may generate conflicts with regional policy which, up until now, has favoured the reconstruction of these weaker conurbations. For this reason it is imperative that the trade-offs between these desirable, though different, strands of national policy should be made explicit and choices made openly rather than covertly.

More generally we see it as inevitable and desirable that conurbations develop their analytical and policy-making capacity in the field of economic development. Since it is unlikely that central government will cede power to the local level over financial subsidies to economic activity, local policies for economic development must focus upon making certain that greater priority is given in land-use allocation decisions to economic development; for using local authority expenditures to support economic development; for meshing local promotional efforts into the activities of development agencies such as the National Enterprise Board, and Scottish and Welsh Development Agencies and for effectively exploiting the range of central inducements, initiatives and guidance available to support the development of local economic activity.

Whether local authorities in the British conurbations will continue to receive major financial support from the central government during this period of downward adjustment is another major uncertainty. That they have received preferential treatment in recent years via the rate support grant, transport supplementary grants, inner city partnerships and other specific grants, is beyond dispute. What is in dispute is whether this preferential treatment adequately compensates conurbations for their heavier spending needs. In particular it has been alleged that there are heavy marginal costs associated with population decline since services and capital cannot be operated at their most effective level. At the same time, so it is alleged, central cities face increased demands from a population which has become ever more dependent upon public support due to the weakness of the central city economy. We have no way of measuring whether this compensation from the centre has been inadequate or too generous. What is certain is that the preference shown to the conurbations via the rate support grant has generated countervailing pressures from smaller towns and the 'shire' counties. And if this pressure results in a relative diversion of central funds away from the conurbations they will be faced with a number of alternatives which they may find unattractive – continued central support but in the form of central/local partnerships for specific programmes of action, expenditure reductions, increases in local revenues through the unpopular and relatively inelastic rating system or the need for a herculean effort to destroy the Treasury's opposition to a local income tax. One other option, the enlargement of the fiscal boundaries of conurbations to take in some of the more prosperous economic activities and domestic rate payers, seems an unprofitable route at present though even here the central government may judge it opportune to change the rules of the game.

It is only five years in England and four in Scotland since local government boundaries were changed. And yet in both countries an adjustment of political/administrative boundaries is distinctly possible. Certainly in England the present allocation of responsibilities between metropolitan districts and counties is fraught with potential conflict. Scotland, having failed to endorse devolution, may be in a less committed mood for change. However, on one aspect probably all conurbation authorities would agree. Over the last few years there has been a marked fragmentation of decision-making via specially appointed agencies of the central government. Such agencies, with their explicit remits and special boundaries, sit very uneasily within the same territory as local government which more and more recognises the importance of responding corporately to social and economic change

Of course we could be sanguine. Economic and social adaptations of the conurbation may necessitate the trying out of many solutions each with their own institutional framework. It is also fair to conclude that central government has tried increasingly to free local authorities from fussy bureaucratic controls over capital allocations, most noticeably in transport, and has genuinely tried to resist local pressures for it to intervene on every major decision affecting localities. And yet there is a constant danger that piecemeal allocation of responsibilities, for whatever good reasons of specialisation, innovation and control, may generate petty demarcation disputes over who has a legitimate right to formulate and implement policy. The institutional 'locking of horns' over territory rights may make good copy for the newspapers but it is highly unlikely to concentrate official minds on the problems to be solved.

When we consider the operation of policy *within* the conurbations two principles stand out in sharp relief. Every conurbation will be faced by acute problems of fixed capital adjustment. What to declare redundant, when to write-off assets, how to make use of under-used capital, what type and location of new capital to employ, all of these questions are central to the future size and use of the public housing stock, the road and transport system, the school system and so on. None of this can be done in discrete stages. In conditions of a growing surplus of publicly-owned houses, for example, the creation of new houses will increase the pressures for residents to quit areas already beginning to show signs of being rejected. Thus there will be a premium upon strategic thinking based on seeing the interrelations between capital decisions not only within individual programmes but across policy areas as well.

A second principle is variety and enhanced consumer choice. Population reduction and a freeing of many fixed assets will be an aid to the deep and pervasive pressures for citizens to participate in decision-making. Tenant management schemes, school council activities, local planning involvement, even such pressures as tenants' requests to make internal and external modifications to public housing – these will be the visible signs of a deep desire for variety and for greater choice over public goods provision. Monolithic solutions, often buttressed by the bland assumption that 'it's better than what it replaced', will give way to multiple solutions, to no clear answers, to variety and to a loosening of bureaucratic control and responsibility.

One other major theme in this book has been policy in relation to deprived groups – those in poverty, suffering unemployment, facing difficult transport circumstances, living in slum areas, attending worn-out schools, and so on. We have shown that the very strong spatial bias in much recent thinking about the deprived may have been overdone. The evidence relating to unemployment, for example, tends to show that high inner-city levels of unemployment are more to be explained in terms of local authority housing allocations which affect the composition of those who live in local areas and that for *any given type* of worker the level of unemployment in inner areas is no higher than in other parts of the conurbation. The evidence on poverty does not suggest that it is highly spatially concentrated but instead strongly focused on the old and spread throughout many parts of the conurbations. We have also shown that much physical renewal of particular deprived areas may have been carried out in a way which leaves the welfare of many former residents worse off after clearance and rebuilding.

All of this might push us in the direction of solutions which attack deprivation in terms of support for particular types of client group *wherever* they are located within the conurbation. It may also push us along the road to rejecting Inner City initiatives, area management schemes for particular deprived areas, educational priority areas and so on.

Such a total rejection of spatial selectivity would be inappropriate. Most local government services designed to help the deprived have a spatial dimension and thus there will be a continuing need for micro-spatial initiatives. Urban renewal, based increasingly upon rehabilitation, efforts to coordinate the sensitive delivery of services to particular deprived populations, selective demolition of parts of housing estates which were erected at standards which are no longer tolerable, all of these and more will bring a strong and continuing spatial element into policy for deprivation. But it will not be enough to leave it at that. Ultimately any serious local attack on deprivation must define targets in terms of clients *and* space, must delineate the availability of real resources, both financial and manpower, must identify the inter-relationship between national and local policies and must allocate budgets in ways which are amenable to *ex-post* evaluations of policy effectiveness. In all of this of course it is realistic to assume that the major determinants of the welfare of those in need will be shaped by national social security policies but that local actions can make marginal improvements to the welfare of particular groups.

What then of the overall prognosis? Continuing economic adaptation, increasing uncertainty over central financial allocations, uneasy alliances between local governments and appointed agencies, increased choice in public service delivery, complex decisions over the use of infrastructure, a continuing need to integrate local attempts for the amelioration of conurbation deprivation with national objectives, and perhaps above all else the development of new frameworks for budgeting which allow for proper policy analysis and review – these are the strands of a conurbation future which may be fraught but will never be dull.

Index